SCHOOLCRAFT COLLEGE LIBRARY

W9-AFS-968

CT
788
.R534
E42

Emblen, D. L.
Peter Mark Roget

BRADNER LIBRARY
SCHOOLCRAFT COLLEGE
LIVONIA, MICHIGAN 48152

Peter Mark Roget

PETER MARK ROGET

The Word and the Man

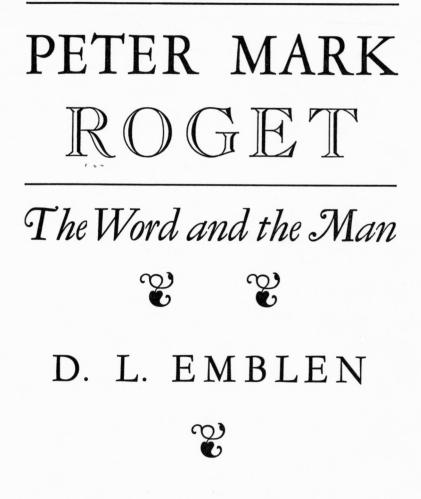

D. L. EMBLEN

Thomas Y. Crowell Company

NEW YORK

Established 1834

CT
788
.R53Y
E42

Copyright © 1970 by D. L. Emblen

All rights reserved. Except for use in a review, the reproduction or utilization of this work in any form or by
any electronic, mechanical, or other means, now known
or hereafter invented, including xerography, photocopy-
ing, and recording, and in any information storage and
retrieval system is forbidden without the written permission of the publisher. Published simultaneously in Canada
by Fitzhenry & Whiteside Limited, Toronto.

DESIGNED BY VINCENT TORRE

Manufactured in the United States of America

L.C. Card 72-109902

1 2 3 4 5 6 7 8 9 10

FOR CLARA E. BREED

librarian, friend,
encourager of innumerable
readers and writers,
including one in an
outrageous orange shirt

Contents

Illustrations

The London Institution
St. Pancras Church
Page from Mary Roget's journal
Page from Roget's optical studies paper
Somerset House, headquarters of the Royal Society
Peter Mark Roget, 1839
Title page of the first edition of Roget's *Thesaurus*,
  1852
Title page of the original *International Thesaurus*,
  1922
Peter Mark Roget at eighty-one
John Lewis Roget
Samuel Romilly Roget, 1917
John Romilly Roget and Ursula Roget
Bookplate used by Peter Mark Roget

GENEALOGIES

Preface

Don't be surprised that my letter is so greasy. As I was writing it at the window a sudden breeze took it and carried it into the street, and a little dirty boy, taking it, I suppose, to contain matters of great importance to the Emperor his Master, seized it and in spite of all the signs I could make, ran away with it. I pursued him down two streets into his house, where he gave it to his father, a soldier, from whom I fortunately rescued it.

So wrote Roget's uncle from somewhere in France in 1781 as he carried his three-year-old nephew from London to Geneva, where the boy's mother was nursing a dying husband. In this instance the uncle retrieved his letter; but the same whimsical breezes, and the counterpart of a legion of dirty little boys—political and social change, fire and death and war, travel, and that most irresponsible urchin of all, time—have carried off the remnant scraps of Peter Mark Roget's life into a thousand side streets of history. So irretrievably scattered are these relics that we can claim, at the most, to have rounded up but a partial account of a long and an extremely varied life. Hopefully the publishing of this effort will be the means of turning up many more letters, documents, and artifacts that might eventually make it possible to write the life of Peter Mark Roget.

The fact that this, the first attempt at a biography of Peter Mark Roget, does not appear until one hundred years after his death and very nearly two hundred years after his birth may suggest some of the frustration and fascination that were the mixed reward of our efforts to piece together, from this distance, the work and times of a man whose life span embraced the last of the Age of Enlightenment, the French Revolution, the Romantic movement, and the first half of the Victorian period. Although we expected to contend with the inevitable loss of letters and other materials through the intervening years, we were not prepared for what seems in retrospect almost a conspiracy of silence, which has robbed Roget of his rightful place in modern encyclopaedias, literary histories, and the like.

Fires have taken incalculable toll of the Roget papers. Especially depriving were those fires of World War II that destroyed the warehouses of Longmans, Green—Roget's original publisher —and the papers of the Manchester Literary and Philosophical Society, and the fire in 1891 that burned the Romilly family home to the ground. Other collections of letters and pictures have been lost and scattered during the many moves of the family since Roget's day. But still, considering the millions of copies of the *Thesaurus* even now being purchased throughout the English-speaking world, and considering the fact that generations of schoolchildren have grown as used to the name Roget as to the name Webster, it is more than passing strange that there has been so little published about the man.

To our best knowledge there have been, since Roget's death in 1869, only four works published that have made any substantial contribution to the world's knowledge of Peter Mark Roget: *Continental Travel in 1802–03: The Story of an Escape,* by Herbert Philips (privately printed in 1904), a collection of letters to and from Roget during a youthful adventure in Geneva (see Chapter V in our volume); *Sketches of the Lives and Work of the Honorary Medical Staff at the Manchester Infirmary, 1752–1830,* by Edward Mansfield Brockbank (1904), which gave a good account of Roget's years at that institution, from 1804 to 1808; *Travel in the Two Last Centuries of Three Generations,* edited by S. R. Roget (1922), a curious collection by Roget's grandson of letters, travel notes, and sketches by various members of the family, from the late 1700's to the late 1800's; and the *Dictionary of National Biography* (1922), whose three-page sketch, despite a number of misleading errors, provides many useful starting points. Working from the names and dates dropped into the two travel books and from the excellent, if partial, bibliography of Roget's writings printed by Brockbank, we gradually began to flesh out the skeleton account offered by the *DNB,* and put together a fairly complete picture of Roget's public life. That this was possible only through the continuous and unstinting expert assistance of many librarians in the United States and

England will be obvious to anyone who has attempted any similar project. There simply is no adequate way to thank these generous and talented persons. And how can one express his appreciation to whole institutions—the British Museum, for example, or the wonderful interlibrary loan system of the United States, which brought us books from every corner of the land? We can list here only the establishments and individuals whom we beset most often and most demandingly with our unending questions and appeals:

Santa Rosa Junior College Library, particularly Miss Lois Newman, Miss Elinor Mohn, Mr. Howard Shipman, and Mrs. Ruth Kelley.

San Francisco Public Library, particularly Mrs. Avis Stopple.

Santa Rosa–Sonoma County Public Library, particularly Mr. David Sabsay.

University of California Library.

California State Library, particularly Mrs. Carma Leigh.

Sonoma State College Library, Rohnert Park, Calif.

North Bay Cooperative Library System, Santa Rosa, Calif.

University of Missouri, Kansas City, Mo.

New York Public Library.

National Library of Medicine, Bethesda, Md.

Library of Congress.

Huntington Library and Art Gallery, San Marino, Calif.

The British Museum.

The University of London Library, particularly Miss Joan Gibbs, Mr. A. H. Wesencraft, and Dr. L. L. Pownall.

National Central Library, London.

The Royal College of Physicians Library, particularly Mr. L. M. Payne and Dr. Charles Newman.

The Royal Society of London Library, particularly Mr. I. Kaye.

The Wellcome Historical Medical Museum and Library, particularly Dr. F. N. L. Poynter.

The Royal Society of Medicine Library, particularly Mr. P. Wade.

The Public Records Office, London.

The Public Records Office, Liverpool, England.

The Royal Institution Library, particularly Mr. Oliver Stallybrass.

Somerset House, particularly the staff in the registry of wills.

The University of Edinburgh Library, particularly Mr. Charles
P. Finlayson and Mr. D. Bisset.

The Manchester Public Libraries, particularly the Central Library.

Camden Public Libraries, particularly the Holborn Central Library, London.

The University College Library, London.

Finding material that would allow us to treat Roget's
personality and private life was quite another matter. A few libraries had a few of his letters—including the British Museum,
University College, John Rylands, Huntington, Edinburgh, Wellcome, Royal Institution, and Royal Society—but nearly all of
these had to do with professional matters. We developed a series
of what we called "proximity charts," which looked like a cross
between a schematic drawing of a molecular structure and a patent application for a Ferris wheel. Finding Roget at a given
place on a given evening with named individuals, we took that
particular moment as the point of contact of several wheels—
each wheel representing the known circle of acquaintances of
each of the individuals named. We realized, of course, that because A knew B and B knew C, it did not necessarily follow that
A knew C; but this scheme became a fascinating and sometimes
profitable device—until we tried to employ it in correlating *all*
of the hundreds of men and women Roget knew in his extremely
active life. Then our diagrams became so hopelessly complex
(another feature of them was that we tried to show, by distance
from the central name, the degree of intimacy between the persons) and so intermeshed that the whole machine ground to a
halt. The device did teach us, however, how small was the circle
of movers and doers of nineteenth-century England.

Despite our best efforts, there remain several serious gaps in
this account of Peter Mark Roget. Roget's tour of duty as secretary to Lord Grey, Roget's courtship, and, most baffling of all,
Roget's preparatory work on the *Thesaurus* are among those aspects of his life and work that remain to be uncovered and described.

It was not until we established contact with Mr. John Romilly
Roget, the great-grandson of Peter Mark and the last surviving
male Roget, that any real light was shed on the private life.
Thanks to Mr. Roget's interest and kindness, we were able to peruse a priceless cache of letters, journals, childhood notebooks,

and memorabilia, and it is due to his generosity that much of this material is published here for the first time. Throughout the project Mr. Roget extended us many courtesies and constant assistance, and his hospitality and hearty encouragement were in themselves among the chief rewards of the labor. Particular thanks must be expressed, too, to Mr. Craig Sinclair of London, who had begun working on a rather different Roget project and whose gracious cooperation facilitated our examination of the Roget papers.

As to the Roget papers, an absolutely essential aid was the generous grant awarded us by the Chapelbrook Foundation of Boston, which made possible the all-important period of study in England in 1967.

We have taken the liberty of modernizing somewhat the spelling and the punctuation in the manuscript materials of the Roget papers, leaving upon occasion original locutions that seemed to be interesting in themselves. We relied very heavily upon a private corps of translators—our friends Dr. Jay Louis Hall, Mr. Geoffrey Selth, Mr. Howard Shipman, and Miss Christianne St. Jean Paulin—whose skill and insight in working with the often peculiar French of the various Rogets were matched only by their generosity and eagerness to help.

Throughout the four years that we have worked on this account, we took advantage of many encouraging friends and colleagues who made important contacts for us, suggested sources, supplied necessary information, read proofs and criticized portions of the manuscript, wrote letters, helped set up the several filing systems necessary, and good-naturedly tolerated what must have seemed at times an obsessive pursuit. We would like especially to mention, in addition to those already named, Dr. Randolph Newman, Mr. Brook Tauzer, Mr. Marvin Sherak, Mr. Gordon Dixon, Mr. Cott Hobart, William and Nancy Booth, Mr. Milton Hoehn, Mr. James Churchill, Mr. John Soares, Miss Ann Elmo, Miss Beryl Hurst, Harold and Susan Hill, Howard and Chris Shipman, Mr. David Harrigan, Mr. Harvey Hansen, John and Darlis Bigby, Garber and Madeline Davidson, Mr. Hugh M. Smyth, Dr. Dorothy Overly, Mrs. Ruth Parlé Craig, Mrs. Mina Curtiss, Lee and Bea Fidge, Mr. Hugh Rawson, Miss Barbara E. Smith, Miss Clovis Emblen, Miss Cirre Emblen, and Mr. Herbert V. Emblen. Certainly in a special category is our indebtedness to our friends Fred and Sue Manalli, who invited us up into their U.S. Forestry Service fire lookout tower high in the Sierras and there patiently sat through a reading, over a period of a week, of the bulk of the first-draft manuscript. Their perceptive criticism was enormously helpful; their kindness is unforgettable.

We are also grateful to Mrs. Barbara McCrimmon, of the *Journal of Library History;* Mr. David V. Erdman, of the *Bulletin of the New York Public Library;* Mr. William F. Irmscher, of *College Composition and Communication;* Mr. William B. Todd, of the *Papers of the Bibliographical Society of America;* Mr. Stanley M. Elam, of the *Phi Delta Kappan;* and Mr. Nicolas Barker, of *The Book Collector* (London), whose acceptance of preparatory papers on certain specialized aspects of Roget was a source of considerable encouragement. Some portions of those prior publications are reprinted herein with the kind permission of these journals.

Finally, it will be noticed that the personal pronouns "I" and "we" are used in this book with an apparent disregard for literary convention. The problem has been that of acknowledging throughout the account the constant aid of my wife, Betty Jane Mitchell Emblen, without attributing to her my own obvious shortcomings as a researcher and writer. Roget has become, through these years, so much a presence in our household that our friends have begun to whisper about a *ménage à trois,* and it is literally impossible to sort out what part of the product is hers and what is mine. I shall not extend this preface to the length necessary to set down the tasks she has cheerfully taken on or the innumerable times her insight and judgment have made sense out of a particular jumble of detail or have given point to what might have been a mass of inert material.

D. L. EMBLEN

Santa Rosa Junior College
Santa Rosa, California

The man is not wholly evil—
he has a *Thesaurus* in his cabin.

—Sir James Barrie
describing Captain Hook

Peter Mark Roget

I [1779–1793 🎶

Birth and Childhood

Judging by the way the word "Soho" now rings all sorts of dubious changes on the themes of irregularity and vice, drawing the curious and the sensation-seeking from all over the world, it is the first irony of a long lifetime of ironies that Peter Mark Roget—surely one of the most straitlaced and high-minded Englishmen who ever lived—should have been born in that squalid district. But a native of Soho he was, and he spent the great bulk of his life within a mile of it.

Named for his two grandfathers—Peter Romilly, a successful jeweler with a shop in Frith Street, Soho—and Jean Marc Roget, a Swiss clockmaker—the newest bearer of an ancient if not distinguished name was born on January 18, 1779, in Broad Street (now Broadwick Street), running westerly from Wardour Street to Marshall Street, only a few blocks east of Regent Street and west of Soho Square. His father was Jean Roget, pastor of the French Protestant Church in Soho—not in Threadneedle Street, as earlier accounts have insisted.[1] His mother was the former Catherine Romilly, sister of an earnest young law student who was to become perhaps the brightest light in British law reform as Sir Samuel Romilly. Jean Roget was twenty-eight in 1779; his wife, twenty-four. They had been married on February 12, 1778.

Roget's forebears have been traced back as far as 1447, when the first Jean Roget was recorded in Swiss documents as a *"bourgeois de Genève"*; and the name Roget (which means "little red man") is found in feudal records as early as 1380, according to a study done by Peter Mark's grandson, S. R. Romilly.[2] The genealogical chart drawn up by the last surviving male Roget,

Peter Mark's great-grandson, John Romilly Roget (see pp. 4–6), shows the full development of this sturdy family.

Jean met Catherine Romilly through his friendship with Samuel Romilly, some six years his junior, who was attracted to the young pastor when Roget was elected minister of the little French church in Soho. In his autobiography, Romilly tells of the refreshing difference in churchgoing made by the arrival of Roget:

> Instead of the stammering monotony, and the learned, but dry and tedious, dissertations of Monsieur Coderc, we heard from Roget, sermons composed with taste and eloquence, and delivered with great propriety and animation. He was, indeed, possessed of the genuine sources of eloquence: an ardent mind, a rich imagination, and exquisite sensibility.[3]

Roget took a liking to the Romilly family, frequently visiting their home, and apparently the liking was mutual. Samuel, two years younger than his sister, enjoyed discussing his studies with Roget, who warmly encouraged the young man and often made predictions about his inevitable success—"predictions," said Romilly later, "that have never been fulfilled, but which, as is often the case with prophecies of another kind, had a strong tendency to bring about their own accomplishment." He readily attributed his decision to enter law to the encouragement of Roget.

Although Jean Roget was immediately taken with Catherine's bright personality, he was a long time in proposing, for his friends warned him that his suit would not be favorably received. He had no property nor any real prospects of gaining any. His father, a clockmaker in Geneva, had no fortune to pass along, and what little he had would have to be distributed as well among two unmarried sisters and an older brother. By contrast Catherine was wealthy. She had been left a legacy of £3,000 by a friend of the family, and her expectations were even greater, for her father's jewelry business was at the time taking in about £20,000 a year. But Jean finally broached the subject delicately to Catherine's father. Not only did the old man not object, but he welcomed Roget's intentions, and the whole family was delighted when the marriage was celebrated.

Little is preserved of the Rogets' home life beyond a few comments in Samuel Romilly's autobiography. He often dined with them at their modest house in Broad Street:

I shall never forget the charms of our little frugal suppers, at which none but us three were present; but where we never were at a loss for topics that went to the hearts of all of us: where each spoke without the least reserve, nay, where each thought aloud, and was not only happy in himself, but happy from the happiness of those most dear to him.[4]

A few months after the birth of his son, Jean suffered a severe attack of tuberculosis. Doctors, unable to aid the sick man, argued that his only chance for life was to return to his native Geneva. Catherine made arrangements with her father, Peter Romilly, to take care of the baby, and she took her husband to Switzerland.

The closeness of Romilly and Roget was nearly matched in both of them by their affection for another young Genevan, Etienne Dumont, whom Romilly met during one of his visits in Switzerland with the Rogets, and who became, with Romilly, a second father to Peter Mark upon his father's death. Dumont was later to achieve prominence as a speech writer for Mirabeau and a translator of Jeremy Bentham's works. As Romilly wrote to his sister upon the news of his brother-in-law's demise, "It is the duty of both of us to guard, to instruct, and protect the children which he has bequeathed to us; those dear children who have not lost, but only changed their father." Thus young Peter's life was inextricably entwined with those of Romilly and Dumont, who again and again made good that solemn promise.

Before Jean Roget's death, the four young people—Catherine, her husband, her brother, and Dumont—were often together, much of the time in lively political and philosophical arguments. The world was young along with them, and much needed sorting out. The American Revolution was still under way, but it was obvious that the colonists would win, for the British, dogged by conflicts with three or four other countries at the same time, waged the war in America ineptly. Geneva was in a political turmoil that in a few years would drive Dumont to England a political exile, and conditions in France were rising toward the climactic Revolution.

Romilly's many letters (1780–1783) to his friend Roget, preserved in the Romilly autobiography, record some of the most fascinating moments of English and American history. Romilly, still reading for the law, spent his nights listening to debates in Parliament, then writing detailed accounts of them to his friend

ROGET FAMILY GENEALOGY

(compiled by John Romilly Roget)

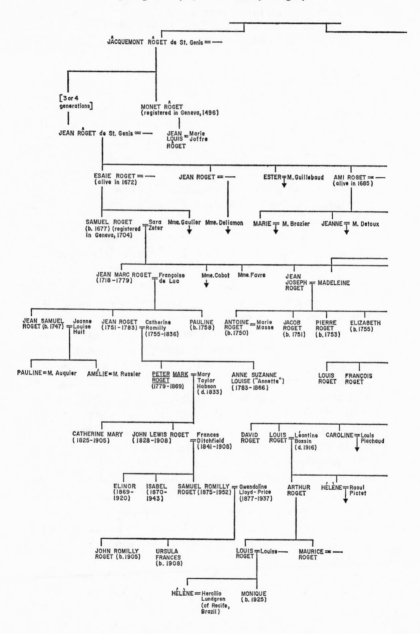

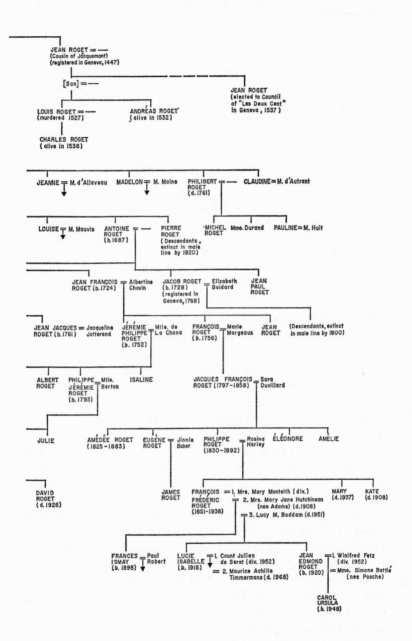

in Lausanne. The Gordon Riots, during which Romilly had to stand guard duty in front of Lincoln's Inn; the debates over motions to end the war with America; the trial of Benedict Arnold; the difficulties with Holland, which was harboring John Paul Jones and aiding and abetting the American revolutionists; the savage acts of a repressive ministry; and the violence of an ignorant populace—all were reported in the midst of their happening. The letters are shot through with affectionate notes to his sister, "Kitty," and concerned remarks about Roget's health and state of mind. Romilly was reading avidly and widely, and he often commented critically upon some book that had just come to him. He was appalled by Machiavelli, for example:

> The picture this Italian politician gives of human nature is the blackest that ever was painted. . . . When he says that men are by nature hypocrites and cowards, ungrateful and rapacious, this may possibly be as exact a copy of the manners of Italy, in an age just emerging from barbarism, as his gloomy imagination could trace; but for a representation of the human species, how false and preposterous it is! [5]

Within this determined idealism and social consciousness Peter Mark Roget took his first steps and learned his first words. Living in the Marylebone home of his grandfather and attended by his young uncle, being passed about affectionately among French and Swiss friends, the child might have been expected to take in by osmosis the same interests and concerns. Yet despite this family heritage, and despite repeated and lengthy associations with other men who were to be in the forefront of political and social reform, Peter Mark Roget, for all his useful and hard-working life, remained outside the raging political currents that in his young manhood changed the face and future of America, France, Britain, and ultimately the world.

After a year in Lausanne, it became clear that Jean Roget could never return to England. Catherine had been living with him there, all the while hoping that they could return soon to reclaim their young son; but early in 1781 she decided that if her husband was to know his son at all, Peter Mark would have to be brought to Switzerland. The grandfather, Peter Romilly, had become thoroughly attached to the baby by this time and would not hear of sending him abroad alone with strangers, so Samuel Romilly, in company with six or eight other travelers and a nursemaid, set off on June 16, 1781, to take young Peter to his parents. It was during this trip that Romilly met Dumont in Geneva.

Young Peter bore the trip better than all the rest of the party, as Romilly reported in a letter from Ostend:

I am just arrived, my dear sister, at this place with your dear little boy, who is in perfect health and excellent spirits. He is quite delighted with his journey; he plays till he is tired and then sleeps for two or three hours together upon the road. Of all the passengers, he was the only one who was not sick upon our little voyage and the only one who could sleep well. His sleep was quite as sound the whole night as if he had been on shore. It is happy it was, for we had a tedious passage of twenty-six hours.[6]

After a lengthy stay with the Rogets, where the four friends thoroughly enjoyed themselves arguing over Jean's projected history of the American Revolution, Romilly took occasion to visit Paris. There he met Diderot, d'Alembert, and Madame Delessert, a close friend of Rousseau, as well as many other politically active figures who were to be important connections for him and for the Rogets in later years.

In 1783 Samuel Romilly was called to the bar, but instead of following the usual circuit court in England, he had to make another journey to Switzerland—a far less happy one than that of 1781. Catherine had written that Jean had suffered another seizure, and that she despaired for his life. Moreover, she herself was not well—the birth of her second child, Annette, on April 29, 1783, had left her exhausted and terribly melancholy. A month later on May 29, before her brother could arrive, Jean Roget expired, and she was left alone with the two children. Romilly's letters to his sister, for all their eighteenth-century stiffness, are poignant, convincing, and entirely expressive of the affection and dedication which characterized his relationship with Catherine and her children the rest of his life. Romilly urged his sister not to try to avoid speaking of their loss—"it cannot but be always before us, nor can we wish it were not"—but he tried to console her with a reminder of their faith. "He is now assuredly rewarded for his virtues by that God in whom he has always firmly believed, and he now partakes of that immortality for which he showed, by the whole tenor of his life, that he knew he was created." Romilly prayed that she would look to her own health—not only for the sake of the children but for that of her

many fond relations in England, who had constantly worried
about her and enjoyed their lives less for her absence. "Hitherto
your life has been most unfortunate; what remains of it you have
the prospect of spending, not indeed joyfully, but unruffled with
tears and anxieties, in a calm and pleasing melancholy."

On his trip to Lausanne, however, young Romilly could not
resist staying a few days in Paris, where he expanded his acquaintance among important men—including Benjamin Franklin, who impressed him enormously. Then living at Passy, Franklin granted Romilly a lengthy interview. "Of all the celebrated
persons whom in my life I have chanced to see, Dr. Franklin,
both from his appearance and his conversation seemed to me the
most remarkable." Franklin read Romilly some passages from the
American Constitution, which had just been published and had
produced a considerable sensation in Paris. Romilly also met
Mirabeau and Lord Lansdowne, who influenced both Romilly's
and Peter Mark's lives so strongly in later years.

But the long journey home, begun on September 24, 1783, was
melancholy and uncomfortable. To avoid the pain of passing
through places that Catherine and Jean had enjoyed together,
Romilly, his sister, and the two children, all under the care of a
Swiss guide, made a circuitous journey via Soleure, Berne, Basle,
Louvain, Malines, Antwerp, Breda, and Rotterdam. There was
none of the excitement of Paris, where great changes were in the
making, but despite their cares the young widow and her brother
found something worth comment in almost every city, town, and
village they passed through.[7] The final stage of the journey, the
voyage across the channel to Harwich, took them fifty-three
hours because of a calm. They arrived in London on October 18,
1783, after twenty-four days of travel.

After some weeks with the Romillys at Marylebone, then the
merest outskirts of London, Catherine began a series of peregrinations that for the next ten years carried her restlessly about
southern and central England. Stopping six months in this place
and a summer in that, she sought the ideal environment for her
children. Her brief life with Jean Roget had encouraged an independent attitude in her that made the loving importunities of
the Romillys unbearable. Moreover, she wanted to put into practice some of the educational theories that she and her husband
and Dumont and her brother had argued in recent years. She
early decided that the metropolis was no place for the rearing of
young children; so instead of using the Romilly home as a head-

quarters, she based her operations in the suburb of Kensington, two or three miles west of the city proper, placing the green buffer of Kensington Gardens and Hyde Park between her little family and the dirt and noise of Piccadilly. All together, if one adds up the many prolonged stays there, she lived several years as a paying guest of the David Chauvet family in their comfortable home in Kensington Square. Chauvet, another Genevan, was an old friend of Jean Roget, and with his wife and daughter provided a warm and generous home for Catherine and her children. He was also a teacher—mainly of the children of other Huguenot families in London—and as such he was the first to start Peter Mark on the long educational road that he was to travel the rest of his life.

Surprisingly, Kensington Square is now, as it was then, a quiet little enclave, seemingly remote from the thronging city that has, of course, long since surrounded and bypassed it. If one walks around into Derry Street, opposite the Kensington Town Hall, and follows the one longish block of that street, he finds himself in one of the most charming cul-de-sacs in all of London. All but isolated and with practically no through traffic, Kensington Square is an island of quiet residences in a sea of metropolitan busyness. The square itself is a short, rectangular block of lawn, shrubs, and trees, surrounded by the usual fence that is locked to all but local inhabitants. The square is ringed by sizable old homes. When Catherine and her children came to live there, the neighborhood was already a haven for French *émigrés,* and it became increasingly so as the Revolution progressed. Among others, Talleyrand spent some time at the house of Archbishop Herring on the south side of the square.

It was in this quiet and protected scene that Peter Mark spent most of his young childhood, playing no doubt with other children on the grass plot, and walking sedately with his mother on Sundays up to the church on Kensington High Street.

Catherine and the children spent some months of 1786 in Worcester at the foot of the Malvern Hills, where Peter's long life was to end so many years later, and then moved to Southampton, Chichester, and other places along the Sussex coast. Dumont visited them in Southampton and wrote to Catherine later, complimenting her on the children's health and optimistically stating that he was sure she would find leads in Southampton that would allow her to "discover a little town where you might find what you are seeking." What precisely Catherine was seeking

is not clear from the letters; it is doubtful that she knew herself.
Dumont added, in the same letter, a lengthy postscript to Peter
himself:

I am glad that you have had a good time at Southampton and
that now you can swim without a float. I am waiting to receive
from you a description of the town and of the surrounding
area, and some details on your other interests, in particular in
Latin and Geography. You have no doubt observed the eclipse
of the sun, as is fitting for an apprentice astronomer and a
good almanac maker. I forgot about it all together, and then
there were some clouds which hindered our observers. Their
smoke-blackened glasses were not necessary. People who do not
know the cause of eclipses are afraid of them. They think that
the sun is going to go out. Please explain to me how you understand they take place.[8]

That Peter was indeed more than casually interested in astronomy at the age of eight is proved by the one surviving artifact of
his boyhood education. This is a notebook entitled

Peter, Mark, Roget.
his Book,
Thursday, Nov. the 21st. 1787

Roget many years later gave this same notebook to *his* son, who
promptly corrected the title page. The unnumbered pages of the
notebook were about evenly divided between miscellaneous astronomical information and classified lists of Latin words and their
English equivalents under such headings as "Beasts," "Of the
Weather," "People," "Parts of the Body," "In the Garden," and
a marvelous miscellany called "Different Things."
    On the reverse sides of pages in the back of the notebook is a
very carefully written essay, presumably by Catherine: "Advice
from a Mother to Her Daughter, Translated from the French."
In an almost copperplate hand, Catherine recorded about sixty
pages of such wisdom as the following (I have not corrected
Catherine's errors here, which, incidentally, are typical of her letters throughout her life):

Let the authority you use over your familly be mild and gentle.
    You should not always threaten without punishing least your
    threats become contemptible; and never use power but when
    persuasion fails. Reflect that Christianity makes us all level.
    The ardour and impatience of youth, lead by false notions,
    makes [us] regard Servants as being of a different species. How

contrary are these sentiments to the modesty you owe yourself
& the Humanity due to others!

Should you my Daughter be so unfortunate as not to profit
from these instructions, they will at least be useful to myself. . . .[9]

Dumont's letters, full and affectionate, were a mainstay to
Catherine in these years, particularly in those moody moments
when she convinced herself that every small domestic crisis or irregularity in her boy's health or manners was evidence that she
was quite unfit to be a mother. In a letter to her at Chichester,
Dumont tried to calm her anxieties. Idleness was natural in
young boys, he said, and she should not fret because Peter did
not pursue his studies as consistently as she thought he should.
He urged her to encourage physical activity in the boy—"running, games, exercises, fatigues of the body—there are the true
occupations of his age." Again he alluded to her quest for some
ideal environment and delicately suggested that she didn't quite
know what she was looking for. He recommended for her son a
place with a garden:

A little piece of earth to work in is almost the first necessity for
him. An animal is worth more than a book, and a carpenter's
tool is the most interesting present you could make him. If you
have nearby a turner or a wheelwright, he could profit from
them to learn to handle the most useful instruments.[10]

Dumont's letters are full of commonsense advice. Over and over
he reminds her that Peter is a very young boy, that his temperament is being formed within her constant embrace, that his chief
business is physical maturation—"being hardened by the air, the
sun, and the rain"—and that she should not expect more from
him during these boyhood years.

Another source of advice was Catherine's brother-in-law, Jean
Samuel Roget, a merchant in yard goods at No. 6 Lower German
Street, Geneva, who wrote a long series of letters to her from
1783 to 1788. Jean Samuel's letters, much of them illegible, are
full of detail on the Geneva branch of the family and on fluctuat-
ing conditions in Geneva—and how those conditions might affect
a bequest of £300 to Catherine from her husband Jean and her
receipt of a larger amount, £6,400, the source of which I have
been unable to determine.[11]

In 1789 Dumont spent some time with Catherine and the chil-

dren in Chichester and enjoyed it immensely, to judge from his
letter of September 3. "What charm indeed is provided by the
hospitality of that little city—its people gathering together, its
little game of cards, its good old women, its aristocrats, its senate
and its citizens. . . . My only fear is that neither of you will be
able to leave it." He was pleased to see that Peter was getting
plenty of exercise on horseback, and told Catherine not to worry
so about Peter's health. She doctored the boy herself with all
sorts of patent medicines and folk cures—such as ass's milk—but
Dumont told her, "The happiness he enjoys is the best regimen
for both body and soul."

That was the year of the French Revolution, which the young
friends had observed abuilding as long before as 1781. Like most
young liberals of the day, they had looked forward idealistically
to the Revolution as the best hope of sweeping away corruption
and tyranny and of establishing a truly enlightened society. But
as the early events—the formation of the National Assembly, the
Tennis Court Oath, the storming of the Bastille—gave way to
the September Massacres, they became more and more fearful of
the fate of the people and their ideals.

A few years later, when the Revolution all but drowned in the
crimson tide that was the Terror of 1793-94, Romilly, again like
most British liberals who had supported the movement, was hor-
rified at what the Revolution had wrought. He recalled and destroyed a pamphlet he had written with Dumont and another
friend, James Scarlett, and issued under the pseudonym "Henry
Frederic Groenvelt," in which he had urged changes in England
similar to those in France in 1789-90.[12] But unlike many of his
one-time liberal friends, his devotion to the ideals behind the
Revolution did not give way. Instead, his faith in law was all the
more reinforced, and he simply resolved to work the necessary
changes through a reform of the law itself. In early November
1789, Samuel Romilly wrote a lengthy commentary to Catherine,
who was back again in Worcester, expressing his anxiety over the
chaos that was emerging in France. The same letter urged Catherine to return to London, or at least to Kensington, reminded
her to keep up Peter's Latin, and advised her against investing in
the Irish tontines.[13]

From Gloucester, Catherine wrote to her brother that they
kept up on the events in France as well as they could, through
the papers and through occasional letters from Geneva and
France:

Peter and myself can talk of nothing else, and we quarrel with our good neighbours continually. They call me a *Wandering Rebel* and laugh at my zeal. . . . I really am very impatient to hear how the National Assembly will act. Poor Mirabeau's talents would have been serviceable . . . I have no doubt it will end well. Is Dumont a spectator at Paris? [14]

In the same letter, Catherine gave a charming survey of the family:

How does my Dear Mother, may we flatter ourselves that things mend and that my good Aunts descend the hill of life with more glee and good humour, notwithstanding the encumbrance of an old tottering mansion over their heads? Take our family in a group—what an odd mixture we should make! both as to variety in dress, manners, etc. We have the Gay and Worldly, the grave and sensible, Children-spoilers, dog-and-cat-lovers, house fanciers, Country-ramblers, . . . You know better than myself the catalogue, so pray give my love to them all. . . . I don't like being absent from you all; I think you will see us in the winter, and yet I know the first pleasures over, I shall grow as dull and stupid as ever. On account of Peter I must choose Kensington, which in other respects cannot suit me. I should like to take a Lodging near you, but there the air is not so good; near Frith Street [in Soho], it is still worse, and My Dear Mother would wish to live with us. I have too many good reasons to not foresee unhappiness—therefore what is to be done?

As to what was to be done, Catherine continued to be a "Country-rambler." She left Gloucester for Cheltenham but was disgusted to find it full of summer visitors, and "a crowd of *stares* is my aversion." By the end of September, however, most of these seasonal residents had left, and Catherine found the town more to her liking. It was clean, nicely paved, and well lighted, "which you seldom find in country towns." In Gloucester, she tried putting Peter, then twelve, in the local school, and was confirmed in her dislike of such institutions when he promptly got into a fight and came home with an angry red mark on his breast. The next day, his chest hurt when he moved, and the pain continued for some days, starting up in Catherine alarmed memories of her tubercular husband:

I imagine a slight cold he caught might have added to it, but he has now neither cold nor cough. In every other respect he is in perfect health, his spirits excellent and only I think too noisy.

Do you think, Dear Sam, if it [the pain] proceeds only from
the blows, that riding is just now so good as keeping quiet for
a few days. Unfortunately, he is violent in every thing he does.
If he does ride out, he shall go gently at first.[15]

In her next letter three days later, she apologized to her brother
for having alarmed him; the pain had lessened and finally disappeared. "Peter (who now pretends to understand anatomy) always said it was lower than the lungs. I applied my *Beaume de
Chison* and he now neither feels it when he blows his nose or by
any motion of the arms."

After a comfortable Christmas in Cheltenham, Catherine again
reported on Peter's health—"as usual thin and pale"—and came
to some interesting conclusions about what her observations had
taught her of his intellectual skills and interests:

Peter ever eager after new studies, has for this while left this
    world and lived wholly in the Starry regions. He hired Fergu-
    son on Astronomy, and has been copying off tables and making
    circles ever since. He gave us yesterday a three hours lecture on
    Astronomy—Nanette and myself (his only auditors) began at
    last to be quite weary. What Mr. C [probably Chauvet] re-
    marked of Peter was certainly very just. He does not promise
    to have that *goût* for the Belle Lettres as we might wish or ex-
    pect. Everything is *Calculation,* and a desire to know more.
    He is very young, and there is no knowing how things may
    turn out, but the hopes of his constitution mending has led me
    to think better things. I sometimes fancy him much cleverer
    than he really is, from having a poor Judgment and small ca-
    pacity myself—*dans le pays de aveugles les bouves sont Rois.*
    [In the land of blind men, the cattle are kings.] [16]

A year later she added to this judgment:

I sometimes fancy Peter is aspiring to a vocation which does not
    suit a very small fortune. . . . His mind will, I see, never bend
    to business except it was nearly connected with books. He is
    still very often trifling in his pursuits. But he is young. Two or
    three years will show us whether he is clever and has a good
    headpiece. You will be surprised when I tell you I think he
    promises less than he did a year ago. With concern I have
    often remarked it—that we must expect either that way or a
    great alteration, which I impatiently wait for.

After another sojourn with the Chauvets at Kensington, Catherine carried her children off to Dover, which thronged with

French refugees, either escaping their native country or trying to find a way to return. Catherine was asked by a French family to sign a certificate before a notary that one of their menservants, who was at Dover, had served as a servant for seven or eight months. By this means the man could get permission to reenter France. But Catherine could not do it. "The unjust severe decree against servants belonging to emigrants may excuse some deceit, but not in my mind a palpable falsity." She did however, through a friend secure for the man another kind of permission.

Despite the expense and inconvenience of Dover, Catherine apparently found it fascinating, and she and the children stayed on there well into 1793. Many of her letters provide vivid vignettes of the plight of the French refugees and of the Dover coast natives. French and British relations deteriorated, and on February 1, 1793, the Legislative Assembly declared war on Britain, Spain, and Holland:

The vessels are stopped, and this week all Foreigners are to leave [Dover]. . . .
The good people here are frightened out of their wits. They are sure the French will land on our coast and expect every night to be awakened by the Castle cannon. The streets are patroled every night, but what is seriously of consequence, we have no soldiers in the Castle. They were ordered from this place when the riots were expected in London.[17]

In another letter she described a ship in the harbor loaded with passengers from France, who were being kept prisoners on the vessel. "Not one of them has passports. The Captain says they got into his vessel by stealth and by force, seized the helm, and obliged them to take them across. They are supposed here to be Jacobins sent to fire the town, poison the water, etc. . . ." [18]

But she was far more concerned with the effect of the war on her own little family. As usual, she worried excessively about her living expenses, although Sam repeatedly wrote her urging that she need have no pecuniary fears. In addition to managing her investments carefully, he bought the lease of the house in Frith Street for her as a present, and it would bring in about £70 a year. He also arranged for Catherine to receive the rent from another house in St. James Street [19]—so that with her regular quarterly dividends of £40, Catherine was receiving regularly about £200 a year.[20]

Catherine was sorry to lose Peter's teacher in Dover, for the boy had taken a sudden, much stronger interest in his studies, particularly chemistry—"it engrosses all his thoughts, and from the ardour he pursues it, makes the time appear long which is devoted to Latin and Greek." Apparently, the teacher was an odd, unpredictable sort. "He has made us laugh heartily this winter and has cost Peter so many *Diables!* I fear I shall have much trouble to break him of this exclamation." The loss of the teacher led Catherine to make another move, still seeking some quiet, inexpensive rural hideaway. In April 1793, they landed in Rochester, and there she learned from her brother that the financial matters in Geneva had been finally sorted out. Whatever monies due her had been settled at something less than five shillings to the pound. Sam had received for her £875, which with her other investments gave her a total of nearly £2,000—"If it should not amount quite to so much, I will make it up to that sum." The bulk of this he had put into 3 percent consols,[21] he said, and again he urged her not to worry so much about her living expenses:

I hope indeed to do a good deal more for you as I grow richer, but you know that I don't deal much in promises. In the meantime I hope you won't suffer your Circumstances to give you the least uneasiness or make any alteration in your way of life. Your present income must I think now amount to about £100 a year more than you spend.[22]

Catherine thanked him in a prompt reply but said that the war was making her expenses greater than they had ever been, and that she was living at the rate of at least £160 a year.

Peter's studies were proceeding more encouragingly, she wrote. He seemed to be working on the Greek and Latin with more industry and more pleasure. He was cheerful, if somewhat rude upon occasion; all in all, he seemed to be much more promising than a year ago. But Rochester, like most of the towns between London and the Channel, was becoming so filled with soldiers that Catherine had to move on. Moreover, she felt the need for a long conference with brother Sam about Peter's future. Thus, toward the end of May, she packed up their battered trunks again, left Rochester, and moved in for another lengthy stay with the Chauvets in Kensington Square. She still disliked London as much as ever, but she felt it necessary to make some decisions about Peter, and she relied strongly upon her brother's advice.

After the pleasure of reunion with the Chauvets had worn off, Catherine found their situation there increasingly uncomfortable. The Chauvets' house was already crowded with other guests (Mrs. Chauvet had had to turn the place into a rooming house), some of whom did not like the children. Catherine found her little family something of an embarrassment to Mrs. Chauvet, who dropped occasional hints that although their house was full, they were able to save nothing. Catherine, who was all her life painfully sensitive to any slight suggestion that she might be a burden to others, talked long and hard with her brother and with Dumont, who was with her part of that summer at Kensington Square.

Their conversations apparently became at times rather stormy. Mrs. Chauvet and Dumont quarreled; Dumont left and wrote a lengthy letter to Catherine, begging her to "accept my power of attorney for a peace treaty, even if the first condition should be the humiliating confession that I make people weep when I want to make them laugh, and that I make them laugh when I want to make them weep." But finally, after considering a number of propositions, it was decided that Catherine should take Peter north to Edinburgh, where he would be enrolled at the university. In such circumstances of formal study, they could then observe the boy and see what could be made of him. Catherine was stubbornly sure, against the recommendations of the Chauvets, that Peter could make no success in business. Her brother agreed with her that the boy also showed no particular literary talent, and that his work with classical languages was considerably less than promising. The boy's one consistent interest seemed to be science and mathematics—"calculations," as Catherine put it— but there was in 1793 no occupation such as "scientist." Thus there was no prospect that even if he did prove talented in computational and experimental skills, he could make a living with such abilities. There was, of course, medicine, a subject Catherine herself found fascinating, and a field which she knew all too well was profitable to the practitioner, even if not to the patient.

Peter's scientific interests were varied and general. He certainly had not settled on medicine at that date. But he was not averse to the suggestion either, and he was young. Give him time, his Uncle Samuel said. Put him to work under first-rate teachers in Scotland; keep him at it—every day and all day—and see what would happen. Perhaps his vague inquisitiveness would focus on

medicine as he associated with other young men already dedicated to taking the M.D. degree, and as he realized that Edinburgh drew talented men from all over Europe and America to
attend what was widely regarded as the best medical school in
the English-speaking world.

II   [1793-1798 ℰ

Education—Edinburgh

O N the evening of September 18, 1793, Catherine and her children took a hackney coach in Kensington Square and set off across London to the Bull and Mouth Tavern in Aldersgate Street, just north of St. Paul's, and very close to St. Bartholomew's Hospital, where Peter was to study some seven years later. This was the first and the shortest leg of the journey to Edinburgh, a four-hundred-mile trip by mail coach and post chaise.[1]

With her usual care, Catherine had made extensive inquiries about the journey, had formulated and discarded several plans, and had commissioned her brother to report to her on the geography, the weather, and the nature and cost of lodgings in Edinburgh.

The 196-mile run from London to York, via Enfield, Ware, Huntingdon, Stilton, Stamford, and Doncaster, with only one good meal—eels, goose, and mushrooms at Newark—took them slightly over twenty-four hours, and the little family was exhausted. They lay over nearly two weeks in York, resting, sightseeing, and worrying about the confusion at the local stage office. Reservations, apparently, meant nothing, and Catherine soon concluded that they must pack their things each morning so that they could leave on the shortest notice. She also had Peter run to the York Tavern whenever the mail coach horn was heard as it entered the town.

Finally, on October 2, he dashed back to say that they could have three seats on the mail from York to Edinburgh. But by the time they had scurried down to the tavern, there were several persons clamoring for places on the coach and none were available. After much confusion the following arrangement was settled: there would be some places opened on the mail coach when it reached Newcastle, 82 miles to the north; thus, those interested could take places in two chaises leaving York a few hours after the departure of the mail coach. Whichever party had the faster horses and could catch the mail coach at Newcastle could then have the seats for Edinburgh. Under these conditions, the northward trip was something less than comfortable; there were breakneck races along level stretches and, whenever the two carriages arrived at a post station at the same time, a great shouting and jostling (all the men in the other chaise, Catherine said, were drunk). The last stage, from Durham to Newcastle, was a free-for-all race at full gallop, which, by virtue of better horses, Catherine's carriage won. It arrived at the station, Hall's Inn, in Newcastle just as the horses were being put to the mail coach. "With a light heart and an empty stomach, we set off, well pleased." A cold supper at Berwick provided their only food during that long day, and after another night of travel, via Houndwood, Dunbar, and Haddington, the little family arrived at Edinburgh at 7 A.M. October 4.

After several temporary quarters, Catherine, Peter, and "Nanette," as Roget's sister was called, settled into a small third-floor apartment in Rose Street, in the center of New Town, which Catherine had heard was much more fashionable than the older city south and east of the Castle. During the next couple of years, they apparently alternated between Rose Street and the suburban village of Fountain Bridge. Peter was quickly enrolled in the university and took up a formal study of classical literature, which necessitated his putting in extra hours on his Latin. Catherine tried to make their meager funds stretch over ordinary and extraordinary expenses, and judging by her letters to Sam, money matters were second in her mind only to Peter's health. A letter dated December 2, 1793, is typical:

. . . I am absolutely pennyless, with using all the economy I am master of I find myself always behind hand. I was in hopes as I do not pay my month's lodging before next Friday (1 gn. per week for two bedrooms and a dining room) that I should not have been in want of cash 'till the end of last week (as I mentioned) but some new and unavoidable expense always crosses my endeavours and drains my purse. If you have not already sent me some money, pray do immediately on the arrival of this. I am vexed that I am greatly exceeding what I ought to spend, and more so as I know no way of avoiding it at present. A small family like ours in Ready Furnished Lodgings cannot spend less here than £200 a year, without the strictest economy. I shall endeavour, with £40 every quarter, to make things do. . . . I make no apology Dear Sam for tormenting you with my fears and concerns—you must and ever have known my thoughts at all times and in every situation of life.[2]

Nearly every one of the approximately forty letters surviving of those written by Catherine to her brother during the Edinburgh years includes some reference to their impecunious state, and many of them include direct appeals for money, often an advance on her quarterly payments of £40. In nearly all of his answering letters, Samuel Romilly urges Catherine to ease her mind about money matters, assures her that he is growing rich and can easily afford to help her, and encloses additional amounts of money, ranging from £20 to £50. In addition, he frequently sent presents of books and clothing, and on at least two occasions made her a present of additional shares of government securities so that her regular income was substantially increased.

Little Nanette is simply a quiet little ghost in the house, as far as the letters are concerned. Catherine mentions her frequently in passing—"Nanette is well," or "Nanette is terribly thin," or "I find it necessary to give Nanette a glass of port each day"—but in the whole series of letters, it is obvious that from first to last the center of Catherine's attention was Peter: his health, his education, his state of mind, his prospects.

The only surviving letter by Peter during 1793 is the following, written on December 31, presenting a fairly informative sketch of his routine at the university. Peter was then just two weeks short of his fifteenth birthday:

Dear Uncle, We have a week's vacation from Christmas to New-Year's day: I take this opportunity of writing you. Mr. Dalzel [3] has given us a Greek verb to write out in all the Moods and Tenses, in order to prevent us from being idle, as he says: but I find it very tedious, and it takes up so much of my time that I have hardly any holidays at all. Dr. Hill has given us nothing particular to do. As the Medical Classes have no vacation, I often hear Dr. Monro who reads lectures on Anatomy in the College. He has a subject at every lecture, which he dissects in the Class: the smell is sometime offensive, when the dead body has been kept too long, as was the case yesterday.

I believe I did not tell you that Dr. Hill reads lectures on Roman Antiquities in the Second Latin class. As I was told they were useful and entertaining, I asked Dr. Hill if he would

permit me to attend them: he complied on condition that I
would tell nobody, which I promised to do. He lectures twice
a week from 11 to 12. I have likewise obtained the same favour
from Mr. Dalzel, who reads lectures on the Greek language
and literature in general, in the second Greek Class. He lectures the same days with Dr. Hill, from 2 til 3. So that Tues-
days and Thursdays I am in the College from 8 til 9 in the
morn. and then from 10 til 3. The other days only from 8 to 9;
from 10 to 11, and from 12 to 2. Mr. Dalzel's class is at the top
of the College; and as we live up two pair of stairs, I every day
go up at least 320 steps.

The beginning of December all the students were matricu-
lated, and their names called over in alphabetical order, and
we all signed our names in a book called *the Album,* and paid
half a crown for the support of the library. Any student may
take out a book on depositing its value and returning it in a
fortnight. It is open four days in the week, from 10 to 1, and
the librarian attends to lend out the books. I borrowed a few,
but as I have no time to read at present, shall defer it till the
summer. Since our matriculations, we meet at Dr. Hill's on
Saturday's from 8 to 9 for Latin phrases; and at Mr. Dalzel's
from 11 to 12. Dr. Hill explains the different idioms and
phrases of the Latin language and which I find very useful, at
the former hour.

The new college they are building is discontinued at present
for want of money. They had not made a just calculation of
the expenses; the funds with which they had begun are already
used, and a stop is therefore put to the building of it.

Give my love to Uncle Tom, My Aunt, etc., and
believe me ever your affectionate nephew

P. Roget

P.S. I am learning to write Short-hand, which I find very useful
for taking notes at the classes and especially at lectures; it will
be still more so when I shall have made greater progress in it.[4]

The costs of Peter's education at Edinburgh are difficult to determine precisely. At the end of the eighteenth century, professors relied for the bulk of their earnings on fees paid them by
students who attended their lectures. The fees varied from two to
three guineas, and the system was held to have a salutary effect
on the productivity of the professors by various reformers, who
argued that that arrangement minimized the treating of profes-
sorial chairs as sinecures. The system favored the medical faculty,
especially those of chemistry and anatomy, for their courses were

ROMILLY FAMILY GENEALOGY
(compiled by John Romilly Roget)

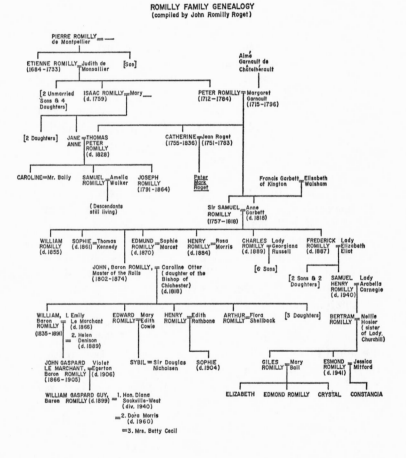

regularly attended by hundreds of students each year.[5] Both
Peter and Catherine make occasional reference in their letters to
class fees—about three guineas per class. We can conclude that
however straitened their budgetary ways became, the family was
not (or did not allow itself to admit that it was) in the category
of a few of Peter's classmates: those who had to apply for gratis
tickets.

Peter received considerable assistance indirectly from his Uncle
Samuel because of Romilly's close friendship with Dugald Stewart (1753–1828), who for a quarter of a century distinguished
the Moral Philosophy Chair. Both Professor and Mrs. Stewart
went out of their way to make the Rogets feel a little less alone
than they certainly were in the northern city. During various periods, Peter regularly breakfasted at the Stewarts' home in Can-
onsgate Street, a few blocks south of Calton Hill, where Stewart
is still remembered by an impressive statue. And through Stewart, Peter was extended many kindnesses by other members of
the university faculty.

Meanwhile, Catherine marshaled her resources, financial and
pharmaceutical, and, fully sensible that she was living through
some sort of exile, established certain priorities—the first of
which was Peter's health. In *all* of her letters, she reports the
state of the weather, and beginning in February 1794, she details
a series of major and minor illnesses that Peter suffered through
the five long, wet Scottish winters they spent in Edinburgh. He
was rarely without a cold, a cough, or a fever, and she was rarely
without a description of the symptoms or an explanation of the
treatment she was following. In her letter of February 1, 1794,
she noted that a deluge of rain had made the roads so bad that
the London mail, which normally arrived there between 7 and 8
A.M., had arrived for several days at 6 P.M.—with six horses instead of four.

By April of that year, Catherine concluded that "on the whole
I think him better for change of air and the constant exercise he
is obliged to take in all kinds of weather." She wrote that "Peter
continues to stoop and grows so fast with it that I have had a
high writing desk made for him, with a stool, such as are used in
Compting Houses [sic], which he likes much and keeps him very
straight." [6]

To Etienne Dumont, Catherine wrote chiefly of the poverty of
their social life, of the seeming impossibility of making friends,

of the long, dreary years ahead. A brief sample of Catherine's lugubriousness is found in a letter written on Nanette's birthday:

Nanette is eleven years old today—*Time,* whether in Grief or Joy, still steals on us, and blends the events of life into harmony—I shall soon be mumbling my hard crust, and talking of the past as of a dream!

Presumably she found some satisfaction in Dumont's genial, if urbane, assurances:

Your attachment for Scotland is now only a matter of the will. That is very clear to me. Your desire for it is no longer there. Inclination is lacking . . . but a few years will pass like a few months, and you are there like a merchant in India, not liking it, thinking of going back home, and for his consolation, reminding himself of the profits of commerce. Your profits will be in Peter's success. I have no doubts in this regard. You have no reason to be anything but pleased. He wrote his uncle a very fine letter, which I saw, where he accounts for his occupations, and in which it is obvious that every hour of the day is well-employed, for time given to exercise, to conversation, and to walking is not lost time. He can, as he walks, give you an account of his lessons, of his reading, and thus engrave them in his mind and in his memory. One learns by talking about what one has learned.[7]

In the same letter Dumont promised to send a dictionary of Latin synonyms.

Both Peter and his mother were disappointed not only with the lack of sociable friends in Edinburgh but in the paucity of intellectual resources there. Both of them complained of the libraries—Peter of the university library, which he said was poorly stocked and inefficiently managed, and Catherine of the circulating libraries in town, where, she said, she was laughed at for requesting books that would have been available in the smaller towns of Devonshire. They had both expected something on the order of the libraries at Oxford and Cambridge.

In the fall of 1794, Catherine reported that they had moved to a little house near Fountain Bridge, a suburb; and several successive letters are filled with observations on the progress of the Revolution and of the fortunes of the war with France, the effects of which were often drastic even in Edinburgh. She and the children visited a large cotton mill that had been shut down for lack

of trade; they observed large numbers of jobless workmen ship-
ping off for America; they witnessed street demonstrations
against enforced celebrations of British naval victories, and
watched a large military force depart to put down mutinous re-
cruits in Glasgow. Enlistment bonuses had risen to 20 guineas,
but even such an inducement—a huge sum for an unemployed
workman during a particularly hard winter—failed to attract
men for the unpopular war, and recruiters were obliged to take
boys of thirteen and fourteen, after getting them drunk. Letters
from her friends in Southampton confirmed Catherine's dismay
at the effect of war on all of England: "Party affairs run high, the
ladies are violent when they talk politics, the men rude, and the
good lament in silence the unhappy times." 8

Meanwhile, Catherine had her own trouble to worry about as
well. The severe winter of 1794-95 (the coldest, she was informed, in forty years) locked them into a hermit's life at Fountain Bridge, prevented them from taking their daily walks, and
gave them all bad colds. Peter was worst of all, with fever and
chills; and finally, sitting bundled up by the fire, he overturned a
kettle and severely scalded his foot. Nonetheless, he insisted on
attending classes. The blisters became infected, and Catherine
had to nurse him through a lengthy and complicated illness,
which caused him to miss some weeks of work.

Recreation in Edinburgh was, for the Rogets at least, limited
to walks in fine weather, an occasional visitor—the Stewarts or
James Scarlett (one of Romilly's protégés)—and, on very rare
occasions, a short expedition into the Scottish countryside. In
July of 1795, Peter enjoyed two "water parties," as the guest of
the family of a schoolmate. One excursion was to Inch Coombe,
the other to Inch Keith—two islets in the Firth of Forth. In autumn of the same year, Samuel Romilly and Etienne Dumont
made a long-promised visit to Edinburgh, and before they left,
they took Peter on a week's walking tour of the Highland country north and west of Edinburgh. Catherine's letters frequently
mention plans for a journey here or there, but invariably she
found that lack of ready cash prevented their going. Sketching
was her chief release. As she put it, "For draw I must in spite of
old age [she was then just forty]. My sketches serve as memoran-
dums of my life and are far more expressive than journals of
dates and years." Nanette spent hours at the piano and in spinning and drawing. Reading, of course, was a prime source of recreation.

One year, Romilly sent Peter a little present of money, to be used specifically for the purchase of twenty tickets at a riding school. Catherine at least was grateful, because Peter so little understood the management of horses, she said, that she was embarrassed for him should he be invited to a country place; he would appear very foolish.

That they were distinctly outside any social life of the city is made clear again and again in Catherine's letters to her brother. She wrote frequently of the comings and goings of the gentry at Stewart's house, but she felt keenly the fact that she was not part of that circle. She bravely kept up her spirits with expressions like "Edinburgh is very dull now," "Absolutely *everyone* has departed," and "The weather prevents our friends from visiting"; but in unguarded moments, she revealed that they simply had no friends in Edinburgh, no, nor any prospects of winning any. An incident concerning a watch that London friends had supposedly sent to Nanette is illuminating:

> The fate of Nanette's watch still hangs in fearful suspense. Mrs. Fisher [Catherine's London friend] has lately informed us that Lady Eden had left the watch with Lady Riddle. Peter consequently called on her Ladyship, who sent him down a verbal message that the watch was sent to the house of Mrs. Mackie, who on Peter's visit to her, refuses to deliver it 'till she inquires into his character, to satisfy which he left with her the names of Mr. S—— [probably Stewart] and Dr. D—— [possibly Dalzel]. We laugh with Peter and tell him he must have a *fort mauvais façon,* and it reminds us that once at the Post Office last winter, happening not to have silver enough to pay for some letters, the gentleman good-naturedly called out, "Never mind, your *Mistress* will pay the first time she calls." I comfort myself with the remembrance that *son digne Oncle l'avocat* was once taken for a *lackey.*[9]

The strain of maintaining the appearance of a genteel life with none of the compensatory successes often told on Catherine, and she occasionally displayed this in melancholy admissions to her brother—statements which she was quick to qualify, however, sometimes in the same letter. Given her background, her social and intellectual aspirations, and the minimum conditions that she rather insisted the family satisfy themselves with, her survival in Edinburgh from 1793 to 1798 must be put down as a supreme act of will. This was often assisted by her propensity for role-playing: sometimes the elegant lady temporarily cast among near-savages and the "honest vulgar"; sometimes the philosopher, grateful for the unadorned life they led and the absence of temptation; sometimes the martyred mother, sacrificing her talent and her happiness for the sake of her children.

A severe blow to Catherine's pride was the belated discovery in November of 1795 that they had been living in a rather shady neighborhood:

> I am sorry to inform you we are in a sad low life neighborhood, *encore passé pour la salate de nos voisins;* but we are surrounded with women of bad character. I was not a little vexed when I heard this Street is famous for them, but a stranger may be supposed I hope to be ignorant of it. The Lodgings in the other great streets are so immoderately dear that there is no changing. Our Hostess is very civil, and as we are entirely to ourselves, I shall make myself easy in our apartment for this winter.[10]

She did not comment on the possibility that the location might have accounted for the failure of Edinburgh acquaintances to drop by for a dish of tea or a bite of mutton.

While Catherine's social life was severely restricted, Peter made several good friends among his classmates, some of whom he met a few years later during his first assault on London. One of his new acquaintances was Lovell Edgeworth (1776–1841), a brother of the novelist Maria Edgeworth and son of the Irish eccentric, inventor, and writer, Richard Lovell Edgeworth (1744–1817). Young Lovell, who spent the winter of 1794 in Edinburgh, was full of life and spirits and apparently brightened the Rogets' evenings considerably. Through Edgeworth they learned of conditions in Ireland, often in tumult owing to expected rebellion of the poor, invasion by the French, or both. Peter was to retain his friendship with Lovell, who in 1802 would accompany him on his Geneva adventure.

Another friend was a young Lord Ashburton, another protégé of Samuel Romilly, who was attending the university and boarding at the Stewarts' home. Clearly, Catherine was somewhat jealous of this young man's closeness to Romilly and to Stewart, and she frequently commented on his tendency to talk too much and too loudly. But she had to admit, finally, that he offered a much more impressive appearance than her own son:

> I fear Peter's sheepish looks ill agreed with his [Ashburton's] open manners. I met him in the meadows on Friday, and he

assured me he had set out to call on us. Perhaps it was mere civility, but we find him quite polite compared to the proud rich you meet here in company. They do not even touch their hat when they see you again.[11]

Still another new friend was Arthur Aikin (1773–1854), a son of the physician and author Dr. John Aikin. Young Aikin arrived in Edinburgh during the winter of 1795 and took lodgings with Scarlett. "I thought him rather heavy and not polite," wrote Catherine. Aikin's friendship was to be of real value to Roget during his London career, for Aikin became a scientific editor and the chief moving force in the founding of the Geological Society.

Early in 1796 Peter joined the student Medical Society, which, of course, improved his social life and brought him into contact with many older medical students and doctors. The society met regularly once a week during term and offered additional library privileges to its members. "The only disagreeable part of the business," wrote Catherine, "is that the Society often does not break up till very late, and twelve o'clock is the soonest you are permitted to retire without being fined." In several other letters, Catherine spoke disapprovingly of the late hours being kept by the society. She preferred Peter to be in bed before 11 P.M. Again, it is ambiguous whether her concern sprang from worry over his health or from an active jealousy toward any activity that would take him from her.

An important function of the society was that of offering M.D. candidates an opportunity to try their all-important theses on a critical audience. As others had before him, Peter was to read his thesis to the society before working it up into its final form.

Shortly after the death of her mother in the spring of 1796, which brought her an additional £400 in 3 percent consols, Catherine decided that they could no longer tolerate Rose Street. The many stairs, the dirt, the dubious activities of some of their neighbors, the lack of a garden, all drove her out to seek more pleasant quarters. On June 15, 1796, she wrote Romilly that she had been successful in locating a lodging house at the end of Hope Park Street, only seven minutes' walk from the university, yet surrounded by trees and pasture lands:

To enjoy this spot as we do, it would be necessary to pass as many months as we did at Fountain Bridge and Rose Street, in particular the latter place; the uncommon dirtiness of our neighbours and Landlady made me, as the summer advanced, live in fear of all manner of filth. . . . Hope Park End is not *fashionable* so that I have the happiness of not making one soul break the 10th Commandment on my account. The New Town carries the day: all is vulgar that is out of its boundaries. The exorbitant price of house rent, the great distance from the markets, the exposure to hurricanes of wind (which never do any essential damage but in the New Town) are trifles light as air, compared to the advantage of having for neighbours My Lord and Lady This and That. The *only* draw back we have heard since our arrival at Hope Park End is that the meadows surrounded with trees are thought by some damp in the winter. We live on the first story, and I should think cannot find any inconvenience on that account. They have a great prejudice about trees and fancy every green leaf produces damp.

But, as though to counter this improvement, Catherine had a new worry: Peter was now attending lectures and observing patients at the Royal Infirmary, which was filled with fever victims. She had noted that many young students became ill during their first tour of duty at the hospital, and she insisted that Peter be careful not to feel the pulses of the more serious cases. Moreover, attendance at the infirmary cost Peter an additional £3 3s. annually.

On the other hand, Peter was now a bona-fide medical student and as such was entitled to the best medical advice without charge, for it was the custom that neither the physicians nor the surgeons charged fees for treating medical students. Of course, Catherine sometimes knew—or believed she knew—more than the doctors about her particular patients. Writing Romilly on March 8, 1796, about Nanette's ill health, she said she was obliged to administer her favorite patent medicine, Godbald's Syrup, which as usual had wonderful effects:

How she caught her cold I cannot tell, but hope it is now in a fair way of going off. She has been otherways so weak that on the whole I was so alarmed I was near sending for Dr. Duncan, but knew he would not order my favorite, Godbald's remedy, which has immediately relieved her cough, lowered her fever, and given her an appetite.

Unfortunately, Catherine's impecunious and lonely time in Edinburgh was unleavened by any sense of humor. Even in reporting the charge of a cow, who ran at the three of them one rainy day as they were walking—"Nanette bid me push the umbrella at the beast, which I did just in time, as Peter came running with his stick"—Catherine was unable to find anything amusing in their situation; and large sections of her letters are boring exercises in self-pity.

In March 1797, Catherine carefully planned their budget for Peter's final year at Edinburgh. His summer and winter classes would come to about £35 or £36, and the printing of his thesis and additional fees to professors would bring the total to not less than £40. Shaking her head at her presumptuousness in bringing Peter to Edinburgh on such a shoestring budget, she again thanked Romilly for his constant support. "Without the kindness you have shown me, how could I have supported it?" She was glad to report that Peter's interest in the profession seemed to be strengthening day by day and that, contrary to her fears that he would be fascinated only by anatomy, he was eagerly pushing forward in the other branches of medicine as well:

> I hope he will be happy enough to do some good in his life. For in whatever chaos of constitution we are driven into [sic], Physicians are still of use. Poverty brings disease as well as riches, and however well frugality may steer our frail bark, it will crack, grow old, want mending, and fall to pieces at last.[12]

Peter's and Catherine's anxiety was not eased by the common knowledge that only a small minority of students who began the course of study with the Medical Faculty actually graduated. An average of only twenty-two students out of a class of four to five hundred were awarded the M.D. degree. In May of 1797, the Rogets were encouraged by the success of two Genevan friends, Alexander Marcet (1770–1822) and Gaspard Charles de La Rive (1770–1834), who were passing their examinations handily. They were granted their M.D. degrees in June. Peter and Marcet were to be close friends and colleagues in London ten years hence, and twenty years later Roget was to write his friend's obituary. All of the candidates submitted themselves to the hands of a "grinder" in prepping for the examinations.

But toward the end of May, two events occurred which killed any small seeds of optimism and brought Catherine to her knees in despair. First, young Scarlett's bid for his doctorate was rejected, and he, incensed, announced that he would publish a pamphlet attacking the faculty. Second, and far more serious, what Catherine had feared for so many years struck: Peter became gravely ill, apparently from tuberculosis.

After the seventeenth consecutive day spent at Peter's bedside, Catherine wrote on June 10:

I have been so unhappy since I wrote last to you that it was impossible for me to take a pen in hand, nor till the last extremity would I for the world have made you share my uneasiness. The very day after my letter, he lost appetite, grew weaker than ever, coughed a great deal, and began spitting up dreadful matter mixed with blood. I immediately knew his danger: I thought an abscess was formed on his lungs—God knows whether it was so, but day after day the cough increased and he began to have night sweats, which after a fever of ten days which had before exhausted his strength, I knew must soon bring him at death's door. I entreated him the day before yesterday to try Godbald's Vegetable Balsam, which has, God be thanked, caused so great a change in his complaints that yesterday he ate heartily some rice pudding and a little beef. He has had two good nights and his cough is greatly decreased. Mr. De la Rive assured me but yesterday that the spitting came from the throat and not his lung, which I cannot think, though I must own during his whole illness he complained of his throat. Be what it will, a return of appetite is the most favorable symptom. I have not as yet mentioned to Dr. G. [probably James Gregory, appointed to the Chair of Medicine in 1790] that I am giving him the balsam, but as he only ordered since the fever a little Julep, it is of no consequence.

Slight as their circle of acquaintances was in Edinburgh, the Rogets' friends rallied round. The Stewarts called several times —as did Scarlett, still blustering about his pamphlet, which Catherine tried to convince him it would be a mistake to publish. Friends in London wrote consoling letters. Dumont, sojourning in Dover, sought out the advice of a locally famous healer and sent it along to Catherine. Doctors from the Medical Faculty were generous with their time, especially Dr. Gregory. Repeatedly, Catherine supervised the meager diagnostic tests that the doctors could make for tuberculosis. Gradually her fears abated: Peter suffered no pain in his chest—she thought that a hopeful sign—and slowly the cough eased. By the end of June, he was sitting up for a few hours a day. His appetite was good, and Catherine had supplemented the roast beef and mutton that he craved with ass's milk and porter. She delighted in seeing him take the nourishment, for he had become terribly thin and weak.

She had moved his bed into the dining room, which was large and airy, and this seemed to improve the boy's spirits.

After a summer's convalescence at Queen's Ferry, a smoky little industrial town about ten miles west of Edinburgh, Peter returned to Hope Park End in great spirits. The sight of his books, the prospect of walking again to the university, the visits of three or four classmates, all gave him great delight, and he began at once to resume his studies. Catherine, of course, monitored his work severely. "I am daily preaching to him on the usefulness of being *ignorant* and sober—that is, little study and more exercise —and doing every thing *moderately*." She was glad to report to Romilly that he seemed sensible of the need to take better care of his health than he had before:

> When he first got out of his sick bed, we thought him grown tall, owing no doubt to his being such a skeleton, for we now think he is growing short. He begins to fill again. His breeches at first hung on him such a manner he was ashamed of them, and his legs, two sticks. He was even obliged to have a pair of smaller shoes made for him.[13]

There was only one relapse and that was psychological, resulting from Dr. Gregory's informing Peter that the cause of his illness had indeed had something to do with his lungs and that he had had a narrow escape. "You cannot conceive the impression it made on him," Catherine wrote. "For two or three days he was very dull, as he knows too well from his physical studies the little relief any medicines can afford."

As a final attempt to strengthen Peter (and herself) for the rigorous winter's work ahead, Catherine dipped into her savings and took the little family on an eight-day excursion of the country north of Edinburgh. They left the city on Monday, August 14; visited St. Andrews, Dundee, and Dunkelt on the Tay (the farthest north they traveled); and returned, with stops in Perth and Kinross, to the ferry and back across the Forth.

Catherine was bolstered in her attempt to slow Peter's eager return to his studies by a thoughtful letter to the boy from his uncle, who told of a similar illness he had suffered when he was Peter's age and how he had learned through sad experience that to sacrifice his health to success was the height of folly. In reply, Peter assured Romilly that he was getting adequate exercise, and he rather proudly described a system he had invented which combined both study and exercise: he simply habituated himself to

walking backward and forward across his room while he was
reading. Moreover, he had acceded to his mother's demand that
he stay away from hospitals until he completely regained his
strength.

Despite the delay and retardation of his work caused by his
summer's illness, Peter was in September working on two papers
that he proposed reading to the Medical Society during the winter term:

> One of these I shall, as is the common custom, convert into my
> thesis. In the subject I had formerly chosen and for which I
> had collected many materials and projected a number of exper-
> iments, I had unluckily been anticipated by another person,
> who had prosecuted it by experiments with great success and
> who intended to publish them in his thesis the same year that
> I am to graduate. As I was unwilling to appear ambitious of ri-
> valling him, and could not expect to offer any thing new on
> the subject, I gave up my former intention and was for a long
> time unfixed as to my choice of another. I have at length, how-
> ever, determined to write on *The Laws of Chemical Affinity*.[14]

In this same letter, his last from Edinburgh, Peter's mature
style in his description of the Highlands tour suggests that he
had done a good deal of growing up in the preceding three years.
He was, he reported, attending an apothecary's shop at the other
end of town to make himself familiar with medicinal drugs and
preparations. Finally, he said, to add to his concern over his
forthcoming examinations, he had very nearly been drafted:

> I have had a great deal of trouble lately in getting my name
> taken out of the list to be ballotted for the new militia that is
> to be raised in Scotland, but I have at length succeeded by the
> help of a certificate of my age. The common people, finding
> that it is in vain that they make any resistance, now quietly
> submit to the measure.

Catherine's next letter to Romilly confirmed Peter's anxiety
about his studies. She had talked him out of studying at night, although the other students could not imagine how he could complete his work and cram for the examinations without burning
the midnight oil. And as Scarlett, who had decided to try again,
turned to his work with twice the energy and time that Peter
could muster, the young Roget became more and more despond-
ent, more and more convinced that he could not possibly complete his work during the winter months.

Meanwhile, Catherine's social life quickened somewhat as the building they occupied filled with additional families. On November 11, 1797, she wrote that there were ten families living in the place, and that of the ten they were acquainted with three:

Perhaps we shall reap some benefit from the fourth, newcomers whom we are going civilly to call on. They live just under us and are so very pious that we hear them sing psalms morning and evening. Supposing them to be Methodist, I declined calling, but have since heard that the strict Presbyterians do the same. What is more singular, the husband, a Captain Pratt, was in the army. Such men would please Mr. Wilberforce,[15] whose sanctity appears daily increasing. My God, 'tis mocking the Prince of Peace to be praying to him with hearts full of war!

In December, Samuel Romilly married Anne Garbett, daughter of Francis Garbett and Elizabeth, and the several surviving letters from the end of the year are largely taken up with discussions of the wedding and the new bride. Romilly had met her at Bowood, the Wiltshire estate of Lord Lansdowne.

As the time for Peter's graduation drew near, a different line of advice began to flow from family and friends. As eager as he was to step out on his own and establish himself professionally, he was pointedly reminded of his age and his lack of experience. Dumont, for example, writing from Kensington Square, advised Catherine:

I understand how important and yet at the same time how difficult it will be to usefully fill up the four or five years from the time of his reception of the doctorate until the time when we will have some chance to put him into the ranks of practicing physicians. For it will be impossible to gain confidence of people before he has attained the complete stature of a man, and it would be unfortunate to aspire too soon. . . . I would advise him to consider his studies already made as it were merely a first sight of the country, which gives him a means of choosing, of beginning again, of learning the very method he must use in order to complete that which is lacking for him. One studies twice . . . the first time serves only to direct one for the second time.[16]

Dumont passed along the advice of doctor friends of his: that Peter especially give attention to anatomy, "which is much too neglected by doctors in general," and that Peter be very careful of his own health.

Peter wavered apparently, through the spring of 1798, between
heeding this good advice about his health and following his own
desires, which urged him to bear down on his work and secure
the degree in June. Catherine was ambivalent, too. If he did not
finish in June, her summer plans would be interrupted, and she
was completely fed up with Edinburgh. On the other hand, she
would not have him intensify his efforts at the risk of damaging
his health. To give her due credit, she was even prepared to accept Peter's ideas of taking his degree in June and remaining in
Edinburgh for another winter of study.

Hearing nothing from her brother in answer to questions
about conditions in London, Catherine appealed to Dumont. He
replied promptly, after conferring with medical friends, that
what she had heard was true: books on medicine were hard to
come by in London; there was no public library; courses given in
the hospitals were very expensive—as much as £50—and they
could not compare with courses given in Edinburgh. But, he
pointed out, the important subject for Peter was still anatomy,
and London was the place for that. "A dissection is the most useful book for a doctor, and this kind of book is found only in the
big cities."

Among other difficulties facing the young medical student in
Edinburgh was that of acquiring subjects for dissection. The
time was a little too early for the exploits of William Burke and
the other infamous "resurrectionists," but restrictive laws in Edinburgh made the supply of cadavers a very unpredictable factor
at the Medical School. Catherine herself had long been aware of
this problem, as evidenced in one of her many reports on Peter's
health:

The dreadful bad smell from the Subjects used in the Anatomi-
    cal lecture is dreadful—particularly in close warm weather.
    They are often quite *green*. There can be nothing so absurd as
    to have made procuring of dead bodies to dissect *criminal*—it
    occasions it being often *mortal*. The church yards here are
    fenced in on every side, and all but the poor pay for a watch
    to guard the lifeless lump of clay—which tho' perhaps of little
    use when living might have afforded instruction when dead.[17]

The spring of 1798 became too hectic for correspondence. In
the surviving family papers, there are no letters between Dumont's of February 20 and a congratulatory letter from Romilly
to Peter, written July 7. We thus have no idea whether Peter ran

into trouble in presenting his thesis or in satisfying his examiners. Trouble or no, he completed the requirements, and on June 25, 1798, at nineteen years of age, Peter Mark Roget was awarded the M.D. degree at the old College Hall (originally erected in 1616).[18] His diploma was presented and signed by all his medical professors, who attended in full academic regalia. Twelve young men received the degree on that day.

The long, lonely years, the determined self-exile, the thousand and one economizings, the fearful survival of yet another cold Scottish winter with all its discomforts and dangers to health, the constant watching and guarding and nursing and guiding—all of these daily, in the face of nagging, second-thought fears that it all should be somehow done differently—were finally past. Catherine, and Edinburgh, and the advice of brother Sam and Dumont, and of course the Divinity Faculty had at last turned out their young man.

III   [1798-1799 ❧

Postgraduate Wanderings
—Bristol

PHYSICALLY, Peter was worn out. The illness of the year before, the winter's grind in preparing his thesis, the constant anxiety of his mother, which made itself always felt, had reduced him to a state of fatigue that bordered on desperation. To some extent young Roget asserted himself in a mild revolt against the family planning that had, all these years, considered him a thing in the process of making. Even his uncle's congratulatory letter upon Peter's graduation made it clear that Peter was not done with the planning, the arranging and rearranging, that had been his lot all his life. So over the objections of his mother, Peter took several sightseeing jaunts during the summer and autumn of 1798—to the falls of the Clyde and to the English Lake District—and made several visits to scientific men who might give him a leg up: Dr. Erasmus Darwin at Derby; James Keir, the chemist, near Birmingham; and Dr. Thomas Beddoes at Clifton, near Bristol.

At Clifton, where Beddoes, an eccentric[1] doctor of many talents and former professor of chemistry at Oxford, was establishing the famous "Pneumatic Institution," Peter Roget stumbled into an incredible mélange of scientific and literary activity which might well have sent him off in an entirely different direction from that suitable to a straightforward young English doctor. As it turned out, even though Roget shied away from the highly irregular carryings-on at Clifton, he made many new contacts (and reinforced old ones) there that served him importantly through the rest of his life. An immediate result of his visit was Roget's first scientific publication. Beddoes included in his essay *Causes of Pulmonary Consumption* (London, 1799) Roget's notes on the nonprevalence of consumption among butchers, fishermen, etc.

Dr. Beddoes—whose prize patient at Clifton was Thomas Wedgwood, cousin and partner of the famous potter—married Anna Edgeworth.[2] Beddoes thus combined, along with his own interest in experimental science, representatives of the arts and of industry in his unique effort to establish an institution for the treating of various ailments by the respiration of various gases. Funded by popular subscription (Josiah Wedgwood gave £1,000 [3]), the institution, long a fond dream of Beddoes, was just becoming an actuality in the summer of 1798. It began operations in October of that year, with Humphry Davy (just one year older than Roget) as superintendent and James Watt designing the apparatus used to produce and administer the therapeutic gases. Roget was to meet both men again, and later to share the lecture platform with Davy at the Royal Institution. Davy introduced to Beddoes by Davies Gilbert,[4] who later, as President of the Royal Society, paved the way for much of Roget's scientific recognition, including the secretaryship of the Royal Society. Roget may well have met Davies at Clifton during the summer or fall of 1798.

Also associated with Beddoes' experiments were Erasmus Darwin, Samuel Taylor Coleridge, William Wordsworth, Robert Southey, Lovell Edgeworth (with whom Roget traveled to Geneva in 1802), Dr. Robert Kinglake, Joseph Cottle, J. W. Tobin, and Maria Edgeworth.

In November, Beddoes leased two houses in the upper, or northwestern, corner of Dowry Square in Clifton, had the interior arrangements altered for his purpose, and installed the machinery that Watt had designed. By early spring of 1799 everything was ready, and the project that Beddoes had proposed six years before opened officially as the Pneumatic Medical Institution, endorsed by the Royal Medical Society of Edinburgh.[5] An announcement in the Thursday, March 21, 1799, *Bristol Gazette and Public Advertiser* declared, "Patients will be treated gratis," and "Attendance will be given from 11 till one o'clock by Thomas Beddoes or Humphry Davy."

The institution was an immediate success. Shortly after its opening, Beddoes wrote, "Upwards of 40 are become out-patients

within this fortnight, and we could immediately fill the house
with in-patients." [6] But the success was short-lived. Both Beddoes
and Davy by 1800 had realized that further progress in pneumatic medicine was blocked by lack of knowledge in physiology
and chemistry.[7] Davy left to take a post in the Royal Institution
under Count Rumford, and Beddoes closed the Clifton establishment. But many of their theories were seized on by later investigators who developed these pioneer efforts into the first anaes-
thetics.

Meanwhile, experimentation with gases continued to amaze
and amuse. Davy, in London, wrote late in 1799 to a former colleague at Clifton, "Tomorow a party of philosophers meet at the
[Royal] Institution to inhale the joy-inspiring gas. It has produced a great sensation." [8]

Interest in pneumatic medicine was revived again, between
1829 and 1833, owing to a series of clinical experiments carried
out by J. A. Albers of Bonn. (In 1816, Roget collaborated with
this same investigator in producing a paper, "On a Change in
the Colour of the Skin Produced by the Internal Use of Nitrate
of Silver.") "Albers' work attracted sufficient attention from researches on the inhalation of chlorine to be undertaken by others,
both in Great Britain and in the U. S." [9]

What was this gaseous marvel with which Roget himself experimented, much to the dismay of his mother? Priestley called it
"dephlogisticated nitrous air"; French chemists, "gaseous oxide
of azote." Dr. Samuel Latham Mitchell of New York contended
that the gas caused contagion, producing sepsis, and he called it
"oxide of septon." The interested public referred to it as "laughing gas," "releasing gas," "joy-producing gas," etc.

As early as 1795, Beddoes and Watt collaborated in publishing
a two-part volume, *Considerations on the Medicinal Use and on
the Production of Factitious Airs*. Part I, by Beddoes, was a complete description of nitrous oxide and its medical application;
Part II, by Watt, comprised detailed drawings of the apparatus
for generating the stuff, and the silk bag and mouthpiece used in
administering the gas. The book closed with a long series of testimonials from doctors and others on the efficacy of the gas. Beddoes and Watt even envisioned commercial possibilities and set
out a package deal for the interested public: a simplified and
portable form of the gas-generating apparatus cost £6 16s. 6d.,
with an additional £3 6s. for auxiliary articles, such as a special
cap shaped like a beehive to use if one had trouble holding the
mouthpiece so that no ordinary air was taken in.[10]

Fascinated by the gas, Davy experimented extensively. He found he could breathe nine quarts of nitrous oxide for three minutes from and into a silk bag, holding his nostrils closed; twelve quarts for more than four; but never in any quantity so long as five minutes. Invariably, Davy reported, the inhalations produced an apparent intensification of visual and auditory perception and

> . . . a sensation analogous to gentle pressure on all the muscles, attended by a highly pleasurable thrilling, particularly in the chest and the extremities. . . . The sense of muscular power became greater and at last an irresistible propensity to action was indulged in. But whenever its operation was carried to the highest extent, the pleasurable thrilling . . . gradually diminished, the sense of pressure on the muscles was lost; impressions ceased to be perceived; vivid ideas passed rapidly through the mind, and voluntary power was altogether destroyed so that the mouthpiece generally dropt from my unclosed lips.[11]

Davy also found that the inhalations improved his poetry, and one of the interesting sights of Clifton in the fall of 1798 was Davy walking the hills, composing verse while breathing nitrous oxide from a bag. Here is a sample of the result:

> Not in the ideal dreams of wild desire
> Have I beheld a rapture-awakening form:
> My bosom burns with no unhallow'd fire,
> Yet is my cheek with rosy blushes warm;
> Yet are my eyes with sparkling lustre fill'd;
> Yet is my mouth replete with murmuring sound;
> Yet are my limbs with inward transports fill'd;
> And clad with new-born mightiness around.[12]

The fact that both Wordsworth and Coleridge were among the young enthusiasts sampling the nitrous oxide at Clifton might well give rise to an entirely new—and startlingly literal—interpretation of certain phrases in Wordsworth's famous definition of poetry:

> . . . a selection of the real language of men *in a state of vivid sensation* [italics added] . . .

> . . . Poems to which any value can be attached were never produced on any variety of subjects but by a man who, *being possessed of more than organic sensibilities* [italics added] had also thought long and deeply. . . .[13]

Davy and Beddoes, eager to add to their growing notes on effects of the gas, talked nearly everyone who visited the Pneumatic Institution into breathing the gas and giving an account.
After Robert Southey tried it, he wrote to his brother (July 12,
1799): "Oh Tom! I have had some; it made me laugh and tingle
in every toe and fingertip. Davy has actually invented a new pleasure, for which language has no name. Oh Tom! I am going for
more this evening; it makes one strong and so happy! So glo-
riously happy!" [14] Coleridge also felt "an highly pleasurable sensation of warmth over my whole frame," and noted that "the
only motion which I felt inclined to make was that of laughing
at those who were looking at me." On another occasion he could
not "avoid, nor indeed felt any wish to avoid, beating the ground
with my feet."

When an anonymous young lady tried the gas, after a few inspirations, to the astonishment of everybody,

. . . she dashed out of the house, when, racing down the square,
she leaped over a great dog in the way, but being hotly pursued by the fleetest of her friends, the fair fugitive, or rather
the temporary maniac, was at length overtaken and secured
without further damage.[15]

The effect of the gas on Roget was less spectacular, but interesting enough to prompt comparisons with present-day reports of
the effects of LSD and other hallucinatory drugs. For all the
polysyllabic solemnity of the young doctor's language, it is clear
that the experience shook him to his boots:

The effect of the first inspirations of the nitrous oxide was that
of making me vertiginous and producing a tingling sensation
in my hands and feet: as these feelings increased, I seemed to
lose the sense of my own weight, and imagined I was sinking
into the ground. I then felt a drowsiness gradually steal upon
me, and a disinclination to motion; even the actions of inspiring and expiring were not performed without effort, and it
also required some attention of mind to keep my nostrils
closed with my fingers. I was gradually roused from this torpor
by a kind of delirium, which came on so rapidly that the air-
bag dropt from my hands. This sensation increased for about a
minute after I had ceased to breathe, to a much greater degree
than before, and I suddenly lost sight of all the objects around
me, they being apparently obscured by the clouds, in which
were many luminous points similar to what is often experienced on rising suddenly and stretching out the arms, after sitting long in one position.

I felt myself totally incapable of speaking, and for some time lost all consciousness of where I was, or who was near me. My whole frame felt as if violently agitated: I thought I panted violently; my heart seemed to palpitate, and every artery to throb with violence; I felt a singing in my ears; all the vital motions seemed to be irresistibly hurried on, as if their equilibrium had been destroyed, and everything was running headlong into confusion. My ideas succeeded one another with extreme rapidity; thoughts rushed like a torrent through my mind, as if their velocity had been suddenly accelerated by the bursting of a barrier which had before retained them in their natural and equable course. This state of extreme hurry, agitation, and tumult was but transient. Every unnatural sensation gradually subsided; and in about a quarter of an hour after I had ceased to breathe the gas, I was nearly in the same state in which I had been at the commencement of the experiment.

I cannot remember that I experienced the least pleasure from any of these sensations. I can, however, easily conceive, that by frequent repetition I might reconcile myself to them, and possibly receive pleasure from the same sensations which were then unpleasant.

I am sensible that the account I have been able to give of my feelings is very imperfect. For however calculated, their violence and novelty were to leave a lasting impression on the memory; these circumstances were for that very reason unfavorable to accuracy of comparison with sensations already familiar.

The nature of the sensations themselves, which bore greater resemblance to a half delirious dream than to any distinct state of mind capable of being accurately remembered, contributes very much to increase the difficulty. And as it is above two months since I made the experiment, many of the minuter circumstances have probably escaped me.[16]

Potentially useful to medicine as those experiments in consciousness might have been, they were, to that young man from Edinburgh, bewildering and frightening. For one so properly, so assiduously, trained to be a model professional man as Peter Roget had been, such an experience in which his equilibrium was destroyed and "everything was running headlong into confusion" was plainly destructive. If he had learned anything in the five years at Edinburgh, in his dim awareness of the chaotic state of the eighteenth-century world, Peter had been convinced that his future lay in regularity and order—not in disequilibrium and confusion. Moreover, he saw no controls on the experimentation. Most of the brightest lights in Clifton were very close to his own age (Davy was twenty; Coleridge, twenty-six; Southey, twenty-four; Wordsworth, twenty-nine), and they were ramping about in more fields than one. They were, for example, quite capable of coming up on a bright morning with an extraordinary scheme like forming a utopian "pantisocracy" on the banks of the Susquehanna. Combining these features with their radical political leanings, one need not strain the imagination to see Roget (and Catherine) deciding that this place was hardly the beginning of the trail to a secure future for him and his mother and sister. By the end of summer 1799, there were distinct signs that the Pneumatic Medical Institution was not long for this world. Puzzled and disgruntled, and feeling an unaccountable sense of failing his first opportunity, young Roget went off with his mother for a brief vacation at Ilfracombe, where he promptly became ill.

Catherine again applied her home remedies and restored the young doctor, whose spirits were given a boost by an invitation that Dumont had arranged for him to spend the month of September at Bowood Park, Lord Lansdowne's elegant Wiltshire estate near Calne.[17] This indeed seemed propitious, for the Marquis of Lansdowne, better known in British politics as Lord Shelburne, who served as George III's Prime Minister on condition that the King seek a reconciliation with the Americans, was one of the most powerful men in a patronage-ridden nation. Lansdowne's circle of acquaintances was enormous, and his estate was a mecca for liberal politicians, jurists, and students. It was at Bowood, for example, that Romilly met Anne Garbett, and it was there that Bentham met Romilly. Dumont was another familiar at Bowood, as were members of the family of Charles Fox. Moreover, Lansdowne's town house on Berkeley Square was a center of artistic, literary, and political activity. If Roget was to find the opening he sought into greener pastures, he could not have asked for a more useful entrée.

Meanwhile, Catherine was busy, planning and evaluating, as seen in this reply to one of her appeals to her brother. Romilly's sober, reassuring advice is typical:

> I approve highly of your decision to quit Bristol. It is quite clear that your residence there will not be of any use to Peter. . . . Peter has no reason, I think, to regret that Dr. B's Institution has not been successful to him. It could not, you say, be profitable, and as to any Reputation to be acquired by it, it could not, I think, have answered—not only for the political reason you give, but for others. I am only sorry that P is out of spirits

about it, though I am not very much surprised. The first Disappointment which a man meets on his onset in life is generally felt more sensibly than it ought to be. I really think the only thing P has to do for some years is to pursue his studies and grow older. . . .

Since I have come to town I have seen Bentham, and he told me what he hinted at once before: that he had a project respecting Peter. What it is I don't know, but I conjecture from some things which he said that it is some discovery in Chemistry which he has made—or thinks he has made—which he considers as very important and which he wishes to communicate to some person in whom he can have entire confidence, and who may, by experiments, ascertain the merit of it. He speaks of it as a thing which may be of great use to P, and he asked me whether I thought P could be induced to come to town about it as it would be necessary that he should see him often. I told him I really did not know, and so our conversation ended. It is possible there may be nothing worth thinking about in all this, but if anything else should lead Peter to town, I would have him certainly see Bentham and ascertain what it is. B. is a man of so original a genius that it is possible the discovery or whatever it is may be very important. If P wishes, I will have some more conversation with B on the subject. . . .[18]

This connection with Bentham was secured by Romilly's suggesting to Bentham's ever-curious mind that Peter could tell him all about the experiments at Clifton, which had become the subject of much public interest. Peter responded to Bentham's inquiry in a lengthy letter on January 9, 1800, not only recounting his own experiences in inhaling nitrous oxide but describing other experiments he had made, showing the effect (lethal) of the gas on mice and other small animals. Roget also gave Bentham explicit directions on how to prepare the stuff, and some practical advice in the handling of the gas, thus confirming the idea that Roget had been no casual observer but had worked as both a physiologist and a chemist in the Clifton laboratory. Roget's letter included one querulous remark that suggests still another reason for his disappointment at Clifton:

In July last, I gave Mr. Davy, the discoverer of this air, an account I had written at his request of the effect it had upon me. This account, I find, has been suppressed.[19]

Roget had yet to see Davy's volume *Researches*, published in 1800, which printed Roget's report.

Before abandoning the provinces, Roget, Catherine, and Annette moved from Bristol to Cheltenham, to survey the possibilities of making a start in that Gloucestershire town. He found it a pleasant enough place, but he was lonesome and not at all optimistic about his prospects there. In his idleness, Peter took the opportunity to begin a correspondence with an Edinburgh classmate, Dr. Alexander Marcet, which was to grow into the nearest thing to an intimate friendship that Roget had. He congratulated Marcet on his recent marriage, using the same stiffly formal style that characterized his writing the rest of his life:

Dear Sir,

I am happy in having an opportunity of beginning a correspondence I have often wished to establish, but have too often delayed to begin, at so auspicious a moment. Permit me to send you my warmest congratulations on your marriage; an event that must so essentially add to your happiness, and of which the news would not fail of giving us the greatest pleasure. Our pleasure has been greatly heightened by the very favourable accounts we have heard of the character and accomplishments of the amiable object of your choice. That you may long enjoy happiness is my sincere wish; that you well deserve it is my firm conviction. . . .[20]

Shortly after writing this letter, Roget packed his trunk and went up to London—alone—presumably to "pursue his studies and grow older," as his uncle had advised. He studied at Dr. Robert Willan's dispensary in Carey Street, and at St. George's Hospital, Hyde Park Corner, he attended a course of lectures delivered by Dr. Matthew Baillie, one of the most successful and influential physicians in London. Talking with Dr. Baillie must have given the young Roget some assurance that he was indeed beginning to find his way, for Baillie, in addition to being Physician Extraordinary to George III, had inherited the Great Windmill Street School of Anatomy from his uncle, the famed William Hunter. Later, Roget himself was to teach at the Great Windmill Street School, but in 1799 he saw Dr. Baillie as the respected mentor of most of the prospective doctors in London.

That Catherine did not approve of her son's separation from her is suggested by a letter from Dumont, writing from Bath, where Dumont was guest of Lord Lansdowne. He pointed out that it was a serious matter and that Peter could get nowhere languishing in the provincial towns:

. . . Peter must present himself; he must make connections; he must profit from a stay in the Capital where ideas are in circulation far more than in Bristol or in Cheltenham. I am more convinced than ever that London is the only city where he can settle successfully. In the smaller cities monopoly is obvious. Let a newcomer arrive and immediately an unpleasant sensation is produced among his dear colleagues. They bustle around, they elbow each other, they attempt to drive him away. They have a thousand little methods of intrigue which do not take place in the grand arena. There are here [in Bath] 34 doctors who, it is said, share among themselves nine to ten thousand pounds sterling; but that is the lion's share. Dr. Perry takes £400 for his share, the others as much as they can. At Bristol it's about the same, and proportionately in the other towns. But London—London! That is the great gate of salvation. Lord Lansdowne often asks me for news of the young doctor; he is very interested in him.[21]

Catherine resigned herself, temporarily at least, to accepting this advice from her worldly friend Dumont, and for the bulk of the next two years made her (and Annette's) home at Sidmouth, on the Devonshire coast. She would not live in London, despite repeated pleas from Dumont, Romilly, Chauvet, and Peter himself; but, as she often put it herself, she would not stand in the way of Peter's success. Thus she and Annette rusticated in the resort town and contented themselves with secondhand news of the political, literary, and scientific events that they might have witnessed at first hand. An example of what she was missing is provided in a letter from her sister-in-law, Anne Romilly, who on May 16, 1800, described an attempt on George III's life as he entered the Drury Lane Theatre. Anne's hope that the would-be assassin would pay with his life is somewhat ironic, in view of the fact that her husband was to devote much of his life to eliminating capital punishment from the English penal code.

Peter of course came down to Devonshire for his holidays, but in the main Catherine had to learn to satisfy herself with his long letters of life in London. He was a loyal correspondent, unstinting in describing his own domestic arrangements, his health, the weather, his progress as a student. His letters, commonly running longer than a thousand words, arrived about every other week. Moreover, he took the time and effort to write most of these lengthy reports in French, partly to increase his own facility with the language and partly to please Catherine, who wrote the bulk of her own letters in French and encouraged Annette to do the same.

In all the materials left bearing on Roget's life—published or private—nowhere is there a clear-cut statement of Roget's political views, nor even any evidence that he *had* any such views. In the considerable correspondence from London, for example, during the next year, the young doctor's remarks on political matters could be printed on one page. Occasionally he alluded to the hostilities with France or to the prospects for peace; two or three times he mentioned the debates under way in Parliament; infrequently he wrote a line or two on the bread riots or rick burnings that were becoming more and more common; once he cautioned Catherine not to listen to the misinformed and malicious rumors that the grain shortage was caused by profiteering merchants and brokers. But in the main, he showed practically no interest in foreign or domestic policies, in the vicious infighting among the Whigs, in the deteriorating conditions of the city poor as they were jammed tighter and tighter into fantastic slums, or in the plight of the rural poor, who were driven off the land by the enclosure system. Why such an obviously talented young man—one who was a university student during the French Revolution, and one who was influenced by such politically active men as Romilly, Brougham, Dumont, Bentham, and Lansdowne—should not have shown early and active interest in politics is one of the mysteries of Peter Mark Roget.

A few glimmerings are thrown on this perplexing question by later events, but at this point—the end of the eighteenth century —Peter was preparing to begin his assault on London with only his own future, and that of his immediate family, on his mind. From his letters he seems to have been almost completely unaware of the fact that he was bobbing about in a stream that was to become a torrent and sweep away forever the eighteenth-century England he had been prepared to serve.

IV [1800–1801 ❧

Postgraduate Wanderings
—London

Before he returned to London in the fall of 1800, Roget resumed his correspondence with Bentham, who had sent him details of a scheme to build a "Frigidarium." [1] The young doctor answered that he was flattered that Bentham should ask his advice. In a second letter, written October 5, Roget said he only awaited a note from Bentham to come on to London, and would Bentham please send the number of his house.

Thus, when Peter Roget journeyed back to London, sometime in October of 1800, he had an exciting destination—Bentham's famous residence in Queen Square Place, just off Southampton Row. He was to stay with one of the most talented—and most eccentric—minds in all of England. There is some evidence that the highly charged atmosphere of the "Hermitage," as Bentham called his home, was, in a very different way, as alarming and as disturbing to young Roget as was that of Beddoes' Pneumatic Institution in Clifton.

A detailed and highly laudatory description of Bentham's establishment is provided by Richard Rush, American envoy extraordinary and minister plenipotentiary to the British court from 1817 to 1825. "If Mr. Bentham's character be peculiar," wrote Rush in describing a dinner engagement with Bentham on July 27, 1818, "so is his place of residence." [2] In a series of three letters—November 7, November 17, and December 7, 1800—Roget told his mother that the Bentham household was not at all orderly: all sorts of people came and went; he enjoyed no pri-

vacy; only rarely could he see Bentham himself; the conversation
often bordered on the sacrilegious; politically, Bentham's place
was a hotbed of radicalism. Peter saw nothing of the graciousness
that impressed Rush. He reported that Mrs. Bentham (Jeremy's
brother's wife) was so pedantic and so domineering that she
drove people quite off.

Bentham's Frigidarium scheme, which he sent Roget on September 4 in the form of a large parcel of notes, diagrams, and
references to printed works,[3] proposed the construction of

> . . . a sort of ice-house, for the purposes of preserving fermenta-
> ble substances of all sorts, from prejudicial fermentation, by
> excluding the degree of heat necessary to that process. The
> commercial plan therein deducible includes, you see, all provi-
> sions except grain, with different degrees of advantage.[4]

The parcel of notes Roget received was typical of Bentham's way
of working: he pushed forward several projects at once, filing
ideas and data away on each of them as he came across such contributions through the years. In the instance of the Frigidarium,
Bentham had collected information for four or five years before
he felt it was time to bring the scheme into fruition. The packet
included not only his initial and modified theories about the
thing, but notes on proposed dimensions, locations; problems of
construction, size, weather; hastily scribbled sketches to illustrate
these several points; sheets of statistics on annual price fluctua-
tion of perishable foodstuffs; calculations of presumed profits to
be gained by the operation of the thing; reports of distantly related experiments, etc. As he pointed out in a covering letter to
Roget, the file was a clutter of repetitions and "absurdities" that
he had no time to sort out. In short, he apparently was hoping
that Roget could study the materials and bring them into some
sort of order so that an application of the scheme could get
under way.

Bentham was fairly specific about what he wanted in the finished product:

> . . . My Frigidarium I think of making semiglobular (or rather
> a frustrum of a globe mounted on a cylinder) about sixteen
> feet diameter clear in the inside: estimated expense, by an able
> and confidential architect, about £170. It will form a mount in
> my garden, and will be pretty well shaded by tall trees. Vessels
> and instruments may make up the expense, say £250; and sub-
> ject-matter of the experiment for the twelve-month, perhaps
> £100.[5]

Bentham's plan depended critically upon establishing proper relationships among the several factors: space, surface, amount of ice, types of perishables, outside temperature. He was not interested in freezing the goods, since he had learned from correspondents in Russia that freezing broke up and destroyed the texture of many food products and impaired the flavor: "The object is to keep the subject-matter unfrozen in a temperature not higher, say, than 36." He also saw the possibilities of an adjacent "Tepidarium," but conceded that he had not had time to think this through sufficiently to warrant their working on it at the moment.

Methodically, he set forth what he wanted from Peter Roget on the project:

1. Does any matter-of-fact or consideration present itself to you as opposing an insuperable bar to success?
2. Item, anything as necessary or particularly conducive to success?
3. Does the course of experiments and observations I think to engage in (unless you should show cause to the contrary) strike you as sufficiently interesting in any point of view, to produce an inclination on your part to observe and attend the progress of them?
4. Could you make it convenient to give me your company at the time of planning the building and other arrangements?—a business which could not, I think, well be deferred (in respect of the season and weather) beyond the first week in October? [6]

More specifically, he wanted Peter to calculate the amount of ice required for the year's experimentation, determine its disposition in the building, and plot the comparative periods of fermentation and decay of various foodstuffs at various temperatures. He pointedly asked about Peter's competency in mathematics.

Roget answered this appeal promptly, on September 9. He said that, after studying the project, he was struck "with the extensiveness of the views they seem to open"; he felt that the "proposed experiments must lead to a wide field of investigation on various subjects, scientific as well as economical." He did add, however—and this must have at least irritated Bentham, who thought of himself as a thoroughgoing Utilitarian—"The only discouraging reflection that presented itself to me is, that the immediate *utility* that may result from the scheme does not, as yet, appear in so clear a light as the possibility of carrying it into execution does."

Bentham came back immediately in a lengthy letter written

September 13, clarifying the "utility" of the scheme by citing present market prices of fruits, vegetables, meats, and fish, and by pointing out that the present purveyors made their profits only after absorbing heavy losses due to spoilage. What, said Bentham, if the spoilage were eliminated? What, too, of the terrific seasonal variation in prices?

> . . . the same peach or parcel of green peas which at one time may be had for 1 shilling, shall at another time only by being a few months or even weeks earlier, fetch a guinea. What would they fetch at Christmas? [7]

Bentham went on for a couple of pages, detailing the enormous profits to be made of various meats, fish, etc., if they could be offered to the market out of season. In short, what he envisioned was nothing less than the whole cold-storage industry.

He concluded his letter by referring again to the need for reliable calculations of ice supply, etc., and by pointing out again that he would rely entirely upon Roget for this contribution. He offered Peter exclusive use of two or three rooms in the Hermitage for as long as he might need them.

But Roget found that Bentham's place was badly located for his purposes. "The distance is terrible," he wrote to his mother early in November. "More than three miles to Pratt Place [Romilly's father's home, where Roget took most of his meals]; also St. Bartholomew's hospital two times a week has exhausted me from the beginning. I'm getting used to it, but I hope I never again have to walk as much. Although I've often taken a fiacre, I lose half the day on the road." Peter had invested 20 guineas in a course of lectures by John Abernethy, the great surgeon at St. Bartholomew's, and he was afraid that he would not learn much "without spending all my time there."

The domiciliary arrangements at Bentham's were not satisfactory either, Roget said:

> . . . Since General Bentham [Jeremy's brother, Sir Samuel Bentham] came, I am obliged to go out on the road to pass to my bedroom, and to make it worse, the passage needs repairs. Thus, for a long time I've been obliged to walk across the library of the General where he and his wife have been each time that I have had to wash my hands. It's even more disagreeable in that I don't even know them. . . . Also very disagreeable is that there are no locks on any of the doors in this house, none except those on my suit-case and a small drawer. All my papers are exposed. [8]

As to work on the Frigidarium, Roget met further disillusionment:

> Mr. Bentham is absorbed in some work that occupies him without letting up. We still have the building, but it is of no use until we can get ice, and we cannot do that until the end of December. The success of the experiment, which will be done there, is already doubtful. I assume that I will have all the responsibility. Mr. Bentham will contribute very little because he understands nothing of it. [One of the first experiences Roget had with the project was Bentham's admission that he had never been inside an icehouse!] I am resolved to lose no time in it because I can't believe that it will be useful. I have tried certain experiments on my own on heat which haven't succeeded. There are many instruments of iron and wood in the out-house in the garden, but all of it is in such great disorder and covered with such a pile of dust that I will only be able to use it very little. I have already lost a lot of time making the most simple preparations for my experiments.[9]

In short, the Frigidarium, Peter felt, was a sample of the thousand and one schemes of a man "not calculated to finish what he starts out to do." [10]

Despite the fact that Bentham's house was a gathering place for many leading political figures of the period, Roget was lonely there and left largely to himself. The political arguments that flourished in the Hermitage (Bentham has credited Mill with awakening him to politics and his future involvement in the hopes and plans of the Philosophical Radicals) sometimes disturbed the quiet young doctor from the provinces. Bentham's wit was sharp-edged, and his sentiments toward such things as religion and literature—always capitalized in Roget's mind—could not have assured Roget of anything but that he had fallen into another highly irregular way of life. Bentham, for example, was fond of using the word "jug"—short for "juggernaut"—to refer to orthodox Christianity; thus his conversation was often sprinkled with various derivatives—"auto-jug," "juggical," for "church" or "Christian." [11]

The last straw may well have been a scheme developed by Bentham and James Mill to emigrate to Venezuela—shades of the Coleridge-Southey pantisocracy! [12]

By the end of the first week in December, Roget had had all he wanted of the Frigidarium and of Bentham too. He found no difficulty in acting on his uncle's advice and leaving the Hermi-

tage. After staying a week at his uncle's house, No. 27 Gower
Street, Peter found a small apartment of his own at No. 3 Titch-
field Street, where he paid 17 shillings a week for two rooms and
a small dressing closet. He was within a few blocks of Middlesex
Hospital, and within easy walking distance of Sunday dinners at
Gower Street.

Through the next year, Roget, his mother, and his sister wrote
regularly and voluminously back and forth between London and
Sidmouth, and of this correspondence more than a score of
lengthy letters survive. Invariably, they discussed each other's
health in detail, described the weather, kept track of who was in
and out of town, and wondered about Peter's chances of becoming established. Catherine stubbornly remained in Devonshire,
and apparently she kept suggesting that Peter leave the metropolis and return to her. Almost desperately, in a letter to his sister,
Roget complains of his mother's lack of understanding about
how difficult it is for a young doctor to make a good connection
in the country:

> . . . You [Annette and Catherine] don't seem to have formed any
> determined plan. You speak of a sacrifice of five years, but you
> don't tell me how you wish to profit from this sacrifice. What
> advantage is it that I can have at the end of five years passed
> in the country that I would not necessarily have had if I had
> passed them in any place? I would have aged five years more,
> that is all. I would only have been able to advance very little
> in my studies. I would have had less to occupy myself than in
> any other situation. I would have probably lost the habit of
> work and the habit of acting for myself; it would be too late to
> regain it. If I have to quit London in the spring, just when I
> will have commenced to make my career, it seems to me that
> this would be very much against my interests. . . . When one
> returns to London, one has to begin everything again. I've
> sensed that very well this winter.[13]

A few days after Christmas 1800, he moved from the Titchfield
Street address to No. 46 Great Russell Street, Bloomsbury, directly across from the British Museum. It seemed that his landlady at Titchfield Street, recommended to him by his mother,
"gets drunk regularly every evening, and often the mornings
too." The Great Russell Street rooms cost the same amount and
were better situated, he said. "I will be much closer to my uncle
. . . the air is purer because there are no houses at all between
the gardens of the British Museum and Hampstead. . . . My

uncle will procure me an order to allow me to read when I want
to go to the Museum." [14]

He dined regularly with his uncle on Gower Street, with the
rest of the Romillys at Pratt Place, and with the Chauvets out in
Kensington, and not infrequently was a dinner guest of some old
Edinburgh friend or professor, or some friend of the family,
where he often met interesting figures. In December 1800, for example, he dined with Johnson, "the librarian," and met John
Henry Fuseli. "He speaks with a lot of animation; his face is on
fire when he describes something that interests him. He talks a
lot, and with his mannerisms, is, by consequence, rather amusing." The same Johnson (whom I have been unable to identify)
gave young Roget that evening an opportunity to earn, for the
first time, some actual cash:

> . . . I received from Johnson a package containing a thesis written
> in English for the translation of which into Latin he offered
> me five guineas if I wished to undertake it and finish it in 10
> days. I had a lot of trouble to read it and even more to under-
> stand it. Many of the sentences were entirely incomprehen-
> sible. I went to see Johnson and tell him that. He asked me to
> mark a few passages that I didn't understand, and he would
> send them to the author by letter. I sent them yesterday. But
> in order not to lose time I translated a quarter of it the next
> day, good or bad, and by evening I'd finished half of it. It's the
> most barbarous and most unintelligible style I've ever seen. It
> is impossible that the writer knows English—phrases that don't
> finish, strewn with parentheses that include other parentheses,
> often an entire page without a verb! I won't go farther until
> I've had a response.[15]

Christmas 1800 he reported as a "superb day." He took a long
walk, beyond Hampstead, drank his mother's and sister's health
at Pratt Place, and accepted his cousins' invitation to a New
Year's Eve ball. His report on the ball comprises the bulk of a
letter to his mother written on January 16, 1801:

> . . . We were invited for five in the afternoon (this was ridicu-
> lously early for a dance that was going to pass the century.)
> We went, my cousins, Sam, my aunt, and I, at six. I saw sev-
> eral friends from Edinburgh. We commenced to dance at 7; at
> 11 we supped for half an hour. We danced during the rest of
> the century and continued until 4:30 A.M.! There is something
> that surpasses by far Annette's ball! I did all the dances except
> one. Admire, if you will, how I can dance nine hours running

and have myself on my feet afterwards. I had engaged a bed at
a tavern across from uncle's in Pratt Place. They had promised
to wait up for me, but no matter how I knocked no one
opened. I continued to walk in the snow in front of the door
during a half hour before someone opened the door for me.
The next day I was very tired; however, I wasn't able to refuse
to go have dinner at Robinson's, near Blackfriar's Bridge. It
was a month ago that he had invited me. . . . It was 2 in the
morning before I got home. The day afterward had been fixed
with my aunt in Gower Street to go alone with Margaret and
Caroline to Covent Garden. . . . We saw Cooke,[16] the new
actor, in Shylock. . . . My uncle finds him the best actor in
tragedy now in England. He pleased me a lot as Shylock, but
he has as many enemies as admirers. . . . On the 4th, Sunday,
dined at Kensington. The 5th and 7th had lessons with Abernethy. The 8th went again to the theater with Edgeworth at
Drury Lane to see Kimball [17] in King Lear and the new pan-
tomime. The 9th went to a club that we have formed—myself,
Robinson, Dr. W. Robinson, Dr. Fullaston, and Dr. Moffat, to
meet one evening a week. We take tea and dinner together. As
the dinner is a modest affair, I have judged that it would be
well to make this little expense every five weeks for the pleasure of their society. The 10th, at dinner with the family at
Pratt Place. On the 11th, dined at my uncle's—Dr. Marcet and
his wife were there, as well as Constant [Benjamin?].[18]

With all this dissipation, Roget did not forget his commission
from his librarian friend, Johnson. He put in two solid days at
the task, "finished it, edited, corrected, and copied all in a reada-
ble hand, and I have carried it to Johnson and received my five
guineas, which gave me an inconceivable pleasure since this is
the first money that I have gained with my own work." [19] He
was then twenty-two.

Roget lived frugally. His mother had given him some money
when he left her in October, and his uncle had offered to give
him a semiannual allowance of £15. The trip to London cost £5,
plus another £1 15s. 3d. for a suitcase. He saved his little capital
for his medical education—expenses of dissecting at St. Bartholomew's, for example. It is clear that he relied heavily upon dinner
invitations and upon his hopes that he would fall into some profitable situation soon. These hopes were frequently stimulated by
remarks of old family friends. David Chauvet, for instance, in
writing Catherine (January 19, 1801) spoke glowingly of the
young man's prospects:

. . . I am more pleased than ever with our young doctor and furthermore I am pleased to see that everyone who knows him thinks the same. I have not the least doubt about his future success.

But a few weeks later it was obvious that these hopes had been unable to sustain themselves. Peter, who was so disgruntled that he forgot himself momentarily, told his mother exactly how miserable his indecisive state made him feel:

. . . I would have written you long ago and you would have received letters much more frequently if there had been anything in London to interest me. But sadly enough everywhere that I find myself, I find nothing but boredom and disgust. I have passed few agreeable moments since my arrival here. I detest London as cordially as you do. Not having had a fixed plan, not having seen anything stable or certain for the future, I have not been able to enjoy anything. Nothing being arranged, I have not been able to apply myself to study. You have written me not to become worried, but never having given me satisfactory reasons, nor having shown me any plan the pursuit of which would make me succeed, I have not always been able to follow your advice. I haven't made any new acquaintances since I was here at first. I lack the means. I haven't had anyone to introduce me. But principally I haven't had the courage to form temporary relationships which would be broken in so little time. . . .[20]

Roget continued in this letter, which he was soon to regret, pointing out that he was learning many things about the family that Catherine could not know: that his aunt openly criticized Catherine for remaining in Devonshire and hinted that she was depriving Annette of social opportunities; that his uncle disapproved as well; that friends of the family were becoming less solicitous and more pointed in their questions about Catherine's refusal to come to London. In short, Roget could see a serious difference developing between Catherine and the rest of the family.

He alluded to the possibility of succeeding a young Dr. Reid at the Finsbury Dispensary. Reid, it seemed, was planning to leave London for two or three months and would consent to Roget's substituting for him without Roget's having to pay the customary gratuity of £50. Roget saw this as an opportunity to gain experience treating the sick, and to further his career by writing the necessary reports for Reid and by making useful acquaintances with the directors of the dispensary. Despite the strongest antipathies toward the city, he said, he should remain.

Roget was never to speak his feelings so freely to his mother again. While her answer to his February 22 letter is not preserved, his next two letters, of February 27 and March 2, make it painfully clear that Catherine's response had bordered on the hysterical. His letter of February 27 reveals a sensitive young man burdening himself with a fearful load of guilt and contradicting the very plans he had laid out in the original letter:

It is, by my faith, impossible to tell you, my dear mother, the sadness that your letter gave me. . . . I hasten to destroy the effect of that fatal letter, which a single moment of sadness pulled out of me, and of which I am now so bitterly repentant, and of which I do not hope to really make up for as long as I live. If ever, from now on, you see me abandon myself to sadness, to malcontent, or letting myself be knocked down by my imagination, . . . show me [the letter] with its tearing response. In whatever situation, the remembrance of the impression which it made will calm me in an instant, will open my eyes, will make my reason act, and will take me out of all sombre images that my imagination might form. No, this lesson will never be forgotten. Never again will my imagination have empire over me.

You say that my letter has pierced you with sadness and nothing will efface it. No, I can't believe it. I don't want to believe it, because such a thought would break my heart. . . . I cannot pardon myself . . . that I have been tempted to exaggerate to you the inconveniences of my situation for a false motive. I wanted to show you how I would have found myself better if we were together. I was carried into telling you more than was real.

. . . All the rest of which I spoke to you in my letter will only be temporary and depends upon the long habitude I have had in living with you which makes me sense the inconveniences of living alone. A great source of bother is that I don't know if I have spent too much or not. I don't know that every penny that leaves my pocket doesn't put you in straits. I am not the master to form any plan. I do not know what to hold myself to, not knowing what my means are. That is why I have proposed nothing to you. That is why I have been held in suspense about what I ought to do. In all sacrifices it is necessary to weigh the advantages and disadvantages. But how can I do it, not having the means to estimate the breadth of our resources, nor to judge the expenses of different styles of life. Only you can tell me all that.

Tell me first if we *can* live in London, because, if not, the question is decided. I am so much in agreement when you say that one must not spend more than our revenues, that I would find it of the last absurdity any plan that would oblige us to do it.

. . . You fear for my health at the moment when I am stronger and carrying myself better than ever. I represented London as being disagreeable to me, but when have I found any place agreeable for the first four months after I came to live there alone for the first time? I had unfortunately represented it as more disagreeable than it is only to show you how much I would find it advantageous to pass a few years there, how ready to submit myself to all annoyances and to make all sacrifices in order to obtain this advantage.

How could you believe that it is the *place* that I liked or disliked? The *situation* in which one finds himself makes all the difference. If you come here next winter, I am sure that I would be as happy as I've ever been. But we will have plenty of time to talk about that, to judge if it is *possible,* if you would find yourself well here, and if that would suit us. I believed that you knew me long enough to know that a small cause often produces in me a grand effect for the moment, but that these effects are temporary. If it doesn't take much to knock me down, it doesn't take much to pick me up either.

. . . I hope more and more—I'm almost sure—to be able to join you in the summer if you desire it the least in the world. I pray you to write me that you are relieved of the sadness of Wednesday. I've thought of an easier way of correspondence. If you heat the envelopes of the newspapers near the fire, you can read that which I will write with a solution of ammoniac salt and water. I will thus send you more detailed news of what I am doing.[21]

Roget's next letter, that of March 2, went on in much the same way, and shows clearly the strong pull of his mother, who, like a pale sort of distant moon, altered the tides of his fortunes:

. . . I cannot believe that you are being serious when you say, "You prefer to sacrifice your happiness, mine, and that of your sister in order to gain the esteem of your friends in London." A long time ago I renounced the idiotic project of pleasing my friends and of following their counsels [not so long ago, apparently, as February 22!]. You are wrong, thus, to believe that I have a sombre idea of the future. I promise myself a very agreeable summer at Sidmouth . . . I am pleased extremely by your plan to pass the winter at Bath. When you proposed it to me at first, I did not pay enough attention to it. The more I reflect on it, the more I find advantages in it.[22]

Peter continued in this same letter, discounting any concern over the state of opinion at Gower Street. His aunt and uncle, he said, really had little idea of his plans or his feelings, nor he of theirs; furthermore, "I don't trouble myself about them hardly." As to the Chauvets, well, "they are at present half-way in my opinion —I persuaded them, when I dined there last, that we cannot live at London." He disposed of Dumont's counsel brusquely: "He does not seem to me that one can have confidence in his judgment. His sentiments are easily influenced by the last person who talks with him. In our last conversation he abandoned to me almost all that he had maintained before."

Notwithstanding all these declarations of independence, young Roget asked his mother to burn his letter!

Roget planned to come to Catherine at Sidmouth as soon as Abernethy's lectures were concluded, around the beginning of May. At that time they could talk about her idea of moving to Teignmouth, a few miles south on the Devonshire coast. Apparently this projected move was prompted by Catherine's and Annette's boredom at Sidmouth. Roget's sister wrote, in March:

. . . Sidmouth grows every day more stupid, and the few parties here are extremely unpleasant. A spirit of gambling has introduced itself among us, and a *vingt-et-un* table attracts everyone who wishes to lose or win a great deal of money. All the mothers exclaim against it, but all the daughters take care to show that their mamas have not the slightest influence over them. The mothers, finding their remonstrances vain, are content to help their dear children in countenance and go to add one more to the list of gamblers. In short, there is not a single person who does not rail against the game and not a single person, your humble servant excepted, who will refuse playing at it. I, alone, remain uncorrupted, . . .[23]

She was reduced, she said, to reading the *Encyclopaedia Britannica,* volume by volume.

Roget's next letter, of March 17, reported that he had a patient! One of Lord Lansdowne's menservants had been languishing away, and all that the apothecary could do was to drug the man. Roget, who was called in on the case on the recommendation of Dumont, conferred with the apothecary and diagnosed the complaint as "a rheumatism complicated with symptoms which threatened to be consumption." Roget prescribed some medicines and warm baths and proudly reported to his mother, "he commenced to get better from the moment when I saw him, and last Sunday I saw himself plant himself behind my chair and serve me expertly at the table." [24] This cure was the subject of conversations at Lansdowne House for some days, Peter said, and no doubt influenced Lord Lansdowne a few years later in retaining Roget as his private physician.

Now that he was going to leave London, he was becoming more aware of its advantages, Roget wrote. He continued dining with friends and relatives, and met a stream of new acquaintances, including Edward Jenner (1749–1823), discoverer of smallpox vaccine—one of Roget's little cousins, Sophie, was one of the first to be treated by Jenner; Mungo Park, the scientist and explorer of Africa; George Heaviside, great-grandfather of the British physicist; Benjamin Constant, the French statesman and writer. He saw the latest newspapers and magazines regularly, and frequently went to the theater, mentioning with particular pleasure seeing Cooke again, this time as Iago, and "the new play of the deaf and dumb." The latter production might well have stimulated an interest in him which prompted him to produce, in 1818, a definitive treatise on the deaf and dumb for the *Encyclopaedia Britannica*.

Roget's last surviving letter from London, that of April 11, reveals his ambiguous state of mind with respect to leaving the city. His social life had settled into a pleasant routine: Sundays at Lansdowne House, Thursdays at Constant's, Fridays at Heaviside's. He frequently dined with professional men of influence, such as Dr. Rhoades, and had met a number of M.D. graduates from Cambridge. He was often entertained by Edgeworth, who had taken up a fashionable lodging in Pall Mall. But all the while he was making preparations to leave London in May. Dr. Reid had definitely asked Roget to take his place in the Finsbury Dispensary. "It would be too bad to neglect so favorable an occasion to advance myself in the knowledge of disease," he wrote wistfully. But in the next sentence, he is "tempted to use a few guineas in buying new books of medicine in order to study at Sidmouth." Moreover, Peter had published again:

. . . Have you noticed in the paper of Monday, April 6, a paragraph touching the planets? I'm the one who sent it to the newspaper office. I'm perhaps the only one who noticed their peculiar position. I'll ask you to keep this paper.[25]

So much for Peter Roget's short-lived independence in London.

Good to his word, by June he was in Sidmouth with his mother. We have no record of Roget's summer there, but by the end of July, Catherine, Romilly, and Dumont, via several letters back and forth, had converged on the young man and agreed that his best course was to join the stream of fashionable travelers to the Continent, which had opened again upon the incipient peace with France. Even Peter seemed to have acceded to this plan and, in the face of this alliance of his elders, given up his hopes of making an early start in his career. A letter from Dumont, writing from Bowood Park, apprises Peter of "a plan in which I have involved you without consulting you, but we cannot finish it without you." He explained that Scarlett had become worried about his sixteen-year-old ward, who, he feared, had been spoiled at London. Scarlett was seeking a suitable governor to accompany the boy to Geneva. Dumont, of course, suggested Roget for the position and immediately consulted Chauvet, who was about to return to Geneva. Letters flew thickly back and forth between Roget and Dumont, Dumont and Romilly, Romilly and Catherine. However, after much negotiation, much speculation, much convincing of Catherine that she could, after all, survive the year without Peter, the whole complicated arrangement fell through. It seems that Scarlett's young man finally insisted on going up to Cambridge.

But in all these letters, young Roget at least had the advantage of some straightforward advice from his uncle, who thought that Peter should "follow [his] own good sense and good disposition rather than be led by the examples or the suggestions of others." There were, however, Romilly wrote, a few "trifles" about the young M.D. that the uncle would see altered:

> . . . Your dress, principally, to which you are much too inattentive—not for me but for those who think dress more important than I do, which is almost all the world or at least that part of the world which you will have to do with. I don't tell you that I could wish you to be a little more cheerful than you are because I know that gaiety is not to be put on like one's coat, but I know by experience that melancholy may be very much increased by being indulged.[26]

After some rapid shifting of plans—Roget, it was first decided, was to go on to Edinburgh; then, on his uncle's advice, he was to

travel alone to Paris for the winter—the young doctor was bundled off to Manchester, with a letter of introduction to the owner
of the largest cotton mill in Manchester and possibly in England,
John Philips. Romilly, it seems, had set up a plan with Philips to
hire Peter as tutor and companion for Philips' two sons, Burton,
seventeen, and Nathaniel, sixteen, and to conduct them on the
Grand Tour.

Roget stopped over at Birmingham, again by his uncle's arrangement, and was entertained so thoroughly that it wore him
out. The most notable event in Birmingham was a pleasant resumption of his acquaintance with James Watt, whom he had
first met at Clifton. On Christmas Day, 1801, Peter dined with
the famous chemist Keir at Hill Top, near Birmingham; and in
the course of a few days in that city, paying his uncle's respects to
friends there, he toured "ten or twelve different manufactories,
which afforded me much gratification and instruction."

In Manchester, he was taken warmly into the Philipses' elegant
home, and he was pleased with everything he saw of the family:

. . . I now find that the purpose intended to be answered by my
coming to Manchester, was that Mrs. Philips and others of the
family should see me. Mrs. P has been very slowly brought to
consent to the scheme of sending her sons to France. . . . A
year is the time proposed for their stay on the continent. Mr. P
had at first only proposed their residing at Paris, but from
what I have told him of Geneva, he has readily entered into
my views. . . . He seems to place great confidence in me and to
leave a great deal to my discretion. . . . I shall leave Manchester in about ten or twelve days and wait for them in
London.[27]

Roget wanted very much, before returning to London, to visit
Liverpool, where he wished to meet, among other figures, Dr.
James Currie, the Scottish physician and editor of Robert
Burns's poetry. As resident physician, Currie was largely responsible for the development of the Liverpool Infirmary, and Roget
may well have hoped to make a useful professional connection
there. Roget's subsequent friendship with Dr. Currie, who was
something of a favorite in influential social and political circles
(he was, for example, family adviser to Thomas Creevey), may
have been important in Roget's meeting his future wife, daughter of a Liverpool merchant.

Roget's letters during this period are fretful and impatient, despite the fact that he was enjoying himself. He lived with the

Philips family, alternating with them between their town house and The Dales, a country place some six miles outside of Manchester. He was invited to many parties and included in all of the social functions that the family enjoyed. He traveled to Liverpool with a couple of doctors and, despite himself, began to see real possibilities for his future in the Birmingham-Manchester-Liverpool area:

. . . Manchester is the largest city and the most populous one after London. It contains about 90,000; however, there are only four or five doctors. The apothecaries and surgeons have a lot of practice . . . I have been told that the country around Manchester is flat and ugly, but it seems that they have calumniated it somewhat. Within a few miles there are pretty enough places, although woods seem to be missing. The town itself is horrible: dirty and black, paved only with small stones, the air always heavy by the smoke of the factories.[28]

After a savage "hurricane" that did great damage to buildings in Manchester and wrecked many ships at Liverpool, the weather took a turn for the better late in January. (Mrs. Philips had refused to let her boys set off during the winter storms.) Roget even pinned Philips down on their financial arrangements, which had been vague up to this point. Bolstered by a letter from Romilly, telling of another young friend who was making a good thing as a traveling companion (£500 for his first trip, £1,200 for his second, and £1,500 for his third), Peter finally insisted on talking terms:

. . . He didn't wish to name a sum, and I named £400 per year as my salary outside the reimbursement of all my expenses. He didn't make any objections, so I regard this sum as agreed upon between us. The only thing that remains to be arranged is when that ought to begin.[29]

Considering the fact that a single man could live on an income of £100 a year, and that for several years Catherine, Annette, and Peter had got along on about £200 a year, a salary of £400 plus expenses—double what Scarlett had agreed to—was more than satisfactory.

That money was important to his sense of his own worth was evident throughout Roget's life. He was delighted that he himself had settled such an important detail, which was even more satisfying after all the arranging that had been done for him. At last he was about to embark on a project of considerable responsibility and very lively interest, and to be thrown at last on his own resources, with no anxious mother or uncle hovering at his shoulder. The prospect gave young Peter Mark Roget a lift of spirits that was to carry him triumphant through a remarkably complicated and dangerous adventure in Napoleon's Europe.

V [1802–1803 ❧

Postgraduate Wanderings —Geneva

THE rising threats of revolution and invasion that had for years terrified the British establishment were dimmed by the rockets and flares of jubilant illuminations held in the fall of 1801 to celebrate the Peace of Amiens. Henry Crabb Robinson noted in his diary that the peace had excited "a tumult of joy such as I never before saw equalled . . . [has] risen almost to madness." [1] But the gritty problems that had made the previous decade such a grim one, especially for the poor, were still there. Violent outbreaks by the poor and savage repression by the government belied the promise of the peace, and international power plays underscored the emptiness of that promise. The Peace of Amiens was proposed by Napoleon in October 1801, ratified in March 1802, and shattered in May 1803. But for Peter Mark Roget, flushed with the prospect of life beginning for him at last, the opening of the new year 1802 seemed a rebirth. He had passed the anxious scrutiny of Mrs. Philips, had long since satisfied John Philips that their two boys would be safe with him as tutor and guide, [2] and was actually packing his suitcase for the grand adventure.

In February 1802, Philips and his sons made the coach run to London, posting through via Macclesfield, Leek, Ashbourne, Derby, Loughborough, and Woburn. After a week of sightseeing in London, and a dinner with Sir Samuel and Lady Anne Romilly, John Philips relinquished his boys to Roget. Roget immediately mobilized boys and luggage, secured passports through

Lord Pelham, and got the three of them down to Dover, where they had booked passage on the *Elgin* under Captain Sampson.[3]

But the travelers had not reckoned with the traffic. The small packet boats—most of them 60- to 70-ton sloops fitted out to accommodate from ten to twenty passengers—were jammed to the gunnels with travel-starved British tourists who had begun swarming across the Channel almost the same day in October that the peace was announced. While many adventurous souls had dodged across and back again in the last few years before the peace, it must be remembered that the hostilities between England and France had been almost constant since 1793, so that for all practical purposes travel in France had been closed to Englishmen for nearly ten years. It is not surprising, then, that Roget found it necessary to stop over for a day in Dover until he could talk himself and the boys aboard another of the busy packet boats.

When all conditions were ideal, the Channel trip was accomplished in three to four hours, but apparently conditions were something less than ideal in February of 1802. Roget's party did not reach Calais for fifteen hours, and then, because it was 3 A.M., they had to wait in a kind of post house another four hours for the gates of Calais to open. They were then introduced to French officialdom: first, they were taken to a room at the harbor, where their names were officially registered; second, they were directed to the town hall, where their passports were examined; and third, they were required to be present for the opening and inspection of their luggage. They lay over the rest of the day in an inn.

A good night's rest did wonders for the travelers, and the boys' interest was revived next morning by their examination of the chaise in which they were to post to Paris.

"It looks clumsy," wrote Burton.

The body is something like those of England, but more confined; the wheels like those of a common cart. The rest like a gig, with the newly-invented springs. . . . The horses go three abreast when there are three persons inside. The postillion has something very ridiculous about him. He wears immense jack-boots, one of which you could hardly lift up with your hand, and carries a long-lashed whip with which he announces his entrance to a town, so that horses may be prepared without delay. Every five to ten miles—which are here called "posts," the horses are changed.[4]

The long ride to Paris carried them through Boulogne, Montreuil, Amiens, and Chantilly, with halts at night in each of the last three towns. Their observations of French life during this journey were limited but specific: many women rode on horseback, on the right side of the horse; the men generally wore earrings and grew prodigious whiskers, and displayed cocked hats, cloaks, and large fur gloves; terrible poverty was evident—wherever they changed horses, crowds of beggars surrounded them; peasants danced on Sunday and people attended plays on Sunday; the French did not know how to build efficient chimneys—the rooms were full of smoke; the houses were mostly built of stone and often extremely dirty inside though often much ornamented.

Roget's first extensive remarks concern what apparently was an important discovery: that Paris was not another London. He and the boys had been prepared for superficial differences in dress and customs, of course, and for many inconveniences—"The French are very awkward in all their contrivances"—but the color and vitality and furious, somewhat disorderly activity of the French capital struck deeply through his well-bred provincialism. He realized for the first time that all the world was not ordered on the English plan. Paris was literally a "new world," Roget said:

> The great height of the houses—six or seven stories high—the narrowness of the streets, the height of the roofs, the walls covered with inscriptions which dazzle and bewilder the eye, the numerous coaches, chaises and cabriolets [characteristically, Roget noted with care the actual numbers: he estimated from three to four thousand hackney vehicles operating in Paris] which drive with amazing rapidity over an irregular pavement with a deafening noise, splashing through the gutters which run in the middle of the streets. . . . The total want of foot pavement renders it really dangerous to walk in the streets, til you are trained to feats of agility. You are required every instant to hop from stone to stone and to dart from one side of the street to the other. The poor foot-passengers are driven about by the cabriolets like a parcel of frightened sheep. The only security is large stones close to the houses, which scarcely allow you, by sticking close to the wall, to escape being hit.[5]

Methodically, Roget ticked off the differences of Paris, most of which he disapproved: pictures painted on the walls of shops rather than forthright signs ("a garland is a sign that wine is sold within"); iron gratings on the windows; courtyards separating the better houses from the street; little or no attempt to display goods in the shop windows; many things sold in stalls in the streets; women walking about without hats; women, as well as men and boys, wearing large wooden shoes; many people sitting about in markets under large red oilcloth parasols; poor lighting of streets; poor design of the common two-wheeled carts—the hubs projected one or two feet from the wheels and often became entangled with other carts in the narrow streets; a general fondness for the spectacular and a general indifference about the dirt of their persons and houses.[6]

Roget and the boys took rooms at the Hotel de L'Europe, Rue de La Roi, and immediately began the required round of social calls, a convention which at least helped to shake Paris down to manageable size. They wrote home that they had received great civility from everybody they met, in particular de Lessert,[7] Lord Henry Petty,[8] Etienne Dumont, and Madame Gautier,[9] and their first few days in Paris were taken up with afternoon calls, fashionable dinners, and visits to the theater. This sort of activity Roget was prepared for; he came equipped with letters of introduction from Philips, Romilly, and his old teacher Chauvet, which gave him and the boys ready access to upper-class French families, where they found life reassuringly like that at home. Moreover, Samuel and Anne Romilly came over to Paris in April.

It would take more than a noisy foreign place to interfere with a well-trained Englishman's methodical way of going. After a few giddy days living in the hotel, Roget moved them to a respectable rooming house near the Montmartre, hired a French tutor and a manservant, and started the boys to keeping the inevitable journals. "Having seen the principal objects of curiosity," Roget reported to the boys' father, "we are applying ourselves with great steadiness to study. . . . Now that we are settled, we are able to apply to business without interruption." [10]

Every day they visited the botanical gardens and the museum of natural history, after first preparing for what they were to see by studying Buffon's *Histoire Naturelle*. Both boys made copious notes of what they observed—"a plan which at once exercises the memory and gives an exercise in composition," said Roget sententiously. Their French master came for lessons on alternate days, but every day the boys translated a couple of pages of French into English and afterward back into French. They dutifully took dancing lessons. They attended plays with determination, after reading them beforehand. They took in the Louvre and carefully counted the items in the several rooms: "The large room contains 209 statues and busts . . . above this is a gallery of pictures, and at present there are 980 of them." [11]

Throughout the three-month stay in Paris, Roget and the Philips boys successfully maintained their British prejudices. Typically, they wrote home describing the theaters but not mentioning the plays they watched; they counted the pieces in the Louvre without mentioning the works themselves; they lived in a French home, but were careful not to interest themselves in French family life. They counted the 309 steps of the tower of Notre Dame, noted that the organ had fourteen bellows, 3,800 pipes, and six rows of keys, but apparently did not hear that great instrument play in that holy place, and apparently took no note of the importance of Catholicism to the Frenchman's way of life—despite the fact that they must have been aware of the bitter struggle in England over the thrice-proposed and thrice-rejected Catholic emancipation.

Their letters reveal no serious concern with nor understanding of the condition or nature of the people or the fantastically fluid state of French politics. The relationship of what they saw to the problems of social, economic, and political organization which bedeviled both England and France—a relationship that seemed to have been suggested by the ruins of Condé—faded into insignificance as the two boys and their young tutor filled their days with familiar and approved pursuits:

We went to the Bois de Boulogne the other day. It extends four miles, and is the resort of all the gay company of Paris between the hours of 3 and 6 P.M. It is absolutely necessary to go to these public places. You are always asked if you have visited them.[12]

Toward the end of May, as they prepared for the next long leg to Geneva, Roget, after much fussing and consultation, bought a large, double-sprung carriage for £50, apparently unable to face another cross-country joust with the French chaise. On the top of the carriage was a valise to contain their linen, under their feet a large well for storing their portmanteaus, and on the boot in front a trunk for their books.[13]

They also acquired a new member of the party. This was Lovell Edgeworth, Peter's old Edinburgh friend, then twenty-five.

Edgeworth's joining Roget is representative of the way in which circles of acquaintances overlapped throughout Roget's life, sometimes expanding, sometimes severely limiting his experiences. The Edgeworths were part of still another circle, which included the Wedgwoods, the Darwins, and the Baillies—each of whom in turn touched on still other groups, thus linking loosely such disparate individuals and interests as the atheistic Bentham and the devout Whewell; the revolutionary Dumont and the aristocratic Duke of Sussex; the scientific Humphry Davy and the romantic Coleridge; the professional John Cooke and the socializing Berrys; the connoisseur Samuel Rogers and the pragmatic James Watt. It is little wonder, then, that Roget moved as though under a protective canopy that delimited and shaped his world, whether he be jouncing through a French countryside or dancing attendance at a de Staël soirée. It is understandable why so little of the real life of Paris penetrated that amorphous umbrella.

After a good many letters back and forth and conferences with family friends, in and out of Paris, Roget's little cavalcade was ready to leave the capital on May 22, 1802. Ominously, however, they were able to depart only after a prolonged and fatiguing bout with French passport officials—a reminder of the customs tangle at Calais and a foreshadowing of the much more serious struggle they were to engage in at Geneva.

At last, with Roget's carriage in the lead and Edgeworth and his squire close behind in a chaise he had brought over from England, the young Englishmen left Paris by way of the boulevards to Charenton, where they crossed the Seine. All of them were distressed by the heat of mid-May in central France—"almost as great as during the dog-days in England," said Roget.

Because of the delayed departure, the party spent the night at Fontainebleau, where they prowled briefly about the ruined château. But beginning with the next day, they rose punctually at 3 A.M. and pushed on to Lyons via Nemours, Croisière, Fontenay, Montarnis, Commodité, Briare, Cosne, La Charité, Moulins, Gerand Le Puy, Droiturier, Roanne, and Tarare, covering some fifty to eighty miles each day.[14] Their letters and journals commented occasionally on the countryside—they did enjoy the valley of the Loire—but they kept up a steady barrage of remarks about the shortcomings of French inns, French roads, French people, even French weather. Roanne was disposed of in one sanitary sentence: "It is a clean town." A brief visit to a church where there had been a wedding gave Roget an opportu-

nity to comment on the ineptitude of French inventors. He noticed friction wheels under the snuffer pan, and remarked, "ingenuity lavished to facilitate motion in a machine not intended
to be moved." At Cosne they were struck with the cleanliness of
the inhabitants and the neatness of their dress—"sure tokens of
comfort and domestic happiness." At the inns, they were often
plagued, Roget said, "with a number of women asking us to buy
knives, corkscrews, gloves and trinkets." They took real satisfaction in the disappointment in several towns of blacksmiths who
could find nothing needing repair on their carriages. Roget's
comments on the evening they spent in Moulins include one of
his rare essays at humor:

> In the evening, as we were walking around the ramparts, we
> were serenaded by a Dutch concert. Among the great variety of
> musicians, of which it would be difficult to enumerate even the
> kinds, a few of the ablest only can be particularized. The prin-
> cipal performers were the frogs; ducks bore a leading part,
> crows and grasshoppers frequently intermingled their melodi-
> ous notes; peacocks lent their aid, and asses occasionally joined
> when there was a full chorus. Each in turn bore away the palm
> of loudness, but the frogs seemed most ambitious of distinc-
> tion.[15]

But Lyons was something else. The effect of that shattered city
broke through Roget's defenses as nothing had thus far in all his
twenty-three years. The many evidences they had seen of the fury
of the Revolutionary and counter-Revolutionary throes—the
ruins at Condé, the vandalized Château Fontainebleau, the gardens gone to seed, the barred windows of Parisian shops—apparently all were reborn in his mind's eye as he walked about the
rubble-strewn streets of what had been the finest parts of the
town. Lyons was one of three cities (Lyons, Marseilles, and Tou-
lon) that were selected to be made into object lessons by the radical Jacobin regime, which had been infuriated by these cities' resistance to what has been called "radicalism carried to the point
of anarchy." The National Convention, "which by the exercise of
a little moderation could have easily restored order without
bloodshed . . . proclaimed as the primary object of the government the complete extermination of all domestic opponents, and
directed its commissioners to subjugate Lyons." [16]
Roget's party spent a long afternoon and evening there, listening to stories of the besieging of Lyons by the army of the Na-

tional Convention in 1793. The siege had lasted sixty-three days; the town, reduced by famine, capitulated October 9, 1793, and hundreds of its inhabitants and defenders were marched out and shot en masse. Roget was told that over three thousand youths had been killed in the course of the long action, that the town had been broken only long after the inhabitants had eaten their dogs, cats, and horses, and that the besieging troops even fired at the hospital, the sick escaping as best they could.[17]

The failure of trade did not escape Roget's notice; indeed he had commented on a similar slackness and token activity elsewhere—glass beads as the prime industry at Moulins, for example. But what stopped him at least momentarily in his optimistic tracks was the way in which the tragedy of Lyons clashed with his conviction that man was, and ought to be, constantly—no matter how slowly or ineptly—on the upward climb. Destruction he could understand, and even a lack of cleanliness, but there must be efforts to repair and overcome. True, one could not expect of Frenchmen what one would take for granted in an Englishman, but there must be, even in Frenchmen, the will to improve.

And in Lyons this will was gone. He wrote that Bonaparte himself had come to Lyons and had laid the first stone of a rebuilding program that he had offered to subsidize:

> . . . But the inhabitants have no perseverance to continue rebuilding. With a population of 150,000 none has the courage to step forward. The spirit of enterprise seems totally extinguished, and all is at a stand. *Events like these are enough to shake to its foundation our confidence in the course of things, and by making us mistrust all views into futurity, teach us to confine them to present and more immediate concerns* [italics added].[18]

Roget's dismay goes much deeper than the superficial, provincial criticism that he had voiced so frequently of French life. It does not even stop with the petulance of the complaint that the Lyonese were not willing to help themselves—the kind of complaint that one might expect from an upstanding, thoroughgoing Englishman. It sounded deeply down into his fundamental vision of man on earth, man in time, man and God. With the blind mask of Lyons staring him in the face, what could Roget make of the fine schemes of such meliorists as his uncle, Samuel Romilly; of that father of scientific social improvement, Jeremy Bentham;

of Dr. Thomas Beddoes and his optimistic scientism? Or, scrapping all such visionary notions, how could one salvage even the security and rigidity of the status quo as a means of making men become better than they are? What of plan and purpose, of order and pattern?

It was thus a sober Peter Mark Roget that chivvied his little company into their carriages on the morning of June 4 and pressed on for Geneva. They followed the left bank of the Rhone most of the day, bowling along on good roads through fertile and well-cultivated country, but Roget's mind was still poised over the lesson of Lyons.

Rather suddenly, the road became an ascent, and at the small village of Cerdun they were forced to halt while additional horses were harnessed to the two carriages. Because of the steepness of the road, the young Englishmen climbed down and took the final rise on foot, commenting the while on the fine view. But Roget excused himself, walked rapidly on ahead of companions, guides, horses, and carriage, and thus stood alone for several minutes on the summit, staring out at the great expanse of valleys and hills, then back toward Lyons. He could not bring together the beautiful promise of the land with the depressing fact of what had happened in it.

Roget and his pupils completed their 355-mile trip from Paris the next day, June 5, 1802, and were greeted warmly by Chauvet, Roget's childhood tutor. Chauvet insisted that they stay for a few days with him at Paquis, just outside Geneva, then found them a place nearby. Later, in the fall, they moved in with the Chauvets at their town house in the Rue Beauregard. Housing was a problem in Geneva that year, and this fact gave Roget some reason to compliment himself on the thoroughness of his preparations.

Geneva in the summer, autumn, and winter of 1802 was bright, busy, filled with French and English, nervous with each gust of war rumors, gay with each respite, and determined to pursue its pleasures: concerts, balls, gala trips to the glaciers, picnics on the lake. Roget was delighted to find Chauvet an excellent entrée to "the best company in Geneva—in the winter we shall know everybody in town." He notes that "the French are, in a manner, excluded from society—they are held in universal detestation"—understandable if one recalls that a few years before, Napoleon annexed Geneva to France after a period of internal disorder. "On the other hand, the very name of an Englishman is an introduction." Roget enjoyed a double welcome—as an Englishman and as a descendant of a respected Genevan family.

But, conscientious fellow that he was, Roget kept their social life well within reason and held the boys to their studies. As he had promised John Philips, once in Geneva they got down to the serious part of the boys' schooling: mathematics, geology, chemistry, and other courses at the local college. Roget saw to it, too, that they attended church regularly, and was pleased to report that the boys followed the French sermons very well.

During August they made a tour of the glacier district near Chamonix and, according to a letter from Burton to his sister, climbed Montan Vers and the Brévent. Beneath them was a view of the Jura and Saint Gothard ranges. Seventeen-year-old Burton's reaction to the scene is reminiscent of his tutor's studied description: "I cannot describe the scene; it was so sublime." Their guide (according to S. R. Roget's account) was the celebrated Jacques Balmat, reputed to be the first person to conquer Mont Blanc.

But the green glasses that one wore in 1802 to protect the eyes from glare on pleasure jaunts to the glaciers did not effectively reduce the glare of the deteriorating political situation, nor did all the cultural and social activity they could muster diminish the increasing rumbles that bespoke the doom of the Peace of Amiens. As early as October, Roget learned that a packet of British newspapers sent to them by John Philips had not been admitted by the French at Calais. Young Burton wrote his father, urging him not to try to smuggle papers to them: "They are forbidden and not worth concealing, for, if found, we should suffer the consequences." [19] A few weeks later, Roget reported, "Geneva is now garrisoned by 3,000 French soldiers. The gates are shut at 10 P.M., and any person found without a lantern after that hour is put into the 'Corps de Garde,' and in the morning taken before the Mayor." [20]

Napoleon's moves, each of them countered, or in some instances antedated, by Parliament's strengthening of the British army and navy, troubled Roget, but even more troubling to him was the refusal of his Genevan friends to take these developments seriously:

. . . I found in all the companies I went into that the general opinion was that matters would be accommodated, and if I ever ventured to express opposite sentiments, they were treated

with the ridicule attached to him who views evil in everything
and delights in contemplating the dark side of every picture.
During the whole period of subsequent negotiation they
seemed very reluctant to admit the continually increasing
probability of an event which from the beginning might easily
have been anticipated.[21]

Roget became more and more uneasy as his friends became
more and more confident that no possible inconvenience, far less
danger, could be incurred by their staying on in Geneva. Roget
was assured that even if war did break out again, he and the boys
would be allowed to stay or go as they pleased. The Government
would play the game, he was advised. "Whatever might happen,"
he wrote, "the Government could not do otherwise than give us
timely intimation if they wished us to depart, and allow us the
necessary time for leaving the territory."

It was all very well to talk about playing the game, but the ex-
perience of Lyons was too fresh in Roget's mind for comfort.
What had happened to the game at Lyons? He noted, uneasily,
that a good many Englishmen had already left Geneva, including
Lord Cholmondley, Lord Brook (son of Lord Warwick), and
Lord Henry Petty, as well as assorted Irish baronets.[22]

By Christmas 1802, the optimism of autumn had worn thin,
even in Manchester. John Philips, observing that trade had become very dull owing to the unsettled state of Europe, declared
that "it is very necessary for this country that all differences upon
the Continent should be immediately adjusted." [23]

New Year's Day—a holiday that the Genevans made more of
than they did of Christmas—was enlivened by the accidental receipt of a packet of six British papers. But among the news items
was a report that Edgeworth's father, who had been in Paris with
his daughter, was ordered by the French Government to leave
the city in twenty-four hours and France within eight days. This
was the first of several warnings that young Edgeworth, still lux-
uriating in the congenial society of Geneva, was to ignore—much
to his prolonged misfortune.

Shortly after Roget's twenty-fourth birthday (January 18), a
series of events made it clear that the carefree days were over—
both for the Chauvet family and for the English in Geneva. After
a short illness, Chauvet died, and Roget and his pupils, in defer-
ence to the widow, reluctantly left the comfortable Chauvet town
house. They took rooms with a Madame Peschier. About the
same time an epidemic of *"la grippe"* swept through Geneva. To

completely blacken the dying winter, Paris newspapers began whipping up reaction to what they called war preparations in England. Napoleon reported to the legislature in February, for example, that political opinion in England was divided: those in favor of peace as opposed to those who were hostile to France. A half million soldiers, said Napoleon, must be kept in readiness by France against the possibility of victory of the second of those parties.[24]

On May 24 John Philips wrote, "I must confess to you my mind, as you would perceive, has all along been made up that a war would be avoided; but the die now seems to be cast, and it is, I fear, in vain to hope for a change. *We live in an era when we cannot foresee events even for a day, and can only act as circumstances fall out* [italics added]." [25] Echoes of Roget's comment at Lyons!

Within a week, Napoleon issued an order by which all Englishmen above eighteen years of age were to be detained as prisoners of war. It would appear that that order was part of Napoleon's answer to England's demand that he respect the neutrality of Switzerland, supposedly guaranteed by the French-Austrian Peace of Lunéville early in the year.

On first getting wind of Napoleon's order, Roget proposed that he and the boys immediately slip across the lake into Switzerland. John Philips had already arranged with a business associate in Lausanne to prepare the way for them and had ordered his bank to establish credit for them in Hamburg. But on attempting to make arrangements for an escape, Roget discovered that the French had already taken active precautions against such flights. Not only was every possible avenue into Switzerland guarded by gendarmes, but the order of arrest was found to extend to that country as well as to Geneva. Moreover, Roget learned that any attempt at such a move would be summarily punished: the would-be escapees were to be sent to the Castle of Montmelian, in Savoy.[26]

With his usual foresight, Roget had struck up an acquaintance with the Commandant of the town, a General Dupuch, who, as it turned out, lived beneath their rooms, on the ground floor of the Peschier house. As the net drew tighter around them, Roget took some assurance in the friendly protestations of General Dupuch that they would enjoy complete safety under his immediate protection.

After weighing the chances of making a dash for Calais and

very likely being interned somewhere en route, Roget decided that his best course was to agree to the Genevan Commandant's suggestion that he give his word not to leave the territory. He thus became a *"détenu en parole,"* despite his fiercely patriotic feelings that

> . . . to accept protection from a foe, to eat of his bread, to be sheltered under his roof, was repugnant to every feeling of delicacy. The idea that you are treading upon hostile ground, that you are surrounded with persons who are breathing hatred towards your country and plotting its destruction, is particularly grating to every sentiment of patriotism. To remain by choice in such a situation was voluntarily resigning a title of which we ought to be proud, and to disclaim all the ties which bind us to our country.[27]

On May 27, Roget and the boys attended a party given by Commandant Dupuch. Roget noted that they were the only English present, and he thought he perceived a coldness in the Commandant's attitude. Before they retired that night, they were handed a vague report that all of the English in Lyons had been arrested.[28]

Roget meanwhile sent a petition to Paris, asking permission to leave France, and John Philips enlisted the aid of Sir Samuel Romilly, who during the Terror had befriended Talleyrand. Roget tried every angle he could think of to secure an exemption from the detaining order. He urged a claim as a doctor of medicine, another as a man who had never been enrolled in the militia, and still another as a tutor in charge of pupils under the prescribed age. These appeals were not even answered by the local authorities. Another letter to Paris, signed by several influential Genevans on behalf of Roget, came back with a plain negative.[29]

After about six weeks of fruitless appeals and increasing anxiety about the intention of the French with respect to the Philips boys, Roget learned of a decision to deport all the English prisoners at Geneva to Verdun. He then concocted the following plan of escape:

> My project was to send the Philipses to Constance; then to revoke my parole [promise] to the Commandant and declare myself entitled to the rights of a citizen of France, as being the son of a native of Geneva; and, upon this, without giving time to the authorities to deliberate on my claim, to leave the town in disguise, and proceed across Switzerland by a route not likely to be suspected.[30]

This was, in fact, only one of several escape schemes Roget dreamed up as he and the boys, along with Edgeworth and other Englishmen and sympathetic Genevans, gathered in hotels, in restaurants, and in private homes to try to make sense out of the conflicting reports from the Mayor, the Commandant, the Prefect, and the couriers from Paris. That they all enjoyed, to a certain extent, the conspiratorial atmosphere is undeniable. Note, for example, Roget's report of one lively morning:

About eight o'clock Burton entered my room, followed by Moré, a person who let our horses, informing us that all the English at Sécheron [a village about one mile northeast of Geneva, just inside the frontier], had set off early that morning for Switzerland, certain intelligence having reached them of the "arrestation" of the English at Lyons. He offered horses at any time that we should want them, and left us to consult as to what we should do. I did not hesitate to attempt an escape if it were not already too late. We had our carriage at Voirembé, two miles from Geneva; thither I determined to go, and ordered horses to be sent there. I took fifteen louis in my pocket, and looked everywhere for the key of our chaise, but in vain. Having each put a couple of shirts in a bundle, and ordered François to take it to Edgeworth at Sécheron, and there to leave it, we were going to sally forth, but reflected that it would be better, in order to prevent confusion, to apprise Mme. Peschier of our intention . . . and to give some of our friends notice of their danger.[31]

In making these rounds, Roget and the boys became convinced that Moré's news was no better than any number of other rumors currently afloat. In fact, in returning to their place, they were confronted by the Commandant, who assured them that no orders for either deportation or arrest had been received. Moreover, he said, if and when he received such orders, he would let Roget know at least twenty-four hours before they were put into effect. At that point, the whole group sat down for breakfast, and Roget's fears were quieted by the laughter that attended their discussion of the whole affair.

On still another occasion, the three conspirators had a fine time designing Roget's escape costume:

. . . I was to walk out of the town shabbily dressed in my greatcoat, old hat, crab stick, dark pantaloons, and red handkerchief around my neck, wearing my night shirt without a frill and a dirty waistcoat.[32]

But the cloak-and-dagger playtime was rapidly running out. Roget was shocked to realize that he couldn't trust the Genevan Commandant, who had assured them for weeks that there was nothing to fear. Added to this was the anti-British sentiment that had become unpleasantly evident in Geneva. Roget reported that the soldiers sneered at them as they passed, and the Jacobins eyed them with even darker scowls. "We were beset with spies. One called on us under pretence of charity. I discovered that our German teacher was a rank Jacobin. Every time we walked out we were followed, and all that we said was listened to." [33] If two or three stopped to talk on the street, it was reported in town that the English had assembled and talked in high terms against the Government. Various reports were circulated against them: that they were meditating escape; that some had actually escaped; that one had fought a duel with a French officer and killed him. Their house was marked, and rumors abounded that it was a political den.

On Saturday, July 16, 1803, Roget was tipped off by a source he could not ignore—the celebrated Madame de Staël herself. She had been ordered out of Paris by Napoleon, and had stayed that year at her ancestral home in Coppet, near Geneva, with her father. Through her influential connections in Paris, she continued to receive early notice of Napoleon's intentions and movements. In fact, her establishment at Coppet became a great center of refugees, many of whom owed their lives to her help.[34] Roget describes the encounter:

I was crossing the dinner salon to go to my room when I perceived Mme. de Staël in the parlour with the Peschiers and Davidsons. I entered. I had not sat down two minutes when she suddenly turned to me and said in English: "I have very bad news for you. You are going all to be sent to Verdun. I have it from an unquestionable source. No reclamations will be attended to. You will set out in about a week." She then turned to Mme. Peschier and talked French. Soon afterwards she added in English: "All the English in Switzerland are arrested. Lord J. Campbell and Dr. Robertson have been stopped at Baden; the former has escaped in woman's clothes, the latter is in confinement." She then apologized to Mme. Peschier for talking English, saying that she could not resist every opportunity of improving herself in the language. She soon left the room. I accompanied her downstairs, and she spoke to me a few words more on the subject, especially enjoining secrecy. I begged permission to communicate it to Edgeworth, to which she, after some hesitation, consented.[35]

Roget no longer hesitated. He went immediately to his rooms and directed the Philipses to prepare to leave the next day for Morges. They would follow Plan A, and Tuesday was the day fixed upon. He then walked to Sécheron in a burning sun and told Edgeworth, who refused to believe the urgency of the situation. On Sunday Roget tried all day to confer with the Commandant, but was unable to find him.

Early in the morning on Monday, Roget had a stormy interview with the Commandant. The young Englishman told the General that he was sending the Philips boys away. The Commandant shouted, threatened, ordered him to keep them in Geneva. Roget told him he had received orders from the parents to send the boys on. The General shouted louder, finally admitting that he had, indeed, received orders to confine all Englishmen over eighteen.

Roget was shocked at the Commandant's duplicity. The young tutor drew himself up and took that moment to "reclame [*sic*] myself." That is, he withdrew his promise not to leave Geneva. Earlier he had considered doing this to force the Commandant to send him off to Verdun; Roget's scheme had been to bribe their escort en route and thus effect his escape. But Roget now played what he thought was his trump card: he announced that the Commandant could not interfere with him because he was, in fact, a French citizen, *"et je ne me considère point comme votre prisonnier* [and I do not at all consider myself your prisoner]." [36]

Roget's claim to Genevan (and thus French) citizenship was simply that he was the son of his father, who had, it is true, been a Genevan. It was a shaky proposition, but anything at this point was worth trying. Besides, he had the force of this same suggestion from his mother. "I wish he would for a time Genevese himself," she had said in letters to friends, mentioning that her brother-in-law, Jean Samuel Roget, had persuaded her many years ago to continue paying *"les gardes,"* a small tax that somehow perpetuated Peter's status as the son of a citizen of Geneva.[37]

Roget had considered this move before but had rejected it, he said, because it impugned his honor—"it was renouncing my English character." Ironically, then, in almost the same breath with which he "reclamed" his honor from the Commandant, he gave up his identity as an Englishman.

Once he had made up his mind, Roget moved quickly. He drew up and presented a petition to the Prefect, claiming rights as a French citizen. The Commandant stormed into the room, interrupted this interview, and declared that unless Roget could

produce, by 7 A.M. the next day, a variety of documentary evidence of his citizenship, including a certificate of his father's bap-
tism and an act attesting his own identity signed by no less than
eight witnesses, he must go with the rest of the British to Verdun. Roget then began what would seem an impossible assignment in any country—to get papers from bureaucrats after office
hours:

> I had literally to run about the whole town all the evening until
> half-past ten o'clock. By dint of recommendation, persuasion
> and insisting on the thing, I got one of the papers, the certifi-
> cate of my father's birth. The other act (acte de vérité), at-
> testing the identity of my person, was to have been done
> before a Juge de Paix, but he was ten miles in the coun-
> try. I found his substitute in a remote corner of Plainpalais; he
> was playing at bowls at his club. I had great difficulty in get-
> ting him to listen to me. At length, by tickling the palm of his
> hand, he promised to be ready for me by six the next morning,
> and in the meanwhile I was to collect eight witnesses, and to
> be sure of finding them all at home the next morning, and to
> bring him their Christian names, etc. Luckily it was the night
> of the parson's society. I went there with M. Peschier, and got
> four at one visit.[38]

On Tuesday Roget got the Philips boys up before dawn and
sent them to Neuchâtel, via Lausanne. He accompanied them as
far as Sécheron. It was still early enough for him to be pounding
at the notary's door by 6 A.M.:

> He was in bed. I called him, however, and he slowly rose and fell
> to work, and in half an hour the deed was executed attesting
> that I was really the son of the person I called my father. I had
> now to run about for signatures. I found many of the witnesses
> in bed. Some got up for me, others signed in bed. Another dif-
> ficulty now occurred. The Bureau d'enregistrement was shut,
> and nothing could be done without it. I waited on the secre-
> tary of the Prefect. He seemed to think it absolutely necessary
> to get the paper immediately. With great difficulty I got the
> Notary to let him see it before it was registered; then, and not
> til then, was I safe from being sent to Verdun.[39]

Roget still did not have a passport, but his new identity as a
French citizen served as a stay of execution, and he was allowed
the freedom of Geneva.[40] During the next few days, he watched
the doleful departure of the remaining Englishmen, including
Edgeworth, for Verdun. They remained there, interned, for
eleven years.

Reports on young Edgeworth's fate during his long internment vary. According to his famous sister, Maria, in her *Memoir*, Edgeworth bore his tribulations like a man, constantly striving to be released from custody, and succeeding at least in being transferred to Saint-Germain-en-Laye and finally to Paris. But a letter from Edgeworth to Roget, posted from Verdun, gives a little less glowing picture of the effects of internment:

Happy as I was, my dear friend, to hear of your safe escape from the hands of these ruffians, yet I could not help feeling a sense of pain at the first news of it, so selfish are we all. . . . Nothing in heaven above, earth below, nor the waters under the earth can be more truly melancholy and abominable than this spot. Perhaps I shall be allowed to go back to Geneva, but I think more likely Montpellier will be the place to which I shall be sent. . . . To my bitter surprise and great despair, not one line have I yet received from Ireland. There were some reports in the papers of great disturbances there, but they have since been quieted. Can anything be equal to the bad conduct of my family? . . . If I don't get away from this place, I cannot conceive anything more melancholy than my winter prospects, and even if I get permission to go, how can I get away, or how can I travel without money? My health is getting worse and worse. My stomach has been very bad ever since I came here; so that in time I think that the best and cheapest plan will be for me to lay me down and die—but then poor William [his servant] will be left totally friendless. *The only way is to have, if possible, no thought at all, and no care, for the morrow*—Farewell, my dear friend.[41]

Meanwhile, as Edgeworth began his long, languishing time as an internee, Roget in Geneva managed to get a reassuring note through to the Philips boys, urging them to stay in Neuchâtel and under no circumstances return to Geneva. He was greatly cheered by a letter from Etienne de Lessert, who reported that Romilly had written directly to Talleyrand, who in turn had promised to lay that letter before the Chief Consul himself.

On Monday, July 25, Roget called on the Mayor, showed him de Lessert's letter, and asked him to give him a passport. The Mayor told him to come the next morning. At noon on July 26, 1803, Roget stepped out of the Mayor's office with a passport; by four he had left Geneva in a cabriolet, reaching Morges at midnight. He started at 4 A.M. the next day and, driving hard, reached Neuchâtel at 7 P.M., finding the Philips boys after many inquiries.[42]

In Neuchâtel, Roget learned that, despite the fact that the boys were under age and had obtained regular passports, General Dupuch had sent express orders to stop them at the frontier. In spite of the orders, they had slipped through, having by accident some papers bearing the signature of the Commandant. Moreover, Roget learned that the Commandant had also ordered his arrest on the ground that since Roget had established Genevan citizenship, he was required under the law to serve in the French army! Enraged by this villainy, Roget set down in his diary a rare outburst, probably the most extreme in his whole Victorian life:

. . . How can any honest mind conceive the concatenation of perfidy and malice which, spread unseen before, behind, and on every side, and drawn by gentle degrees closer and closer, lays hold first of one limb and then of another . . . ?

He went on for some pages, describing the insulting hypocrisy of Napoleon's agents:

. . . One can bear open hatred; vanity excited our contempt; a gust of passion leaves no impression on the mind; but the sneering compliments of a pretended friend, offering us consolation and holding out to us his protection, when we know the malice that rankles in his heart, that he considers us as his dupe, gulled by his smiles, decoyed by his fair words, and that when offering us friendship, he is all the while plotting our destruction. . . .

He had, it seemed, to get it all out:

. . . Thank God I have at length escaped from their clutches! The Tygers [sic] of Africa are less to be dreaded, are less ferocious than these. Monsters vomited up from the deep are less terrible. Demons commissioned from Hell to execute some infernal purpose and overrunning the earth, spreading wheresoever they go the calamities of plague, pestilence, and famine, are milder and more to be trusted than they. The land is blasted which they tread upon. The air which blows from their accursed country is loaded with infection. All is blighted and corrupted by their envenomed touch. Dissimulation and corruption are in the van, perfidy and treachery pave the way, and ruin and horror are in the rear. Their track is marked by devastation and destruction. Death pursues their footsteps and swallows up what they leave. . . .[43]

Although relieved by his outburst and by rejoining his charges, Roget's troubles were far from over. Neuchâtel, a principality of the King of Prussia, was full of English who had flocked over the Swiss border to avoid arrest by the French troops. The town was seething with rumors, conspiracies, elaborate escape plans, and despairing fugitives. Passports or other releases obtained from the Geneva authorities were worthless. Napoleon had placed garrisons in nearly every town in Switzerland, with orders to seize and return all Englishmen. The safety of Germany could only be reached by careful planning of an escape route that would not pass through any town.

Roget had brought a Genevan servant with him who knew the byroads of Switzerland. Roget and the boys dressed themselves as peasants, carefully avoided speaking a word of English, and stopped only at obscure villages, traveling in this way to pass the gates of Seleure, which they managed by tiptoeing by at 3 A.M., without challenge by the sleepy sentry.

The fourth day was the most critical. They had to take one of two roads. One passed through Baden, where some Englishmen had already been arrested. The other took them through Brug, a small town but one where a French garrison had recently been placed. They discussed their chances and chose Brug. Here is Burton's account:

We rose at 3 A.M., walked with a guide and our faithful servant six or eight miles, and crossed the river Aar in a common boat a little below the town—having sent on the coachman, who had travelled these roads for twenty years. He was stopped by a sentinel who asked him to whom the carriage belonged. He answered, "To some gentlemen of Neuchâtel who crossed the river some days ago, and are waiting for me in Germany." "Very well," says the sentinel, "you must stop til the Commandant is up," for it was 5:30 A.M. So the coachman gets down and goes to the innkeeper, who, knowing all, says to the sentinel: "Let the carriage pass; I know the persons, and am answerable for them and their carriage. You come and drink a bottle at my house when you come off duty." Thus did this fellow, for a bottle of wine, betray his trust, and so our carriage got through happily. It might have been confiscated had they known it belonged to an Englishman. Indeed we ourselves had to pass through a corner of the town, which we did not expect to do, and we saw this same sentinel with his back turned toward us. It is probable that had he seen us, he would not have said anything to us, as we were dressed very shabbily, with

pipes in our mouths, and long sticks. When the carriage over-
took us, we recrossed the Aar, hastening before the Commandant at Brug could have time to send after us. In half an hour
we found ourselves on the banks of the Rhine, the great
boundary between Switzerland and the German Empire.[44]

Roget's version tallies exactly with Burton's, but is a little more
expressive of their great relief to escape the French:

. . . It is impossible to describe the rapture we felt in treading
on friendly ground. It was like awaking from a horrid night-
mare. We could scarcely yet believe our good fortune, and hastened away from the border of that inhospitable land where
we had met with such persecution.[45]

The exhausted fugitives lay over in Stuttgart for a few days to
rest and refit and to congratulate themselves on being freed. "I
repeat to myself frequently," Roget wrote, " 'I am free. I am on
my way towards England. I am once more a man.' "

In Frankfurt, a few letters from home caught up with them, affording them a grim sort of amusement, since the letters were
full of family chitchat; obviously the Philipses still thought the
trio safe in Geneva. Finally, however, exactly a month from the
day Roget streaked out of Geneva in a rented cabriolet, a letter
arrived from the boys' father:

Good God what an escape! Although you are at present in perfect safety yet the perusal of your letter was almost too much
for poor Mrs. Philips. . . . If it could be contrived I should
wish that Mrs. Philips might not know when you are likely to
be at sea. . . . The accounts we receive from your part of the
world are so contradictory that we cannot judge how the
Northern Powers will act. You will now have the opportunity
of seeing English papers. I am called away. Adieu! May that
providence which has hitherto attended you conduct you safely
to your native country! [46]

The remainder of the journey was delayed by Burton's falling
ill of "brain fever," necessitating their remaining in Frankfurt
from August 12 to October 6. Writing to his uncle again—he
carefully avoided telling his mother anything about his dangers
until they were past—Peter reported that the fever finally had
subsided but had left the boy very debilitated, "and what is
worse, completely deranged in his mind. At times indeed he is
quite rational, but he varies so astonishingly from hour to hour
that it is extremely difficult to form any opinion as to his pro-

gress." Luckily, Frankfurt was the home of Dr. Samuel Thomas von Soemmerring (1775–1830), the internationally known anatomist, who heard of the case and gave Peter every assistance. An added complication was the necessity of conducting the whole drawn-out affair without letting Mr. Philips know of Burton's illness.[47]

Furthermore, Peter's own mother was beginning to suspect that all was not well. "Do you know," she wrote to Anne Romilly, "I begin to be uneasy. . . . A letter may indeed have miscarried, but why is he so long en route? I don't like his staying some days at Stuttgart . . . I fancy it is not far enough from French trammels." [48]

After correspondence between home and travelers had been reestablished, Philips Senior smoothed their way by seeing that funds and friends were waiting for them at various points along the escape route: Heidelberg, Mannheim, Frankfurt, Leipzig, Wittenberg, Potsdam, Berlin. From Berlin they rode north into Danish territory to their embarkation point, the seaport of Husum, arriving in "sight of the sea on October 31 with a feeling akin to that of Xenophon and his soldiers." [49]

At each stopping place along the way, they picked up news of the resumed hostilities and, as usual, were confused, sometimes frightened, by the rumors that passed for news. Some of the more persistent rumors were that Napoleon had mounted his long-threatened invasion operation against Britain, that the French navy had established supremacy in the North Sea, and that Englishmen were being impressed from all vessels leaving northern European ports. Thus, during a three-week delay in Husum, caused by storms and contrary winds, Roget and the boys entertained themselves with guesses on whether, once they did embark, they would arrive in England or be dragged off by French marauders.

The account of the last lap of the twenty-month journey is told by Roget in third person, possibly indicative of a new maturity or a new objectivity, or both:

Embarked on board a pilot skiff at 4½; got to the packet *Diana* (Captain Stewart) at 6. But the dangers of the sea had yet to come. For six days they were tossed on the North Sea. When at length the little vessel was making good way for Harwich, a suspicious-looking sail made its appearance in the offing. Growing larger, it took the shape of a frigate, which showed no colours, but brought the *Diana* to by firing a gun. The passengers

on board watched, with no small anxiety, the lowering of a
boat for the purpose of boarding her, and it may be believed
that to none of our three fugitives was a sound more welcome
than the voice of the Lieutenant in command of the boarding
party; for, as he approached near enough for them to hear
him, he shouted to his crew with a round and unmistakeably
British oath. The frigate was *H. M. S. Unicorn* (Capt. Hardi-
man). Friendly greetings followed and an invitation to dinner,
which was virtuously declined by Capt. Stewart on the ground
that he had five mails on board. These, together with our
three travelers, were safely delivered at Harwich on the following day, November 22. There they lodged at an inn whose
landlord bore the singularly appropriate name of Mr. John
Bull.[50]

VI [1804-1808 ❦

Professional Beginning
—Manchester

As good as the foggy, windswept estuary of the Stour looked
to young Roget and the Philips boys, they lost no time in book-
ing places for the hundred-mile journey to London. There they
were heartily welcomed at No. 27 Gower Street by the Samuel
Romillys, who insisted that they spend a few days with them before taking the long coach trip to Manchester. Catherine, winter-
ing again at Ilfracombe, on the Dover coast, was anxious to see
her boy, but Romilly agreed with Peter that she would have to
wait until he had delivered his charges safely home. Romilly got
them places on the fastest mail coach for the two-hundred-mile
run to Manchester. They arrived at the Philips residence in
Bridge Street on December 10, 1803. Peter, writing to his Aunt
Anne on December 15, sounded relaxed and pleased with himself:

. . . For these ten days past we have been doing nothing but receiving visits and congratulations on all sides, and partaking of
the feastings and rejoicings in honour of their [the boys'] return. I find at length that there is no end to the dinners and
invitations, and that I must sooner or later make my escape
from this hospitable place and retreat to the more tranquil
and sequestered vales of Devonshire.

Peter wintered in Ilfracombe with his mother and sister, but in
April was back in Manchester, looking the place over with a critical eye as to what it might offer a young professional gentleman

about to begin his career. Writing his uncle, on April 25, on the results of his inquiries in the area, he sounded definitely interested, particularly since there seemed to be a vacancy coming up for a physician at the Public Infirmary. Such a position would indeed be a plum for a beginner, but Peter was confident that with the weight of the Philipses' recommendation behind him—Philips was Chairman of the Board of Trustees for the hospital—he had an exellent chance. In addition, he was struck by the possibilities for a good practice in the town:

> The number of physicians at Manchester bears certainly a less proportion to the population than in most other towns. For 100,000 inhabitants, six or seven physicians seems scarcely an adequate number. The prodigious and sudden influx of inhabitants during the short interval of peace may in some measure account for this under proportion; and the great reputation of Dr. Percival and Dr. Ferriar [1] may have deterred such as were ambitious of advancing rapidly into extensive practice.

Peter's letter continues in a sensible, analytical way, concluding that, all in all, the circumstances in Manchester at that time seemed the most propitious he could hope to find anywhere. Dr. Percival, growing old and blind, was about to retire from the infirmary, and had already given up all his out-of-town practice. Peter was sure that when news of Percival's impending retirement were known, "no doubt many would immediately pour in to supply the place—but surely a person already fixed on the spot, and who had been previously known, would have a much better chance than any new adventurer could possibly have." Moreover, he was sure that Catherine would be more than content to come to Manchester, where her acquaintance with such a prominent family as the Philipses would give her immediate access to the best of Manchester society. Peter determined to make the most of these opportunities, but to improve his own qualifications he decided to spend three or four months in additional anatomical studies in Edinburgh.

Meanwhile, in Ilfracombe, formerly an important seaport but in the nineteenth century one of the most fashionable watering places in Devon, Annette enjoyed what was probably the happiest year of her life. She and her mother had been there nearly a year and, in the way of British summer resorts, were solidly established in the ranks of the "better society" of the place. Annette's letter to her brother on May 20, 1804, fairly bubbles with life and pleasure. Surrounded by friends, both male and female, Annette's days were entirely taken up with horseback riding, walking tours, picnics, dances, card parties, amateur musicals.

Annette described lively horseback excursions with young friends to nearby points of interest—some of these being expeditions of two, three, or even five days' duration, all properly chaperoned, of course, and most of them charmingly interrupted with luncheon dansants. She was very fond of riding and spoke frequently of her "little grey," a horse that apparently her brother had ridden the preceding winter. On Fridays, Annette and her friends regularly held musical parties, apparently the function of an amateur orchestra group which they called "The Mail Coach": "They go on very well, being supported by Miss Lee, Miss Walters, and myself, females, and Mr. Hodgson and his delightful flute, Mr. Vie and his voice and bass viol, and Mr. Baker and his violin. Next Friday we are engaged to a large music meeting at Mr. Lock's; we are all learning and practicing our parts." Annette reported a party that she and Catherine had held in their house—"above twenty, two rooms open, cards and music." [2]

Through the next four or five years, Catherine's, Annette's, and Peter's letters abound in gloomy references to the departure from Ilfracombe, which was so painful to Annette that her mother warned everyone against the mere mention of the place. Moreover, leaving Ilfracombe plunged Annette into such a sustained despondency, lightened only very occasionally in the following years, that more than once she had the whole family—the Romillys too—seriously alarmed for her health and sanity. Annette's health deteriorated rapidly, she gave up her usual activities (the piano, her drawing, needlework, reading, riding), lost weight, became again a pale, unhappy ghost trailing along after her mother, from watering place to watering place. Again and again in Catherine's letters are cryptic phrases such as, "we can never return to Ilfracombe," or, "our present situation is pleasant enough except that we are too close to Ilfracombe," or, from Tenby, "she stares tragically across at the Devon coast."

We have repeatedly studied the approximately fifty letters written between Peter's return from Geneva (1803) and his removal from Manchester to London (1808) in an attempt to find enough facts to explain what amounted to the ruin of Annette's life. But the results of this study are far from satisfactory. Up to and including her last letter from Ilfracombe (August 28, 1804),

Annette seemed to be full of life, completely occupied with her
sizable circle of friends, and marvelously happy, despite the fact
that they had already planned to leave Ilfracombe and locate in
Manchester. It would seem, then, that the mere departure from
Ilfracombe, although the loss of her friends would certainly
dampen her spirits temporarily, could not bring about the deepening gloom that characterized her life from that time on. She
was, after all, to spend the next few years in places just as lively
as Ilfracombe, places just as filled with pleasure-seeking young
people, with whom she presumably could have found no difficulty in associating. Moreover, they were setting off to rejoin
Peter, an event to which both Catherine and Annette had looked
forward for years.

Subsequent letters from both Catherine and Annette include
several veiled references to Annette's being mistreated by one of
her Ilfracombe admirers. Annette herself, in a letter dated December 6, 1804, sends Peter some forty lines of rhymed couplets,
including these:

> I hate your coxcomb beaux who flutter
> And in your ear soft speeches mutter,
> Pretend how much your charms give pain
> And shed false tears like show'rs of rain.
> Oh how I hold such puppies low!
> Their hearts as cold as ice or snow:
> What marry one? Rather than risk it
> I'd live for life on bread or biscuit.

Her poem then takes up the tale of a certain "Louisa," who,
wounded by false love, retreated to a rural hiding place to spend
her life extolling the beauty of nature and lamenting "Fate's
cruel laws":

> But sighing deep and seized with sudden pain,
> "And thus was I," she cried and sigh'd again.
> "Young, blooming, happy, pleasing all I pleas'd,
> "Till cruel love his hapless victim seized.
> "Esteem was pleaded—under this disguise,
> "My heart was stole a willing prize."
> Thus with her future peace a woman parts
> Deceiv'd by looks, by *words* and winning arts.

Her emphasizing of "words," and occasional references in the
letters to deceitful speeches of heartless men, of course suggest
that Annette's melancholy was the product of a broken heart.

But who was the man? Fragmentary references in Catherine's letters through the next three years narrow the field to a "Mr. L——." Subsequent mentions of Mr. Lee and his sister, favorites of both Catherine and Annette, seem to eliminate him. That leaves us, then, with a Mr. Lock, who was Annette's most constant escort at Ilfracombe. But in backtracking again to Annette's last letter from Devonshire, we find that she tells Peter of an "impetuous idea" that she and Mr. Lock had just had: "The Picks,[3] Mr. Lock and me propose drinking tea in the country by way of a change." Thus, if Mr. Lock is to be regarded as the villain of the piece, he must have deceived Annette (or, perhaps, merely disappointed her) sometime in September, for by early November Samuel Romilly was writing Peter, after entertaining Catherine and Annette in eastern England, to warn him that Annette's melancholy was only making her physical ailments worse. It is possible, of course, that Annette's break with Mr. Lock occurred as a result of the impetuous tea party in the country. But whenever or whatever, something certainly happened that changed Annette within a few short years from a happy, mischievous young woman into a dour and lonely, often neurotic, spinster. She never again opened herself to the world; she became more and more a moody companion to her perambulating mother. Annette never blamed her mother for taking her away from Ilfracombe, but Catherine, in at least two letters, described Peter's settling in Manchester as "a tragic mistake for all of us," as though she attributed Annette's unhappiness to her (Catherine's) compulsive need to be near her boy.

Peter followed through with his plan to study at Edinburgh during the summer of 1804 and took rooms at No. 5 Nicholson Street, very close to the university.[4] However, he had barely accustomed himself to the old college yard when he received an urgent summons from Dumont and Lord Henry, the son of Lord Lansdowne. Lansdowne was seriously ailing, and Dumont, no doubt with some assistance from Romilly, had arranged for Peter a position as private physician to the old nobleman. Peter hastened south and joined Lansdowne's entourage at Bath, where his wealthy patron was taking the waters. Roget then lived briefly at Bowood, Lansdowne's nearby estate at Calne, and accompanied Lansdowne at least once to Harrogate. Peter's association with Lansdowne, while brief (Peter returned to Manchester in October upon the death of Dr. Percival to accept a physicianship at the Public Infirmary), was cordial and, in the long run, extremely profitable for the young doctor. He made close friends with the nobleman's son, Henry Petty-Fitzmaurice (1780-1863, almost an exact contemporary), who, upon his father's death in the spring of 1805, became the third Marquis of Lansdowne. In later years in London, Lord Henry materially assisted Roget in securing important posts.

Precisely why Peter left the elderly marquis is not known, but it would seem reasonably clear from the letters that two factors entered into his decision: 1) Lansdowne's health seemed to be on the mend by the autumn of the year, and 2) Peter's advisers (especially Dumont) did not want him to miss the opportunity at the Manchester infirmary.

Following Lansdowne's death in May 1805, Catherine, writing in French to her son, indicated that she was outraged at the bequests. Her good friend Dumont, who had been of long-time service to the old marquis, got nothing. Peter also received nothing, as did little William, Romilly's son.

After spending a few weeks at the Philips town house, Peter found suitable rooms at No. 18 Oldham Street, which terminated at Piccadilly, then the location of the infirmary. He had known Dr. John Ferriar before that summer, and he quickly accepted Ferriar as a dedicated and able mentor. It may well be that this early association with Ferriar was the beginning of Roget's lifelong interest in public health and medical education, for Ferriar, in addition to carrying on a prodigious practice, was a pioneer in public health, at a place and time when his efforts could not have been needed more.

A discussion of the profound physical, industrial, political, and social effects that the introduction of power looms and machine cotton-spinning had had on Manchester at the end of the eighteenth century would be out of place here. But in order to understand the opportunities available to young Dr. Roget when he walked into the wards of the Public Infirmary for the first time in September 1804, one should realize that the execrable working and living conditions of the working classes probably cannot be duplicated by the worst circumstances to be found in modern Europe. Paralleling the misery of the many was the opulence of the few, as there emerged a small, plutocratic class of immensely wealthy merchants and manufacturers, all of them operating on a strictly laissez-faire basis.[5]

The primitive state of medicine itself and the unparalleled congestion and lack of sanitation in the teeming poor sections of

Manchester were quite enough to challenge any number of young men just entering the medical profession. Roget joined Ferriar in his determined attack on the epidemic fevers, particularly typhus, that struck down thousands each year. As late as 1842, in the famous *Report on the Sanitary Condition of the Labouring Population of Great Britain,* Manchester was highlighted as one of the worst pestholes of the nation. That report calculated the average age of death for mechanics and laborers to be seventeen—and it *followed* several public health and reform efforts first begun more than thirty years before by Ferriar, Roget, and other physicians at the infirmary.

The huge mill of John Philips, Roget's patron in Manchester, was considered an outstanding example of enlightened management. He provided separate buildings for the housing of the boys and girls, many of them parish children sent from London. The children were fed generously with oatmeal porridge at breakfast and supper, and broth and beef for dinner. Philips provided a master to teach them to read and write, in the evening hours after work, and saw that they were all marched to church on Sunday. While most of the textile factories were dark, badly ventilated places, Philips' plant was one of the first to be lighted by gas, a phenomenon so innovative in its day that it was the subject of a paper read to the Royal Society in London.[6]

But Philips was the exception to the rule. Ferriar and his small circle of friends and colleagues formed a "Board of Health" and, undaunted by the reluctance and outright antagonism of the mercantile barons of Manchester, fought on for such reforms as a system of licensing and inspection of lodging houses, provision of nurses, proper ventilation and cleaning in mills and factories, and the covering of wheels and gears of machinery. Volume III of Ferriar's *Medical Histories and Reflections*[7] includes an excellent account of the board's establishment of fever wards, along with records of the same from 1796 to 1806. The board also went directly to the people, as evidenced by what must surely be a unique document in the history of public health, a short broadside entitled "Advice to the Poor." Roget undoubtedly assisted Ferriar in its preparation (if, indeed, he did not write it himself). The whole of the short paper is appended here.[8]

Still another front on which Ferriar's board fought a difficult but slowly successful battle was that of formal medical education itself. In his first letters after his appointment, Roget mentions that he may be asked to prepare a series of medical lectures on chemistry. In cooperation with Ferriar; William Simmons (1762–1830), senior surgeon to the infirmary; Benjamin Gibson (1774–1812), surgeon; John Hutchinson, surgeon and apothecary; and the venerable and durable Charles White (1728–1813), chief moving force in the founding of the infirmary in 1752, Roget delivered courses of lectures in the rooms of the Manchester Literary and Philosophical Society. Such lectures, which had been offered sporadically through the years under the auspices of the College of Arts and Sciences, were, in effect, the beginnings of a medical school in Manchester.

Correspondence with the Literary and Philosophical Society and with the Central Library of Manchester has confirmed the fact of Roget's contribution to the founding of a medical school in that city. Roget's course, some eighteen lectures in all, was offered beginning on January 29, 1806, to medical students, and was repeated the next year for a more general audience.[9] A third series may have been given at Charles White's medical museum in King Street.[10] The one positive evidence of Roget's lecturing to the medical students, aside from the letters themselves, is a printed copy of the syllabus of his course of lectures. Roget was solely responsible for the latter half ("Physiology") of the syllabus, a thirty-page booklet.[11] In his "prefatory observations," Roget showed that his chief interest in the new science of physiology lay in the *organization* and *order* of the several aspects of that subject and in the *relationship* of the subject to such kindred fields as anatomy. This keen interest in relationships and classification was to develop into Roget's characteristic way of work and to lead, eventually, to his culminating attempt at classification, the *Thesaurus of English Words and Phrases.*

Roget's syllabus is "probably the earliest printed outline of lectures delivered to medical students in Manchester." [12] In fact, Roget extended his subject to a course on comparative anatomy and physiology. He presented a series of evening lectures, again at the Literary and Philosophical Society, beginning in January 1807, and these "were attended by a large and respectable audience." Roget was elected a member of the society on January 25, 1805, "probably on the recommendation of John Philips," and was Vice-President in 1807 and 1808 when Thomas "Magnesia" Henry was President and John Dalton was Secretary.[13]

In the year of Roget's appointment, the infirmary was deep in several kinds of trouble. Financially, it was on the brink—expenses exceeded income by £1,300.[14] There were also some problems among the personnel. Roget's associate Hutchinson, in charge of the hospital medications, was accused of incompetence; he seemed to be the target of the several surgeons, especially Simmons. Hutchinson, who was also in charge of the library, retaliated by charging the others with negligence in use and return of the infirmary books. He ordered wire fronts made for the bookcases and kept the keys in his pocket. Animosities reached such a pitch that Philips, as Chairman of the board, threatened to resign for lack of support. The board prevailed on him to stay and upheld Hutchinson after a long series of meetings and acrimonious letters, and the institution survived. Roget apparently was careful to stay out of the thickest part of this fray. His Aunt Anne, writing on January 11, 1805, comments:

Your most entertaining letter amused your Uncle and I very much although we cannot help feeling sorry that you have got into such a hornet's nest. If anybody can avoid being involved in those disputes, I think you will, and it will be no little merit if one can judge by your letter of the acrimony of the disputants.

In view of Roget's later involvement in many battles with and for the Royal Society, he must have looked back with amusement on this letter.

Roget's progress, for all of the work with Ferriar and the Literary and Philosophical Society, was slow, and he was occasionally moved to suggest in a letter to his uncle or his mother that he should pull out of an unpromising situation without further loss of time. But they consistently advised him to stick it out a little longer. Romilly, particularly, insisted that he give Manchester a fair trial, pointing out the advantages that a successful sojourn in the textile city would offer when he was finally ready to make his bid in London. In addition—and this is significant in light of the tragic events that were to befall both Romilly and his sister—the uncle warned the young doctor not to give way to melancholy:

Despondency is, I have always thought, the great defect of our family, and I do not think that you are more exempt from it than the rest. I have been apprehensive ever since I first heard of your intention of going to Manchester of the effect of the first impression which your residence there would make upon you all.[15]

In the fall of 1806, Roget impulsively took up an opportunity that presented itself through his uncle's wide friendships among the nation's political leaders. Without resigning his position at

the hospital, he accepted in November an appointment as private secretary to Lord Howick, then Secretary of State to the Foreign Department, and afterward to become Earl Grey. Two of
Howick's attributes might have attracted Peter: he was a stalwart, liberal Whig, and he was publicly opposed to the course
taken by leaders of the French Revolution. The former would
have fitted well with Peter's admiration for his uncle's dedication
to reform, and the latter would have touched Peter's own conclusions about violent revolution, conclusions drawn from his recent
adventure in Napoleon's Geneva. Peter's association with Lord
Lansdowne no doubt figured too in his being offered the position
with Howick, for, with Romilly and Fox, Howick was a frequent
guest at Bowood.

Roget spent a month at Lord Howick's family seat, situated
about a mile from the sea on the rocky eastern coast of Northum-
berland, some thirty miles south of Berwick and forty north of
Newcastle. Unfortunately no letters survive to describe Peter's activities or state of mind at that northern redout. We are left
simply with the note that he did not like the work and thus returned to Manchester in time to begin one of his lecture courses
in January 1807.

Meanwhile, Catherine kept up a constant stream of letters
(many of them in French) to Peter, describing her and Annette's
mournful pilgrimage. From town to town they moved, staying a
few weeks here, a month or two there, as they sought the ideal
place to spend the indefinite interim period before they could be
reunited with Peter. Their demands for the optimum habitat apparently were far more exacting than could be met by the succession of small towns and villages that formed their itinerary during the five years Peter remained in Manchester: Ilfracombe;
Park Gate, just across the Mersey from Liverpool; Bangor, on the
northern Welsh coast; Aberystwyth, a beach resort on the west
coast of Wales; Tenby, on the south coast of Wales; Swansea, a
busy smelting center on the south coast of Wales; Chepstow, a
seaport on the Monmouthshire side of the Severn River at its
confluence with the Wye; Abergavenny, north and inland from
Chepstow; Derby, on the Derwent River in the southernmost
portion of the hilly Derbyshire resort area.

In all of her perambulation, Catherine was nursing Annette
through various physical and psychological ills, at times so severe
that the mother despaired of her daughter's survival. Annette's
physical complaints were a recurring intestinal problem and a
persistent discharge of the eyes. Catherine tried an impressive list

of home remedies and patent medicines, reporting the dosages and results meticulously to Peter, and begging him for additional ideas. When he did make suggestions, she more often than not rejected them—"It is difficult, I know, for one so far away to realize the conditions as well as one who has been with her all this while." In the course of these three or four years, Catherine employed the following specifics on her daughter: vinegar-and-water wash, calomel pills, analeptic pills, Phipps & Ball's Remedy, Smellowe's Eye Salve, serpentaria, bark, Goulard water, powder of Valerian ("it smells terribly and draws the cats to our room"), cream of tartar, opium, calcined white vitrio and camphor (an eyewash), "Scotch pills," port wine (three times a day), porter, tincture of castor, lozenges of ching (for worms), calibrate water, iron remedy, rhubarb, burgundy pitch plaister.

Catherine's running medical correspondence with her doctor son is sometimes amusing (she was often simply interested in his agreeing with her) and often pathetic, as, quite alone and in some remote spot, she grew desperate to relieve Annette of pain or discomfort. In some letters, her descriptions reveal a real talent for objective, detailed observation. In others, she provides Peter with surprisingly shrewd psychological advice in regard to a doctor's bedside manner, or the prescription of placebos, or the need for a doctor to keep his patient's spirits up: "A physician surely ought to say much even if he does not say much to the purpose. It amuses the sick." [16] Fearful of Annette's despondency, Catherine often resorted to having Peter use a kind of code so that Annette, who read all of the letters from him, would not be worried by certain specific discussions. For example, in a discussion of a salve that Peter had recommended, Catherine asked him if he would not, in his next letter, write a small "M" in one corner of the page if the salve contained, as she suspected, mercury.

Few of Peter's letters from this period survive; in fact, judging by his mother's frequent pleas to write more often, he did not keep in touch with his family as he might have. It may have been, too, because of the similarity of Catherine's repeated complaints—of weather, of society, of ill health, of lack of funds—that he simply didn't know what to say. Rather standardly he preached optimism and patience to them, assuring them that one day they would all be together again:

> I am sorry to see that you are so troubled and that you yield so
> easily to discouragement. Believe me, my dear Annette, take a
> little more heart; try to awaken within yourself some moral

courage. Look upon your present trouble as an opportunity
which has been presented to you to exercise your patience, and
use the offensive passages to fortify your constancy in undergoing the *real* evils in life. One should not expect to enjoy the
pleasures of life without a little self-preparation, without some
salutary self-discipline. The flowers which beautify spring are
sown in winter; the gardener must not neglect his cares and
abandon them in despair because he sees the snow arrive.

. . . For a moment forget yourself and cast your eyes about
you: have not others their troubles, their sorrows? the poor,
victims, of the caprices of the tyranny of the rich, the rich tor-
mented by their passions, always reviving themselves, always
far from being satisfied; people in mediocre stations working
without let up, exposed to the risks of commerce, after losing
all their fortune and forced to submit to straitened circumstances.

. . . You are not the only person to whom independence is
dear and who hates constraint and want. You are not the only
one whose sensitivity is wounded by coldness of manners and
who does not feel a terrible worry in not being able to have all
his time at his disposition. Have I not experienced myself a
thousand impositions? I would have been only too happy to
have had three hours a day to myself.

. . . Forget the past and begin again to take courage. Worry
no longer about pleasing others and you will better succeed in
this. Think only about being natural and meanwhile the rest
will come. Never despair or abandon yourself to discourage-
ment and the despondency which, more and more, will take
possession of you to the degree that you indulge yourself in it.
Even force yourself sometimes to be gay, and persevere in your
attempts. Cheerfulness depends more upon habit than you
think, and a habit is established only slowly and by force of
will and a multiplicity of efforts. I will say to you that you will
gather the fruit of your pains in more than one manner, but
time is necessary for fruit to ripen, and one only succeeds in
obtaining it by accepting the penalty it exacts.

Look, therefore, toward the future with more confidence.
Whatever may be your present worries, they will not last very
long. In a little while we will be re-united in our own affairs;
we will be the masters of our own time. If you wish to advance
yourself and cultivate your mind and your talents, you have
every means of doing so. . . .[17]

Painful as it is to read this self-righteous and secondhand
avuncular advice, one must see it as a genuine portrait—not necessarily of what the twenty-nine-year-old Peter Mark Roget was,

but of what he thought he was, or what he thought he ought to be. Nor is it difficult to trace most of these ideas back through the letters of his mother, his uncle, his aunt, and earlier in the long series of letters of Dumont to his mother following the death of Jean Roget in Lausanne. The same ideas are, of course, present in the autobiographical volumes and letters of many another figure of the late eighteenth and early nineteenth centuries. At their worst they express an impossibly stuffy, self-congratulatory Pollyanna attitude and an incredible insensitivity toward the real trouble of others. At their best, they reveal a stubborn strength of will, a faith in salvation through work, and a pervasive confidence that in a God-propped world, good will be eventually rewarded.

By midyear 1808, Peter felt that he had gone about as far as he could go in Manchester. He had learned, in those years, that if one wished anything more than a mediocre success, one must seek it in London. Although there was still much to be done in Manchester—both in the way of public health projects and in the way of private practice—he had found that the exciting prospects of 1804 had simply disguised the underlying rivalries, private feuds, closed territories, and general apathy toward medical reform. Moreover, sociologically, conditions were worsening. More of the poor were starving; economic and political power was being concentrated into fewer and fewer hands. Manchester, for all its 110,000 inhabitants, was not to have an organized municipal government nor to secure any representation in Parliament until after the great reforms of the 1830's. Rick burnings were on the increase, as were brutal reprisals from factory owners and landholders against the semiorganized mobs of unemployed men who struck out blindly in their desperation. The reign of General Lud was about to begin.[18] The Peterloo Massacre was less than a decade away. The London papers were full of the violence and tumult in the textile towns as the marked gap between the masters and the poor widened.[19]

Romilly, too, was aware of Peter's growing dissatisfaction with the limitations of Manchester, and in several letters he suggested that perhaps the time had come for Peter to try his luck in the metropolis. Anne Romilly also urged him, in an affectionate letter, to stop throwing away his time and talents in Manchester. A room for him would always be ready in their new place at No. 21 Russell Square. Romilly also made an arrangement for Peter to act as tutor for the eldest of the Romilly children, William, then nine. Roget's comments on this experience are interesting; his letters offered him a real exercise in tact—how to assure his uncle of his undying devotion to William but at the same time point out that the boy at the moment was quite uneducable. The letters do not make clear whether the boy was sent to Roget at Manchester, but it would seem so, for Roget was still writing from Manchester as late as October 6.

In November, Peter made his decision, and by the beginning of December the little family was together again, in temporary quarters in London. A note from Romilly to Catherine on December 4 assures her that she and Peter will have his full support throughout the London experiment, for she insisted that their coming to London be seen simply as an experiment. Romilly was satisfyingly specific:

> Indeed, it always was my intention (though I have never mentioned it to you or to him and of course not to any other person living) that all the risque [sic] of it should be exclusively my own. I wish him to try what a residence in London will do at least for three years, and I will undertake that at the end of that period neither you nor he shall have incurred any debts or broken in upon the capital of either of your property by the Experiment. I have no doubt that I shall run very little risk myself. I have no doubt that you will be able to live upon your income, being as I know you both are careful without being parsimonious, but whatever the risk may be I am anxious that it should be mine. I don't undertake that you shall be gainers, but you certainly shall be at the worst at the end of three years only just where you were. I hope that this assurance will induce you to lay aside all those fears and anxieties which it is but too evident you have too much indulged. . . . I wish you to be quite secure, to be careful and economical, but not to consider it as a matter of importance if you spend more than your income amounts to.

On the next day, December 5, another note from Romilly provided convincing evidence of the genuineness of his assurances. He entirely approved of a new house Catherine and Roget had located, and he stood willing to advance the purchase price—some £1,500.

On January 14, 1809, four days before his thirtieth birthday, Roget received his first letter in his new home—No. 39 Bernard Street, which was to be home, office, study, and retreat for the next forty years. On this day, his mother and sister were comfortably installed in their own rooms. A cook and a maidservant had been hired. New clothes had been purchased for the young doctor from the provinces. When he surveyed the world from his front step in Bernard Street, Peter Mark Roget, M.D., might have been pardoned for rubbing his hands together with a brisk kind of satisfaction that the metropolis was his for the taking.

VII [1809–1815 ❦

Establishment in London

*The night nursery of the Darling family, which is the scene of
our opening act, is at the top of a rather depressed street in
Bloomsbury. We have a right to place it where we will, and
the reason Bloomsbury is chosen is that Mr. Roget once lived
there. So did we in days when his Thesaurus was our only companion in London; and we whom he has helped to wend our
way through life have always wanted to pay him a little compliment. The Darlings therefore lived in Bloomsbury.*

*It is a corner house, whose top window, the important one,
looks upon a leafy square. . . . Since the days of the Darlings,
however, a lick of paint has been applied; our corner house in
particular, which has swallowed its neighbor, blooms with the
awful freshness as if the colours had been discharged upon it
through a hose. Its card now says, "No Children," meaning
maybe that the goings-on of Wendy and her brothers have
given the house a bad name. As for ourselves, we have not
been in it since we went back to reclaim our old Thesaurus.*[1]

CHARMING as Sir James Barrie's tribute to Roget may be, it is
unfortunately incorrect in at least two respects: Roget's Bernard
Street house was not a corner house, nor did it look out upon a
leafy square. It was by the narrowest of margins (about four
doors down the street) in Bloomsbury, at least as that district is
presently defined by the *Survey of London*.[2]

When Roget (or, more accurately, Samuel Romilly) bought
the place in December of 1808, Bernard Street was new and raw,
being simply a connecting way between Russell Square and
Brunswick Square. The street was named for Sir Thomas Bernard, active in the administration of the Foundling Hospital, the
management of which was at that time in the midst of a specula-

tive development of some fifty-six acres surrounding the hospital. The houses in Bernard Street were put up by an amazingly successful builder, James Burton, who is credited with building the bulk of the Foundling Estate houses as well as the lion's share of the property between Bloomsbury Square and Euston Road. Burton put up nearly £2,000,000 worth of houses.[3] He began work on Bernard Street in 1799 after an arrangement had been made with the Duke of Bedford to open the street into Russell Square, at that time simply the private gardens of the Duke. By 1801, Burton had eight houses on the rate books; by 1820 the street was completed.[4]

The houses along Bernard Street were nearly identical, built of brick from local clay of a light ochreous shade, with slate roofs, chimney pots from the factory at Bagnigge Wells, and a minimum of exposed woodwork. Typical of Burton's cheaper grade of construction, No. 39 was long and narrow, consisting of four floors above street level and a semibasement. The tops of the windows could just be seen above one of the submerged service "areas" that still guard the fronts of thousands of London houses like miniature, fenced moats. One excellent study of Georgian London describes a similar house as typical of the city:

> Practically the whole population lived in one version or another of such houses. A handful of aristocrats had their isolated palaces; and the unemployable and criminal classes had their centuries-old rookeries; but the remainder, from earls to artisans, had their narrow slices of buildings, now called, for no very good reason, "terrace-houses."
>
> The vertical relation of the terrace-house to its site is not as simple as it seems. All houses except the poorest have basements. But the basement represents only a shallow excavation [in Bernard Street, the earth so excavated was made into bricks for the subsequent construction] while the roadway is partly *made up*. That is why the front basement room of a London house invariably looks into a deep "area," whereas the back room has a door leading straight into a yard or garden. The roadway and the garden are at different levels. The garden level is the "natural" level, whereas the roadway represents an "artificial" level.[5]

No. 39 Bernard Street does not exist today, but identical houses—now converted into small hotels—remain along the opposite side of the street. As one emerges from the Russell Square underground station, he stares directly across the street at the former

location of Roget's home. When I tracked down the spot in the
summer of 1967, I had to be content with a very large hole in the
ground. The whole area between Bernard Street on the south,
Coram Street on the north, Brunswyck Square on the east, and
Herbrand Street on the west, formerly a three-block neighborhood solidly built with Burton's houses of the 1800-1820 period,
was in the last stages of demolition. I stood there one afternoon
and watched the huge iron ball cave in the last of the houses
with a great smashing of bricks and tearing of timbers. A steady
stream of dump trucks hauled away the debris, and along the
Bernard Street side, workmen were already pouring foundations
for what the estate agent told me was to be a new hotel-and-shop-
ping center complex.

But in 1809, Bernard Street was spanking new. Its cream-col-
ored brick must have stood out attractively against the green of
the surrounding meadows. It was certainly a promising location
for a new doctor, particularly a new Dr. Roget, for he was less
than a full two-block walk from his uncle Sir Samuel Romilly,
then Solicitor General, who had been in his new home, No. 21
on the north side of Russell Square, less than four years. Some of
Roget's closest friends and associates—Alexander Marcet, John
Bostock, John Yelloly, Abraham Rees—were to take houses in
the immediate neighborhood. Roget was within easy walking distance of the British Museum, of the Bloomsbury publishers' offices, of the soon-to-be-organized London University. In the street
directly behind his house, then called Great Coram Street, a
group of influential people of the neighborhood, headed by
Romilly, Scarlett, and Francis Horner, endowed and erected the
Russell Institution, a kind of social and cultural center.

Roget's new home was a short block north of Queen Square,
where he had so unsatisfactorily tried to work with Jeremy Bentham, and a mere four- or five-block walk from Great Russell
Street, where he had lived, during his first unsuccessful assault on
London, in rented rooms across from the British Museum. By
London standards, he was a satisfactory distance from the teeming alleys of Soho, and he could take some pride in the symbolic
distance between that ambiguous district, thronging with refugees,
and the wide streets, open spaces, and elegant new construction
of a district obviously restricted to professional persons on their
way up.

Roget lost no time in seizing the many opportunities that presented themselves. He immediately applied for and was granted a

licentiate from the all-powerful Royal College of Physicians, the kingdom's licensing agency of the medical profession. One of his first professional cases was the treatment of Romilly's youngest son, Edward, for which Romilly later sent him a draft for 10 guineas and his heartfelt thanks.[6] Early in 1809 he also accepted an invitation to participate in the first season of lectures at the new Russell Institution, where he shared the platform with John Pond (1767–1836), the Astronomer Royal. Roget delivered a course of twelve afternoon lectures on animal physiology. These were so successful that he was asked to repeat the course in the following year. (This was essentially the same material he had worked up for his lectures in Manchester.) For thirty years thereafter, Roget was to lecture on this and related subjects so eminently that he was widely regarded during his lifetime as an important and influential lecturer.

Roget wrote his friend Alexander Marcet on November 14, 1809, describing in detail his part in the organization of the Northern Dispensary, typical of the neighborhood charity clinics that served the poor in various sections of London. Roget; John Want, a surgeon; and Charles Whittell, another physician, were to provide medical treatment in that area, including Somers and Camden towns, Pancras, and the territory bounded by New Road (now Euston Road); Bagnigge Wells; a line through Guildford Street, Russell Square, and Keppel and Store Streets; and Charlotte Street and Fitzroy Square. The charity was sponsored by such gentlemen as Sir Samuel Romilly, Francis Horner, James Scarlett, Sir Arthur Pigott, and Sir H. Fitzherbert. Roget wanted to include Marcet, who was at that time supervising a temporary military hospital at Portsmouth, then crowded with the fever-ridden troops being brought home after the disastrous Walcheren campaign in July 1809.

The dispensary opened the following June at No. 9 Somers Place, north of New Road, and there Roget performed the duties of physician gratuitously for the next eighteen years. As late as 1861 (Roget would then have been eighty-two), he was listed in London medical directories as "Consulting Physician of the Northern Dispensary and for Diseases of the Eye, 126 Euston Road." [7]

While his work for the dispensary brought in no direct compensation, the project was an excellent one for a newcomer to London since it brought Roget into innumerable contacts with future patients and persons of influence, and undoubtedly contributed importantly to the "considerable practice" he had built by 1813. In the beginning, remembering the enviable ratio of physicians to population in Manchester when he was there, Roget must have felt that he needed something like the dispensary to gain a foothold, for there was then about one doctor for every thousand Londoners.[8]

Roget's next step was to associate himself with one of the most famous of the early London medical schools—the Great Windmill Street School, at No. 16 Great Windmill Street on the southernmost margin of Soho, just around the corner from what was to become Piccadilly Circus. In 1810, Roget began lecturing regularly there on "The Theory and Practice of Physic." The building had been rebuilt in 1766 to the specifications of William Hunter, who installed a large lecture theater, a museum, a dissecting room, a house containing three rooms, and a coachhouse and stables. The school enjoyed a steady popularity through the remainder of the eighteenth century under such notable men as William Cumberland Cruikshank, John Sheldon, Matthew Baillie, James Wilson, and Dr. John Cooke. Important men at Great Windmill when Roget began teaching there included Charles Bell, Benjamin Brodie, and John Shaw. According to Sir Zachary Cope, Great Windmill was the first building in London constructed for a school of anatomy.[9] After several decades of service, the school dwindled away, and the building was let to various enterprises: a printer, a billiard hall, a French restaurant (Le Café de l'Etoile), and finally, about 1878, with suitable remodeling, the present Lyric Theatre, featuring another kind of anatomy demonstration—girlie shows. The neon-lighted front wall of the Lyric is one of the original walls and bears a plaque commemorating William Hunter's school.

Roget delivered two courses of lectures a year at Great Windmill until 1815, when he was apparently eased out of the school by a reorganization. Charles Bell leaves an interesting letter giving some idea of the efforts to make the place a going concern:

> I was sitting here drawing yesterday when first Brande,[10] then Dr. Cooke, then Wilson, Brodie and Roget came in upon me, to lay our heads together about advertisements and hours of attendance. Wilson you know . . . Dr. Cooke is an elderly man, wears spectacles, a scholar and in good society; Brande is a very young man—he succeeds Davy in the Royal institution, has made discoveries, written good papers in the Society's *Transactions* and is a favourite with Sir Joseph Banks,[11] Dr.

Peter Mark Roget at age sixty, ten years before he began to write the *Thesaurus of English Words and Phrases.* (Dr. William Brockbank)

Title page from the notebook kept by Roget as a boy of ten. The additions are those of his son, John Lewis Roget (1828–1908). The notebook was filled with astronomical information and drawings and lists of Latin words. (J. Romilly Roget)

David Chauvet (d. 1803). During much of his childhood, Roget and his mother and sister lived with Chauvet, who kept a private school in Kensington Square, London. Many years later, Roget stayed with Chauvet in Geneva. (J. Romilly Roget)

Portrait of Roget's uncle, Sir Samuel Romilly (1757–1818), by Sir Thomas Lawrence. Romilly became virtually a father to Roget, paid for his education at the University of Edinburgh, and set him up in medical practice in London. (National Portrait Gallery)

TENTAMEN PHYSICUM
INAUGURALE,

DE

CHEMICÆ AFFINITATIS LEGIBUS;

QUOD,

ANNUENTE SUMMO NUMINE,

EX AUCTORITATE REVERENDI ADMODUM VIRI,

D. GEORGII BAIRD, SS. T. P.

ACADEMIÆ EDINBURGENÆ PRÆFECTI;

NECNON

Ampliffimi SENATUS ACADEMICI Confenfu; et

Nobiliffimæ FACULTATIS MEDICÆ Decreto;

PRO GRADU DOCTORATUS,

SUMMISQUE IN MEDICINA HONORIBUS AC PRIVILEGIIS

RITE ET LEGITIME CONSEQUENDIS;

ERUDITORUM EXAMINI SUBJICIT

PETRUS M. ROGET,

ANGLUS;

SOCIET. REG. MED. EDIN. SOCIUS EXTRAORD.

NECNON SOCIET. NAT. STUD. EDIN. SOC.

" See plaftic Nature working to this end,
" The fingle atoms each to other tend ;
" Attract, attracted to, the next in place
" Form'd and impell'd its neighbour to embrace.
" See matter next, with various life endow'd,
" Prefs to one centre ftill, the gen'ral good."

POPE, *Effay on Man.*

Ad diem 25. Junii, horâ locoque folitis.

EDINBURGI:

EXCUDEBANT ADAMUS NEILL ET SOCII.

M DCC XCVIII.

Title page of Roget's M.D. dissertation at the University of Edinburgh. Roget was nineteen when he was awarded the degree. Dedicated to Romilly, the dissertation dealt with "the laws of chemical affinity," one of many interests that Roget pursued throughout his life. (Royal College of Physicians)

PASSE-PORT. Nº 136.

Liberté.

Egalité.

DÉPARTEMENT DU LÉMAN.

Lois des 10 Vendémiaire, 17 Ventose an IV, et 28 Vendémiaire an VI.

Mairie de la Ville de Genève.

Laissez librement passer dans l'intérieur de la République pour aller à *Paris*

le Citoyen *Pierre Marc Roget* — *inscrit* —

au Tableau de la Ville de *Genève* — sous le Nº. *2862*

domicilié à *Genève* — profession d *—*

âgé de *vingt quatre ans 6 mois* taille de *un Mètre 700 Millimètre,*

cheveux *bruns* front *moyen* yeux *bruns* —

sourcils *bruns* nez *long* — bouche *moyenne* —

menton *à fossette* visage *ovale*

et prêtez-lui aide et assistance, aux offres d'en faire autant en pareil cas.

L-dit Citoyen *P. M. Roget* a déclaré savoir signer.

Délivré par nous Maire et Adjoints de la Ville de Genève, le *Septième Thermidor* an *onze* de la République Française, une et indivisible.

Le Maire ou Adjoint, *Maurice Me*

Porteur du Passe-port *Pierre Marc Roget*

Garriod Secrétaire en Chef.

Hawker Hill Street, Chepstow, on the west bank of the Wye near its junction with the Severn. Roget's mother Catherine and his sister lived in Chepstow and a dozen other, similar country towns and watering places during the years he was establishing himself in Manchester. (*South Wales Argus*, Newport)

Roget's Genevan passport, finally granted him after he had been detained by Napoleon's agents in 1803 and threatened with conscription into the French army. Roget and the two teen-aged boys he was guiding through Europe on the Grand Tour made their escape through Germany and Denmark. (J. Romilly Roget)

The Public Infirmary in Manchester, where Roget began his professional career in 1804. In addition to his work as physician in the
infirmary, he became active in public health projects and prepared
lectures which gave impetus to the founding of the first medical school
in Manchester. (Dr. William Brockbank)

TOP RIGHT: Roget's home at 39 Bernard Street, just off Russell Square,
London. Roget lived there from 1808 until 1843. This building was
demolished in 1967 to make way for new construction. (Holborn Central Library, London)

BOTTOM RIGHT: Facade of the Royal Institution, Albemarle Street,
London, where Roget was a prominent lecturer with Michael Faraday,
Humphry Davy, and other leading scientific figures of the early nine-
teenth century. (The Royal Institution of Great Britain)

II. *Description of a new instrument for performing mechanically the involution and evolution of numbers.* *By* Peter M. Roget, *M. D. Communicated by* William Hyde Wollaston, *M. D. Sec. R. S.*

Read November 17, 1814.

To abridge that species of mental labour which is required in conducting arithmetical computations, has been the professed object of a variety of mechanical contrivances. But the greater number of arithmetical machines, as they have been called, are more ingenious than really useful, and have been recorded more as objects of curiosity, than as admitting of convenient or ready application in the actual practice of arithmetic. The machine invented by PASCAL, and others constructed on the same principle, were, strictly speaking, limited to the simpler operations of addition and subtraction, and were incapable of being applied to the finding of products or quotients in any other way than by effecting a number of successive additions or subtractions. Still less did they aim at the immediate performance of the higher operations of involution, which, even by the most compendious methods of arithmetic, is a laborious process; or of the extraction of roots, to which the common rules furnish but a circuitous and slow approximation.

The only instruments which promise to afford real assistance to the practical calculator, are those founded on the theory of logarithms: a theory, which has been the fertile

MDCCCXV.   C

First page of the mathematical paper that won Roget a fellowship in the Royal Society in 1814. The subject was his invention of a device that later became the log-log scale on the modern slide rule.

Baillie, etc; Dr. Roget, who takes part of Cooke's lectures is, you know, the nephew of Sir Samuel Romilly, a well-informed, active young man, and I have no doubt by his own industry and friends will do remarkably well; Benjamin Brodie is an assistant surgeon of St. George's Hospital, and in good estimation as a young man.[12]

Great Windmill, which, for all practical purposes, served as medical school to the Middlesex Hospital, was doomed in the 1830's when the new university, after a break with Middlesex, erected its own teaching hospital in Gower Street.

Before he left Great Windmill, Roget made the acquaintance of another influential Londoner and one of the most successful physicians in the city—Dr. A. B. Granville, later an associate of Roget's in the Royal Institution, at the Royal Society, and in the Athenaeum. Granville, a prolific writer of pamphlets and treatises who was later active in a discussion of the attempts to reform the Royal Society, was a friend of Alexander Marcet and of Pictet,[13] and was a member of the Manchester Literary and Philosophical Society as of 1812. He taught briefly at Great Windmill under Brodie.[14] His subsequent advice to young doctors trying to get a start in London might well have been directed at Roget himself: "A man of science who was also a physician seldom succeeded in settling himself down profitably in practice if he insisted at the same time in maintaining the character of a savant." [15] Granville was also a close friend of Brande's, and regularly attended Sir Joseph Banks's famous Sunday evening *"conversaziones"* of 1812–13, held at his lavish Soho Square residence, along with Brande, Marcet, William Hyde Wollaston, Humphry Davy, Dr. Thomas Young, Henry Brougham, Lord Henry Petty, Joseph Herschel, William Whewell, David Brewster, Henry Ellis, William Laurence, Leonard Horner, Count von Humboldt, Augustin de Candolle, Dr. Matthew Baillie, Astley Cooper, Everard Home, George Birkbeck, Dugald Stewart, and John Playfair. There is no evidence that Roget was a member of this group, but considering his acquaintance with many of these men, including Banks himself, it would be strange if he were not at least an occasional guest at the Banks soirées.

Much of Roget's time, from 1809 on but particularly in those first few years in London, was taken up promoting the newly formed Medical and Chirurgical Society, an important and long-lived attempt to bridge the gap between the physicians and surgeons, not only of London, but of the whole nation. With his two friends, Alexander Marcet, then Physician to Guy's Hospital, and John Yelloly, Physician to the London Hospital, Roget is credited as being a prime mover in the promotion of the society, which was originally formed in 1805, the second-oldest medical society in England. Another close friend, John Bostock, joined the triumvirate later. The society survived for more than a hundred years, until it was amalgamated, along with many other specialized societies, into the Royal Society of Medicine in 1907.

The first volume of *Transactions of the Medical and Chirurgical Society* included two papers by Jenner; a paper by Marcet— "A Case of Hydrophobia, with an Account of the Appearances After Death"; and a paper by Yelloly—"A Case of Tumor in the Brain." [16] Roget, Yelloly, Marcet, and Bostock all contributed papers to Volume II, as did Dr. Martin Wall, Professor of Clinical Medicine, Oxford, who wrote on "Premature Puberty in a Female"—in Latin! Roget appeared for the first time in the *Transactions* with "A Case of Recovery from the Effects of Arsenic, with Remarks on a New Mode of Detecting the Presence of This Metal." [17] This was an account of his attending a nineteen-year-old girl, "of sanguine temperament and delicate constitution, having met with a severe disappointment, [who had] formed the resolution of putting an end to her existence. She purchased 60 grains of white oxyd [*sic*] of arsenic, left her house at 8 P.M., strewed the powder upon a piece of bread and butter, and eat [*sic*] the whole." Marcet assisted him in the case, making several calls on the girl with Roget; and Roget also acknowledges, in notes, papers by his friends Bostock and Yelloly.

Subsequent volumes of the *Transactions* show Roget continuing as Secretary, a responsibility which he fulfilled energetically and capably for twelve years. The job included the laborious task of editing the annual volume of the *Transactions,* which in turn often involved stirring up members to write papers, helping authors of accepted papers to draw them up in publishable form, reading proofs, and wrangling with printers. Roget is credited with editing and preparing for the press the first twelve volumes of the *Transactions.*[18] He often chaired meetings of the society, was Treasurer in 1827 and 1828, and in 1829 and 1830 was elected President and Treasurer. He was Treasurer again in 1832, and remained on the Council through 1835. With I. A. Albers, Roget published a second study in the *Transactions* —"Observations on a Change of Colour of the Skin Produced by the Internal Use of Nitrate of Silver" [19]—in which he described treating a twenty-five-year-old woman for epileptic fits by giving her nitrate of silver, gradually increasing the daily dose until, after nine or ten months, she was taking 18 grains per day. The treatment was successful except for one detail—the patient's face and tongue turned an indelible blue. Roget cited another, similar case in which, five years after the patient stopped having fits, the skin turned "a deep violet, approaching to black and having a complete similitude to the negro or to a bronze bust."

In 1812, Roget had the pleasure of seeing an honorary foreign membership bestowed on Samuel Thomas von Soemmerring, the German anatomist and friend of Goethe. Soemmerring had provided kind and skilled assistance to Roget in treating Burton Philips, when the boy fell seriously ill in Frankfurt during the escape from Geneva in 1803.

Roget's interest in the Medical and Chirurgical Society seemed to know no bounds. On March 7, 1810, his Housing Committee (Roget, Marcet, Yelloly, Cooper, and C. R. Aikin) recommended that the society take a large house at No. 3 Lincoln's Inn Fields, renting for £115 10s. per year, with part of this to be paid by the Geological Society, which was to take the second floor.[20] The recommendation was accepted, and Roget was appointed to carry out the leasing arrangements. Once in the new quarters, the society was happy that Roget would take on the additional job of librarian, and he set about classifying and arranging the society's considerable library.[21]

Several surviving letters between Roget and Marcet, who was traveling much of this time, lend further credence to the idea that Roget was spending every available hour on the business of the society. He took care of all manner of housekeeping problems, such as straightening out the finances after the society's clerk, a Mr. Yeoman, defrauded it of about £335 by the simple expedient of taking in members' dues, pocketing them, and then posting the members as delinquent.[22] Roget investigated, and, accompanied by a couple of lawyer friends, marched on Yeoman's house and forced him to sign over a bill of sale for all the personal possessions therein. They didn't come to more than £100, but the society was gratified by Roget's decisive action. This incident led to a detailed examination of the accounts of the society, and Roget served, as he had on several other occasions, on the auditing committee. The committee's chief resolution was that no person should be appointed clerk who could not post £300 bonding money.

The *Minute Books* of the society show that until the mid-1820's Roget rarely missed a meeting either of the society or of the Council, which met at least once a month. On several occasions, Roget, Marcet, and Yelloly were the only members present and they conducted business as usual, alternating in the chair.

Roget was active in the society's first attempt, in December 1812, to obtain a royal charter, an attempt that was defeated by the opposition of the Royal College of Physicians. A second attempt in the next year got Roget, Marcet, and Yelloly into hot water by their failing to inform such old stalwarts of the society as Halford, Baillie, and Saunders of their project. The charter was finally secured in 1835 after a considerable campaign and an outlay of £500, for which the members were assessed (Roget contributed £2 2s.).

Roget had the painful duty of judging the actions of his former colleague at the Northern Dispensary, the surgeon John Want, who, contrary to the bylaws of the society, published in the December 4, 1814, issue of the *Medical and Physical Journal* a notice of a paper read at the November 22 meeting. Mr. Want, apparently a somewhat disputatious gentleman, was already in trouble with Roget for not returning a library book, despite a 5s. fine. The affair occupied some three special meetings in December and January, devoted primarily to deciding how to proceed against Want. Finally, Roget was asked to write up the following motion to be put to the Council: "Are you of the opinion from the whole of the circumstances which have come before the Society relative to the subject in question, that Mr. Want has made himself liable to ejection, and that he be ejected accordingly?" [23] In the minutes for February 1, 1815, Roget wrote that Mr. Want had been ejected.

Other letters between Roget and Marcet discuss various problems of the Medical and Chirurgical Society, with Roget serving more than once as Marcet's editor and as editorial assistant to Marcet's wife, Jane, author of the remarkably popular *Conversations on Chemistry*, which appeared in 1806 and went through sixteen subsequent editions. Again and again in these letters, the four names Roget, Marcet, Yelloly, and Bostock occur, until it is perfectly clear that the four men held each other in high esteem over a long period of time and that they aided each other in their several personal and professional activities. Marcet, despite the fact that he was nearly ten years Roget's senior, seemed to be the closest to Roget, for it is only in letters to Marcet, and then only very occasionally, that Roget writes in anything like an informal or intimate manner. Usually, his letters are as stiff as his professional writings. The following excerpt might serve:

. . . Bostock has been at Liverpool for the last two months and has very thoughtlessly locked up all the papers and books of accounts, etc. relating to the Society which have been much wanted and are not to be got at till his return. With all this you will not wonder that the affairs of the Society have engrossed [?] as long a portion of my time as they have of this sheet of paper, in which I had intended to convey to you intelligence on the other subjects of your inquiries, on which I must be very laconic. I am well in health, my practice tolerable, but not increasing. I am, however, detained in town by two or three patients, whom I expect soon to cure and then take the Home Circuit in the humdrum style you so justly satirize. But I cannot venture on the delightful but unprofessional amusement you hold out to me, tho' you may be assured nothing would give me greater pleasure. For various reasons, and your absence is among the principal ones, the summer is uncommonly dull to me. My mother and sister have been in Devonshire for the last six weeks, and my domestic economy sadly discomposed by painters. Longmans informs me that the sale of the Conversations goes on exceedingly well.[24]

Having returned to Geneva for a long stay, Marcet apparently had invited Roget to drop his professional worries and join him in Europe. Marcet had married the daughter of Haldimand, one of the richest merchants in London, and a few years before the letter quoted above had inherited a huge fortune on the death of his father-in-law. He had promptly resigned his office of physician to Guy's Hospital so that he could devote himself to private research. Roget, too long schooled by his economy-minded mother, could not imagine himself holding up his end of the expenses in an international junket with Marcet.

It seems clear that it was his varied experience and numerous contacts made during work with the society in the first few years of his long career in London that formed the broad base for Roget's subsequent successes. A mere glance at the membership list of the society, in almost any year from 1809 on, shows a catalog of the most able, the most prominent, the most influential medical men in London.[25] These and dozens of others on their way up were Roget's regular associates at the society meetings, on committees, in the writing and selection of papers to be published.

As important as the Medical and Chirurgical Society was to Roget, it did not by any means absorb him completely in those early London years. He had quickly placed other irons in other fires.

A ledger entitled "Members of the Royal Institution, Commencing 1810" includes the following entry for March 2, 1812: "Roget, P.M., M.D. £57:15:0." Roget's entrance fee was money well spent, for we have his letter of May 29, 1812, to J. Guillemard, Secretary, Committee of Managers, Royal Institution, accepting Guillemard's invitation to Roget to present a course of lectures at the institution. Roget thus shared the 1812 lecture platform in the institution's famous Lecture Theatre on Albemarle Street with Humphry Davy (chemistry), Thomas Campbell (poetry), John Pond (astronomy), and J. E. Smith (botany).[26] His lectures were so popular that he was asked to give another series in 1813, and again in 1814.[27] The list of Managers and of Visitors (the governing boards of the institution) for the years 1811 to 1814 included many influential men that Roget had already become acquainted with (e.g., Leonard Horner, Marcet, Lord Henry Petty, Davy, Wollaston), and many more who were to be important friends later, such as the Duke of Bedford, the Earl of Hardwicke, General William Thornton, Viscount Palmerston, Richard H. Solly, the Earl of Selkirk, Lord Teignmouth. Most important among these was Davies Giddy (later Gilbert), the "discoverer" of Humphry Davy, and afterward, as President of the Royal Society, a sponsor of Roget.

It should be noted that the Royal Institution was at that time exciting the educated world with its popular and practical demonstrations of scientific and artistic discoveries. Established in 1799 through the efforts of Count Rumford and formally organized at a meeting at the home of Sir Joseph Banks, with the approval and assistance of the Royal Society, the institution, often called the "workshop of the Royal Society," encouraged new work in a variety of scientific, artistic, and literary areas.[28] Its early success was due primarily to the energetic Humphry Davy, who accepted Rumford's offer of the superintendency after foreseeing the limitations of Beddoes' Pneumatic Institution in Clifton. Banks was the first Chairman, and Thomas Bernard (of Bernard Street) the first Secretary. The Royal Institution was, of course, best known in its early years for the work of Davy, Michael Faraday, Brande, and Wollaston, but more to our purpose here is the fact that Roget's participation in the lively proceedings on Albemarle Street brought him into working contact with an additional circle of talented and successful men.

Roget's personal life at this period is practically unknown,

aside from the occasional glints of light thrown by the surviving
letters, and these are few. Roget's mother is completely silent
through the second decade of the new century. After the correspondence with Romilly, in December 1808, about the move to
London, there are no letters from Catherine until 1820. This is
also true of Annette, whose earlier letters to her brother were
often revealingly frank. The fact that both of them were living
with Roget in Bernard Street of course accounts for much of this
silence, but there were opportunities for letters. Catherine, after
her fashion, continued to visit the better watering places, especially during the late summer months when anyone who *was* anyone fled London, either for the Continent or for the seacoast resort areas of Devonshire, Dorset, Hampshire, and Sussex. Dr.
Holland, for example, perhaps the frankest society doctor of the
period, and an inveterate traveler, explained that he selected his
clientele from the classes who were normally absent from London in these months.[29] Invariably Catherine took Annette with
her, and, judging from occasional remarks in Roget's letters, she
suffered the same inconveniences and disappointments that filled
her chronicle of the years up to 1809.

Roget himself spent some of his summers at places like Sidmouth, Brighton, and Teignmouth, but during most of his first
ten years in London, he stayed on in Bernard Street, working at
his several projects of improvement. He spent long, quiet days
and nights alone, studying and compiling the notes that he kept
of particular medical cases; his reading of the increasing flood of
scientific publications was thorough; he prepared diligently,
carrying out much library and original research, for his several
lecture commitments; he carried on some experiments—chemical,
optical, physiological, mathematical—in his own home and in
the laboratories that were open to him at places like the Royal
Institution. He walked a good deal about London and kept some
notes of his observations of new developments, such as the new
gas lights on Pall Mall (1812), and on conditions of the poor; he
was alarmed at the frequent uprisings, such as the violence that
broke out with the arrest of Sir Francis Burdett in April 1810,
for his daring to criticize Parliament in Cobbett's *Weekly Register*. He was an avid chessplayer and entertained himself (and, as
he put it, improved his mind) by trying to apply his mathematical expertness to the solution of classic chess problems. He was a
regular churchgoer—the Established Church of England—and
studiously read such theological works as William Paley's *Natural Theology*.

His work was his life; life was work—and not solely in the sim-
plistic Calvinist notion that identified work with virtue and virtue with happiness. He seems to have been genuinely curious
about many things and genuinely satisfied to spend his days
pursuing his own and others' questions. He was excited by the
enormous city about him, which was growing prodigiously in the
early nineteenth century, and he wanted to understand it. That
he saw himself eventually as a kind of latter-day Renaissance
man is fairly obvious in later expressions. He was excited by the
emergence of whole new sciences, by the bombardment of all
sorts of discoveries, and he wanted to be a part of them all.

He was well started in writing the stream of scientific treatises,
reports, and books that were eventually to make up a total bibliography of over one hundred items. In July 1812, the *Edinburgh
Review* printed his review-essay of Huber's work on ants, and in
October 1815 another, similar discussion of Huber on bees; and
he had a letter from the editor, asking him for more. These articles, like all of them in that famous journal, were unsigned, but
in the tight circle of the British intelligentsia of the day, their
authorship was quickly known.[30]

Roget was no recluse. When he could tear himself away from
his books, he indulged his fondness for the theater; and his widening circle of acquaintances involved him in many dinner parties, teas, and home musicals. Henry Crabb Robinson, for example, speaks of meeting Roget in 1812 at the home of William
Porden (1755–1822), the architect, during a meeting of the
Attic Chest Society, a social and literary club whose chief activity
was the production of poetic effusions expressive of classic
mythology.[31] None of Roget's contributions, if he made any,
have survived, but I have found a more-than-generous sample of
Miss Ellen Porden's work in a five-page review of her *The Veils:
Or, The Triumph of Constancy, a Poem in Six Books*.[32] Miss Porden noted at the head of her poem that she considered herself a
pupil of the Royal Institution, having profited from the lectures
given in Albemarle Street by "Sir Humphry Davy, Mr. Brande,
Dr. Roget, Sir James Edward Smith, and other eminent Lecturers." Roget was an enthusiastic lecturegoer, no doubt partly for
professional reasons, as he early saw himself as a professional on
the platform. One series of lectures that he attended with more
than customary interest offered an excellent example of what
Roget meant in his frequent advice to his sister—"never lose an
opportunity to improve yourself."

The lecturer was one Gregor von Feinagle, who entranced (hypnotized?) audiences in London in 1810 and 1811, and whose *New System of Memory* appeared in print in 1812. Roget was fascinated by the problem of memory—a practical problem for a rising savant—and he not only followed the lectures eagerly but mastered Feinagle's system at least sufficiently to be capable, in his very old age, of amazing his friends by reeling off the value of "pi" to forty or fifty decimal places.[33] But Roget's interest in the memory system was far deeper than that of simply entertaining his friends. His analytical mind, constantly seeking *systematic* ways of understanding natural phenomena—he was most proud of his efforts to systematize the study of physiology and comparative anatomy—was attracted by any device employing classification or categorization. Thus Feinagle's imaginative scheme, even when spun out to make a four-hundred-page volume, seemed to offer some sort of key to the problem of organizing human knowledge.

Feinagle reported that his study of memory proved that far and away the most efficacious mnemonic device was that of associating the item to be remembered with a given place or location, particularly in relation to other like items. He therefore proposed an elaboration of an ancient idea: the student was to imagine his mind as a room, with four walls, a floor, and a ceiling. Each of the six planes then was to be divided into nine equal sections, which were to be numbered or named or identified by a fanciful symbolic figure, depending upon the type of information to be remembered.[34]

Beginning with simple lessons (on one wall of one room), Feinagle's course worked on through succeeding ramifications to, for instance, one hundred places in two rooms, showing with lengthy examples how the system could be applied to mathematics, linguistics, historical chronology, and geography. Feinagle's text was accompanied by several marvelous foldout schematic drawings, showing how the several rooms of the mind were to be laid out and designated by arbitrary symbols.

Roget may well have been intrigued originally by the mathematical manipulation by which Feinagle was able to accommodate indefinitely long series of items to be remembered in a given operation. Roget's interest and accomplishments in mathematics continued through his long life, and he found many opportunities to advance his career by the application or demonstration of his computational skill. The most important of these, as far as his career was concerned, was the writing of a paper in 1815 which won him election as a Fellow of the Royal Society.

Roget had been working for some time on a device that would eliminate much of the drudgery of certain mathematical operations involving the use of logarithms. Moreover, he had gone to the trouble and expense of having a sample made up by a machinist. It is this mechanical device that is described in his paper "Description of a New Instrument for Performing Mechanically the Involution and Evolution of Numbers." [35]

His paper was "communicated" to the society by Wollaston, then Secretary. It was read at the meeting of November 17, 1814, and was published the next year. Typically, Roget begins his paper:

> To abridge that species of mental labour which is required in conducting arithmetical computations, has been the professed object of a variety of mechanical contrivances. But the greater number of arithmetical machines, as they have been called, are more ingenious than really useful, and have been recorded more as objects of curiosity, than as admitting of convenience or ready application in the practice of arithmetic.

Subsequent commentators on Roget's instrument point out that it was nothing less than the invention of the log-log scale, still used on modern slide rules.[36]

The paper is expressive not only of Roget's interest in mathematics but of his mechanical bent. In a few years another savant with an even greater facility in mathematics and mechanics— Charles Babbage, inventor of the first mechanical computer— would collide head on with Roget over Babbage's attempts to reform the Royal Society. But at the moment—particularly that triumphant moment of his election on March 16, 1815—Roget's intelligence and industry had won him the most coveted title in the nineteenth-century scientific world. Within five years from his appearance in London, a promising but obscure young doctor from the provinces, Roget had won acceptance by the most exclusive club of the metropolis, election to which many a more famous man had worked, not always successfully, for the bulk of his life.

He could now write his name, as he meticulously did thereafter, "Peter Mark Roget, M.D., F.R.S." Those three letters must have seemed to him—as, indeed, in many respects they were—the keys to the city.

VIII [1815-1818 ℘

Loss of Romilly

In 1815, and 1817, Roget worked hard on a series of articles for the famous *Supplement to the Fourth, Fifth, and Sixth Editions* of the *Encyclopaedia Britannica*, articles that were important in increasing his stature as an authority in physiology and as an all-around savant. He seized the opportunity offered him willingly, as he had learned by this time that publication was one of the major roads to scientific success in London. This particular opportunity was due to the kindness and respect held for him by his former Professor of Philosophy at Edinburgh, Dugald Stewart, as seen in the following letter to Francis Horner in London:

Allow me to introduce to your acquaintance, and to recommend to your good offices, my friend Mr. Macvey Napier, who goes to town for a few weeks with the view of enlisting contributors for the Supplement to the *Encyclopaedia Britannica*. Constable [1] has prevailed upon him, after much solicitation, to undertake the laborious task of being the Editor of this work. . . . The principal object of this letter is to request your advice about the individuals to whom he should apply. I have mentioned to him the names of Mr. Malthus,[2] Mr. Hamilton,[3] Mr. Tennent,[4] Drs. Marcet and Roget, and of a few others; but I have been so long a complete stranger to the literary society of London that my list must necessarily be very imperfect.[5]

Some of Roget's articles, particularly those on phrenology and the deaf and dumb, got him into some serious controversies later, but when the six volumes of the *Supplement* began to appear in 1816, he was gratified by the recognition they brought him. One mark of this recognition was his election on June 12, 1816, as a member of the Royal Society of Arts. He was proposed for membership by John Frederic Daniell (1790–1845), physicist and chemist.[6] Founded in 1754, the Royal Society of Arts was created, as its full title declares, "for the Encouragement of Arts, Manufactures and Commerce." It still thrives, as it did in 1816, in the handsome building erected for it in the old Adelphi by the celebrated Adam brothers in 1774. Because of the breadth of its interests, the society attracted an amazing variety of members, and as one of the two learned societies in England when it was formed, it served many of the functions now carried on by governmental agencies of public health, agriculture, forestry, art education, etc. Increasingly valued as a member of the Royal Society of Arts, Roget became Vice-President in 1832, a post he retained until 1855.

Meanwhile, Roget was becoming even more active in his work with the Royal Institution, which in many ways was an imitation and a competitor of the Royal Society of Arts. With J. F. Daniell, Roget was elected to the list of "Visitors" for the institution, a kind of supervisory group that, with the board of "Managers," was responsible for the successful operation of the institution. I have read minutes of meetings at which Roget was present and helped decide the fate of the worn carpet in the reference library and resolved that "the paper cases over the models be repaired by Mr. Faraday, the assistant in the laboratory." [7]

Roget suffered some setbacks during this period. A letter to Marcet records a reorganization which terminated his association with the school in Great Windmill Street. Writing from Manchester, where he was taking a holiday, Roget also spoke of difficulties in bringing out the new Medical and Chirurgical Society *Transactions,* including Marcet's paper on the analysis of chyle, which Roget was working over for him with the assistance of George Birkbeck.[8] But as though to counter this disappointment, a much more important recognition came Roget's way in 1817— he was appointed Consulting Physician to Queen Charlotte's Lying-In Hospital, an office he held the rest of his professional life.[9]

In the same year, Roget's good friend Bostock moved from Liverpool to London and joined Roget in his work with the Medical and Chirurgical and other societies. He took a house at No. 22 Upper Bedford Place, just a few doors from No. 18, which Roget was to buy in 1843, and just two blocks from Roget in Bernard Street. The two friends spent much time together, often working quietly in the study at one or the other of their houses, each pushing forward one of the many papers that they were both writing in those years. Bostock was a classicist as well as a scientist, and his projected translation of Pliny's *Natural History* no doubt produced much conversation between him and Roget on linguistic matters. Bostock, as eager a promoter of the Geological Society as Roget was of the Medical and Chirurgical, became associated with Arthur Aikin, credited by the *Dictionary of National Biography* with taking a foremost part in founding the Geological Society in 1807. From 1817 to 1819, Bostock assisted Aikin in editing *Annals of Philosophy,* which subsequently published many of his papers and some of Roget's. Bostock was at this time working on his monumental *Elementary System of Physiology,* which also would have drawn him and Roget into frequent conversation and joint study.

In May 1818 *Annals of Philosophy* published a short article by Roget on the recent patenting of an optical invention by David Brewster (1781–1868), Scottish physicist, who called the thing a "kaleidoscope." Roget, who later wrote a longish article on the instrument for the *Encyclopaedia Britannica,* was fascinated by various optical phenomena, and on seeing Brewster's description, he immediately began experimenting. The results of his experiments were reported in this brief article in the *Annals,* a highly technical discussion of refinements that Brewster might have made in the construction of the kaleidoscope, involving several mirrors:

Those [kaleidoscopes] composed of more than two mirrors, and which may be denominated *polygonal kaleidoscopes,* have not, however, been so particularly noticed by the inventor, as their superior practical utility when applied to the arts would seem to deserve. Some inquiry into the principles on which they should be constructed may, therefore, be not unworthy of occupying a place in your journal.[10]

The concise article, which he illustrated with small schematic drawings, well displayed Roget's knowledge of optics and geometry as well as his own inventiveness.

Because of the absence of actual statements of Roget's income at this point, it is impossible to do more than guess at how his practice was prospering. Beginning with the Royal Society statement that by 1813 his practice "began to be considerable," [11]

and recalling Marcet's pleased comment in October 1818 that
Roget's practice was still growing rapidly, we might make use of
figures recorded in the recollections of one of Roget's associates,
Henry Holland. Holland began practice in London in 1816; he
was then twenty-seven. Roget began in 1809, at the age of thirty.
Holland said that from the beginning his professional income
had always exceeded his expenditures, usually double them: "As
early as the fourth year of my practice in London, it exceeded
£1200 a year. . . ." Holland, who loved to travel, resolved to
keep his practice under £5,000 a year, but this, he said, took
some doing.[12] It is true that Holland specialized in society doc-
toring and would appear to have paid more attention to developing a profitable practice than did Roget, who was spending much
of his time with the Medical and Chirurgical Society, the Northern Dispensary, the Royal Institution, and his writing. But he
was fast making friends among the wealthy as well as among the
scientific, and his uncle would probably have helped him garner
at least some affluent patients. It would seem reasonable, then, to
put Roget's practice, at the end of eight years in London, at half
Holland's income, say £2,500 a year, surely a handsome living for
a man as frugal as Peter Mark Roget. It should be remembered
too that his lecturing and writing brought in at least an additional £200 or £300 a year. In February of 1817, Romilly apparently considered that Roget's income was such that he no longer
needed the quarterly allowance payments that Romilly had been
making. Typically, rather than put Roget to any inconvenience
over suddenly cutting off the allowance, Romilly asked his
nephew to accept a lump sum of £500 in lieu of the continued
payments. Moreover, from that moment on, Romilly said, Roget
should be expected to be compensated for his professional attendance on Romilly and his family.[13]

Roget rose early, worked hard all day, read on into the evening, and still had time for the theater and for developing his
widening circle of friends. He was in the habit of advancing several projects at one time, a multiplicity of effort that was made
possible at least in part by his highly organized approach to his
many interests. He had no time at all for the dandyism that had
infected London society in the years immediately after Waterloo,
and his capacity and fondness for work frankly dismayed his
competitors. Catherine and Annette lived with him, of course,
and managed his house, arranging occasional dinner parties, but
seeing to it that he was not disturbed when he was particularly

engrossed in a given project. Catherine, Romilly, and Dumont seemed to have forged an engine in Peter Mark Roget that knew no stopping and admitted no territory closed to it.

But in the closing months of 1818, Roget's quietly running machine nearly stopped. After a long and painful illness, his aunt Anne Romilly died. Four days later his uncle, upstairs in his Russell Square home, cut his throat and gasped out his last bloody breath in Roget's arms. The almost unbelievable event proved such a shock that Roget's expanding world all but collapsed.

The effect of Romilly's suicide on Roget can only be understood against the dismay felt by nearly all of political and intellectual England over the loss of a man regarded by both liberals and conservatives as a statesman of conscience and principle—perhaps the brightest living prospect for rational change of a graft- and privilege-ridden system. If such a man could so violently express a loss of hope and faith, where did that leave the thousands of lesser men? What of the sure, steady improvement of society that hard work, principled action, and unremitting faith were supposed to bring?

Romilly had devoted his adult life to a determined, reasoned, humane reform of British law, as is simply but fully shown in his diary. Right up to the summer of his wife's fatal illness, Romilly maintained his steady, determined pressure to change the conditions of life for the average Briton. A champion of religious liberty, freedom of speech, an end to slavery, an end to capital punishment, relief to the poor, and, above all, just law, Romilly came back again and again to Parliament and the courts. Defeat of a given measure seemed only to strengthen his resolve, and he returned to the battle, as he was prepared to do at the dissolution of Parliament in June, when his last speech expressed

. . . my fervent hope that England would never see another Parliament as regardless of the liberties of the people, and of the best interests of mankind, as the present.[14]

There was little doubt that Romilly would be returned to Parliament; the only question was which of the many districts beseeching him to represent them would be successful. He had resolved not to accept any of these offers, but he received such a mandate from the City of Westminster that he could not refuse. Some sixty prominent electors of that constituency requested permission to put Romilly in nomination and paid him the rare compliment of requesting him not to bother with any sort of campaign:

> We require from you no pledge, since the uniform tenor of your honorable life, your known attachment to the Constitution, your zealous and unremitting efforts for the amelioration of the laws, the correction of abuses, and the support of the cause of freedom, justice, and humanity, wherever assailed, are a sure pledge to us of your qualifications for our service, in common with that of the country at large.[15]

An odd occurrence during the campaign, in which Romilly took no part, was the action by Bentham, Romilly's long-time friend. Bentham did not vote, but he wrote a handbill for one of Romilly's opponents, the radical Sir Francis Burdett, attacking Romilly as a "mere Whig" and "a friend only to moderate reform." Romilly noted in his diary that he felt no resentment, that "I know he [Bentham] is too honest in his politics to suffer them to be influenced by any considerations of private friendship." [16] Moreover, Romilly gladly accepted an invitation to dine at Bentham's Hermitage shortly after the election.

In his acceptance speech, Romilly directly attacked Castlereagh, Sidmouth, and all those who had supported their recent repressive "Gagging Bills," which suspended the habeas corpus, forbade public meetings to be held without leave of a mayor, sheriff, or magistrate, placed all public reading rooms under license, and gave magistrates extensive power to imprison any speaker whose observations they did not like.

The jubilant Westminster electors insisted on the ceremony of chairing Romilly through London. He demurred, but finally acceded to the wishes of the crowd, but when the procession was temporarily halted in front of Burlington House, he quietly slipped away and walked home unobserved through the immense crowd which thronged all the streets. Commoners and aristocrats alike hailed Romilly's victory; both saw him as a thoughtful, judicious, knowledgeable man, unafraid to confront the most powerful and reactionary Government forces, yet who could be counted on not to plunge England into the chaos that France had suffered. The Duke of Sussex, the liberal-leaning, out-of-favor son of the King, held a sumptuous dinner in Kensington Palace to celebrate the occasion.

It was in this great upsurge of support and recognition—perhaps the most gratifying moment in his public life—that

Romilly was forced to admit a fact that demolished all hope, all gratification: his beloved Anne was dying.

Although no one had been willing to admit it, Anne had been failing since March, when she had been too ill for the family to spend the holiday at Tanhurst, their country place. She spent most of April and May at Brighton and returned apparently much improved, but by the middle of June she was bedridden again. In July Romilly rented a small cottage for her on Hampstead Heath with the hope of sparing her the muggy heat of the city in summer. In September, with Anne obviously declining, they accepted an invitation from their architect friend, John Nash, who had already begun to cut a swath through London with his Regent Street project. Nash invited the Romillys for an indefinite stay at East Cowes Castle, a country estate he had built on the Isle of Wight.[17]

Marcet, writing to Roget from Paris in early October, said that he had been told by their old friend Madame Gautier that "Lady Romilly was now making rapid progress towards her entire recovery." [18] But upon his return to London, Marcet found a letter from Roget reporting that Anne's illness had taken a very serious turn for the worst. Moreover, Marcet observed disturbing signs in Romilly that he urged Roget to watch with extreme care:

Any symptom of declining firmness of mind is doubly alarming in a man of his stamp. Pray try to prevail upon him to occupy his mind, even with occasional business, if the common modes of diverting one's attention fail him. . . .[19]

Roget, keeping in close touch by letter not only with Romilly, but with Dumont and other members of the family who had gathered on the island in the Channel, and keeping in mind Marcet's warning, grew alarmed over signs that Romilly was faltering. Roget took a fast coach to Cowes, where he observed with pain some evidence that Romilly's stability was being eroded by his refusal to accept the imminent loss of Anne. Roget found that through September and October Romilly's mind had hovered closer and closer about a central preoccupation with death and that he had fussed and patched at his will until it became a long, closely written document of five pages.[20] Originally drawn on August 19, 1815, the will left Romilly's major properties—estates, personal possessions, the house in Russell Square, etc.—to Anne and to his brother Thomas. It released Catherine and

Peter Roget from any debts, and bequeathed £1,200 to Roget, £500 to Catherine, £400 to Annette, and various amounts to his several nephews. Romilly named John Whishaw (1764–1840), long-time lawyer friend and fellow Whig, as guardian of his children if Anne should die before they reached their majority.

But through September and October, at Cowes, Romilly kept adding codicils every week or so, constantly amending and refining the terms of the document. One such codicil, added on October 9, particularly alarmed Roget and Dumont:

> I am at the present moment of perfectly sound mind and in the full possession of all my faculties, but I am labouring under a most severe affliction and I cannot recollect that insanity is amongst the evils which mortal afflictions sometimes produce without observing to myself that that unhappy lot may possibly at some time be mine. If I ever should become insane (which God forbid), it is my earnest desire that while I continue in that state the following bounties may be paid to different relations out of my income during my life and may be considered as part of the expenditure which I certainly should have made if I had continued capable of managing my own affairs: to my brother one hundred and fifty pounds a year, and to my nephew Peter Roget one hundred and fifty pounds a year. . . .

The whole company at Cowes was wracked by Romilly's state and his desperate grasping for any sign of Anne's improvement. At one point she rallied sufficiently to be able to spend two or three hours a day sitting with her guests, but in mid-October she suffered a severe relapse. No one but Romilly could still maintain the fiction that she would recover. He was nearly out of his mind, through anxiety and lack of sleep, and, according to Dumont, muttered two or three times about his fear of mental derangement. Romilly had nightmares and considered them proof that his mind was giving way. He alternated between Anne's bedside and his own desk, where he drew up the several codicils to his will and impressed friends and servants to serve as witnesses to the changes.

Shortly before midnight, on Thursday, October 29, Anne Romilly died, and it was Roget's painful duty to report the news to his uncle.[21]

The distraught Romilly wished to remain at Cowes, but he agreed to be ruled by his doctor nephew, and Roget decided that it would be best for Romilly to return to his own home. The whole entourage—Romilly, Roget, Sophia, William, Dumont, Mrs. Davis (sister to Anne Romilly), and servants—set off on Friday by boat across Spithead for the mainland, and then in several carriages for the northward flight. The party rested that night at Winchester, with Roget remaining with his uncle through the night. On the road again Saturday morning, Romilly grew increasingly agitated. According to later testimony, he was constantly tearing his gloves or the palm of his hand, scratching his fingers and his nose, and some blood came from his nose. He squinted his eyes tightly shut, and frequently wrung his hands distractedly. Adding to his nervous state was his obvious effort to subdue such actions. Before the party had been traveling more than a few hours, Romilly was so weak that Roget ordered a stop at an inn in Miller's Green, where Romilly got some sleep and Roget again sat up with him through the night.

He was recovered sufficiently by Sunday morning for Roget to resume the journey, and the travelers—tired, dusty, fearful—arrived at 21 Russell Square at about 5 P.M. Roget and Dumont took Romilly into his library, where he threw himself upon a sofa and gripped his hands together, holding himself rigidly still. After some moments, he allowed Dumont to help him up and, taking Dumont's arm, walked slowly about the room several times. "He appeared to me to be in the state of a man dying of an internal wound," Dumont reported.[22]

An hour or two later, Romilly asked to see Marcet, saying that his nephew, Dr. Roget, had suffered too much. Marcet stayed the night, sleeping in Romilly's bedroom, as did Roget. None of the three got much sleep, however, for after a few tranquil hours, during which Romilly lay staring at the ceiling, his body began thrashing about with increasing violence. Whenever Marcet or Roget attempted to calm him or give him medicine, Romilly drove them off with his wild hands. By morning, he lay silent and exhausted but burning with a high fever.

Roget sent for a third doctor, William Babington, M.D. (1756–1833). Their consultation was fruitless. They could only agree that Romilly should be kept as quiet as possible, and to that end they barred even his old friend Dumont from seeing him. The doctors agreed further that Romilly should not be left alone.

Early in the afternoon, Romilly's daughter Sophia relieved Roget, who went downstairs to the library. Shortly before 2 P.M., Romilly sent her down to fetch Roget. During the few minutes of her absence, Romilly got out of bed, took a razor from his traveling case, and, with one deep stroke, cut his throat, completely severing the windpipe.

Thomas Bowen, Romilly's footman, sitting in the kitchen two floors down, heard a heavy thump, like that of somebody falling to the floor. He dashed up the two flights of stairs and saw Roget standing just outside the open door to his master's bedroom. As Roget stepped into the doorway, Romilly, bleeding profusely, lurched forward, slammed the door, managing to fasten it, and stumbled backward. Bowen thought he saw Romilly throw a razor away from him as he shut the door. Bowen and Roget burst the door open and found Romilly leaning over the washstand in the corner of his room. A shirt and blanket were draped about him, and his blood was flowing copiously. He was speechless, but he made several frantic signs for pen and paper, which were instantly given him as Roget supported him. Romilly tried feebly to scratch something on the sheet, but then collapsed in the arms of Roget, who lowered him to the floor. When C. Maybrey, a surgeon living nearby, came into the room a few minutes later, Romilly was dead, the blood-smeared paper still clutched in one hand—according to Maybrey's testimony before the coroner.

Still another surgeon, John Knox, who had also been summoned from his home at 65 Great Russell Street, corroborated Maybrey's account. Asked by the coroner if the wound might have been inflicted accidentally while Romilly was shaving, Knox replied, "Judging from the circumstances, I should conclude that he had left his bed to commit the deed."

The coroner, hearing the names of more and more important figures brought into the testimony (Holland, Brougham, Lansdowne, etc.), apparently became uncomfortably sensible of the importance of the inquiry.[23] He therefore adjourned the session and directed the jury to reassemble at No. 21 Russell Square, where they could view the body. The whole company—coroner, jury, witnesses, reporters, and a growing crowd of spectators—then filed out of the Colonnade, paraded across Woburn Place, and along the north side of Russell Square. Outside Romilly's house,[24] the coroner had to call on the assistance of constables to keep back the crowd of curious who blocked the sidewalk and steps and tried to get inside the building. Inside, the jurymen warily eyed the body of Sir Samuel Romilly, which lay as it had fallen from Roget's arms, and nervously listened to the remaining testimony.

Following the coroner's summing up, the jury without hesitation returned the following verdict: "We are unanimously of opinion that the deceased cut his throat while in a state of mental temporary derangement."

Marcet had written and signed a statement to the coroner that Roget was in such an agonized state that it was impossible for him to attend the hearing. As a result, Roget himself did not testify. Roget had locked himself away from everyone, leaving orders that he could see no one, but informed of Marcet's efforts, he wrote the following hurried note on the evening of November 2 to Marcet:

My dear friend,
    You are a friend indeed! the best I have left! I had thought myself quite unequal to the interview, but your kindness has softened me, and I should now like to see you. I am almost distracted! Ever your's   PMR [25]

A second note from Roget, on the morning of November 3, the day of the inquest, reported to Marcet that he had had no sleep but was calmer than he was the night before, and that Catherine and Annette had got some rest. He asked Marcet to find out whether he could be excused from attending the inquest: "It would be most harrowing to my feelings." And a third note, written in the late afternoon, after the inquest, thanked Marcet for handling the matter as he had: "I am infinitely better than yesterday, and I shall be very glad to see Dumont this evening. Give our best love to all that are with you."

The inevitable postmortems included some criticism of Roget's professional behavior during his attendance on Romilly between the death of Anne and the suicide. Should Roget have insisted that Romilly make the long, tiring trip home so soon from the Isle of Wight? Once in London, should he have followed Dumont's suggestion and installed Romilly in some place other than his own home, where he was surrounded by intimate memories of his life with Anne? How is it that Roget did not apply leeches or subject Romilly to ice baths? The most serious and persistent criticism was that Romilly had been left alone, even for the few moments it took for Sophia to run downstairs at her father's request and summon Roget. Brougham stated that the doctors were certainly wrong in leaving their patient alone. Lord Grey was highly critical of the doctor's allowing Romilly to travel, and said "that with such symptoms upon him, he should have suffered to remain one minute alone, seems almost incredible." [26]

Grey continued, however:

> I knew poor Roget; he was once my private secretary by Romilly's recommendation; nothing could exceed his attachment to his uncle; that he did everything for the best cannot be doubted; and whatever omission he may have been guilty of can only be ascribed to want of presence of mind and decision from too much anxiety and being exhausted by fatigue.

If there had been attempt to stigmatize Roget for his part in the tragedy—and some of Brougham's and Grey's criticisms appeared in subsequently published eulogies—the effort did not succeed. Friends, associates, and the public in general were quick to sympathize with Roget's agonizing experience: first, having to be the one to tell Romilly of Anne's death, and, second, being the one to burst open his uncle's door and catch his blood-drenched body.

Anne's funeral was delayed, and in accordance with Romilly's will, his body was shipped to Knill Court, where the couple were buried on November 11 following a private service restricted to the family and a few intimate friends.

The impact of Romilly's death on Roget has been merely suggested in the foregoing account. If there had ever been a man whose industry and whose steadfast principles and affection represented a tower of strength, that man, as far as Peter Mark Roget was concerned, surely was Samuel Romilly. His reaction could not have differed greatly from the profound conclusion that shook him as a very young man viewing the ruin of Lyons —symbolically, the ruin of the whole liberal ideology:

> Events like these are enough to shake to its foundation our confidence in the course of things, and [make] us mistrust all views into futurity. . . .

The effect of Romilly's death on the nation was also profound. Newspapers and journals of all descriptions published memoirs ringing with the highest praise for the constancy of Romilly's ideals and the humanity of his methods. Several lengthy pamphlets appeared within a few weeks,[27] and many notable citizens pronounced memorial orations in clubs, societies, and institutions. One interesting event was the attempt of a group of influential

Frenchmen to celebrate a solemn service to the memory of Romilly in the Church of England, and the refusal of the ministers of that sect on the ground that their dogmas were inconsistent with such ceremonies. Nothing daunted, the Libéraux (as the French gentlemen called themselves) held their memorial service in a rented hall, and were gratified to have one of their number, the famous Benjamin Constant, invited by the Athenaeum to deliver a commemorative oration on Romilly at the club's next session.[28]

Many letters survive (such as those from Creevey, Brougham, Holland, Horner, Maria Edgeworth, the Marquis of Buckingham) expressing such grief for the nation that it is impossible to avoid comparing the event with the reaction in the United States to the assassinations of John F. Kennedy, his brother Robert Kennedy, and Martin Luther King, Jr. The three Americans were almost universally seen as bearers of a troubled nation's hopes that intelligent and just means could be found to divert the plunging course of the nation toward internal chaos and international war. Much of the eulogy delivered on Romilly's death conveyed the same profound dismay that a man so distinguished by dedication, ability, and reasonableness should be so violently carried away. There was the same sense that a mighty timber—one that both conservatives and liberals had counted on to shore up a tottering nation—had been senselessly destroyed.

Roget's expanding horizons had encountered their first violent rebuff, and they retracted painfully to the limits of a single room, hung with crepe. He remained there, ill and distraught, the year closing with another dismal event—Marcet had finally made up his mind to return to Geneva permanently:

It is with great regret that I quit England without bidding you adieu and thanking you for all your kind attentions to me. The indisposition which prevents my seeing you increases my concern, but I hope that you are far advanced in your recovery and that we have some chance of seeing you in Switzerland next Summer.

I have taken the liberty, my dear Sir, of desiring a French clock which has long been used in our family to be sent to you, hoping it may sometimes remind you of those whom you have so kindly and carefully attended throughout their suffering and their sorrow.[29]

IX [1816–1840

The
Encyclopædia Britannica
and Phrenology

THE famous *Supplement to the Fourth, Fifth, and Sixth Editions* of the *Encyclopaedia Britannica* began appearing in December 1816 in half-volume form and continued in this serial form until the completion (in April 1824) of six large volumes, containing just under five thousand double-columned pages. According to the *EB*'s own account,[1] the distinguished contributors included James Mill, David Ricardo, Thomas Robert Malthus, Dominique François Arago, Jean Baptiste Biot, William Hazlitt, Sir Walter Scott, Dugald Stewart, John Playfair, and John Leslie. Conspicuously missing in this list is the name of Peter Mark Roget, an important contributor, whose connection with the *EB* provides one of the more interesting ironies in the strange history of silence that has, to this moment, held Roget in almost complete anonymity, except, of course, for the *Thesaurus*. While practically every popular and scholarly encyclopaedia of the present time devotes a paragraph or two to the maker of the *Thesaurus*, the one that would seem most to owe Roget some kind of recognition—the *EB*—mentions him not at all. This irony is further compounded by the fact that in its successive editions, at least well into the 1920's, the *EB* has reprinted without acknowledgement several of Roget's original articles. Moreover, the 1967 edition of the *EB* includes compressed, anonymous versions of some of Roget's original articles written before 1820 for the *Supplement.*

All in all, including his contributions to the seventh edition, which began appearing some ten years later, Roget wrote well over three hundred thousand words for the *EB,* about half of which are accounted for by a major treatise, "Physiology." Articles on "Sir Joseph Banks," "Ant," "Bee," "Cranioscopy," "Deaf and Dumb," "Phrenology," "Apiary," "Baldinger," "Barthez," "Beddoes," "Bichat," "Brocklesby," "Broussonet," "Camper," "Crawford," "Currie," "Kaleidoscope" were comparatively brief, running from two thousand to twenty thousand words.

In the preface to the *Supplement,* the editor, Macvey Napier, introduced the featured articles and writers, mentioning Roget three times:

. . . besides the systematic articles [on zoology], a few of a more popular kind have been contributed by Dr. Roget.

. . . Physiology is fully treated in the Encyclopaedia, in as far as concerns the principal facts relative to the functions of animal life; but there seemed to be wanting a comprehensive view of the general laws to which they are reducible; a defect which has been ably supplied in this work by Dr. Roget.

. . . The art of educating the deaf and dumb—one of the most pleasing results of this branch of philosophy [education] —is fully explained in another article, written with his accustomed clearness and elegance, by Dr. Roget.[2]

Roget's articles were well received by Napier, who sought additional articles from Roget for the *Edinburgh Review,* specifically one on "animal magnetism" and another on Cuvier. Roget regretfully declined on the ground that he lacked the time to do the pieces properly.[3]

That Roget's *EB* articles were more than satisfactory is even more convincingly demonstrated by the fact that they—or slightly edited versions of the originals—were used if not acknowledged by the encyclopaedia through several succeeding editions. A study of the history of these articles, from their first appearance in the *Supplement,* through the seventh, eighth, ninth, and subsequent editions to the present, shows incontrovertibly that the *EB continues* to owe Roget *some* kind of acknowledgement. An example of this is the course of his four-page article on Paul Joseph Barthez (1734–1806), French physician and physiologist. Roget's article was used again in the seventh and eighth editions of the *EB,* and appeared, slightly trimmed but with no acknowledgement to the author, in the famous ninth edition, completed in 1889. The same article was reprinted in the tenth edition.

In the celebrated eleventh edition of the *EB,* sponsored by Cambridge University in 1910, the Barthez article suffered drastic cuts, but that it was clearly a condensed version of the ninth-edition article is shown by the fact that over half of the thirty-seven-line article is presented in exactly the same phrases used originally by Roget in 1818. The 1947 *EB* uses a still more condensed version (eighteen lines) of the eleventh edition, and exactly the same boiled-down article appeared in the 1958 *EB.* By 1963, "Barthez" had dropped out entirely.

Histories of other Roget articles show the same derivative usage through the years. Some of them—for example, that on Marie François Xavier Bichat (1771–1802), French anatomist and physiologist—are still in the 1967 *EB.* It should be noted that, since the seventh edition, completed in 1842, the *EB* has offered no acknowledgement of Roget's serviceable contributions. He was paid 30 guineas by Napier in 1823,[4] and presumably he was paid at least that much more for the treatise on physiology for the seventh edition.

Roget's attraction to earlier researchers such as Barthez and Bichat was twofold. Barthez's 1798 study of motion in animals undoubtedly provided much of the material for Roget's 1822 lecture, "On the Functions of Progressive Motion in Vertebrated Animals," an abstract of which appeared in *The Philosophical Magazine* of that year.[5] Bichat's most important works, *Anatomie générale* (1801) and *Anatomie descriptive* (1802), caught Roget's eye because of Bichat's emphasis on classification of the parts and functions of the human mechanism. Of the first work, Roget writes:

It is founded on his classification of the parts of the body, according to their intimate structure; in order to establish which he decomposes the animal machine, not merely into the larger pieces of which it is formed, but into the organic elements that constitute them. Of these elementary parts or textures, as he terms them, into which every organ may be ultimately analyzed, he enumerates twenty-one different species. He conceives each of these textures to possess a peculiar modification of vitality, from which it derives those properties that distinguish it from dead matter, and that give rise to all the phenomena of the animal economy, both in a healthy and diseased state.[6]

And of Bichat's second great work: ". . . a new work in which the organs were arranged according to his peculiar classification of their functions."

One has only to recall Roget's own breakdown of the functions of the body into neat classifications—in his outline of the course he gave in Manchester 1805—to see again Roget's persistent interest in the problem of applying categorical analysis to the field of physiology and anatomy. Bichat's earlier works included a treatise on life and death in relation to the three central organs, the heart, lungs, and brain. In 1833, Roget published an essay on "Age" (in the *Cyclopaedia of Practical Medicine*), in which he drew on Bichat, among others, in an attempt to survey what was then known about old age and the cessation of life.

But the personal lives of men like Barthez and Bichat must have also attracted Roget's interest. Both of them were successful practicing physicians; both of them were physiologists; both of them also dabbled in chemistry and mathematics; both of them became brilliant lecturers. It is not too imaginative a suggestion to think of Roget seeing himself as following the same course as these French scientists. Like Roget, Barthez had taken his M.D. at the age of nineteen. Barthez was from Montpellier—source of Romilly's ancestors; Bichat was first established in Lyons, where Roget first felt the impact of the Revolution. Like Broussonnet, another of Roget's biographical subjects, both men were forced to flee from enviable positions, losing fortunes, libraries, and commissions because of the turmoil of the Revolution. It is entirely possible that studying the lives of these men merely strengthened Roget's fear of violent upheaval and his apparent determination to have nothing to do with politics.

The opportunity offered by Napier to write for the *EB* gave Roget his first important chance to write on his favorite subject, physiology. In his first attempt, a seventeen-page article for the *Supplement* in 1824, he provides a useful demonstration of the typical scientific mind of the period at work:

Physiology, or the study of the phenomena of life, differs from all the other branches of philosophical inquiry, by its involving the consideration of the *final* as well as the *physical* causes of these phenomena. A new principle of arrangement is thus introduced, which is scarcely ever applicable in the sciences relating to the properties of inert and inorganic matter. Those sciences are formed by applying to the subjects they concern, the rules of philosophical induction. By comparing together phenomena, and uniting in one class such as are of the same kind, we arrive at the knowledge of a certain number of general facts, which we regard as laws of nature, and from which, when once established, we deduce the explanation of a multitude of subordinate phenomena, resulting from the simple or the combined operation of these laws.[7]

Roget goes on to detail the special problems posed by multiplicity of species, difficulty of experimentation, and the impossibility of studying living things isolated from their environments, and explains that, because of these difficulties, physiologists have yielded to the temptation to study and classify organic beings in relation to their apparent purpose:

This proneness to substitute final for physical causes has been the source of frequent delusion, by insensibly leading us to believe that we are really in possession of the physical law on which the phenomenon in question is dependent, when we have merely given it a name with reference to the intelligent agency, by which it was adjusted to its object. . . . When it is said, for instance, in the language of this school, that the coagulation of the blood is occasioned by "the stimulus of necessity," it is clearly the final cause only, and not the physical cause of this phenomenon that is assigned; and it is also evident that no advance is thereby made towards the discovery of the latter.[8]

The remainder of the essay "Physiology" was largely taken up with an analytical classification of the powers that bring about changes in a living system. He argued that the usual description of these phenomena under the two heads "contractility" and "sensibility" was incomplete and inadequate. He therefore proposed four distinct "powers" that activate organic change: "muscular contractility, nervous agency, sensorial power, and organic affinity." With his customary care, Roget then defines each of these terms and then proceeds with explanation and illustration.

The article just described was, we can see now, a trial run for a much more imposing contribution, Roget's "Physiology," an essay that ran well over a hundred and fifty pages in the seventh edition of the *EB*. The first attempt, completed in August 1823, according to a letter from Roget to Marcet, probably appeared sometime in 1824, while the longer treatise was not printed until at least 1837. Thus Roget would have brought to that work the benefit of more than thirty years of lecturing and writing on the subject, including completion of his two-volume Bridgewater

Treatise, and the *EB* article could thus represent his final summary of what was recognized as physiology in the first half of the nineteenth century.

Characteristically, he begins with the etymology of the word *physiology,* finding that its Greek progenitor had a much wider signification than the modern word—namely, the science of nature—and, in fact, the term was often synonymous with "natural philosophy." Roget's explanation of the "modern" meaning of these words is useful in that it sorts out terms that were often overlapping:

> If we were desirous of substituting a term which would accurately express the idea now associated with the word physiology, we should adopt that of *biology,* from *Bios,* life, first introduced by Treviranus, who has written a German work on this subject. Natural philosophy, or physics, is now understood as designating that class of sciences, which have for their object the examination of the properties of lifeless matter; whilst physiology, in its modern acceptation, is in like manner limited to the consideration of the properties which are peculiar to organized and living bodies.[9]

Roget then subdivides "natural philosophy" into mechanics, hydrostatics, pneumatics, optics, electricity, magnetism, the science of heat, mineralogy and chemistry—sciences "which are commonly termed in the present day, *the physical sciences.*" These distinctions are followed by a similar breakdown of the life sciences into various specialties of botany and zoology, which he saw as simply concerned with the external phenomena.

That Roget found it necessary to define and separate terms which are now so commonly taken for granted suggests not only the confusion of nomenclature that was often the despair of scientific men in the early nineteenth century but the amazingly sudden proliferation of sciences themselves in that period. More specifically, what Roget's introductory pages present is a rather prophetic view of the whole process of ramification and subdivision, still proceeding rapidly today, resulting in a splitting of one science into two, of those two into four, of those four into sixteen, and so on into the labyrinthian multiplicity of specialization that has become at once the secret of much modern scientific success and the bane of those seeking a unified understanding of existence. Perhaps the best way to illustrate the acceleration of this subdividing process is to show with a simple list Roget's own participation in the many new sciences that were then emerging, as suggested by the springing up of dozens of institutions devoted, in large part, to the advancement of science. We have already seen his participation in the Manchester Philosophical and Literary Society, the Royal Institution, the Medical and Chirurgical Society, the Russell Institution, the Great Windmill Street School, the Royal Society, and the Society of Arts. Following are the dates of founding of other institutions, along with Roget's first participation in their activities: [10]

1805: The London Institution. Roget delivered a course of lectures there in 1826.

1807: The Geological Society of London. Roget was a member from 1809 until his death.

1820: The Royal Astronomical Society. Roget was elected a Fellow in 1822, served as a member of the Council in 1823.

1824: The Athenaeum Club. Roget was a charter member.

1826: The Society for the Diffusion of Useful Knowledge. Roget was a founding member and served as an important contributor to and an editor of its publications.

1826: The University of London. Roget was Examiner in Comparative Anatomy and Physiology from 1839 to 1842; served on the Senate from 1836 until his death.

1826: The Zoological Society of London. Roget was a member from 1827 until his death.

1828: The Institution of Civil Engineers. Roget was elected an honorary member in 1838.

1830: The Royal Geographical Society. Roget was a charter member.

1831: The British Association for the Advancement of Science. Roget was a charter member and presided over the physiology section of some of the early annual meetings.

1833: The Royal Entomological Society. Roget was a charter member, and in 1834 a member of the Council and the Committee on Publications.

Physiology, Roget declared in his *EB* thesis, embraces a wider field of research, inquires into the connections between the phenomena, and investigates the causes from which they spring and the laws by which they are governed. In short, the botanist and zoologist simply provided the isolated facts, which the physiologist then shaped, through his discovery of relationships, into descriptions or statements or organic laws.

Earlier researchers, Roget said, became bogged down in trying to identify some single principle of life that would then explain all the actions and phenomena which are peculiar to living things. Terms like the "vital principle," "spirit of animation," the "archaeus," the "organic force" have contributed nothing but confusion and a false sense of discovery, he said. "Nothing, indeed, can be more specious than this reference to unknown facts, which have a manifest connexion with one another, to a common principle of action," said Roget in asserting that physiologists have been unable to "obtain results of the same general and comprehensive nature as those which have rewarded our efforts in the purely physical sciences."

It is interesting to note the shift in Roget's views from the early attempt at the "Physiology" article in 1823 to the present treatise in the *EB* seventh. Where in the first article he deplored the tendency of investigators to content themselves with explanations based upon "final causes" or "purposes," in the latter writing he seems to have swung around to that very position:

Living nature is impressed with a character, which at once raises it to a higher order among the objects of human intellect, and invests the science which regards it with a more lofty and ennobling sentiment. Life is peculiarly characterized by the manifestations of INTENTION. Adaptation of means to an end is visible throughout the whole of this animated scene. Express design is palpably discernible in every formation, in every arrangement, in every series of changes which this vast theatre of nature displays. Utility is the governing principle of all; intelligence and power far exceeding the utmost stretch of our imagination, are revealed to us in language not to be mistaken, and carrying with it irresistible conviction. Thus while the sciences of inorganic matter are founded on the relations of cause and effect, physiology takes cognizance more especially of the relations of means to ends, which the phenomena present to our view.
. . . The principal object of physiology, then, is the study of the functions of life; that is, the investigation of the changes occurring in the living system with reference to their respective objects, and in their subservience to the maintenance of life, and the various purposes for which life was bestowed.[11]

Such a shift was expressive of the effects of profound events occurring in both his professional life and his private life between the 1823 and the 1837 "Physiology" articles, events which produced shattering philosophical changes and led him into ambiguity and self-contradiction.

Roget's reading of the literature of his field was broad and versatile (including works in German, Italian, French, and Latin), and he brought his subject up to date by citing abundantly the work of his friends Marcet and Bostock and other associates in London and Edinburgh, such as Mayo, Prout, and Latham. Never a bashful writer, Roget also included substantial quotations from his own works—he referred his readers to his Bridgewater Treatise [12] and to observations he had made on the relationship of nutrition to physiology during his work in 1823 to stem an epidemic at the Milbank penitentiary.[13]

While it is true that Roget's summary of the state of physiology, because of the velocity with which the science was developing at the time, is now seen to have been obsolete almost before it was printed, it was a major work and recognized as such by the scientific world. The treatise, combined with Roget's article "Phrenology," was reprinted twice, once as a two-volume work in Edinburgh in 1838, and again, the next year in Philadelphia, as a single 516-page volume under the title *Outlines of Physiology, with an Appendix on Phrenology.*

Roget's *EB* writings on phrenology were met with lively and persistent criticism that extended over twenty years. The relevance of this running argument, in which a great many scientific men became involved, is the light that it sheds upon Roget as man and scientist. His intelligence, his knowledge, his honesty, and his very intentions were called into question by his increasingly vituperative antagonists.

A letter from Roget to the editor of the *EB* in 1817 dates the beginning of his battle with the phrenologists, since he apparently anticipated trouble when he accepted the assignment from Napier. "I shall endeavour to give quite a fair and impartial statement of the doctrine," wrote Roget.[14] Another letter, dated August 30 of the same year, suggests that "Cranioscopy" was a better title for the phrenology article than the one suggested by Napier—"Craniology." Roget pointed out that he had heard Spurzheim [15] also express a preference for "Cranioscopy."

Roget's article thus appeared under "Cranioscopy" in the *EB Supplement.* It was a seven-page essay, beginning with a definition and a backhanded reference to the ambiguity of the subject:

Cranioscopy, or the inspection of the cranium, is a term recently invented to express the study of the external form of the skull in men and animals, with the view of ascertaining the form, size, and respective functions of the subjacent parts of the brain, and of deriving from thence indications relative to the natural dispositions, propensities, and intellectual powers of each individual. This science, whether founded on a real or imaginary basis, may be said to have originated with Dr. Gall, a physician of Vienna, whose system, matured in conjunction with Dr. Spurzheim, has of late attracted so much attention, and been so keenly discussed both here and on the Continent, that we think it our duty to present our readers with a general outline of its doctrines.[16]

There followed a substantial presentation of the contentions of Gall, Spurzheim, and other phrenologists, along with examples of their experiments and observations. Once this was accomplished, however, Roget seemed to have felt free to "examine the doctrine," which meant express his objections to accepting it as a legitimate science.

Eschewing the weapons of ridicule and satire that had been unlimbered in the popular press, Roget attacked the subject on two grounds: 1) it was founded on an inadequate knowledge of the brain; 2) its proponents used faulty logic in developing their theory:

We shall also refrain from employing the weapons of ridicule against a system so vulnerable to its attacks, and which would have been so capable of affording Swift a new incident for the history of the philosophers of Laputa. The simple exposition of the sandy foundation on which it has been built, of the flimsy materials of which it has been composed, and the loose mode in which they have been put together, will suffice to enable our readers to form their own conclusions as to the soundness and solidity of the edifice.[17]

In the first place, said Roget, "nothing like direct proof has been given that the presence of any particular part of the brain is essentially necessary to the carrying on of the operations of the mind."

Roget's second charge—that of fallacious logic—is twofold. He submits that the phrenologists depended solely upon analogy, and that they were guilty of circular reasoning:

The only arguments in . . . favour [of the departmentalization of the brain] which bear the least plausibility, are derived solely from analogy. . . . Now, the utility of analogical deductions as to what takes place in one department of nature, from our knowledge of what occurs in another, consists chiefly in their affording indications of what may possibly happen, and thus directing and stimulating our inquiries to the discovery of truth by the legitimate road of observation and experiment. But to assume the existence of any such analogy as equivalent to a positive proof which can result only from the evidence of direct observation, is evidently a gross violation of logic.[18]

Roget provided examples of the phrenologist's analogous reasoning—for example, that because the various secretions of the body are produced by particular glands, the various thoughts and emotions must be produced by particular portions of the brain. He then shows his own skill as a logician by pointing out:

> Even in a case where all the analogies are favourable to one side of a question, such a loose mode of reasoning would be entitled to little confidence; but how fallacious must it not prove, when analogies can be pointed out which apply in opposite ways.

And again, he provides abundant examples—for example, that the stomach digests very different kinds of food, yet "we do not find that one portion of that organ is destined for the digestion of meat, and another for vegetable matter." After hammering away at this and other analogies relied upon by the phrenologists for their arguments, Roget attacks the idea that the size and shape of the skull are reliable criteria for determining the size and shape of the brain. Further, he denies that size is a measure of the energy or the efficacy with which a given function is performed by the brain, a contention arrived at, again, by the phrenologists' analogy, "A large muscle is stronger than a small one; and a large loadstone is more powerful than a smaller one —why should it not be the same with regard to the brain?"

Roget refused to involve himself in "that metaphysical labyrinth of the thirty-three special faculties into which the phrenologists had analyzed the human mind." [19] Instead, he came down hard on the logical fallacies that to him riddled the whole phrenological argument.

Despite his promise to Napier to be fair and impartial and his promise to his readers to avoid ridicule and exaggeration, Roget in his summing up could not avoid a satirical bent:

> With minds capable of allowing any weight to such observations, and imbued with such notions of the nature of philosophical induction, as are implied by the grave admission of such frivolous arguments as these, the investigation of the laws of nature must be an easy and delightful task. With the abundant and all powerful resources, which their indulgent method of rea-

soning is ever ready to supply, all difficulties may be smoothed away, all chasms immediately filled up, and all obstacles made to vanish the moment they arise. . . . With such a convenient logic, and accommodating principles of philosophizing, it would be easy to prove anything. We suspect, however, that on that very account, they will be rejected as having proved nothing.

Thus, in "Cranioscopy," in 1817, Roget threw down a challenge that was quickly taken up—not only by the self-announced phrenologists, but by a good many of Roget's own associates—and Roget was unable to extricate himself from the controversy for another twenty years. In the same year that the last volume of the *Supplement* was issued, *Lancet* [20] published a very sympathetic review of *Elements of Phrenology* (Edinburgh, 1819), saying in part:

> We trust it will be perused by those who have so unsparingly abused the science of Phrenology, and we hope in their future attacks they will show us, at least, that they are acquainted with the elements of that science, and not continue, as they have hitherto done, to attempt the refutation of a doctrine without possessing the knowledge of a single one of those innumerable facts from which it was discovered, and on which it is immutably established.[21]

But the phrenologists, chiefly the brothers Combe,[22] needed no *Lancet* to engage the enemy for them. First, George Combe wrote Roget personally a courteous but firm objection to "Cranioscopy," his object being principally to point out that Roget had ignored the principles, not only of phrenology, but of physiology as well. Roget had not stated such principles in his article, but simply attempted to show that further inquiry was unnecessary and that the phrenological system was self-evidently absurd. Combe quietly suggested that it was possible that he had misread Roget's article, and that before Combe's forthcoming book went to press, perhaps there was still time for Roget to reconsider the matter.[23]

Roget answered promptly, refused to bow to the blackmail attempt, and argued calmly that there simply had been insufficient evidence produced to establish the phrenologists' chief tenet: that there exists a uniform correspondence between certain forms of the head, skull, or brain and certain characters of mind. Until this could be ascertained as a matter of fact—inductively through verifiable observation or experiment—the whole phrenological

structure must remain in the category of "speculation . . .
founded on reasonings *a priori* . . . [and] can, in my opinion,
lead to no positive or certain result.[24] He added that he had no
confidence in the proponents of the system "either as faithful observers or as sound reasoners" since their observations did not
match with his own experience:

> I at one time took some pains to make observations on this sub-
> ject; and am persuaded that I met, in the course of them,
> nearly as many exceptions to the rules, as instances in confir-
> mation of them. . . . I have stated some of the sources of the
> difficulty, not with a view of discouraging inquiry, if con-
> ducted on the true principles of philosophical induction, but as
> ultimately contributing to its success, by inspiring a salutary
> caution against a fault, to which it seems to me that the found-
> ers of this system have shown a strong propensity, that of too
> hasty and imperfect generalization.[25]

Roget closed his letter by reminding Combe that the burden of
proof of the phrenological system lay with the proponents, and
that there was little point in his continuing the debate with
those who were satisfied with the questionable observations and
dubious logic of Gall and Spurzheim.

Combe, of course, responded to this letter with still another,
dated May 28. Still respectful in tone, Combe said he hoped that
he had not misinterpreted Roget's intentions in "Cranioscopy,"
but that he could not help concluding that Roget had simply set
out to show phrenology as absurd. He asked permission to publish their correspondence.

Roget replied within the week, assuring Combe that his mind
remained open, and that when and if adequate evidence were
amassed and proper generalizations derived from that evidence,
he, Roget, would be the first to acknowledge the contribution.
Meanwhile, he had no objection to Combe's publishing the
letters.[26]

Getting no satisfaction from Roget, Combe went ahead with
his book and included a lengthy chapter entitled "Objections of
the Anatomists Considered," in which he singled out Roget and
for twenty-nine pages laid into the author of "Cranioscopy" with
a vigor that was hard to match. Combe raked Roget's article
from stem to stern, beginning with the word *cranioscopy*, which
he said was typical of the gratuitous remarks of such authors.
Combe pointed out that Gall and Spurzheim had called their science *phrenology*, and asserted:

This circumstance would not be worth noticing, were it not the practice of some opponents to shew an ignorant contempt of the doctrines by fabricating names which do not indicate the true nature of the subject.[27]

Combe's chief arguments against Roget—"and others of his kind" —were 1) their failure to present evidence of their own observations or experiments, 2) their outright distortion of the phrenological doctrines of Gall and Spurzheim, and 3) *argumentum ad hominem*. Reminding his followers of Spurzheim's warning— "Self-conviction can be founded only on self-observation . . . and this requires the actual observation of nature"—Combe again and again asks why Roget presented no observations of his own to counter those of Gall and Spurzheim.

Contrary to Roget's objection that the phrenologists did not offer enough factual evidence to convince, Combe declared that they had too much:

They would have swelled volumes had they attempted to specify the hundreds of instances on the evidence of which each organ is admitted; and such a specification would have done no good, because we see that their observations are doubted as well as their conclusions.

Roget in the *EB* was as guilty as any writer in any penny weekly, said Combe, of sinking to cheap ridicule and exaggeration:

The author proceeds thus: "Is the transient glance of a passing observer, sufficient for unravelling the complex web of our affections, or unveiling the secret and tortuous recesses of the human heart, so as to assign to each principle its precise sphere of agency?" No certainly; Gall and Spurzheim nowhere affirm that "the transient glance of a passing observer" is sufficient for such a task. Then to what purpose does this observation tend? To throw a suspicion over their statements by a side wind, when the author did not choose to attack them manfully in front.[28]

Combe concluded his counterattack with a lengthy quotation from Samuel Johnson's *Life of Drake* to the effect that there are "some men of narrow views and grovelling conceptions," who thrive on perpetual skepticism and treat every new attempt as "wild and chimerical," and where they cannot find arguments against such an attempt, "treat it with contempt and ridicule." [29]

A good many privately issued pamphlets, including at least

one in Latin in 1822, were hurled back and forth by the antagonists in the battle over whether or not phrenology was a genuine
science, and the argument provided much amusement for the by-
standers as more and more persons were urged to take sides.
John Abernethy, the dean of British surgeons, whose lectures
Roget himself attended during his first assault on London in
1800, declared, "I anticipate nothing but mischief from Gall and
Spurzheim's Physiognomy or Cranioscopy becoming generally
known and accredited," and went on to suggest several hypothetical cases that verged on the grotesque.[30]

The *Edinburgh Review* devoted a large part of an issue in
1815 to a summary of the arguments antagonistic to phrenology.
The author made considerable use of the "able and elegant article of Dr. Roget." The phrenologists responded in kind. They
launched their own publication in Edinburgh, *The Phrenological Journal and Miscellany,* the first volume of which covered the
period from December 1823 to August 1824. Edited by the
Combe brothers, the *Journal* devoted more than half of its first
volume of 655 pages to counterattacks against their attackers.
Possessed of a sharp tongue and an aptitude for epithets somewhat reminiscent of William Cobbett, Andrew Combe took up
more than twenty pages in the first issue with reprints of extracts
from articles attacking phrenology, classified under the following
heads: "Railing & Abuse," "Falsehoods & Malignities," "Imperti-
nencies & Insolencies," "Dull Jokes," "Indecencies," "Nastiness &
Brutalities."

In the second number of the volume, Andrew Combe took on
Roget's *EB* article specifically in an attempt to show that it was
neither able nor elegant, although he did concede that it "is still
regarded in the south [that is, London] as the most formidable
attack phrenology ever had to sustain." [31]

For some eleven pages, Andrew Combe castigates Roget very
much along the same lines laid down by his brother, but with
some extra fillips. For example, Combe finds it laughable that
Roget should use analogy to argue against phrenology just one
paragraph after he has objected to the phrenologist's use of analogy to support the doctrine. The editor proceeds systematically
to demolish, at least to his own satisfaction, all of Roget's arguments, and urges his reader to investigate phrenology himself, for
"we can safely assure him, that insofar as anatomy is concerned,
or, indeed, any other species of general medical knowledge, any
man of ordinary understanding may, in a single day, qualify

himself as thoroughly for entering upon the study of phrenology as the profoundest physician that ever lived." [32]

Meanwhile, the Combe brothers were gaining some support in London. The brilliant and eccentric Dr. John Elliotson (1791–1868),[33] who took two M.D. degrees—one at Edinburgh and one at Cambridge—and who was a close associate of Roget's in the Medical and Chirurgical Society, founded the Phrenological Society of London. Many years later, still an adherent, Elliotson began publishing *Zoist: A Journal of Cerebral Physiology and Mesmerism* and carried on the battle within the halls of the Medical and Chirurgical Society itself.

Lancet began publishing a series of "Lectures on Phrenology by Dr. Spurzheim," with the following prefatory remarks:

> We have this day the satisfaction of introducing to the attention of our readers the first of Dr. Spurzheim's excellent letters on the science of Phrenology, a science which by far the greater portion of the English public have never yet heard mentioned unless accompanied by ridicule, abuse, or misrepresentation. Thousands of individuals will now, for the first time, have opened to their view this beautiful and useful branch of philosophy.[34]

Even Roget's friend Bostock was drawn into the fray when he had to mention phrenology in his three-volume work *An Elementary System of Physiology* (1827). In a lengthy footnote to his discussion of physiognomy, he comments on the recent attacks and defenses of the phrenological doctrines:

> . . . it must be acknowledged, that they [the attackers] have been more characterized by the brilliancy, or perhaps flippancy, of their wit, than by the soundness of their arguments: it would seem, indeed, that the writers did not regard it as a subject for serious consideration. I must, however, except from this censure the article "Cranioscopy," by Dr. Roget, which is truly characteristic of the cultivated and candid mind of its author.[35]

The Phrenological Journal's response to this was to compliment Bostock for his candor and acuteness but to doubt that any unbiased person could agree with his laudatory remark about Roget:

> For Dr. Roget's talents and attainments we, in common with the mass of his educated countrymen, entertain a high respect; but we must be permitted to add that . . . he had not bestowed

upon Phrenology that patient study without which no man, however eminent his abilities and general knowledge, can render himself qualified to form a correct judgment on the questions at hand.[36]

Meanwhile, two additional volleys were fired, one by each side. In his Bridgewater Treatise of 1834, an extremely influential publication, Roget took occasion to state that his views on phrenology had not at all changed since his "Cranioscopy" article of 1818, and George Combe issued one of the more curious pamphlets of the war: *Testimonials on Behalf of George Combe as a Candidate for the Chair of Logic in the University of Edinburgh* (Edinburgh, 1836). In addition to its ostensible purpose, Combe's pamphlet also paraded before the public a truly impressive collection of sixty complimentary statements about Combe and phrenology. Included were signed testimonials by the Archbishop of Dublin; Dr. James Johnson, Physician Extraordinary to the King; D. G. Hallyburton, M.P. for Forfarshire; Charles Maclaren, editor of *The Scotsman* and of the sixth edition of the *Encyclopaedia Britannica;* Dr. Evanson, Professor of the Practice of Physic, Royal College of Physicians, Ireland; as well as some prominent men of Europe and America. Combe's chief opponent for the university chair was Sir William Hamilton, philosopher and sturdy antiphrenologist. Sir William was elected and for twenty years exerted an important influence on young Scottish thought.

It is difficult to appreciate now how widely phrenology was accepted in the 1830's and 1840's. It was regularly taught as a subject in the mechanics' institutes, for example, a fact that G. M. Young used to introduce an interesting comment. Whatever modern scientists think of phrenology, it did, said Young, "help to keep the idea of personality alive under the steam-roller of respectability." [37] Moreover, throughout the arduous educational experimentation applied to Victoria's young Prince of Wales (born 1841), George Combe was one of Prince Albert's advisers. Specifically, Combe was retained to examine the baby's skull periodically and report on what these examinations would show of the infant's adhesiveness, amativeness, combativeness, etc.[38]

All this while an even greater phrenological outcry was in the making, for Napier was about to issue Volume XVII of the seventh edition of the *EB,* and he had asked Roget again to contribute the article on phrenology. As soon as the volume appeared, the *Journal,* newly christened *The Phrenological Journal and*

Magazine of Moral Science, inserted a brief notice promising a
"full exposure of Dr. Roget's conduct touching Phrenology."
The same notice concluded with this contemptuous note:

Some years ago, the name of Dr. Roget would have had weight
with men of science. We believe it has none at this day; the
impressions being that he was unable to sustain a reputation
yielded to him by anticipation. But with the multitude a belief
may linger that the Secretary of the Royal Society [Roget became so in 1827] *must* be a man of talent. On asking a medical
friend what would be the effect of Dr. Roget again coming forward as a writer against Phrenology, he gave us this laconic
reply, containing a severe truth under a jingle of sound:
"Troja fuit: Roget fuit" ["Troy has been; Roget has been"].[39]

Two features of Roget's article, retitled "Phrenology," particularly incensed the editors of the *Phrenological Journal:* 1) while
he had been publicly silent throughout the years of debate over
his "Cranioscopy," in the new article he had now the temerity to
answer the Combes directly; and 2) he had reaffirmed his contempt for phrenology by insisting on reprinting the old article
substantially as he had written it in 1818.

A comparison of the two articles proves Combe to be quite
right on the second point, but then Roget made no bones about
it either. Both privately (in a letter to Napier, February 19,
1838) and publicly (in his preface to the separate book form of
Treatises on Physiology and Phrenology, issued the same year),
Roget acknowledged that much had been published on phrenology since "Cranioscopy" appeared, that he would study the material, but that the "ground work will of course remain as before;
nor do I imagine I shall have to alter any of the opinions with
regard to it I formerly expressed." [40]

The following explanation appeared in his book:

In revising the article "Cranioscopy," . . . I have availed myself
of [the editor's] permission to reply to some of the criticisms
which had been made upon it by Mr. G. Combe and Dr. A.
Combe; it was, accordingly, thought desireable to reprint the
former essays, with no other alterations than a few verbal
corrections and the introduction of a few sentences descriptive
of some modifications and additions that the system of Gall
and Spurzheim contained in Mr. Combe's *System of Phrenology.* In the remarks which I have subjoined to the essay, the
reader will perceive that I have refrained from entering into
the discussion of the numerous objections that might be urged

against the metaphorical part of the modern system of Phrenology, having neither the leisure nor the inclination to engage
in controversies of this nature.[41]

Roget's reply to Combe's criticism ran to twenty-one pages, inserted in Volume XVII, immediately following the "Phrenology"
essay. He remained firm in his conclusions, and with his customary thoroughness, again explained at length why he believed
that Messrs. Gall and Spurzheim, Combe and Combe had not observed a recognized scientific method in arriving at their generalizations. Again he found serious fault with what observations they
did offer and cited some of their own illustrations to bolster his
view that their findings were chiefly interpretative opinions. He
himself had spent some time in Deville's famous museum of
skulls on the Strand—the source of many of the Combes' and
Spurzheim's specimens—and he found that conclusions very different from those of the phrenologists could as easily be drawn as
theirs from the same materials. He declared that the much-
vaunted popularity of phrenology was simply that—easy acceptance among the credulous populace—and that the "science" had
significantly failed, in twenty years, to establish itself among scientific men. This was Roget's last word on the subject—his concluding paragraph:

When we consider that the present age is not one in which there
is any lack of credulity, or in which a doctrine is likely to be
repudiated on the score of its novelty or its extravagance, we
cannot but smile at the complaints of persecution uttered by
the votaries of the system of Dr. Gall, and at the attempts they
make to set up a parallel between its reception in this country,
in these times, and that which, two centuries ago, attended the
speculations of Galileo, and subjected him to the tyrannous
cognisance of the Inquisition; or to establish an analogy between the dogmas of phrenology and the discoveries of the circulation of the blood, and of the analysis of light, which have
immortalized the names of Harvey and of Newton.[42]

Far from being dismayed by the *Phrenological Journal*'s continued and increasingly personal attacks, Roget seemed all the
more confident in his own judgment. He was, of course, not
alone in his views, but was supported actively by the articles and
lectures of such antiphrenologists as Drs. Barclay, Gordon, Holland, Tupper, Kidd, Hope, and Brown, and Sir Charles Bell, Sir
William Hamilton, Jeffrey, Brougham, and Sir Benjamin Brodie.
Arrayed against these outspoken men were proponents such as

Elliotson, Mackenzie, Macnish, Laycock, Archbishop Whately, Drs. James Scott and Disney Alexander, and Sir William Ellis.

The invective reached its highest pitch, apparently, in late 1838 and 1839. Andrew Combe printed, first in the *Phrenological Journal*, and then as a separate pamphlet, two letters: one to Macvey Napier, pointing out how Roget's article had sullied the otherwise good name and serviceability of the *EB*, and the second and much longer letter to Roget, who had come to be the focal point of the *Journal*'s counterattacks. There is little new in Combe's pamphlet, even though he does address himself to Roget's defensive remarks in "Phrenology." The phrenologist's anguish rises, in the conclusion, to an utter condemnation of Roget and a consignment of him to the ash heap of scientific history:

> . . . Your article "Cranioscopy" would have been hereafter held only a pardonable error, having been written at a period when the discoveries of Gall were almost universally disputed in this country; but your article "Phrenology" will cause your name to become a warning against injustice and prejudice. . . .
>
> In conclusion, we must state that, not you, but phrenologists themselves are the proper persons to judge the science they study. If you choose to disregard it, you are at liberty to do so, and the loss is your own. If you misstate it to the public, they are justified in exposing your faults and follies. . . . The publishers of the Encyclopaedia may yet find cause to regret having ever had the disadvantage of your pen.[43]

The shrillness of Combe's *Strictures*, however, was not entirely representative of public opinion, nor was it sufficient to maintain the intense pitch of the controversy. A nonpartisan magazine, *The Aldine Magazine,* selected Roget's volume *Physiology and Phrenology* as its "Book of the Week," and while the reviewer seemed to favor phrenology, there was none of the acrimony of Combe's diatribe:

> Dr. Roget is a determined opponent of phrenology; but abating a slight and only occasionally shewn disposition to sneer, he is a fair and honourable one. As such, and as our present limits will not permit us to moot the point with him, we allow him the advantage of the last word.[44]

The last "word" allowed Roget was the entire final six paragraphs of his response to the Combes, a generosity which perturbed Andrew Combe, for, as he put it in a subsequent summary of "Phrenology and the Periodicals," "The reviewer is favourable to Phrenology, and he is also disposed to be favourable to Dr. Roget, which almost unavoidably leads him into the expression of opinions not reconcileable together." [45]

Attacks and counterattacks continued to appear for several years following, but it is clear that the real fire of the argument had died to a sporadic flicker. More and more frequently, writers and editors attempted to take an intermediate position, a fact that did not favor the phrenologists, who seemed to thrive on controversy. A good example is the position of the *British and Foreign Medical Review*, which in 1840 published a lengthy summary of recent articles and books (including Roget's) for and against phrenology. Again, the writer was obviously pro-phrenology—in fact, he went on to print drawings of the skulls of Michelangelo and "an idiot, aged 20," as materials with which the beginner might take up the study of the new science. He also suggested that the skeptical make a comparison of the skull of Dickens with those of some of his characters, such as Sykes and Fagin. But the same journal next published a highly laudatory review of the American edition of Roget's *Physiology and Phrenology*.[46]

While history seems to have borne out Roget's judgment with respect to phrenology, when one considers the embryonic state of physiology at the time, he also seems to have jumped rather more quickly to his conclusions than his knowledge of physiology would allow. He certainly proved himself quick on his feet in an intellectual scuffle and capable of giving as good as he got in his exchanges with the Combe brothers; nor would he be thrown off the balance given him by his insistence on legitimate inductive and deductive procedures. But it is also true that he never produced his actual observations, which he said controverted the evidence claimed by the phrenologists. That he was correct in pointing out the unsubstantiated claims of the phrenologists seems to me undeniable; but in view of subsequent altercations, in which he refused to give ground when presented with convincing evidence that he should, I must question his intentions in refusing to do further battle.

After 1839 Roget apparently refused to discuss the matter further, perhaps because he was distracted by other problems. A number of other thunderheads had arisen during the twenty years of phrenological argument, and some of these had brought storms that he was hard-pressed to survive. One of these, indeed, became a battle for his life and prestige at the Royal Society.

Loss of Marcet, Milbank
Epidemic

Roget's war with the phrenologists has been dealt with as a single, uninterrupted sequence of events, but it is necessary to remember that when it began, with the appearance of the first volumes of the *EB Supplement*, Roget was all but prostrate with grief over Romilly's suicide. While those phrenological battles were fought—over a period of twenty years—many other events were shaping these prime years of Roget's life.

Perhaps it was his uncle's urgent advice to avoid the family propensity for melancholy, or perhaps it was simply a lesson learned from the long durance of five Scottish winters—something there was, however, that told Roget in those last, gloomy weeks of 1818 that he must act to save himself. His salvation then, as at many another time in his life, was work, and with the new year he plunged into a dozen new projects: articles, lectures, experiments, as well as a resumption of editorial work for the Medical and Chirurgical Society, service with the Northern Dispensary, promotion of his own medical practice, and his own private studies in language, natural theology, and medical jurisprudence.

At the urging of Abraham Rees, who lived in neighboring Brunswick Square, Roget took on an assignment to write several articles for a new encyclopedic work, *The Cyclopedia, or Universal Dictionary of Arts, Sciences, and Literature*. When that thirty-four-volume publication appeared in 1819, Roget had contributed the following articles, ranging from a short paragraph to essays of several pages: "Sweating Sickness," "Symptom," "Synocha," "Synochus," "Tabes," and "Tetanus."

At the same time he renewed his interest in optics and in the operation of the human eye. One of his fugitive publications in 1820 preserves for us the picture of this tall, lonely man, mirror in one hand and candle in the other, observing the motions and reactions of his own eyes as he sat in his study in Bernard Street and subjected them to various test conditions. The short article, which appeared in a medical text by his friend Benjamin Travers, a fellow member of the M-C Council, was preceded by a handsome compliment: ". . . my ingenious and learned friend, Dr. P. M. Roget, in whom, I may be permitted to say, profound scientific knowledge is accompanied by a characteristic aversion to ostentatious display." [1]

Roget's article detailed his experiments leading up to developing the ability to dilate and contract the iris at will. He explained that he could induce these reactions, "which are usually considered as no more under the dominion of the will than the heart or blood vessels," and thus prove that the power was, in him at least, totally independent of the influence of light. While he admitted that he had never met anyone else who could do it, he declared that he had often demonstrated this unique ability to the skeptical. Roget attributed the trick "to no other cause than to my having from my childhood, been much in the habit of observing optical phenomena, and of practicing various experiments relating to vision, a subject which I early took great delight in cultivating." Recalling his work with kaleidoscopes and anticipating a forthcoming paper in the RS *Philosophical Transactions,* one must agree that optics was a persistent and important interest throughout his life.

Through the hot summer of 1819 Roget occupied himself with almost single-handed attempts to hold the M-C Society together. Because of destruction of the building they were in, the society had to find a new home, but the members could not get together to make a decision. Once a decision was forced upon them, Roget could not persuade enough of them to contribute enough money to buy the suggested new home in Lincoln's Inn Fields. There were more housekeeping troubles, reminiscent of those caused by the peculating clerk back in 1819. What worried Roget most was the threat to the society's *Transactions* posed by trouble with the printers and a falling off of contributions from interested members. He and Marcet corresponded frequently about this, and Marcet too became increasingly alarmed:

It would almost seem now as if the Society was going to pieces, without a house and without its volume. . . . I entreat you to attend more diligently than ever to the collecting and printing of good papers and the regular publication of our *Transactions*. Depend upon it, those volumes are the true *pabulum* of our existence, and the regular income of a batch of medical news, which the Society has hitherto regularly afforded to its members, has been the cause of our extraordinary progress.[2]

It is in this series of letters (1819–20) that Marcet interests Roget in a means of improving his London practice, a means which is both mildly amusing and pathetic in that it reveals the maneuvering that attended nearly every step of the rising doctor in the metropolis. Marcet mentions glancingly, once or twice, that Roget might do well to stop in and remember Marcet to the Duke of San Carlos, currently the Spanish ambassador to the English Court. For some years Marcet had held the sinecure of Physician to the Spanish Embassy; not only was it a direct source of revenue, but he found that it had opened many important doors to him. He still held the post, although he was remaining indefinitely in Geneva, where, incidentally, he was one of thirty members elected in the fall to the representative Council. Before leaving London, Marcet had introduced Roget to the Duke, suggesting that the Duke consider Roget as a temporary replacement, but Roget had thought this a mere matter of courtesy and had not paid court to the Spaniard—hence Marcet's reminders.

Complications arose when various indispositions in the Duke's household required the attendance of a physician, and Roget was called for. For the next several months, Roget rendered substantial professional service, and not only was he not compensated for it, but he caused Marcet to suspect that Roget was trying to take over the post. The fact that they straightened out the misunderstanding in their next few exchanges of letters is perhaps the best evidence of their close friendship, for the situation became increasingly complicated. A third doctor,[3] backed by the powerful Duke of Wellington, launched a campaign to get the job at the Spanish Embassy.[4] As soon as that was weathered, the Duke of San Carlos, Marcet's friend, was replaced by a stranger, the Duke of Frias. Marcet then relinquished the position formally and persuaded San Carlos to write a glowing recommendation of Roget. Roget's subsequent appointment was not verified until November 1820; the whole tangle had begun in September 1819.[5] Roget held the post to his considerable advantage until he retired from medical practice twenty years later.

Meanwhile, Marcet and his wife Jane were enjoying themselves in Geneva. In addition to preparing his maiden speech for the Genevan Council, Marcet and de La Rive,[6] whom he with Roget had met at Edinburgh, were giving lectures in chemistry and medicine at the University of Geneva. Marcet's best news, insofar as Roget was concerned, was the announcement that he intended to return to England for a long visit in the autumn of 1821.[7]

Their letters on through the spring and summer are full of gossip about the London societies, as in this sample from Roget:

But the great news with regard to the [Royal] Society is the intended resignation of Sir Joseph Banks, whose health has been declining much this winter. He wishes to secure the succession to Mr. Davies Gilbert! He is certainly not a fit man; but alas! who is? [8] The Royal Institution is very flourishing this winter; it is nearly, if not quite, out of debt, and the lectures go off well. There was a dinner of the members the other day at which Lord Lansdowne presided. The Russell Institution is going down hill. There has been a conspiracy among a low set, who have, by a sudden spring at the last annual meeting, turned out all the old and respectable managers and taken the reins of government into their own hands. The London Institution is next to ruin. The Committee in their annual report propose to discontinue the newspapers and lectures and shut up the house in the evenings.[9]

Jane Marcet's *Conversations on Natural Philosophy* was doing well; Roget had just gone over every page of the proofs for the second edition. Yelloly was back in town from Norwich; Sophie Romilly was spending the winter with Lady Lansdowne; Roget begged to be remembered to old friends—de La Rive, the Chauvets, Dumont.

Marcet's letters were cheering, and on November 16, he explained that he would much prefer to limit his time in Switzerland to long visits, "as I cannot bear to lose sight too long of my English friends and habits, without which I feel that social existence would be most drastically curtailed." These reassurances notwithstanding, Roget had to get through the winter and most of 1821 without his good friend. He had to settle for working out experiments that the two wrote about in their letters and quizzing Marcet on the results. Again, one gains a poignant picture of Roget, alone in his Bernard Street study, solemnly and determinedly making an electrically wired orange light up like a light bulb. "Take an orange, plant two wires through it," directed Marcet, "and cause an electrical discharge with the Leyden bottle to pass through it. The whole orange (if the room be darkened) will appear like a globe of fire, as if it were a transparent body." [10]

Meanwhile, Marcet traveled about Europe with his wife and son, and kept a stream of entertaining letters coming to London. In February 1821, they were checked in their progress toward Rome and Naples "by events of the most momentous kind. But Florence is a noble prison, and we are admirably placed here for marking the events." [11] Roget carried Marcet's reports on Italy with him and read them at their favorite dining club, the Pow Wow, where his audience "with one accord poured down a libation in honor of the writer."

Early in 1821, Roget could report more favorably on the M-C Society with the election of a new President, Dr. John Cooke, Roget's old associate at the Great Windmill Street School. Roget was sure that Cooke would exert himself on behalf of the society more than his predecessor, Astley Cooper, had done. Besides, the society had finally taken a good house on the west side of the square at Lincoln's Inn Fields, their new clerk was attentive and efficient, their annual income now exceeded expenditures by nearly £300, and a new and improved volume of the *Transactions* was due to come off the press within the month:

> I think I shall continue as I am in the Society [he was then Secretary] a year or two longer, although I feel it is a serious encroachment on my time, which nothing but my attachment to the interests of the Society could have made me so long submit to. . . . I think I hear you asking me how I go on professionally—I should answer *tolerably*. I do not feel that I am advancing; nor perhaps am I receding, unless in as far as that a physician who is not advancing is in fact receding when compared with his contemporaries in the stream. Time has not made me less sensible of the immense void which your removal from England has left in my enjoyments—as it has indeed in the whole circle in which I have been accustomed to see you move; and there are occasions when the contrast between present and former times affects me too strongly.[12]

Roget concluded this letter with the news that he had joined the Chemical Club, which he found very pleasant, but hardly a substitute for the lively activities that he and Marcet had shared a few years previously.

In 1822, Roget took on another lecture series for the Royal Institution. Many of these lectures survive in abstracts published in *The Philosophical Magazine,* the *Literary Gazette and Journal of Belles Letters, Arts, Sciences,* and other publications of the day. Typical subjects were "On the Functions of Progressive Motion in Vertebrated Animals," "On Respiration," "The Functions of the Skeleton," "Digestion," "The Capillaries," "Introduction to Perception and Feeling in Animals," "Vision." The *Literary Gazette* was particularly appeciative of Roget's efforts, and after he had delivered the first two of his twelve-lecture series, the journal announced:

> The vivid sensation produced in the scientific world by Dr. Roget's admirable lectures has induced us to obtain further particulars and an accurate summary of his interesting discourses; these we have now the pleasure of communicating; and thus of disseminating more generally the intelligence which they contain and the admiration which they have excited.[13]

In his first lecture, Roget talked of the problems and methods of applying comparative physiology to zoological classification. In his second, "Mechanical Functions," he entranced his audience with demonstrations of the strength of bones:

> He said that if the bones had been solid, instead of hollow cylinders, they would not have been so strong, unless they had been much heavier; and he proved this proposition by an ingenious though simple experiment: he took two cylinders of glass of equal weight, the one hollow, the other solid; he laid each of them on a frame that supported only their extreme ends, and attached weights to their centers. The result was that the solid cylinder broke with a weight which the hollow one bore without bending.[14]

The lectures were so well received that Roget was hired to appear again in 1823, and again he delivered a course of twelve carefully prepared, illustrated lectures at the Royal Institution theater in Albemarle Street. He offered this series as an "Introduction to Comparative Physiology," and again the *Literary Gazette* published generous accounts (most of them running well over a full three-column page) of his presentations on such subjects as "Zoophites," "Insects," "Molluscs," "Reptiles," and "Birds."

Finally, Marcet returned to England, and he and Roget rejoiced in being together again. Marcet did not come back empty-handed. For all his reports of his laziness in Europe, he had been working, and on March 5 and 19, 1822, he read papers at the M-C Society. He thoroughly approved the new quarters, the new officers, and the solvency of the society, and he highly praised Roget's stubborn work to keep it alive. Then he and his family set off on a long, sentimental tour of northern England and Scotland, stopping off for a few days with Sydney Smith in Yorkshire, "where we passed two days in attacks of mirth and laughing which those only who know the reverend personage can form an idea of." In Edinburgh, their laughter was cut short by the changes since their student days there:

> If our friends were as much improved as the town itself within the last twenty-five years, this would be a delightful world indeed! But while the old houses are all, more or less, looking cleaner and in better repair, with new and magnificent mansions rising on all sides, the men, alas, decay and pass away. Playfair is gone. Sir James Hall is all but gone (so far as his mind is concerned). Gregory is gone. Hope is what he ever was. Rutherford is no more. Stewart is but a noble wreck —etc. Yet the students are animated by the same spirit which has kept up this university for half a century—and in the absence of more illustrious teachers, they still continue to cast on this falling school some degree of lustre.[15]

Roget's letters to Marcet show that, in spirit at least, he accompanied his friend through all the old, familiar streets of Edinburgh, particularly those near the university: Nicholson Street, Potter Row, Meadow Walk, Bristo Street, and, of course, Hope Park. But Roget was discouraged. As usual, his mother and sister had left Bernard Street for their regular summer sojourn at Ilfracombe, and he faced the long, empty months ahead with little enthusiasm. Yelloly had returned to Norwich; Bostock had left for Liverpool and Scotland, planning to meet Marcet there. The town was empty, the future seemed far away:

> I am, indeed, grown rather weary of forming projects, having become less sanguine as to the power of realizing them. I intend therefore to trust more to the chapter of accidents for what may present itself. I believe it is very likely, for want of some predominant motive to determine me, that I may do nothing.[16]

In fact, he sounded terribly tired, as though the highly efficient engine that was Roget had faltered. While it is true that about this time he had given up a long-dreamed-of project—a book on

medical jurisprudence [17]—actually, he had as many irons in the
fire as usual. In his August 9 letter, for example, he noted com-
pleting the treatise "Physiology" for the *EB Supplement*. And
the new volume of the *Transactions of the Medical and Chirurgical Society* had apparently done a surprising job of reviving interest within and about the M-C Society. Much of that interest,
Roget thought, was due to an article by Marcet, giving an account of an American sailor, one John Cummings, who had
come under his care. Cummings had lived ten years after having
swallowed, on a bet, more than thirty clasp knives and other me-
tallic objects.

On May 10, Roget was elected a Fellow of the Royal Astronomical Society,[18] where he was spending much time observing
and arguing a very exciting project indeed. It was to that society
that Charles Babbage, the mathematician and inventor, was describing, in a series of meetings, his fabulous calculating engine
and trying to drum up support for the construction of the thing.
Roget was to cross swords with Babbage before the decade was
out, but at the moment he was fascinated by the possibilities and
the preposterousness of Babbage's ideas, since they sprang from
two of Roget's fields of interest—mathematics and machines.

One last surviving letter from Marcet may well be his last written communication to Roget. Writing from the village of Dal-
quharn, where Loch Lomond joins the Clyde, Marcet expressed
his disappointment that Roget could not have broken away from
London and met him in Scotland, "where you are justly considered as an oracle of London." Marcet was full of compliments
for Roget's medical advice to his cousin Sophia Romilly Kennedy, with whom Marcet was staying, and for Roget's handling
of a paper by Marcet on seawater. He had not seen Bostock nor
Wollaston in Scotland, as he had hoped, but he had gone on a
grouse-shooting expedition with Humphry Davy. "We have had
a delightful tour and many interesting adventures which you
shall hear in due time. We shall certainly be in London in the
first weeks of October . . . and intend to take a lodging in your
neighbourhood if we can find a suitable one." [19]

Marcet did, indeed, take a place in Roget's neighborhood—
rooms directly behind Bernard Street in Great Coram Street,
next to the ill-fated Russell Institution—but that place was to be
his death chamber.

Marcet had been there only a day or two when he drove out to
Westcombe Park, near Greenwich, to visit his brother-in-law,

Morris Haldimand. The next morning, Friday, October 11, Marcet was suddenly attacked with a violent pain in the chest, shooting like electric jolts to all parts of his body. He immediately attributed it to gout in the stomach, recognized his condition as serious, and despaired of recovery. Marcet's son rode quickly into town and returned in less than an hour and a half with Roget and Dr. Babington. Brandy and laudanum were administered; the pain was removed, and immediate danger subsided. Marcet remained, however, feverish, weak, and irritable, and Roget stayed on, sleeping at Westcombe Park, until Wednesday, when the Marcets decided to return to Great Coram Street.

Instead of the mild and gentlemanly carouse that the two old friends had looked forward to in all the letters back and forth from Geneva, they had only a few hours more together in Marcet's sickroom.

As he was dressing on Saturday, Marcet complained of faintness, sat down on a sofa, and seemed to faint away. Mrs. Marcet, who was in the room, immediately sent for Roget, who was there in five minutes, arriving just as Leonard Horner happened in. Marcet remained unconscious, his hands and feet growing cold as he sank, apparently without a struggle. Despite Roget's desperate efforts—and those of Dr. Richard Bright, another of their M-C Society cronies—to restore circulation, Marcet was gone within ten minutes. He was fifty-two; Roget was forty-three.

Roget did what he could to console Jane Marcet, who sat silent and stunned. When her son returned, she gave way and sobbed inconsolably; the young man himself was in a state of near-shock.[20]

Roget's first duty, after assisting Jane Marcet with her husband's funeral, was to write a memoir of Alexander Marcet for the *Annual Biography and Obituary*. The stilted and painfully proper style of his prose reveals little, if any, of the anguish which the loss of his dearest friend had cost him:

> The great number of objects, both public and scientific, which had thus engaged his attention, alone afford strong testimony of the active zeal with which he was animated for the advancement of knowledge and the interests of humanity. The persevering energy with which he pursued those objects, and the variety of talents and rectitude of judgment which marked his progress in whatever he undertook, are evinced by the success with which his exertions have been attended. Endeared as he was to a wide circle of friends, by the excellence of his heart,

the warmth of his affections, and high sense of honour, his death has left a mournful and irreparable chasm in their society. Gifted by nature with that constitutional flow of cheerfulness which imparts the keenest relish for the enjoyments of life, he conjoined with it that expansive benevolence which seeks to render others participators in the same feelings. . . .[21]

Fortunately, that universal anodyne—a job to do—caught up Roget early in 1823 to the extent that he had little time to brood over the premature deaths of Romilly and, now, Marcet. At the moment his every faculty was suddenly called upon: his professional knowledge and skill, his patience and diplomacy, his ingenuity, endurance, compassion, and determination.

An epidemic had struck the city's new penitentiary—Milbank [22]—located on that bend in the Thames, between Lambeth Bridge and Vauxhall Bridge, precisely where the world-famed Tate Gallery now stands. A contemporary description of the institution, one of the fruits of the amazing mind of Jeremy Bentham, suggests something of the civic pride in the riverside prison:

The plan of this building is principally on the *Panopticon*, or *all-seeing* principle of Jeremy Bentham, and was constructed for the purpose of trying to effect a system of imprisonment founded on the humane and rational principles of classification, employment and reform.

. . . The external walls of this vast building, which resembles a fortification, or rather a continental fortified château, form an irregular octagon, enclosing no less than 18 acres of ground. This large space comprehends several distinct though conjoined masses of buildings, the centre one being a regular hexagon, and others branching out from its respective sides. By this means, the governor or overseer can at all times have the power of overlooking every division of the prison from the windows in the central part.

This institution is to accommodate 400 male and 400 female convicts. . . . The prisoners are allowed a per centage on their labours and the amount is given them when discharged. The expense of building this vast edifice amounted to nearly £500,000.[23]

When reports of the epidemic first leaked out in the winter of 1822–23, there was a general reaction of horror and disbelief. Milbank, or the "General Penitentiary," as it was officially called, was, after all, the ideal prison. If conditions could deteriorate in such a place in so few years of its existence, what hope could one have for social progress in any institution? Finally, in February 1823, Roget and another doctor, Peter Mere Latham, later to become Physician Extraordinary to Queen Victoria, were called in by the prison Committee, which had become alarmed at the obvious inability of the prison medical staff to halt the rapidly spreading disease. Thus, their first difficulty was that of working with the hospital staff, already hypersensitive to outside criticism.

Both doctors began visiting the hospital daily, beginning on March 3. Since neither of them had had previous experience with the prison system, they had not only to examine and treat the sick and inspect the sleeping, eating, and working quarters of the prisoners, but to acquaint themselves thoroughly with the dietary, occupational, disciplinary, exercise, and domestic routines of both prisoners and keepers. In short, they had to amass a considerable amount of information quickly about the building itself, the sanitation, heating, ventilation; and, most important of all, they had to become familiar with the medical histories of the individual prisoners and the institution's records of all other significant diseases that had prevailed in the place since it opened.

Working as closely as they could with the medical officers of the prison—Alexander Copland Hutchison, surgeon, at one time a member with Roget of the M-C Society's Council, and a Mr. Pratt, the prison apothecary—Roget and Latham learned that during the preceding autumn the general health had been seen to decline visibly. Those at the treadmill could grind less corn; those at the pump could raise less water; women working in the laundry fainted at their tubs. But there had been no distinct manifestation of a particular disease, and the number of sick in the prison infirmary had not increased significantly. But beginning in February, an increasingly large stream of prisoners began coming to the infirmary, complaining of diarrhea. By the first week of March, when Roget and Latham began their visits, there were 110 prisoners in the infirmary; by April 5, the rate of incidence had doubled—an additional 225 had been admitted, bringing the total ill to 332. Of these, 11 died.[24]

The two doctors spent most of their time at first examining the sick prisoners carefully, and their almost immediate conclusion was that the diarrhea was a symptom of a type of scurvy. They dissected the bodies of two prisoners who had died dysenteric and found in various parts of the intestines the morbid appearances called ecchymosis, "that is, spots of the same kind as those which on the skin constitute scurvy. We found, in fact, an absolute scurvy of the bowels, of which the diarrhea or dysentery was only a symptom and consequence." [25]

The first report of Roget and Latham, dated April 5, 1823, after reviewing the history and present state of the disease in the prison, concluded that the causal factors were diet and the uncommon cold of the preceding winter. They found that the diet had been changed from what it had been during the early years of the prison:

> The change, which took place in July last, reduced the animal part of the diet almost to nothing. In a soup made of pease or barley, ox heads were boiled, in the proportion of one ox head to 100 male and one to 120 female prisoners; and we found upon an inquiry that the meat of one ox head weighed, upon an average, eight pounds, which, being divided among a hundred, allows only an ounce and a quarter for each prisoner. This new diet has been continued until the present time; and to it we mainly ascribe the production of the disease in question. [26]

The second factor, cold, was included in the doctors' report after they had personally visited all the sleeping cells of the prisoners. They noted, as late as April, severely low temperatures in the cells.

Shortly after they began working on the case, Roget and Latham ordered an immediate change in the diet: in place of pease or barley soup for dinner, they substituted a daily allowance of four ounces of flesh meat and eight ounces of rice daily for each prisoner, and white bread instead of brown. They also prescribed three oranges for every prisoner daily, one at each meal.

Between March 12 and 19, they noticed great improvements— physical signs of scurvy on the legs and arms of the prisoners as well as the dysentery seemed to be on the wane. The doctors stayed on a few more days, wrote their first report, which was immediately published, and prepared to resume their ordinary practices.

But in the last week of March and first week of April, the disease exploded. By April 5, 448 of the 858 prisoners were sick. Roget and Latham rushed back to the hospital, again commissioned by the Committee, which in sudden alarm had fired Hutchison. The two doctors readily admitted that their first report was premature:

> The conviction it expresses, that there is "now no obstacle to the entire re-establishment of the healthy state of the Peniten-

tiary," was proved, by what speedily occurred, not to have been well-founded, and although our opinion respecting the sources from which the disease was originally derived, was confirmed by numerous medical men who were examined upon the subject, and was at the time entirely satisfactory to ourselves, and equally so to the Committee, facts subsequently brought to light have led us to doubt whether this latter opinion was entirely correct.[27]

By the middle of May, the epidemic was raging quite out of control. Not only had all the prisoners who had formerly suffered been struck by relapses, but with very few exceptions, all the rest of the prisoners, including those admitted since the change of diet, had come down with the sickness. To make matters worse, the remedies, which were formerly successful in controlling it, "had not now the smallest beneficial influence."

Roget and Latham set about again to study the symptoms. Surrounded by the groaning sick, who of course had long since exhausted the minimal facilities of the infirmary and were now simply left in their cells, with the doors left open, the doctors examined the patients, analyzed their discharges, consulted medical colleagues and medical libraries, performed more autopsies. They reported symptoms unlike the usual ones for dysentery: uncontrollable discharges, gradually weakening the patient to the point of death. Many were without fever, without pain. Some suffered agonizing pains in various parts of the body. Most simply lay in bed or on the floor, with a turbid water continually running from their bowels and a constant complaint of a sinking sensation at the pit of the stomach—"Pray do something for this dreadful sinking." The chalk mixture and tincture of opium they had used before had no effect on the dysentery.

In desperation, Roget and Latham experimented with dosages of mercury, apparently a rather daring treatment at that time, and one of the sources of difficulty with Hutchison. As Roget later testified, Hutchison had specifically refused to use any of the mild preparations of mercury that the other two doctors suggested. The specific preparation used by Roget and Latham was "mercury in the form of *hydrargyrus cum creta*." [28] Roget and Latham reported:

We began therefore and proceeded with the greatest caution, venturing no further than observation did (as it were) lead us by the hand. Thus, gradually making good our ground, we succeeded, at last, in exploring experimentally a very large field;

and learnt how, by varying its preparations and its dose, and varying also its combinations, to adapt this same medicine safely and successfully to the exigencies of the disease under many different forms.[29]

They found that headache and vertigo were often reliable first symptoms and that the mercury treatment if then applied would often stave off the dysenteric attack. While the mercury treatment seemed to offer their first real hope at bringing the epidemic under control, the doctors had other problems heaped upon them as they struggled—mostly in the dark, as they readily admitted—with an unidentified foe. One of these was the increased difficulty in managing the prisoners. Desperate and terrified by the suddenness and prevalence of the disease, and incapable of working at their usual jobs on the treadmill or in the laundry, or even of taking their usual twenty-minute exercise walks, both men and women prisoners often went into delirium or started up uncontrollably, screamed, staggered a few wild paces down a corridor, and collapsed. Many simply gave up: refused to eat or to clean themselves, turned their heads against the stone walls, or drew their filthy blankets over their heads and stared blankly at nothing. Another complicating problem was the fact that the debilitating disease left the prisoners in such weakened condition that all sorts of other ailments that normally would have been resisted made their appearance.

By the middle of summer, thirty prisoners had died, thirteen men and seventeen women. The newspapers were raging at the prison Committee's inability to effect a quick and lasting improvement. Members of Parliament were investigating individually. The pamphleteers were hard at work. One member of the Committee, G. Holford, M.P., himself published three separate pamphlets, objecting to the Roget and Latham reports and attempting to vindicate the penitentiary staff.[30]

A select committee of the House of Commons was appointed to make a thorough investigation—not only of the conditions in the prison but of the medical procedures being applied. To the latter end, the select committee recommended that the Royal College of Physicians institute a special committee to make its own investigation. Accordingly, Robert Peel, then Home Secretary, directed Sir Henry Halford, President of the Royal College, to appoint such a committee.

Halford's committee report unequivocally supported Roget and Latham and concluded that the disorder "had borne a dysenteric character," that the patients were "already far advanced towards recovery," and that the treatment by mercury "appears to have been very successful." The report was signed by Halford and Drs. Henry Ainslie, Edward Ash, W. G. Maton, Thomas Turner, and Pelham Warren, all of the Royal College of Physicians.[31]

The House select committee carried on its own investigation, and the official record of that inquiry is a bulky document indeed. Roget's testimony alone runs to twelve printed folio pages, and dozens of other persons—doctors, M.P.'s, members of the prison Committee and prison staff—were also closely questioned on every phase of the prison operations. Roget had the satisfaction, at least, of being told that the select committee found no fault in him or in Latham:

> They did not, however, do this [referring to the Committee's calling for the special RCP committee] from their entertaining the least suspicion of the talent, judgment and skill of the medical officers of the establishment, Drs. Roget and Latham; but when a contrariety of opinion was held upon a subject on which the lives of hundreds of human beings might ultimately depend, who had no choice but to submit to the treatment which their medical adviser might prescribe, your Committee considered themselves imperiously called upon to refer the subject to the best medical authorities the country could produce . . . and their Report, which is here subjoined, sets, in the opinion of your Committee, the question at rest and fully confirms the propriety of the practice of Drs. Roget and Latham.[32]

Hutchison, meanwhile, had not taken his dismissal lying down. He issued two pamphlets in May, defending himself against assorted charges and offering a number of testimonials of his excellence. Hutchison had been let go by the prison Committee ostensibly for alleged drunkenness. The wording of the original charge against him is an interesting example of euphemism: "that the directions which you give in cases which come under your consideration after dinner, are marked with haste and precipitation, which are not observable in an earlier part of the day." Hutchison averred that, yes, he took his wine at table, but that he knew how much to take and never was under its influence. Once, he remembered, he had had some wine that was not very good, but even then . . .[33]

Conditions at the prison were still far more than Roget and

Latham could handle. They asked for assistance, and Peel ordered the Royal College of Physicians to appoint four additional
doctors. Of the four, three actually showed up to help at the
hospital: William Macmichael and Henry Herbert Southey, both
physicians at the Middlesex Hospital, and Clement Hue. Southey
was a brother of the poet Robert Southey, whom Roget had met
at Beddoes' Pneumatic Institution.

As summer subsided into fall, the disease was still furiously epidemic despite their best efforts with diet and medications. Roget
and Latham asked to have a sizable group of prisoners removed
from Milbank to see what effect, if any, might be achieved. They
had already rejected the frequently suggested idea that the location of the prison on the river was a contributing factor, but by
this time they were willing to try anything. With the assistance
of many interested parties, including the determined Mr. Peel,
who presumably had had orders to clean up the prison once and
for all, 120 women prisoners were sent to the Ophthalmic Hospital in Regent's Park, and 200 men were transferred aboard the
Ethalion, a hulk at Woolwich. Improvements in health and spirits were immediately noted, and the two doctors quickly recruited more support and letters for the idea and succeeded in
removing the remaining prisoners at Milbank to hulks at Woolwich. On November 14, 80 women were received on board the
Narcissus; on December 8 and 10, 281 men were taken to the
Dromedary.

Again, some immediate signs of improvement were noted. But
in the midst of this satisfactory state, the disease broke out again
among the prisoners at the Regent's Park location. Thus, on January 21 and 23, 1824, the women were transferred to the hulks at
Woolwich. The total then on the hulks was 625—the prison was
empty.[34]

The prisoners continued in a depressed mental state and unable to work, a condition that led to frequent acts of violence and
tumult on the hulks. The doctors finally recommended that all
the prisoners be given pardons, apparently working from an idea
that as long as the prisoners stayed together, they would simply
continue to reinfect each other.

The suggestion of medical pardons created another uproar in
the popular press—what! hundreds of felons let loose upon the
public! But by exerting every bit of leverage—medical, political,
social—they could muster, the doctors managed to get the
women prisoners freed by an act of the Crown. They could not

get a similar pardon for the men, but by arguing the same point again—that the disease would prevail as long as the sufferers were herded together—they managed, again with the aid of Peel, to get an act of Parliament passed on April 12, 1824, which gave them the power to distribute the remaining male prisoners among the whole system of prison ships, which lay like somber markers in the lower reaches of the Thames.[35]

Thus the case was closed—or rather, it simply wore itself out —and an exhausted Roget returned to Bernard Street and his home neighborhood practice. That his and Latham's methods had been exonerated by the Royal College of Physicians, the House of Commons, and even, finally, by *Lancet* was the source of some satisfaction to him. But as a medical man and a scientist, and as a human being who had worked, largely ineffectively, for fifteen months among terribly suffering fellow beings, he was far from content. He was exhausted, discouraged with the state of medicine and the overwhelming evidence of his own ineffectuality, aware that others were forging ahead of him (Babbage, for example, had been awarded a gold medal on June 13 by the Royal Astronomical Society), and greatly in need of a distinct change. That change—an utterly surprising one—was soon to come, but had Roget pursued the Milbank epidemic further, had he and Latham been able to devote themselves and perhaps recruit colleagues at the RCP or the M-C Society, they probably would have made a very great discovery. As it was, they came so close to discovering the germ theory of disease that it is all one can do, in reading their accounts, to refrain from calling out aloud, yes! stop! here! look just a little further!

As they struggled with the disease through the summer of 1823, Roget and Latham frequently recorded observations and reflections that sound as though they were just about to stumble upon that which had to wait for Pasteur's definitive experiments with milk and wine some forty years later:

> Unquestionably, then, we do believe, that some injurious influence has been in operation over and above the causes to which the epidemic was originally imputed. . . . If it consist of contagion (and such possibly may be the case), dysentery will still probably linger in the prison as long as any remain there who have not suffered it; and then, due to the place, to the season, or to the moral and physical condition of people so confined, it may be still capable of renewing the same disease, or of creating another form of epidemic.[36]

Specifically questioned by the select committeemen whether the
disease was contagious or not, both Roget and Latham said, without reservations, that while they were sure that neither scurvy
nor dysentery was contagious, they had grounds to believe that
the unidentified "influence" at large in the prison had made the
disease contagious. They said that their study of the hospital records had convinced them that diarrhea had prevailed in the
penitentiary from its inception:

> Contagion is a very obscure thing; and, so, too, is the noxious in-
> fluence of situation. They are not only obscure in themselves,
> but perpetually obscure the operation of each other in the pro-
> duction of disease. We can never be sure of the operation of
> contagion except under circumstances which exclude the oper-
> ation of local influence. Thus it may take ages to settle the
> question of contagion respecting a particular disease because it
> may not be found under circumstances in which local inju-
> rious influence is unquestionably excluded. It is a subject of
> much controversy, at the present day, whether the yellow fever
> be contagious or not—and for the reasons to which I allude.
>   If I am asked, what would go to the full proof of contagion
> in the disease of the Penitentiary, I should say nothing less
> than this: that various prisoners, under the actual symptoms of
> the disorder, having been set at liberty, various people with
> whom they had intercourse in the several situations to which
> they resorted, had been seized with symptoms precisely the
> same.[37]

Why, then, with this growing conviction of the contagiousness
of the Milbank penitentiary disease, Roget and Latham insisted
on dispersing their patients among uninfected populations is a
question that can only be answered by a study of the remarkably
primitive state of medical knowledge of the day. It is also extremely curious that Roget apparently made no connection between the contagiousness of the disease and his work with Ferriar
back in 1804 in combating the typhoid fever that infested
Manchester.

Three short years later, Roget (and medical science) was to be
tried again as the threat of Asiatic cholera loomed ominously
over England and Europe. Again, his services were to be called
upon by King and country, and in an official investigation,
he was to uncover shocking conditions and suggest the means of
saving thousands of lives—still without any real knowledge of
the agents of infection.

XI [1824–1833

Marriage

WHILE Roget doggedly worked his way out of the depths into which his uncle's death had plunged him in 1818, Catherine, then sixty-three, never recovered from the shocking suicide. She locked herself away from everyone except Roget and Annette for the better part of a year. Her behavior became more and more unpredictable, more and more extreme. She began suspecting the servants of conspiring against her; she had sudden losses of memory during which large chunks of her past seemed never to have happened. Such periods would be interrupted by moments of painful self-consciousness, when she would alternate between extremes of garrulous self-pity and long silences, which seemed almost like vigils, as though she were mutely struggling to regain control.

Roget and Annette relieved each other through long nights and longer afternoons, sitting with their mother, or walking with her about Bloomsbury or Russell Square. On various pretexts, Roget would have his medical friends drop by, but none of them could offer any real aid. Occasionally Catherine would eye them narrowly and refuse to talk with them, as though they, like the servants, were plotting to do her or her family harm. On one or two occasions, Catherine left the house and simply wandered, and this alarmed her son and daughter so much that they knew that a different living arrangement would have to be devised.

In the late spring of 1820, Annette took Catherine off, ostensibly for their usual summer peregrinations about the watering places of Hampshire, Somerset, Dorset, and Devon. They settled, despite Annette's trepidations, in Ilfracombe, and it is from there that all remaining letters from Annette were mailed. There are

only a handful of these in the surviving family papers, but they
are more than adequate to describe a steady disintegration of
Catherine's mental health, and a steadily deepening gloom and
bitterness in Annette's outlook. In 1820, Annette was only thirty-
seven, but her letters sound like those of a lonely, frustrated, em-
bittered woman of at least twice that age. She suspected—and it
is hard to avoid acknowledging her correct assessment of the situation—that she had been victimized: that a poor, a thin, an utterly unpromising life had been palmed off on her. Where, she
wondered, was the gay promise of thirteen or fourteen years ago,
when her chief problem was the sorting out of beaux at Ilfracombe balls? What was the use of the hours spent in music, in
drawing, in other polite studies? Of what value was all her successful brother's pious advice to welcome adversity and disappointment as salutary lessons, if *this* was all she was to be
taught—how to be keeper of a complaining and increasingly un-
balanced old woman?

The last surviving letter written by Catherine (1820) exhibits
her characteristically firm hand and inexact French, but it is uncommonly short. Without a good deal of background explanation, it would not make much sense. She had worked herself into
a painful state of anxiety over reports that John Whishaw, Romilly's close friend and executor of his literary estate, was about to
publish Romilly's journals. What bothered her—and I have yet
to determine why—was that the journal would reveal the date
when Romilly traveled to Lausanne (1783) to bring the four-
year-old Peter to his mother. Catherine wrote that she had
begged Whishaw not to publish the date, and that she was grief-
stricken "that they should not respect my wishes." Abruptly, in
the next sentence, she veered off into another area—her brother's
will, a subject on which she had apparently been brooding, although this was the first mention of it in her letters: "What do
you say if *they* say that he had the generosity to give £100 a year
to his sister [during her life before his death], but when he dies
he leaves me such a small legacy." She continued:

Everyone's already noticed the different way he has treated his
    sister in contrast to his brother. One is living in luxury and
    the other (his sister) with frugality and will always live in fear
    that her expenses exceed her expenditures.[1]

On the same day, Annette wrote to her brother, and she too
beseeched Roget to do something about the forthcoming publication.

I cannot express the grief and worry which your letter gives me regarding Mr. Whishaw. I cannot conceive that a man has the right to speak of living persons in any publication if these people object to being mentioned; it is well known that one cannot do this with honor. If Mr. W. knows that my mother dislikes anyone knowing the date of her return to England, and that she objects being *brought before the public,* and finally, if one tells Mr. Whishaw that it is offensive for everyone to know precisely when and where one was born, it seems to me that he can very easily suppress any mention of *us.* If that cannot be done, I declare that this will make me withdraw from *all society.* . . . I certainly would not wish to attend any parties—I would be recognized as an old woman, and I do not wish to be made fun of for dancing when I have given it up, and for being gay like a young girl. Already, I am so sorrowed that I will no longer go to balls and entertainments here, and I will accustom myself from this moment on to the sad life I must lead when that *wretched life* is published. . . . I had begun to set up house here believing that all will go better, but this is ended, and I repeat: I will certainly withdraw from all society if you are not able to succeed with Mr. Whishaw.[2]

It is difficult to tell which of the two ladies was the more distracted, except that Annette's syntax was better and the whole organization of her letter more sensible.

Roget answered Annette's letter promptly—or at least wrote a rough draft of such a letter—urging her to calm herself and her mother. None too gently, he pointed out that they were alarming themselves over a subject that wasn't worth the trouble.

I firmly believe that Mr. Whishaw will never publish anything regarding my uncle. He has abandoned the thing for the present, and I am persuaded that he is too indolent and too indecisive, and that he has too many other things to occupy himself with to allow him to revise the work for a great many years. Nevertheless, since you attach such importance to the affair, the moment I received your letter, I went to see him. . . . He assured me that he wanted very much to oblige you and that he would think about this when he resumes the work, but that he is going away for the summer and consequently he has put it aside for the present. It is quite clear to me that there is no danger that he will publish at all. I confess that that gives me quite a bit of distress for I am sure that the publication of the memoirs of my uncle and particularly of his letters to my father would have benefited us all infinitely in the eyes of the world.[3]

Roget went on to castigate the opposition of his uncle Thomas
to the publication, charging that Thomas Romilly "insisted on
sacrificing to personal motive and to a despicable sentiment (false
pride) the public interest and the interest of humanity."

> I am sure that you as well as my mother and my self would have
> very much profited from knowing what kind of a man our
> father was and how much my uncle esteemed him. . . . You
> can rest assured, meanwhile, that I will not lose sight of your
> desires on this subject if ever it becomes a question of publica-
> tion. I should not conceal from you that I find these desires
> completely unreasonable, and that the circumstance of the
> dates being made known will never be of the least disadvan-
> tage to you.

Romilly's autobiography, of course, was not brought out until
1840 and then not by Whishaw, but by Romilly's sons. The critical dates, however, were included.

A year after the Whishaw incident, still living in Ilfracombe in
rented rooms, her mother becoming more and more difficult to
control, Annette wrote a long, dismal, complaining letter, one
that sounds remarkably like many of those of her mother during
Roget's Manchester days. Her health was poor, everything (including the water) was too dear, the food was terrible, the social
life unbearably gay (since she felt she could no longer be part of
it), the days were oppressively hot.

> But it isn't of the present that I suffer. If only the future could
> present anything agreeable to me, but since there is nothing
> ahead but misery, I often hope that the sore foot I have would
> be fatal. The picture that I have in front of me—to live al-
> ways, for the rest of my miserable life, in furnished apartments
> in this place worries me so much that I lose all appetite and
> all repose. I must necessarily give a great price for an apart-
> ment poorly furnished without a single comfort, and remain in
> the power of our landlord to chase us out when it pleases him.
> . . . The greatest misfortune of my life has been that of living
> at London, where I wasted my health and accustomed myself
> to luxuries that I was to lose. I cannot accustom myself to the
> common black bread, the stinking butter, and the horrible
> beer here, and my stomach has become so delicate that I exist
> almost entirely on plum pudding and potatoes. Can't you send
> me, with the liniment and the medicine, a pot of prepared an-
> choves for sandwiches? [4]

Perhaps her most bitter remark was one following her expressing
a wild hope that a family friend, who had promised a gift of

HOBSON FAMILY GENEALOGY
(compiled by John Romilly Roget)

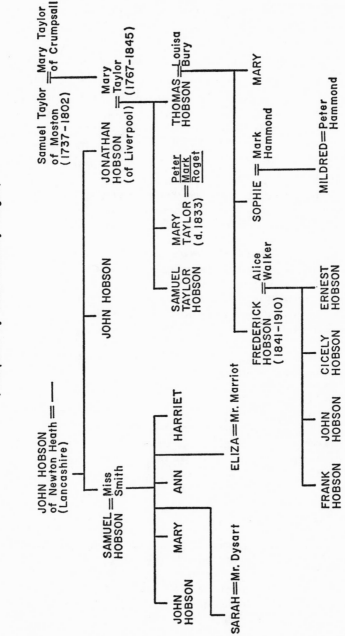

£1,000 on Annette's wedding day, would give her the money any-
how: "It is agreeable to be punished in this manner for remaining a virgin!"

In 1822, Catherine's condition worsened, and Annette nearly
lost her own mind trying to soothe her mother's imaginary fears
and control her erratic behavior. They tried returning to Bernard Street, but that did not work out, and Annette took her
mother back to Ilfracombe. Apparently any sort of travel excited
the old lady to the point where she lost any sense of time or
place. Annette depended heavily upon a maid, Elizabeth:

> Without her, I don't know how I could manage in the inns
> where we sleep. It is then that my mother is absolutely unman-
> ageable, for it is then that she runs upstairs and looks in the
> bedrooms to see if she has left anything in the drawers. It is in
> vain that I tell her that we only entered the place for a few
> moments. As I have already said, she doesn't want to trust me
> for anything, and I always fear that she is going to burst out in
> front of everyone with the extraordinary ideas that have come
> into her head. I have never been able to make her understand
> that we have left London and are traveling to Ilfracombe. For
> several mornings after our arrival, she was packing her things
> to travel again, and what is more remarkable, at the end of
> two days only, she thought we had already dwelt in Ilfracombe
> for several months.[5]

Annette and Roget corresponded frequently about their
mother but apparently could not agree or, at least, they could
not adhere to any single plan.

Dumont, who continued to write regularly from France or Geneva, was not much help. He frequently expressed his sympathy
for Catherine and agreed that Ilfracombe was the best place for
her. But his idealization of Annette's acceptance of her plight
shows how far removed he was from the reality. To Roget, he
writes:

> Your sister rediscovers acquaintances which will compensate in
> part, and the sentiment of duty will succeed in consoling her
> of the sacrifice which she makes in separating from you. She
> has a noble character. She has never said a word of all she was
> experiencing in her trouble and privations. She seemed not
> even to think of these things.[6]

The long years droned by for Annette. She couldn't tell which
were worse—the gay and frivolous summers at Ilfracombe, where
a whole new generation danced, sang, and got up tea parties in

the country—or the cold and silent winters, when the few permanent residents of the town yawned and shivered their way
through to the next season. Their only diversion during the winter was card parties, and Annette had sworn off those. There
were a few scenes with landlords and consequently a few removals. Annette wrote that they simply had to have a place which
could provide at least one locked door between Catherine's room
and the street door, for once or twice Catherine slipped away
and trailed off across the town, hatless and gloveless, her long
skirts dragging in the mud of the streets.

A lengthy Christmas letter from Annette in 1827 presented to
Roget another detailed plea that he help her build a small house
of their own in Ilfracombe. She opposed the idea of an asylum,
and here Annette revealed an uncommonly precise awareness of
her situation:

> You say that I would thus have more liberty, but I do not under-
> stand you. Tell me clearly what kind of life I ought in that
> case to lead, and if this liberty, of which you speak, means any
> more than to live in furnished apartments in one place and an-
> other. . . . The only liberty that I desire is simply that of
> being able to calm my mind with peaceful studies, some agree-
> able daily occupations joined certainly to some household
> duties.[7]

Roget himself was bewildered. He knew his sister too well to
be completely convinced by her complaints. Besides, her next letter would, more likely than not, express a more contented mood.
A particularly desperate letter would often be followed by one in
which she said that life in Ilfracombe, after all, was really quite
pleasant, that she had her oldest friends there, etc. Moreover, he
was too fond of her to let her accept the bleak life she outlined.
He was more and more convinced that the only answer was to
put Catherine in a good rest home, but every time he alluded to
this Annette grew more and more distracted.

The last surviving letter directly dealing with Catherine (January 6, 1832) is a reply to an inquiry from Roget by Dr. Alexander R. Sutherland, physician to St. Luke's Hospital. Roget had
apparently written Sutherland for information on how to get
Catherine committed to a private asylum. Sutherland explained
the procedure. Roget and Annette had discussed this possibility
in earlier letters, but apparently nothing came of the plan. Annette continued serving as her mother's keeper—mainly in Ilfracombe, where, indeed, Roget finally did buy them a small house

—until 1835. There, on August 6, at the age of eighty, with her now famous son jolting toward Ilfracombe as fast as a coach could carry him, the old lady died.

Thus Catherine Roget, aggressive, intelligent, ambitious, who had driven herself and her son so hard through those early years, who had wanted so little for herself yet had needed so much, bereft of husband, brother, and for all practical purposes, son, was no more. Her daughter lived on in Ilfracombe for another thirty years, dying, as her mother had before her, after a long and unhappy exile. Mother and daughter lie buried in the churchyard at Ilfracombe.

Throughout the last ten or fifteen years of her life, Catherine's illness had caused her simply to blank out whole sections of her past and much of the time to be quite unaware of the present. Her relations with the Romillys, for example, had never been cordial—she had, as early as 1800, suspected that the London family had tried to win her son away from her and that, since her brother's death, they had abandoned her—so in her illness, they simply ceased to exist. Another event that Catherine never recognized despite her family's attempts to explain, and which, coming on top of the shock of her brother's suicide, might well have accelerated her mental deterioration, occurred on November 18, 1824. On that day, in the parish church of St. Philip, Liverpool, Peter Mark Roget, forty-five, was wedded to Mary Taylor Hobson, twenty-nine.[8]

While little is known of Roget's courtship of Mary Hobson, there are many references in Roget's letters and in letters from his friends through the four or five years preceding the marriage to the fact that he had many connections in Liverpool. Some of these had grown out of his continued friendship with the Philips family and the infirmary personnel in Manchester, just thirty-four miles away, and others had developed over the years from Roget's own trips to Liverpool and through his friendship with men like John Bostock and James Currie, of the Liverpool Infirmary. In fact, the name of John Bostock appears in Mary's letters as early as 1812, when he, apparently an old friend of the family, took Mary and her mother to an exhibition in town.

In all probability, Roget was fairly well known in Liverpool and enjoyed access to the better society of that city, including the home of the wealthy cotton merchant Jonathan Hobson, No. 1 Nile Street, at the corner of Great George Place. A congratulatory letter from Dumont, shortly after the marriage, reveals that

Dumont had known the Hobsons in Liverpool, a fact that strengthens the supposition that Roget was fairly well known in the northern city. Dumont had no difficulty, he said, in remembering Mary: "No idea of your plans occurred to me then, but I noticed in your young friend an ease and a grace which are not very common, even in the most likeable persons of her age." [9]

Deprived though we may be of actual accounts of their courtship, we are fairly generously provided for with respect to Mary's personality and their married years together. Approximately thirty-five letters, mostly between Mary and her brothers, plus a charming journal that she kept from 1826 to 1831, allow a fairly satisfactory view of Mary's developing personality and of the poignantly happy years of the Rogets' marriage.

The letters begin with exchanges between Mary and her twin brother, Samuel—their birthday was April 15, 1795—during their sixteenth year. The letters, many of them in French, are consistently formal and schoolgirlish and self-consciously correct.

I have some reasons to think that I shall go on learning French under the direction of M. Cizos. In that case, you will be my comrade, and you will not only make my work lighter by your company, but you will help me too in my progress by your sweet and pleasant instructions. You musn't fear that I will not pay attention to your counsels. I shall listen to them with pleasure, and I shall thank you for them. Then we shall soon have botany.[10]

The formality never quite breaks down, as it did occasionally in Annette's and Catherine's letters, but Mary over the years takes on much more attractive outlines than those of either of the other two women in Roget's life. Although she turns aside in a girlish way from time to time to sketch for Sam some little domestic vignette—the family scene in the parlor where she is writing, or her mother and herself caught in the midst of "feathering chickens" by a socialite caller, or her other brother Thomas rubbing their father's aching feet—she never really loses her restraint, or, perhaps, a better word for Mary would be poise. She is always secure, simple, satisfied in her role as girl, daughter, sister, and later wife and mother. Her pride, her humor, and her warmth are often apparent. She might well serve as an admirable model of Victorian womanhood (although her short life ended three years before Victoria came to the throne)—sensitive, perceptive, idealistic, warm and affectionate under a very definite, self-imposed restraint, and secure in her world. Her family was a

fit subject for a John Galsworthy, and despite the differences that
arose within it, the parents and brothers, the grandparents and
uncles and aunts provided Mary with a consistent and firm
framework.

Mary was the only girl in this close-knit, very comfortably
fixed merchant family. The father, a somewhat irascible patri-
arch, became increasingly bent on making money and expanding
his business, into which he expected his sons to follow him. Although he had some ideas of family closeness—he regularly read
Miss Plumtree's Travels in France to the family at night—the
children were early used to the idea of duty and obedience.
Fanny Taylor Hobson, Mary's mother, seems to have more than
made up with her affectionate warmth for the father's "hasty
temper" and singlemindedness. She saw to it that the children
were not frightened or unduly beaten down by the father, and
they responded with an unbounded love. Fanny was an entirely
practical, housewifely woman, energetic, good-humored, fond of
lavishing her affection on the children yet very careful to school
them in all the proprieties and amenities of the age. Mary, for
example, could not accept an invitation to a dancing and dinner
party in 1812 because her mother felt that no proper girl should
attend such affairs until she was eighteen.

The Hobsons maintained a large, comfortable house within a
fairly circumscribed world of relatives and neighbors. They were
not troubled with aristocratic friends so they had no need to
maintain an establishment beyond their very ample means. Hobson was, of course, part of the same rising class of merchants and
industrialists that generated and accumulated enormous economic power in Manchester and other industrial cities of the
north. It would not have occurred to him that, as he became
richer and his family more comfortable, the lives of thousands of
working people were being blighted by a deepening poverty and
insecurity. Roget would have found the Hobsons very much like
the affluent Philips family in Manchester—well fed and cared
for, affable, kind, mildly interested in the arts and sciences, and
utterly blind to that world of stinking alleys and warrens of the
poor.

In the summers, the Hobsons and the Parkses (Charlotte Parks
and Mary were very close friends), or perhaps the Gates family or
the Reids, would retreat to a seashore resort, such as Crosby, a
few miles north of Liverpool, where they rented adjacent cabins
and carried on the same comfortable, uncomplicated round of
life that they enjoyed on Nile Street.

An excerpt from these early letters of Mary Hobson provides a brief glance into the genteel school for young ladies, where Mary and her close friends studied their languages and arithmetic:

We have finally finished Paley,[11] and I believe we are to have a course of ancient history. Lately we have been reading some of the poets with Mr. Reid—Armstrong's poem on health, which is a very beautiful didactic poem, Aikenside's "Pleasures of the Imagination," Thomson's "Seasons,"—and today we are to have the first book. Our plan is this. We read the poem at home, and when we meet, Mr. Reid examines us with regard to the order of the poem, and comments upon it. Then we each read a certain portion aloud. This was the most formidable to me at first, for my heart beat and the blood ascended into my cheeks so that I could scarcely utter a syllable. What we read is examined and explained and particular passages criticized, and so closes our lecture. I like it very much indeed. It improves the taste, and directs the judgment with regard to poetry, and I am sure I have already much more pleasure in reading the poets than I had formerly.[12]

Mary reported later that she liked history as well and found "composition delightful if more difficult." She complained that arithmetic was boring, that she would prefer algebra. She had covered the "grammatical part" of music, she said, and had gone on to the "rhetorical or composition part" and was composing some small pieces herself.

But for all her protected surroundings—or perhaps because of them—Mary was no prig; she did not hold herself aloof from the household chores on Nile Street nor from the earthy pleasures of the family farm at Tyddyn, near Mold, Flintshire. She wrote that she enjoyed taking her turns with the dairy maids at milking the cows, and in one letter described herself as "up to the elbows in black currants for wine."

Moreover, Mary was not deaf to the rising cries of the working and pauper classes. In one letter she described carefully and sympathetically the unemployed workmen who had been forced into visiting houses in gangs of fifteen or twenty, begging for work or meat or money. She was frightened by the Luddite uprisings of 1812, and her letters suggest that she was at least partially aware of the desperation that motivated the violence. Moreover, she was interested in her twin brother's liberal leanings, which she apparently grew to share.

Mary matured into a thoughtful, idealistic young woman who became more and more important to the running of the Hobson home establishment as her father's and mother's health declined. She kept up her studies, apparently, judging from her letters to her brothers, with as much enthusiasm as she had shown as a girl. In fact, the girlish excitement of beginning a new course of study deepened into a genuine respect for learning that no doubt played a great part in making Roget attractive to her.

Both of her brothers had gone off to America and, while still in the service of the family business, left a vacuum at home that increased Mary's importance there. Tom and Sam wrote chiefly from New Orleans, and although they traveled about the new continent a good deal, their chief duty seemed to be that of cotton buyers for the Liverpool and Manchester spinning mills. Sam's journal, from which he copied generous slices into letters to his sister, entertained her highly but seemed as remote from the "real" world of enlightened Liverpool as Lilliput. She no doubt shared many of these accounts with Roget, who all his life had suppressed a hankering to visit the New World. The closest he came to realizing this desire was acquiring a small collection of books and pamphlets by travelers in the wilds of America.[13]

As quietly as they lived, the Hobsons were not retiring folk, and it seems reasonably certain that old Jonathan Hobson would have insisted on their wedding being done up in proper style. Roget carried his bride off to London immediately, and within a few days she was installed as the mistress of No. 39 Bernard Street, where their arrival was duly noted in the fashionable news of the day.[14]

If Mary had not been aware of Roget's enviable position in London, she soon became so, for their little marble-topped table in the entry way was heaped with congratulatory letters from far and near. Roget's friends at the Royal and other scientific societies, his medical colleagues, and various editors for whom Roget was producing articles for journals and encyclopaedias paid their respects, and it was not long before letters from Europe, Scotland, Ireland, and America were arriving. His old comrade in arms, Lovell Edgeworth, wrote from Ireland, where he was trying to hold the old family estates together, congratulating Roget on the event and incidentally enclosing a banknote (amount not stated), apparently part of the £120 he had borrowed from Roget in Geneva in 1803. Edgeworth's talented sister, Maria, also sent brief but hearty congratulations.

The Romillys, of course, sent complimentary messages and gifts; John writing from Rome, averred: "The proverbial lottery of matrimonial connections can not be one with you. I am certain that the lady chosen by you must be both amiable and sensible." Tom Hobson, still in New Orleans, reported that he first got the news from a friend's newspaper, and that he had been moved to tears by his joy: "Mary, I never knew how much I loved you till now, at least I think not, and from my soul I am thankful that the door is at last opened which shut you out from happiness." [15]

Annette wrote from Ilfracombe:

My dear sister

It is very sweet to me to address you by this title for the first time, and though I have delayed for many days congratulating you on an event which has given to each of us so near and dear a relation, it has not been from want of inclination, but of power alone. In fact, I am so constantly harassed with all my various duties, that epistolary ones, in which I used formerly to take particular pride and pleasure, are necessarily neglected or performed in so hurried and slovenly a manner as to make me fear the loss of all my old friends as correspondents.[16]

Annette went on at length, in rather the same long-nosed tone, to disabuse her new sister of the myth that living in the country was pleasant and easy. Supplies were difficult to get, tradespeople required constant nagging, the weather was bad, the streets mudholes, and so much work had simply to be done by hand. Annette descended into a lugubrious melancholy when she mentioned her mother, of whose condition Mary had apparently already been informed:

I trust I have your sympathy though I cannot have your assistance in my perplexing situation. How often have I wished for a sister who could share with me, and lighten my difficulties, and who could convert a melancholy and fatiguing tête-à-tête into a cheerful fireside! . . . I omit the ceremony of sending my Mother's regards—my Brother knows how impossible it is to impress on her mind the event which has given her a daughter-in-law.

It seems likely that Catherine never admitted the fact of her son's marriage. As late as December 1825, when Annette informed her mother that Roget's wife had given them a baby, Catherine cried out, "Who? Who is she?" and Annette found it futile to explain.

With all the polite excitement over their marriage, Roget found some way of letting his wife know that among other recognitions of his worth was his election that year as a charter member of the Athenaeum Club.[17] Founded in 1824 by Sir Walter Scott and other notables, the Athenaeum was, from its inception, the most highly respected club in town—Panizzi was later to be refused membership. Charles Dickens won admittance, in 1836, and his biographer comments that this was the high point, the seal of an almost official recognition of Dickens' conquest of London society.[18]

Two weeks after they had settled into the Bernard Street house, Roget took another important step on his upward path. On the evening of December 9, he read to the Royal Society his "Explanation of an Optical Deception in the Appearance of the Spokes of a Wheel Seen Through Vertical Apertures," [19] a paper that was to have far-reaching effects, far beyond Roget's imagination and far beyond his century. Nearly every modern history of the motion picture film has credited Roget's paper with providing the breakthrough that permitted the invention and development of the cinema. Arthur Knight, for example, writes:

> Once Roget enunciated his theory . . . in 1824 . . . the advance toward motion pictures and motion picture projection was rapid and direct. Almost immediately scientists throughout Europe began putting his theory to the test. Their devices may have resembled children's toys—whirling discs, twirling coins, booklets of pictures flipped with the thumb—but they quickly established the basic truth of Roget's contention that through some peculiarity of the eye an image is retained for a fraction of a second longer than it actually appears. On this peculiarity rests the fortune of the entire motion-picture industry.[20]

One hundred years later, newspaper and magazine writers delighted in celebrating the centennial of Roget's contribution to that exciting new medium, the movies. Among these notices were substantial articles in *The Photographic Journal* (December 1924), *Cinema* (December 11, 1924), *The Times of India* (November 18, 1924), *Bioscope* (December 11, 1924), and *The Film Renter and Moving Pictures News* (December 13, 1924). Similar accounts appeared in *The Illustrated London News* (August 19, 1922), *The Times* (London) (March 19, 1929), and *American Review of Reviews* (January 1925). Wilfred E. L. Day, author of the article in *The Photographic Journal,* concludes his account:

There can be no shadow of doubt that the publishing of this remarkable paper by Dr. Peter Mark Roget started a new train
of thought amongst many of the great scientists of the period,
and the fact that he later received the acknowledgements of
Dr. Faraday [21] in London, Dr. Plateau [22] of Ghent, and Dr.
Stampfer [23] of Vienna, proved that his writings were very
widely read, and but for his data, so clearly given, and his
lucid explanation of the phenomena, the invention of the
phenakistoscope by Dr. Plateau of Ghent and an exactly similar instrument, the stroboscope, by Dr. Stampfer, would never
have transpired. Through following the methods laid down by
Dr. Roget it was a fairly simple matter for them to produce
the two instruments already named, which were the first to
show to an astonished world both the human and other figures
in motion. . . . So much did these two early inventors of mov-
ing-picture apparatus think of Dr. Roget that both of them,
through Quételet [24] in his writings on the Continent, acknowledge these writings in the *Philosophical Transactions* as
being the source which gave them all the necessary data to
achieve their object, and the writer has in his possession several books autographed by Dr. Plateau and presented to his esteemed friend Dr. Peter Mark Roget. It is interesting to note
the wonderful achievements of this great scientific genius. . . .

Roget's paper is a straightforward description of the strange effects he had noted in staring through a venetian blind at a moving carriage wheel. Standing in the basement kitchen and looking
upward through the areaway at traffic on Bernard Street, he
found that the slats of the blinds acted like the frames of a modern motion picture film, breaking up the motion into a series of
still pictures. Moreover, the spokes of the wheels seemed to be
curved instead of straight, depending upon the velocity of the
carriage and the position of his eyes in relation to the slats of the
blinds. He stood there, moving his head up and down, with the
edges of the slats acting like shutters, and became so interested
he forgot about Mary waiting breakfast on him upstairs. With
customary thoroughness, he pursued the phenomenon, gave a
vendor a shilling to move his cart backward and forward in the
street in front of the window. He sketched furiously, later translating these rough drawings into precisely executed plates that
were to accompany his paper. He retired to his study and worked
out mathematical as well as optical explanations for the distor-
tions he had observed. Finally, he reduced his notes in his usual
methodical way to a brief but explicit paper, which began:

A curious optical deception takes place when a carriage wheel, rolling along the ground, is viewed through the intervals of a series of vertical bars, such as those of a palisade or of a Venetian window-blind. Under these circumstances the spokes of the wheel, instead of appearing straight, as they would naturally do if no bars intervened, seem to have a considerable degree of curvature. The distinctness of this appearance is influenced by several circumstances presently to be noticed; but when everything concurs to favour it, the illusion is irresistible, and from the difficulty of detecting the real cause, is exceedingly striking.

Recalling his earlier experiments with the kaleidoscope and after trying another series of experiments—looking at the same wheel through various sets of *vertical* bars—Roget made the all-important observation:

The true principle, then, on which this phenomenon depends is the same as that to which is referable the illusion that occurs when a bright object is wheeled rapidly round in a circle, giving rise to the appearance of a line of light throughout the whole circumference; namely, that an impression made by a pencil of rays on the retina, if sufficiently vivid, will remain for a certain time after the cause has ceased.

It was this statement of the persistence of vision, connected with a simple means of demonstrating it, that led Faraday and the others to create their wheel and disc mechanisms to produce the illusion of motion.

But when Roget returned from that December evening meeting of the Royal Society at the old Somerset House on the Strand, he of course had no idea that his modest observations had initiated a train of events that would lead to what Marshall McLuhan and others have recognized as another dimension for human existence.

Thus Roget and Mary settled into their married life—with the best wishes of dozens of friends and relatives, with Roget's star rising brightly in the Royal Society, with their neighborhood rapidly becoming considered a part of the distinguished and fashionable sections of Russell and Brunswick squares. Dozens of impressive new structures were just recently or about to be erected: Sir John Soane's additions to the Bank of England; the new Court of Chancery at Westminster; John Nash's dramatic Regent Street and Park Crescent; the imposing Pimlico arch and screen structures by Decimus Burton at Hyde Park Corner; the new British

Museum; the new Covent Garden market; the Burlington Arcade; the great clubs—Travellers', United Service, University, Union, Oriental, Athenaeum; Lancaster House; Waterloo and Southwark bridges; London University (now University College), about a five-minute walk from Bernard Street; the London Institution, in Finsbury Circus, where Roget was to lecture so successfully a few years later; and dozens of new churches, including that attended by the Rogets—St. Pancras, put up by W. and H. W. Inwood in 1819–1822, at the corner of New Road (now Euston Road) and Woburn Place. A major effort was being made to clean up open areas like St. James's Park, which well into the century were dangerous places to walk at night. The unenclosed ground about the canal was railed in; shrubberies were planted; light standards were erected; and soon respectable folk were passing the word, "There is gas in the Park!"—a convincing sign of progress and uplift. The Royal College of Physicians was about to move to its new building in Pall Mall East, and just opposite, a short while later, was installed the gallery of the Society of Painters in Water Colours, the history of which the Rogets' yet unborn son was one day to write.[25]

In the process of organization was the energetic Society for the Diffusion of Useful Knowledge, of which Brougham was the chief mover. Roget was a founding member, along with respected men from many fields, including Captain Francis Beaufort, Sir Charles Bell, Dr. John Elliotson, Henry Hallam, Sir J. Cam Hobhouse, J. W. Lubbock, James Mill, John Whishaw, and Lord John Russell. In the spring of 1827, the society began an ever-expanding publication program, issuing treatise after treatise, usually in the form of fortnightly sixpenny numbers, aimed to place in the workingman's hands the best of modern science written in nontechnical language. Of Roget's contributions, the society's publisher, Charles Knight, wrote:

> Amongst the founders of the Society, Dr. Roget was, from his accepted high reputation, the most eminent of its men of science. He wrote its treatises on Electricity and on Magnetism.[26] . . . He was a diligent attendant on its committees; a vigilant corrector of its proofs. Of most winning manners, he was as beloved as he was respected. . . . Upon all questions of Physiology, Peter Mark Roget and Charles Bell are the great authorities in the Useful Knowledge Society.[27]

The next year too—1825—focused still more attention on the hard-working doctor of 39 Bernard Street, who apparently was

not touched by a stock market panic that ruined many Londoners. P. M. Latham published the complete story of the Milbank
epidemic in pamphlet form, an account that was widely read
throughout the city. Roget delivered another series of lectures
at the Royal Institution. In an impressive ceremony, the gover-
nors of the Northern Dispensary presented Dr. and Mrs. Roget
with a beautiful piece of silverplate in appreciation of Roget's
eighteen years of gratuitous service to the charity. Roget was
mentioned on the program of the formal opening of the new
Pall Mall home of the Royal College of Physicians. He published
another interesting paper, a geometrical and philosophical problem, in the *Scientific Gazette*.[28]

On October 27 Mary delivered their first child, a daughter,
Catherine Mary Roget. A few surviving letters between Mary and
her brothers record the happiness brought to the whole family by
the arrival of Kate, as she was to be called the rest of her life. Especially pleased was the crusty old grandfather. Writing to her
brother Sam in New Orleans when Kate was two years old, Mary
was amused to report on one of the Rogets' frequent visits to the
Hobson home in Liverpool:

You know it was our little Kate's first appearance amongst those
who were so well prepared to love her, and we flatter ourselves
she came back with a large share of Lancashire affection.
She is more amusing than when you saw her, and it was touching to see the influence she had unconsciously acquired over
my father. He was, at the beginning of our visit, now and then
as provoking as ever I knew him, but that child led him by the
hand all over the house even when he was tired.[29]

While Roget worked just as hard as ever—in 1826 he brought
out another major work, *Introductory Lecture on Comparative
Physiology,* a book that grew out of his preparations for lectures
at the new Aldersgate medical school—it is obvious that the introduction of Mary and of Kate into his life had a gentling and
easing effect. He became much more inclined to put aside his
work and go off for a weekend jaunt in the country with his little
family, or take longer vacation trips in the north of England, or
write long, gossipy letters to his brothers-in-law in America. Despite the row that was boiling at the Royal Society, Mary even
persuaded Roget to take her on a three-week vacation trip to
Paris. Roget began to fit far more comfortably into the pattern
of life that had been well established for professional and aristo-

cratic classes in London: everyone of any importance lived in London during the Parliamentary session, from February to August; and from then on until after Christmas, London was deserted by the world of politics and fashion. The Rogets were fond of their beach cabin at Crosby, and for several years their appearance there was the occasion for much festivity. A useful letter here is that of Mary's close friend, Charlotte Parks, writing from Crosby to Sam Hobson in New Orleans. Charlotte spoke of the pleasure Mary's mother was receiving from the demonstrative granddaughter—"here she ran to her immediately, kissed her and would not leave her." Charlotte must indeed have been fond of the Rogets, for she even spoke glowingly of lectures given the little vacationing colony by the "dear Doctor," who solemnly discoursed on two evenings on astronomy and on electricity. "He is so very clear in his method of arranging his subjects, and he explains everything so very well that it is quite an intellectual treat to hear him." [30]

In London the Rogets became regular theatergoers, preferring frequently to take inexpensive seats in the relatively unfashionable French theater. One of her letters recounts their pleasure at seeing Molière's *Malade Imaginaire*.

Mary and Roget often took drives together, especially enjoying watching the emergence of Nash's Regent's Park and the elegant stucco villas and terraces surrounding it. They often met friends, sometimes aristocratic and wealthy acquaintances, on these drives, and Mary once admitted sheepishly to some envy for the luxurious carriages and fine clothes.

> I could not help *half*—no, a *quarter!*—enjoying Mrs. Jones-Lloyd who drove past us in her easy carriage reclining at her ease as on a bed, not noticing one humble, and I acknowledge, very shabby equippage. Soon after, we met the rich banker, L. L. himself, on horseback. He was civil and even kind. But I looked at my best of husbands by my side and all my envy vanished.[31]

Mary sometimes accompanied Roget on his rounds in the Bloomsbury and Russell Square neighborhoods, and they often walked in the evening, as they did every Sunday, weather permitting, to services at St. Pancras church in Woburn Place. Mary was a good housekeeper. She managed the place smoothly, was beloved by the servants, and prepared an excellent table (according to the testimony of many friends). She could not fatten up

Roget, however. He remained the same tall, lean, somewhat stooping figure that his mother had been afraid he would be.

To chronicle their life together, Mary kept a daybook in a small paper notebook, with a reddish pasteboard cover. This is, according to the legend at the top of her first page, the "Journal of Mary Roget." Composed hurriedly at the close of each busy day, the journal recorded in the briefest notes the high points of the day: who came to dinner, where the couple drove of an evening, what plays they most enjoyed, why the upstairs window needed replacing, etc.

Mary's hand is not always legible, partly because of her haste in jotting down these entries, and partly because of her fondness for ellipses and abbreviations, whose signification is not always apparent. But for all these limitations, Mary's journal provides invaluable glimpses behind that gleaming door at 39 Bernard Street and often charming views of the good doctor and his wife at home. Unfortunately, she kept this daily record only from April to November 1826. In the following excerpts, I have provided most of the punctuation:

Sunday, [April] 9th [1826]: St. Pancras in the morning. At home the rest of the day after calling upon Mrs. Bostock with Mrs. Reid. Uncle Potts and Eliza called. Read *Emile* [32] to Roget in the library while he examined the constellations on the globe preparing to make a transparent planesphere.

Saturday, 15th: Sam's and my birthday—Kate put into short clothes. Diorama in Regent's Park, walked there with Sam and to Bazaar. Mrs. Reid lent me a rose tree with two full blown flowers for the Birthday. Had it put on the table with Dessert after dinner. Games in the evening.

Sunday, 16th: At home morning—rain. Read the lessons to my husband, he making drawings for his lectures. Walked with Roget to make a few calls. Henry Potter dined on his way to Paris, also Edward Smith. Uncle Potts, Mrs. Charles, Miss Anne and Eliza called.

Tuesday [May] 2: Drove to Hampstead, called upon Miss Aikin and Mrs. Mallet. Sam and R with me. A most beautiful day— delicious. Looked at lodgings which we liked. Made calls on our return. Mr. Sotheby and Milman, E. Gates and Mrs. Austin dined with me, and we went to the opera in the evening— Mdme. Patti in *Romeo*—Candoni[?]—Julietta. Most beautiful! R dined out and did not go with us.

Friday, 26th: R's last lecture at the London Institution—exhibited two drawings we had made together—one a head illustrative of the eyes described by Dr. Wollaston; the other a convex and concave object in drawing made to descend upon the side the light comes from. Great applause and very gratifying. Discovered that my storeroom had been opened by a second key. Gave my housemaid warning—she suspicious.

Sunday 28th: My dear mother's birthday. Heard Dr. Bloomfield, Bishop of Chester, preach a charity sermon at St. Pancras on the education of poor children—not only taught to read and have the Bible given to them but with it the *right* interpretation of its meaning. Dined at Lordship Lane in the country.

Saturday [June] 3: After translating some Italian from Boccacio [*sic*] made some calls in a carriage with Roget—at home evening.

Sunday 4: Talked much with R and very encouragingly on the better employment of my time.

Sunday 11: Went with R to Walthamstow[?] to see a patient. Called upon Miss Bailley, kindly invited to spend next Sunday with them. The drive was delicious. R promised to teach me mathematics in good earnest—had a first lesson in algebra this evening.

Sunday 18th: Dined at the Bailleys. A pleasant drive in Mrs. B's gig to Epping Forest. Beautiful country. Since last Sunday have had a lesson every day and have arrived at simple equations. R says I am quick and I now try [to find?] time to practice or I shall forget what I have quickly understood.

Saturday [July] 1: Wrote to my sister [-in-law]. Find we can't go to Ilfracombe next week as we intended on account of patients not to be left.

Friday [October] 27th: Dear little Katie's birthday! One year old —quite recovered her illness. Fat and merry—cannot walk or bear her own weight, but put one foot before the other very prettily. Tries to imitate everything she hears, and says "Papa," "Mama," "Ta," "Pitty," "Ba"—has a good memory and is fond of music. Not at all shy, and like most children preferring gentlemen to ladies. Inclined to be passionate but seldom cries and is not fretful. Mrs. Haines who wet-nursed her came to [the first?] tea in the nursery. Each maid servant had a new white cap ribbon. The man a pair of gloves.

There were, of course, clouds that occasionally darkened the Rogets' busy, sunny life. Mary's mother became ill in 1827. Roget raced to Liverpool, examined and treated her, and the old lady (then in her eighties) was able to resume her usual energetic and loving ways. A serious difference arose between Tom and his father, a rift that Mary tried patiently to patch up despite the fact that she did not blind herself to the source of the problem—her father's incurable ambition to become ever richer. In 1827, Roget applied unsuccessfully for a professorship at the new London University.[33] Roget himself fell ill, necessitating an operation in 1829, from which he recovered promptly and plunged with his usual energy back into his several projects.

The most serious threat to their happiness—and the only real one—was Mary's declining health. She was a long time regaining her strength after the birth of Kate, and on at least two occasions between 1825 and 1828, she had to "rest" for several weeks at a time, either at Bernard Street or in the old Hobson home in Liverpool. Following each of these occasions, there were little signs that Mary, though announcing herself completely recovered, was not quite as well as she had been before the illness. Despite this gradual decline, however, she looked forward to delivering her second child, and on April 28, 1828, Roget announced to family and friends the birth of a "fine boy"—christened John Lewis Roget.

With the arrival of John, Mary of course became preoccupied with her two children; and a few months later, on the evening of November 14, 1828, she turned to a fresh page in her journal, abandoned the hurried notes she had daily scribbled, and with a lively flourish, inscribed at the top of the page "Annals of the Nursery." From that page forward, she confined her writing to reports of her observations of the children, and of her and Roget's experiments to inculcate certain attitudes in their young. The manuscript notebook is a poignant, sometimes amusing, always earnest and precise record that exhibits perhaps in the most direct way possible the values by which Roget and his beloved wife attempted to live.[34]

November 14, 1828: I have often wished that I had kept a journal of the progress of my dear babes, both in health and intellect, and a circumstance occurred this morning which determined me to begin. It is so very agreeable to remember the anecdotes connected with our children and the dates attached to them. So very slight often are the early indications of propensities which strengthen by time and become permanent peculiarities of character. Kate Mary was three years old the 27th of last month and without being forward in book acquirements is a very intelligent child and as tractable as one could reasonably expect a child of quick feelings to be.

I was this morning telling her of Ulysses' dog Argus knowing

his master after a long absence and dying at his feet on his return. She said, "Poor dog! It died."

"Yes, for it was very old, and you know when it died, nothing could hurt it any more."

"No," she said, "but I'll tell you something, Mama. When
we die we can't feel, but we can't see either. We lie down—
so—" putting her head against the chair—"and we shut our
eyes and we can't see." Surely this was very intelligent.

Once begun, Mary pursued her subject faithfully, noting, and
usually describing, every bit of behavior that seemed significant.
She recalled, for example, Kate's first conscious experience with
colors, a year before, and her and Roget's subsequent experiments with bits of colored paper cut into circles, squares, tri-
angles, and spirals, the main product of which seemed to be that
Kate could, by two years three months, distinguish and name several colors and shapes. Mary kept close account of teething dates,
first walking dates, the nature and duration of infantile ailments.

Although the Rogets watched every sort of behavior of their
two children, and instructed the maids to report anything of interest to them, they seemed particularly concerned in the children's intellectual development. The Rogets' devotion to self-improvement was an important part of their life together, thus it
must have seemed natural to set Kate, before she was three,
doing lessons every morning with her mother—reading, drawing,
and mathematics. She was regularly quizzed by her father in the
afternoon, and Mary's "Annals" are full of reports on the little
girl's intellectual progress.

In several pages, Mary delightedly reports one or the other of
the children making some association or connection between two
things or events that seemed to her to prophesy an early skill at
finding relationships and analogies:

Two days ago [March 24, 1829] she made the following comparison: "Mama, the arm is like the leg—the hand, the arm, and
the elbow are like the foot, the leg, and the knee. The fingers
are like the toes."

On June 19, 1830, Mary noted that, at four years, Kate was
very imitative, especially of big words, and that she was good at
"deducing clever inferences." At that age, Kate could read *Frank*
(a novel by Maria Edgeworth, 1822) "with a little help for very
long words." But she was not fond of learning by rote and com-

mitting words to memory, "though she remembers the names of things very readily and took very easily to piecing together her map of Europe, which she learned to do last Christmas in three days, with the addition of the names of all the countries except the German states."

In June of 1831, one of the last entries in the "Annals," Mary noted the following as evidence of the liveliness of her young son's mind:

We were telling John the other morning how he could not be in two places at once. "Now for instance, you could not be here and upstairs in the nursery at the same time." He put on a considering look and said, "But if we brought the nursery downstairs and made this the nursery, then we could be in two places at the same time."

While the Rogets' interest in intellectual development seemed paramount, the anecdotes pertaining to emotional and temperamental growth are probably more significant, both for what they record of parents and children and for how they point up their mutual problems in socialization. The favored values of the age, for example, are made plain by Mary's notes on their delight in observing in the children evidence that they were generous, affectionate, honest, obedient, polite, pious, and industrious. Several virtues in the diadem of nineteenth-century British morality are highlighted in this final excerpt. The most revealing single passage of the "Annals," this incident shows better than any other the complex structure of values that Englishmen of the period attempted to impose upon their lives. Happily, the anecdote also reveals, in the interstices of this same rigid construct, a somewhat redeeming awareness of human doubt, tenderness, and hope.

A fortnight ago [written on January 18, 1829] I had a struggle with dear little Kate which I think so characteristic that I am anxious to remember every particular. I think they may in future days afford us interesting matter of speculation.

One morning she came to me in perfect good humor to say her lesson. She was playful, and after having read "go up," the next words were "go in," and she did not choose to read "go" —first from playfulness and afterward from determined opposition. She was to have some apple and comfits if she said a good lesson, and after trying to persuade her to read "go," I told her that she could not have them unless she told me what the word was. She seemed so determined not to tell me for she said, "I can tell it, but I wont," that I felt the importance of taking the opportunity to establish my authority. So I told her if she did not say it, I must put her out of the room and shut the door, which after waiting a while and trying persuasion again, I did—very gently—at which she cried, but in a very short time went upstairs and played very cheerfully in the nursery.

In about two hours she came down again, telling me she was come to say her lesson and that Davis [the nurse] had sent her. "I am very glad of it, love," I said, and kissed her.

On opening the book, however, the sight of the words seemed to bring back the spirit of opposition, and she again refused but with more temper than before. She said, "I *will* go down and I *will* go again to Davis."

I held her firmly but gently on my knee, at which she kicked and screamed, saying she *wanted* and *would* have Davis. She became so violent that I really was a little alarmed and agitated myself, so that I could not conceal my own tears, but I could not yield and walked with her in my arms up and down the room which helped to pacify her.

While I was doing so, she said, "Mama, the room turns round," which at first I thought might be caused by a confusion of her head, but I think it was only that she observed for the first time apparent motion of the wall where we move ourselves. But I rang the bell for the nurse and asked her to bring some cold water. "What for, Mama?"

"That you may drink a little. It will perhaps do you good." She drank a little and was calmer. I then said, "Now, Kate, you may go upstairs with Davis. Perhaps she can make you good."

She was not to come down till she had said her lesson, and I sent her dinner into the nursery instead of dining with me below, which she told Davis she liked. I presently went up to know if she would say her lesson, but she always said, "No."

"When will you say it?"

"Tomorrow morning."

The first thing in the morning I went up as usual. I asked her again, but again she said, "No." I came down to breakfast without her.

Roget and I consulted what had best be done, and he went up after breakfast to persuade her by saying that if Eliza Bostock came to see her, she must not come down.

"Is she coming?"

"I don't know that she is, but she often calls on Sunday."

"Well, I'll come down and say my lesson."

"No, you can't come down till you have said it. You remember you did not say it yesterday when you said you would. I will go and ask your Mama if she will come up and hear you."

I went up and after some difficulties, such as, "But what shall I do with my doll?" she sat on my knee to say it. I opened the book, but *again* the rebellious spirit rose up. She said "go" was *"rat,"* and then she said, "it is not *nog* nor is it *note.*"

"No, Kate, you know what it is." For she even read the word in every place in the page but *the one.* "Why can't you tell me?"

"Because I won't!"

"Now, Kate, you *shall,* or I shall whip you with a rod and it will hurt you badly. But I hope you will tell me for I should like to be able to say that my little Kate was never whipped." She twisted about as if she did not like the anticipation herself. But it was some time before the spirit would yield, and after repeated encouragings and quiet but determined threats, both from myself and from the nurse who was washing little John and who was to find a rod when he was dressed, at least she very calmly read, "go in," which I made her repeat three times.

When I said, "Now you have done it, and you may go down with me," she was very happy and exultingly told everybody she met that she had said her lesson—"go in and go up and go in again." I was struck with her good humour that accompanied her determined resistance and her delight on having at last done the deed we had encouraged all we could. The result is that of the most cheerful obedience and a very evident increase of affection toward me in her manner.

This morning she was playing at being poorly and asked Papa to feel her pulse and look at her tongue.

"Ah, how white it is," he said, "and how blue and red and pink and all manner of colors."

She said, "Then you must have seen it through a prism, Papa."

So grew the young Rogets, and so flourished the family of Dr. Peter Mark Roget.

But this happy, domestic, earnest life of Roget—he who could enjoy giving his wife algebra lessons, who could walk with her in peace and pleasure all about the thriving city, who could, of a sunny morning, jokingly find all the colors of the rainbow in his daughter's tongue—was due for a savage blow that should have destroyed him entirely. Happiness came late to Roget, and to survive the senseless ripping away of that happiness seemed more than should be asked of any man. Moreover he knew it was coming.

Mary's health fluctuated strangely after John's birth. She seemed to surge back to strength after every bout with an insistent, unidentified malady that two or three times in 1830 and 1831 gave her great pain and incapacitated her. Each time, of course, much was made of her recovery, but Roget the physician knew better.

Finally, after a particularly painful siege, Roget's fears broke through his reserve, and he wrote frankly to Mary's brother Sam:

The real truth . . . is that Mary is considerably worse than when you left us. The tumor continues to enlarge and what is still more distressing, is giving her a constant feeling of uneasiness and often of pain. She walks with greater difficulty, and is now quite unable to bear the shaking of a carriage. No perceptible check has been given to the growth of the tumor by the iodine, which, indeed, we were at length obliged to discontinue as it was sensibly impairing her strength. We have now resumed it, but I confess with very little expectation on my part of its doing her any good. It is impossible not to foresee that if this source of irritation is to continue, the constitution must eventually sink under it. Of late, her spirits have flagged much, however cheerful a tone she may have assumed in her letters. I need not tell you, for you may well imagine it, what continued anguish I am suffering, and what efforts it costs me to hide my sufferings from her. The future is to me all mist and darkness through which I cannot yet see my way. My poor children, too —what will become of them! I know it is my duty to be patient and to submit, but the task is hard. I trust I may have sufficient fortitude to go through with it. I know not why I should thus harass you with my own melancholy forebodings and tax your sympathy so severely, except that it is really a great relief to me to give them utterance to one who I know will share them with me, and in whose brotherly affection I can so fully confide. Mary does not know I am writing to you.[35]

In September, Roget wanted to take Mary to their favorite seaside cottage at Crosby, but she couldn't stand the travel. Instead, he hired the best carriage he could find and drove her slowly and carefully to a cottage on the Hampstead Heath, hoping that an escape from the broiling city would help her. Writing to her brother from Hampstead, Mary reported that everyone *thought* she was improving, but she herself wasn't so sure. True, she felt less pain, but she put that down to Roget's halting the application of iodine and other medicines he had tried.

The important question is has there been a reduction of the slight inflammation existing. *We don't know*. The local evil has not diminished, but we think it has not latterly increased —you who know the state I was in when I came here will understand this account.[36]

Sick as she was, Mary did not dwell on her condition nor on that of her father who had been enfeebled and ill for some time. Instead, she regaled her brother Sam with the pranks of the children—rooting up the gravel walks at the place, and John spitting at the cook. "I am told that is certain evidence of his manliness, for all boys have a spitting age. But I place more reliance on his manliness in his telling me the other day he knew how to fight: he doubled his fists and really made no bad attempt. He said he had seen two boys fighting, and that was the way!" [37]

Full of warmth and eagerness to the last, Mary Roget struggled through the winter and saw the first blossoms of the spring of 1833 before she succumbed to the cancer that none of Roget's increasingly desperate measures could check. Her illness prevented her attending her father's lingering death in Liverpool. He expired early in March,[38] and his daughter followed him within the month. Mary Roget died on April 12, aged thirty-eight.[39]

After the funeral, Roget collapsed. Friends and Mary's brothers rallied round and took him home to Liverpool, where he was nursed worriedly and lovingly by the twice-stricken Fanny Hobson. His recovery was agonizingly slow; indeed he seemed to feel little desire to live. What apparently brought him out of this depth was his concern for his children, who were being cared for by the Hobsons, of course, but more particularly by a Miss Catlow, whom Roget had retained as a nurse-governess.

By September he was well enough to take the children on a visit to his sister and mother in Ilfracombe. Back in London in the early fall, Roget stepped fearfully into a house that was deathly empty and, for him, at least, was to remain so for the rest of his life. As his friends had told him, the presence of the children helped, but it hurt as well, for at the most unexpected moments a glance at one of them would remind him of his wife's beloved face. "Their unconsciousness and innocent playfuness," wrote Mary's close friend Elizabeth Reid, "is the first thing that a sorrow-stricken heart can learn to enjoy again." He was to take consolation, she added, "from reflecting that you can never again, while life lasts, suffer so severely again."

But Elizabeth Reid was wrong. In going through Mary's desk in the library at 39 Bernard Street, Roget found something which brought him to his knees. It was an undated letter (probably written shortly before the birth of Kate), sealed, addressed in Mary's familiar hand to Roget, and marked, "to be read after my death":

You have promised, my beloved husband, that none but you shall open my desk if it be ordained that I do not survive the approaching hour of trial. These few lines then will be seen by you alone. They are to repeat to you, my precious, how dearly I love you, and to thank you for the sweet tenderness and kindness which have made the last year of my life so *very very* happy. Do not, love, think of me in sorrow for God will let us be happy again where we need not fear to be separated any more. If I leave you a sweet infant, it will comfort you and you will cherish it for my sake. But more than all, you will be comforted by that firm confidence in the goodness and Mercy of our Heavenly Parent, which we have so often talked of together as the dearest hold of our consoling religion. Our God is a God of Love, and with Him every thing is good—all He does is kind. I pray Him to lead you on to Comfort and Happiness. Think of the many hours of exquisite bliss we have enjoyed together, and oh, my dear husband, remember how dearly I do love you, and let these thoughts be without bitterness, for when you follow me, pain and sorrow will be no more. And God will keep you and bless you till he wills that we may meet again.

My ever precious friend, my darling husband,

your Mary Roget

Comfort my mother.

XII [1827-1830

Royal Society Row,
Water Commission

THREE years after Roget began his long, stormy reign as Secretary of the Royal Society in 1827, he became the target of an attack by Charles Babbage and others, which, however unsuccessful at the moment, proved to be the entering wedge of a movement to reform the entire society. Eventually (1848), not only was Roget unseated, but this rising undercurrent finally and permanently lifted the society to that condition toward which it had labored for two centuries. When the dust had settled after twenty years of protests, exposés, pamphleteering skirmishes, secret sessions by both sides, and a good deal of rather vicious infighting, the Royal Society emerged as a genuine scientific body and left behind those practices and deficiencies which had so long made it vulnerable to charges of dilettantism, private interest, nepotism, and snobbery.

For various reasons, some of them personal, Roget had by 1830 transferred that devoted industry he had formerly expended for the Medical and Chirurgical Society to the fortunes of the Royal Society. He had not given up the medical group—in fact, he was President of that society in 1829 and 1830—but the fact that he was spending more and more of his days and evenings with the Royal Society is made obvious by his record of attendance at meetings, his work with RS publications, and his service on RS committees.

This transfer of his attentions might well have been due, in part, to a series of losses Roget had recently sustained. On June

11, 1828, Dugald Stewart, who had been ailing for many years, died, an event which affected Roget strongly since it was Stewart who had been his real mainstay through those long years at Edinburgh, and who had befriended him so often since. On December 22 of the same year, William Hyde Wollaston died. Wollaston, too, had materially assisted Roget in becoming established in London (it was Wollaston who prevailed on the Royal Society to hear Roget's paper on the logarithmic device in 1814). His death may have suggested to Roget the beginning of the end of an era. In many ways, Wollaston, an old crony of Sir Joseph Banks, was one of the last of the old-style scientists, or "philosophers," as they preferred to call themselves. A product of eighteenth-century rationalism, Wollaston's curiosity about nature ranged through many fields, leading him to make a variety of important contributions. "Variety" is the significant word here, for, in common with others of his kind, and in conformity with a long tradition, Wollaston refused the temptation of specialization. Best remembered as a chemist, Wollaston also did important work in galvanism and electricity, and published papers on crystallography, physiology, optics, and mechanics.[1] He even devised a slide rule for chemists. Not only were all of these activities of immediate interest to Roget, but the variety of them suggests the philosophical hope of investigators of the old school: that if they kept advancing on *many* fronts, an understanding of a *unified* universe would eventually be theirs. It was this kind of savant that Roget aspired to be, and thus the loss of one such as Wollaston might well have suggested that he (Roget) was pursuing a state of excellence and accomplishment that a new generation would not recognize.

A third blow, and an even more severe one psychologically, was the death of Etienne Dumont in 1829. With Dumont gone, the last of those upon whom he had most depended through his childhood and young manhood was no more, and again Roget must have suffered a sudden glimpse of the progression of generations. No longer the promising young man, supported by family and kind friends, Roget now began to see himself as a representative of the older generation. He was, after all, in that year of Dumont's death, fifty years old. The younger men—Whewell, Babbage, Faraday, Elliotson, Grant, Bright—were beginning to crowd up around him on all sides.

The death of George IV on June 26, 1830, also signaled the end of an era and prompted Roget to turn even more to that which seemed to resist the changing times, the Royal Society, formed originally in 1660. The larger reform efforts in the kingdom were coming rapidly to a head at this time, and while Roget had always been proud of the part played in these by Romilly and Dumont, his conservative, antirevolutionary leanings made him fearful of any large-scale change. And change was in the making.

When Oxford and Cambridge proved resistant to a liberal revitalizing of their methods and curricula, a new university was founded—the University of London, that "godless institution in Gower Street" (also called "Brougham's Patent Omnibus," from its motto: *Patens Omnibus Scientia*), where, for the first time, a young man could take a degree without having to sign the loyalty oath of the thirty-nine articles of faith in the Established Church of England. Efforts toward changing the penal code, toward eliminating the slave trade, toward controlling the rapacious acts of businessmen and manufacturers, toward extending the voting franchise, toward changing the archaic and corrupt legislative structure of England—all were beginning to be felt as the nation moved, reluctantly, toward the great Reform Bill of 1832.

Thus, Roget had no sooner become ensconced as senior Secretary of the hitherto untouchable Royal Society than the unutterable security of *that* institution was invaded by a rebel band. To make matters worse and defensive action more difficult, the rebels, at least most of them, were Fellows and thus working from within.

The most conspicuous of these was Charles Babbage, surely one of the most brilliant and eccentric minds of the century. Described by a contemporary as *"the* militant man of science," [2] Babbage had recently (1828) become Professor of Mathematics at Cambridge, where he revitalized the interest in and the teaching of his subject. He had also been a prime mover in the founding of the Astronomical Society and, a few years later, the Statistical Society. His work on the calculating engine is justifiably famous; practically every modern account of the computer credits him as the inventor of the first genuine computing machine. Roget had first met him at the Royal Institution, where Babbage had shared the lecture platform with Roget and later competed with Faraday as the institution's star attraction. He was elected a Fellow of the Royal Society in 1816, and the same volume of *Philosophical Transactions* that printed Roget's paper on the slide rule published Babbage's "An Essay Towards the Calculus of Functions." Babbage's wit, his perceptiveness, and his lively curiosity are delightfully evident in his writings—especially his *Passages from the Life of a Philosopher* (London, 1864). In 1832 he was offered, along with such men as Charles Bell, John Herschel, James Ivory, John Leslie, and David Brewster, a knighthood. Suggesting something of his independent spirit, Babbage refused it.

Roget had had further dealings—presumably amicable ones—with Babbage. In 1820, he had worked out an arrangement with Babbage, acting for the Astronomical Society, for that society to share the new quarters of the Medical and Chirurgical Society at 55 Lincoln's Inn Fields.[3] In 1821, at Babbage's request, Roget wrote him a letter of introduction to Professor Pictet in Geneva.[4] And in 1819, Roget generously responded to a request from Babbage, who was preparing to print a pamphlet of testimonials in support of his attempt to get a professorship in mathematics at the University of Edinburgh. Adding to the laudatory remarks of John Playfair, James Ivory, Sir William Herschel, J. F. W. Herschel, John Leslie, William Whewell, John Pond, Davies Gilbert, and others, Roget wrote:

> . . . I beg leave to state my full conviction of his being eminently qualified to fill that office with honor to himself and advantage to the University. My opinion is founded not only on his extensive knowledge in mathematics and the physical sciences, which has been amply attested by the numerous profound and original researches he has already given to the public; but also on the excellence which I know him to possess in the art of public instruction, and which was remarkably evinced when he was lecturer on astronomy at the Royal Institution in London. I cannot therefore hesitate in adding my recommendation of Mr. Babbage in the strongest manner as peculiarly deserving your choice.[5]

In addition, Roget had followed Babbage's work on the calculating machine with active interest in meetings at the Astronomical Society, at the Royal Institution, and at the Royal Society.

Thus Roget was somewhat nonplussed when, in the spring of 1830, Babbage published a book-length attack on the Royal Society, in which he singled out Roget for a particular assault.[6]

Generally, Babbage's *Decline of Science* took not simply the Royal Society to task, but all of England, for failing to develop a consistent and effective means of promoting scientific discovery. Making many comparisons with the scientific scene in Europe, Babbage charged that England was pathetically far behind France, Germany, and even Italy, and that this delinquency was due to a national indifference to science as seen in the reluctance of schools to train scientists, in the refusal of the nation to reward the work of those who made significant discoveries, and in the influence of such antiquities as the Royal Society. To show 1) that the society was under the domination of a stale and inbred and unchanging group of men, and 2) that the society was composed chiefly of men who made no pretense at performing scientific work, Babbage printed studies of the membership of the Council at various periods, and long lists of the membership at large, showing how few of them had ever published a scientific work. Babbage did not hesitate to name names and, what may have been more offensive, ages, and finally accused the officers, and specifically Roget, with illegal acts designed to cover their own mistakes and inadequacies.

As evidence of illegal acts, Babbage presented two exchanges of letters. The first purportedly showed that Roget's colleague and eventual junior Secretary, John George Children (1777–1852), had persistently pressed a personal friend to be put up for Fellowship in the society against all rules and custom of the society.

The second exchange was between Roget and Davies Gilbert, then President of the society, letters which Babbage printed to bolster his accusation that Roget had been guilty either of failing to write the rough minutes of a Council meeting or of writing the minutes some time later from memory. Babbage's accusation rested upon his contention that the official Council minutes did not include the fact that Captain Francis Beaufort had been proposed for the Council and had refused the nomination. Babbage offered this omission as one evidence of deliberate attempts by the Council to prevent a general knowledge of widespread dissatisfaction with the Council:

The paper preserved amongst our records which professes to be the rough minute of the Council of the 26th November, is a single folio half-sheet, written on both sides; towards the middle of the second page are the names of the persons recommended. If that of Captain Beaufort were founded in this list with a line drawn through it by the pen, and that of Sir John Franklin [who later accepted the position Beaufort refused] substituted, it might have been argued that although the subsequent alteration of a rough minute was highly irregular, yet it could give no just ground to suppose that it was intended to conceal from the Society the fact of the refusal.

But any member of the Royal Society may satisfy himself that the name of Captain Beaufort has *never* been written on that paper. I confess I can see no alternative but to suppose that the paper containing those minutes was written from memory *subsequently* to the date it bears—or that it is *not* a genuine document.[7]

A second irregularity protested by Babbage—and on the same ground as the first—was that the society's records showed no entry at all for a Council meeting held on February 11; therefore, Roget (and the Council) was guilty again either of negligence or of deliberate misrepresentation, or both.

Babbage manfully published Roget's replies to both of these charges just as Roget had originally published them in *The Philosophical Magazine* and *Annals of Philosophy* in June 1830. They appeared in the form of a letter to the President of the society, and his answer. After pointing out that Babbage had "spent an immense time in ransacking the records of the Society with an industry worthy of a better cause," Roget explained the first charge as follows:

A slight attention to the arguments [Babbage's] will show that they all proceed upon the gratuitous assumption that the paper which I gave to the Assistant Secretary to copy into the Minute-book, and which Mr. Babbage says "professes to be the rough minutes" is the identical paper written at the Council on the 26th of November. This it neither is, nor ever professed to be. Every one conversant with business must know that it is generally impossible, during the time of a meeting, to take down more than the heads of what is to form the minutes; and that on many occasions it is requisite that the minutes, in order that they may accurately express the sense of the meeting, should be afterwards written out more fully and more deliberately. At the meeting in question, a rough minute was of course taken down; and it did contain the name of Captain Beaufort. That minute was afterwards corrected. . . . The rough draft itself, being then of no use, was destroyed. The paper which the Assistant Secretary has in his possession, and which Mr. Babbage has mistaken for the original rough draft, is the fair copy of this corrected minute. The whole of his reasoning built upon this erroneous supposition falls, therefore, to the ground.[8]

With equal dispatch, Roget disposed of the second charge:

Had it occurred to him that the persons most likely to give him
   accurate information respecting the meeting of the 11th of
   February were those who were present at it, he might have
   saved himself the trouble of reiterating his imaginary charges,
   and of accumulating hypotheses to sustain them. Instead of assuming that the Council must necessarily have met, merely
   because it had been summoned; and that having met, it must
   have transacted business; and that "the only business it transacted probably was to resolve itself immediately into a Committee of Papers;" and that a minute of such transaction ought
   to have been made; and that consequently, the Secretary must
   have been guilty of negligence in not entering such minute;—
   he would have learned the real fact, that *no meeting of the
   Council was held at all.* The President stated at the time, that
   as there was no business to come before the Council, he had
   given orders to summon a Committee only, and not a Council;
   but a summons for the latter had, by accident, accompanied
   that for the Committee. The Council therefore held no meeting; the mace was not placed upon the table; there was no
   business transacted; no resolving of itself into a committee; no
   minute to take down; no negligence in not recording a
   nonentity.[9]

Gilberts' answer to Roget's letter was simply a hearty endorse-
ment of the accuracy of Roget's version of the affair.

To understand the intensity of feeling that provoked Babbage
to publish his book, it is necessary to step back briefly to 1828,
when Babbage was appointed to a committee established by Gilbert in belated response to increasing pressure for reform. The
committee's work was ignored; Gilbert and other members of the
Council saw to it that its report was simply filed away, and despite Babbage's repeated attempts to get the Council to act on
the report, nothing was done. The frustration of those dissatis-
fied with the society was thus intensified to a point where some
of them felt that their only recourse was to appeal to the public.
Accordingly, in the January 30, 1830, issue of *The Times* appeared a letter signed "Argus," who "accused the President and
the Secretary of the Royal Society of flagrant violation of the
spirit and letter of the laws of the Society." [10] The irregularities
later charged by Babbage in his book were then detailed by
"Argus," who claimed that Beaufort refused to serve on the
Council unless the "Report of the Society's well-known Reform

Committee" were acted upon. Added to Babbage's larger complaints were a number of personal inconveniences, such as the rejection of his request for a copy of Greenwich *Observations* distributed by the society. Roget wrote him a rather stuffy letter advising Babbage that he was welcome to use a copy in the society library any time he pleased, but "The Council regrets that the number of copies placed by Government at their disposal is insufficient to supply the demands already made upon them by various learned bodies both here and on the continent. . . ." [11] On the back of this letter, Babbage scrawled a note saying that Roget's excuses were lies and that every year the RS reduced tons of the *Observations* to pasteboard. In fairness to Roget, it should be noted that in a subsequent letter (February 13) Roget gave an accounting of the *Observations*. Of sixty copies given it by the Government, the society had already distributed fifty-six, Roget said. [12]

Then, in May, Babbage's *Decline* appeared, followed by successive editions. While the book did not, finally, achieve the kind of reform that Babbage and his friends sought, its appearance was like pulling a thumb out of a hole in the dike. There was a great choosing of sides. A group of Roget's friends proposed that Babbage be thrown out of the society. [13] The junior Secretary, General Edward Sabine, astronomer who accompanied Sir John Ross's expeditions in 1818 and Perry's expedition in 1819, resigned, and Roget took over his duties until a new officer could be elected, collecting, incidentally, an additional £52 for his trouble. [14] More letters to *The Times* and an editorial to the effect that *Decline* "has boldly thrown aside the veil which conceals the vices of its management" were followed by lengthy pamphlets, more charges and countercharges.

Perhaps the most outspoken of the materials published by the reformers was *Charges Against the President and Councils of the Royal Society*, by Sir James South, a twenty-three-page pamphlet which first appeared on November 11, and was reissued as a second edition on November 25, 1830, the day of the society's anniversary meeting. South had found it necessary to reissue the pamphlet because, he said, Gilbert and Roget had conspired to refuse an offered copy of the first edition for the society's library:

Whether these personages—the one requited by *honor* for holding the office of President, the other *paid* out of the Society's funds for discharging the duties of Secretary—are to be the

judges of what the Fellows ought to give—or what the Society
ought to receive for its library—is for the body at large, and
not for me, to determine.[15]

South's pamphlet, admirable in its conciseness when compared
with many of the other effusions that were hastily thrown into
the press,[16] consisted of thirty-nine tersely stated charges. In addition to general charges made by Babbage, South accused the
RS officers of refusing Fellows access to records, of deleting from
minutes letters of Fellows critical of RS procedures, of unjustifia-
bly awarding RS medals, of squandering RS funds on dinners
and entertainments, of favoring a relative of the RS President
(as a member of the Council) over the "most profound mathematician of Great Britain" (James Ivory), of back-room bargain-
ing to preserve power in the hands of the old guard. South's
two-paragraph conclusion disclaimed any personal animosity toward any of the officers or Councilors and challenged the society
to do something about his charges, if only to eject him from
the society, for "where admission is no honour, expulsion can be
no disgrace."

Needless to say, South's second attempt to get his pamphlet accepted by the society's library was no more successful than the
first, although it was, apparently, more exciting, according to a
detailed account of the meeting on November 25, before which
he appeared.[17] Apologizing for any lapses in the account, *The
Athenaeum* reported that South's attempt to address the society
was constantly interrupted by "discordant voices, tokens of applause and disapprobation," and by speakers variously insisting
that South had no right—had a perfect right—to take up the
time of the meeting with his complaints. Requesting an opportunity to substantiate his charges, South finally strode forward
amid much tumult, laid a copy of his pamphlet on the Secretary's table, and left the meeting. South was followed by a few
sympathizers, and additional speakers, including Babbage and
Granville, protested the actions of the President and the Council.

Clearly, the more public the revolt became, the more explicit
became the charges, and the more obvious it was that the movement was gaining ground. Sir Nicholas Harris, in a pamphlet entitled *Observations on the State of Historical Literature . . .*
(London, 1830), extended the cry for reform to include the British Museum, the Society of Antiquaries, the Public Record Office, the Rolls Chapel, and the Record Commission. Lumping the
Royal Society in with the rest, Harris characterized the officers of

these agencies as proceeding "in Boeotian tranquillity, effecting nothing, and attended by benefit only to the secretaries, who enjoy comfortable sinecures, the one for doing the very little that is done, the other for assisting him."

Sir Nicholas, who had as quick a tongue for invective as Babbage, lauded the publications of South, Babbage, and others with respect to the Royal Society. He closed his comments with the remark of a Danish visitor to the Society of Antiquaries, an anecdote that received a mighty amen from fellow reformers: Asked his reaction after visiting the society, the Dane said, "I do think it one great humbug." The same question being put to him at the close of the sitting of the Royal Society, he observed, "By gar, I do think this one greater humbug still!" [18]

The letters (public and private), the extra meetings (official and clandestine), the clamoring pamphlets and books led to a focusing of the controversy upon the society elections held in November 1830. When it was learned that Davies Gilbert would not stand again for the presidency, the reformers saw this as a grand opportunity to unseat the diehards and the dilettantes. Gilbert meanwhile was manipulating the Duke of Sussex into accepting the nomination as a means of preserving the status quo. The reformers prevailed on J. F. W. Herschel to enter his name in the lists. Letters between Herschel and Babbage show that Herschel was extremely reluctant to become a candidate. He had had enough of Royal Society politics: "I love science too well to be very easily induced to throw away the small part of the one lifetime I have to bestow it on the affairs of a public body which has proved to be . . . a continued source of dispute and annoyance." [19] But in November Babbage had his way, and Herschel, still denying that he wanted the presidency, agreed to serve for one year. One of his conditions was that Babbage would serve on the new Council.[20]

Babbage's cohorts quickly organized a campaign and printed a handbill stating that, because of Herschel's "varied and profound knowledge and high personal character," [21] the undersigned intended to put him in nomination on the day of the election. The bill was signed by seventy-four Fellows, including Francis Baily, Francis Beaufort, Charles Bell, David Brewster, Benjamin Brodie, Henry Hallam, Charles Lyell, Herbert Mayo, John Rennie, Adam Sedgwick, and William Whewell. Many of the signees were Roget's friends and associates in the Medical and Chirurgical Society and/or Royal Institution, and the appearance of names such as Leonard Horner and Alexander Luard Wollaston, who had been very close to Roget, must have indeed shaken the Secretary's confidence.

Shortly before the appearance of this announcement, the reformers succeeded in getting Gilbert and the Council to hold an *ad hoc* committee meeting. After explaining how it happened that the Duke of Sussex had accepted the nomination, Gilbert left the meeting. In the face of the united force of the opposition, the Council members, without the leadership of Gilbert, wavered and finally passed a number of significant resolutions proposed by the reformers. Among these were that the officers and Council members should be scientific men, and that in place of the President's naming successors to retired or deceased Council members, a list of fifty Fellows was to be circulated from which the society would elect its new officers and Councilors.[22] The reformers were jubilant, and when the Council actually issued the list demanded by the resolution, and the list did not include the name of the Duke of Sussex, victory seemed complete.

But less than two weeks before the November 30 election, Gilbert and his followers outmaneuvered the reformers, and in one swift political move, scuttled the victory ship. Because the election procedure had been changed by an *ad hoc* committee, which had no power to make such changes, Gilbert and his Council were free to alter the resolutions. They simply rescinded that part of the committee resolution which stipulated that the new *officers* would be chosen by the society from the list of nominees circulated. The key word was "officers," since the reformers rightly saw that the officers held the real power of the Council, and hence of the society. However, the Council resolved that the *present* Council recommend persons to fill the officer positions.[23] Thus, while the Council did issue a list of twenty-nine Fellows from which the new members were to be chosen, the deletion of officers from this list was a fatal blow to the reformers' hopes.

The reformers' victory evaporated, and their only recourse was to scrabble about for write-in votes for Herschel for President in the few days they had left. How nearly they succeeded, even after this tactical defeat, is suggested by the fact that, although the Duke of Sussex was elected on November 30, he won by the narrow vote of 119 to 111.

Close as the reformers came to upsetting the old order, the administration retained its power. Gilbert kept a seat on the Council, and the old guard made a clean sweep of the officers:

the Duke as President; Lubbock as Treasurer; Roget as senior Secretary; and John Children as junior Secretary. Hopes for sweeping changes in the RS statutes were frustrated. *The Record of the Royal Society,* a year-by-year account of changes, laconically notes that the new edition of the society's statutes "contains a few changes which are of no great moment." The 1830 election merely confirmed the reformers in their disgust over the state of the Royal Society. Their reaction to Gilbert and friends led the next year to the formation, under the leadership of Babbage and David Brewster, of the British Association for the Advancement of Science. This was undoubtedly seen by many as a further blow to the prestige of the Royal Society, although many loyal Fellows joined the British Association. Roget, for example, was a charter member, and he chaired the physiology section at the Cambridge meeting in 1833 and the medical section in Edinburgh in 1834. In the same year, Roget, still on the publication committee for the Royal Society, read Brewster's paper on the optical structure of the crystalline lenses of animals and, in a brief report, recommended its publication.[24]

It is this kind of juxtaposition that makes it extremely hazardous to generalize about Roget and his stature among nineteenth-century scientists. That he was the target of a good many scientific men during the 1830 turmoil is indisputable, but that his professional worth was soundly recognized is also true. On June 24, 1831, he was appointed *speciali gratia* a Fellow of the Royal College of Physicians, and in 1832 he was chosen to deliver the Gulstonian Lectures at that most prestigious and influential of medical organizations on May 2, 4, and 9.[25] A particularly gracious notice of this event was published in the *London Medical Gazette:*

> This tribute to talent, extensive learning, and those acquirements which dignify the character of the physician, is no less honorable to the College than it must be gratifying to the gentleman on whom it has been conferred.[26]

Moreover, Roget not only continued as Secretary of the RS, where he served on an increasing number of important committees, but he continued to sit on the Royal Institution's Board of Visitors, and, in the midst of the 1830 struggle at the RS, he was reelected President of the Medical and Chirurgical Society. In the same year he became a charter member of the Royal Geographical Society. An increasing record of publications and lec-

tures attests to the respect in which he was held by large seg-
ments of the scientific and medical community.

Meanwhile, larger events were about to break upon England
with a force that all but swept away such minor matters as the alleged administrative deficiencies of the Royal Society. Cries for
national change were rising toward the passage, in 1832, of the
first great Reform Bill. But in 1831, before this social revolution
could take place, the long-dreaded, often-rumored approach of
Asiatic cholera, which had stalked steadily westward across Europe, became a fact in England. Widespread fear and hysteria
seized the nation as whole towns and sections of cities were
stricken. The death list climbed. In Exeter, for example, cholera
claimed four hundred lives in less than four months. Trade and
industry halted. Despite the belated establishment of a Central
Board of Health at the Royal College of Physicians, the medical
establishment was obviously ill-equipped to cope with the epidemic, which all too grimly reminded Englishmen of the disastrous visitations of the black plague in earlier centuries.

Better than most physicians of the time, Roget knew that pre-
ventive measures were some years too late. He had known this, in
fact, since 1828, when he completed the first study of the
metropolitan water supply by special commission of King George
IV. A truly pioneer study, Roget's project antedated by nearly
twenty years the great series of more famous sanitary commissions and public health bills leading up through the midcentury
to the comprehensive Public Health Act of 1875. Roget's commission was the prototype, establishing procedures, goals, and even
the political footwork of similar efforts for several generations to
come. Yet the story of Roget's work, a matter of public record
since the House of Commons ordered his report printed on
March 17, 1828, has, to this day, remained part of the silence
that has shrouded Roget's life.

In 1827, public sanitation was in a very primitive state indeed.
There were, of course, no filtration plants, and in many cases, as
Roget's investigations discovered, water companies pumped directly from the Thames into the mains supplying the London
households. The Thames thus served two functions simultaneously: source of supply and sewage disposal.

Beginning with complaints of fishermen that fish were disap-
pearing from the Thames, and swelling with householders' out-
cries against smelly water at the tap, the demand for inquiry
burst into the London press with charges against the private

water companies that then controlled the city's supply. There were horrendous exposés, and there were polite letters to *The Times*.[27] One old gentleman theorized that the copper bottoms of ships at London Dock were poisoning the fish, an idea that soon became popularly accepted as fact. The penny dreadfuls added more than their bit with stories of the cholera epidemics that were then sweeping across Europe from India. Private citizens met in taverns, listened to speakers (variously informed), drafted collective letters to the newspapers and to Parliament. It was these "addresses," made respectable by being presented to both houses of Parliament, that convinced the King and his cabinet that something had to be done to prevent the water question from becoming that final effective spark in a tinderlike populace, already demanding relief from all manner of sociological and political ills.

If the popular protests alone might not have affected the monarch, perhaps it would have been the unsavory state of the atmosphere at the royal residence in Windsor. Charles Knight, publisher and friend of Roget, gives in his 1864 autobiography an all-too-descriptive account of the sanitary conditions at Windsor. He remembered them "with a qualm in my stomach" from his boyhood there:

> Never was there such a sink of impurity as my native town. Those pleasant fields were in spring, summer, and autumn, pestilent with black ditches. In the Bachelor's Acre we boys played by the side of a great open cesspool, kept brimming and overflowing by drains disgorging from every street. The Court sniffed this filthy reek. . . . Municipal or royal dignitaries never interfered to abate or remove the nuisance. In truth, the word nuisance had scarcely then found a place in our language in a sanitary sense.[28]

As late as 1844, some fifty-three cesspools were found overflowing beneath Windsor Castle.[29]

Responding at last to a rising public clamor against the foul water in London, the King signed a special order on June 25, 1827:

> GEORGE THE FOURTH, by the Grace of God of the United Kingdom of Great Britain and Ireland King, Defender of the Faith, Etc., To Our trusty and wellbeloved *Peter Roget,* Doctor of Medicine, and *William Thomas Brande* and *Thomas Telford,* Esquires,[30]—Greeting: WHEREAS an humble Address has been

presented to Us by the Lords Spiritual and Temporal in Parliament assembled, beseeching Us that We would be graciously
pleased to order a Commission to be issued to inquire into the
Supply of Water in the Western part of the Metropolis. . . .[31]

Having the royal permission to investigate did not constitute a
license to make, or even to suggest, any changes, Roget found.
The fact that the city's water supply was entirely in the hands of
freely enterprising private companies made the situation a
touchy one for a government that had been nourished on an almost exclusive diet of Adam Smith laissez-faire economics. Thus,
the mere creation of the commission represented a not inconsiderable act of political bravery. That there were definite strings
attached, severely restricting the commission's activities, was soon
made obvious to Roget and his colleagues.

During the next few months, a time confused politically by
two changes in prime minister, Roget carried on a polite but
stubborn battle with Whitehall: first, to get the funds needed to
carry out his task, and second, to get permission for the commission to make recommendations as well as simply to report its findings. In a discouraging interview with Sir Robert Peel (then
Home Secretary), Roget was told plainly that he was to limit his
inquiry to the quantity and the quality of the water. He was *not*
to make "any protracted examination which would include taking levels or making surveys"; he was *not* to spend time devising
means of improving the water system of the city. Put into workaday English, this meant, "Don't make waves," since almost any
suggested change would be seen as interference with private industry.

Roget was no rebel, but neither was he to be pushed around.
He found ways of making it clear in his report that he didn't
think much of a government that would stop a scientific inquiry
short of doing everything it could to improve such a fundamen-
tally important resource as water supply. A practical and careful
man, Roget also took pains in his report and in his attached correspondence to identify the parties responsible for so limiting the
inquiry:

> . . . we were about to procure accurate analysis of the Water
> taken from different places, and more particularly from those
> whence the several Companies derive their supply, and in dif-
> ferent states of the tide; but as from the expressions of Mr.
> Peel's sentiments with regard to the nature of our Commission
> . . . we are led to apprehend that he may not sanction our

proceeding further. . . . We beg to be informed whether the expenses necessarily attendant on such an investigation will be defrayed by Government, as we had originally reason to expect they would be. . . .[32]

Roget's letter closed with the wry observation that it would hardly be possible for the commission to give an opinion on the "salubrity" of the water unless it could make analyses of the water. He won his point there and forced Peel to approve funds to hire Dr. John Bostock to analyze samples taken from various points of supply.[33] But that was as far as Peel would go. His correspondence repeats his interpretation of the original commissioning order of the King: that the inquiry limit itself to the reporting on quantity and quality of the water supply. Peel's final word was a none-too-gentlemanly reminder that the commission had been in existence for several months already and that he would like a definite date on which he could expect to see their report.

The commission, after months of conducting hearings, studying water samples, receiving letters of evidence, considering improvement schemes, weighing charges against the water companies and the companies' defensive statements, looking at "disgusting objects" that householders claimed to have found in their water, checking statistics provided by the companies against those offered by such sources as the city firemen, inspecting mechanical equipment—pumps, hoses, pipes, turncocks, reservoirs —experimenting with sand and mechanical filters, designing settling basins, interviewing dozens of persons along the Thames, and establishing criteria for the evaluation of both quantity and quality of the water, filed its report on March 10, and the House of Commons ordered it to be printed on April 21, 1828.

On the first page of the report, Roget again made it clear why the commission had not gone as far as it might have:

. . . it appeared that our attention was required to be directed to three principal points; namely, first to ascertain the *sources* and *means* by which the Metropolis is supplied with water, and their efficiency as to the *quantity* supplied; secondly to determine the *quality* of the water; and thirdly to obtain such information as might enable us, if necessary, to suggest *new methods*, or *sources of supply*, or to point out the means of ameliorating those now in existence. But having since learned, by a recent communication from His Majesty's Principal Secretary of State for the Home Department, that our inquiry is to be limited to the description, the quality, and the salubrity of the Water, and that we are not called upon either to consider new and more eligible sources of supply, or to suggest plans for the improvement of those already existing, we have agreed upon the following Report, respecting the two former subjects.[34]

The report itself occupied a mere twelve pages, but the resourceful Roget and colleagues saw to it that the official printed version included over one hundred pages of supplementary material, including about twenty pages of "plans of remedies."

Thus the commission had the last word after all, and thanks to the determination of Roget and colleagues, scientific advance triumphed over political timidity and expediency. One significant outcome of the report was the establishment, a year later, of the first sand filtration system at the Chelsea Water Company—a system which became the almost universal method of water purification. It is still called, appropriately enough, the "London method," and it was better than even Roget thought.

In the report, Roget conceded that even though sand filtration would be an immense improvement in removing suspended impurities, that method would not take care of pollutants held in solution. Since filtration could not contend with substances dissolved or chemically combined, "it will follow that the most perfect system of filtration can effect only a partial purification." What he was worried about, besides chemical pollutants, was disease-carrying agents. In other words, while he did not discover bacteria—in 1828, Pasteur was only six years old—Roget had sensed a significant connection between environmental agents and disease. What he did not know then was that sand filtration does, in fact, remove bacteria.

With his customary systematic approach, Roget took up in turn each of the eight existing water companies: New River, East London, West Middlesex, Chelsea, Grand Junction, Lambeth, Vauxhall, and Southwark. His report concisely summarized, first, the commission's findings on source of supply and quantity, the conclusions being that about half of the metropolitan supply was drawn from the Thames, and that generally "there appear to be no just complaints respecting the quantity of water furnished by any of these companies, except in cases of fire, when there has occasionally been a serious deficiency."

On the second major point—quality of the water—the report was largely negative. Quality of the water fluctuated markedly,

Roget reported, depending upon several factors: the state of the weather, the state of the tide, the rate of use. At low tide and in good weather and when reservoirs had been full for some time, the water from the Thames was "comparatively clean and clear," but if any of the three factors were adverse (and it was rare when at least one of them wasn't), "the water was loaded with various matters in mechanical suspension rendering it more or less coloured and turbid . . . and manifestly unfit for immediate use."

Surprisingly enough, the chief problem was not the fact that into the river Thames was dumped every imaginable sort of industrial and domestic refuse, including raw sewage and dead animals—although these sufficiently polluted the stream to account for the disappearance of fish in certain reaches. More directly responsible for the vile product delivered to the kitchen tap (or, what was more common, to the public pump) was anything—weather, tide, or heavy use—that stirred up the water, either in the river itself or after it had been pumped into holding basins or mains.

Under the pressure of complaints, some of the companies had built reservoirs to allow the untreated water to settle. But in the best operation of this system, there were three built-in failings, Roget reported, that all but canceled the beneficial effects: 1) the mud and other material that was thus allowed to settle out of the stored water clogged and fouled the cisterns and the pipes from or near the bottom of the reservoirs; 2) the agitation which accompanied every fresh influx of water became a renewed source of contamination of the whole mass; 3) stored water was particularly susceptible to bacteriological action, especially in warm weather. Added to this were relatively minor problems—such as the water companies having no real way of preventing the public from bathing in their reservoirs.

The commission did not ignore the enormous quantity of contaminants that was dumped into the Thames. Following up the fishermen's complaints, they found that such pollution had indeed "led to the almost entire destruction of the fisherman's trade between Putney Bridge and Greenwich." They found that the purity of the Thames had "suffered a gradual deterioration within the last ten or twelve years," that, for example, "the eels imported from Holland can now with great difficulty be kept alive in those parts of the Thames where they were formerly preserved in perfect health," and that "the fishmongers in London find it impossible to preserve live fish for any length of time in water taken from the same district."

In addition to the increased sewage resulting from a heavy population rise in the past decade, another important source of pollution was the increase of "certain manufactories, amongst which those of coal gas are the most prominent, polluting the river by their refuse." Other important sources were the slaughterhouses, the streetcleaners, and the apparently increasing erosion of farmlands in the suburbs.

Roget's commission even pursued the popular theory that the copper bottoms of ships were an important source of pollutants, but he gave the Navy and the merchant fleet a clean bill of health on that particular point. Roget directed Bostock to study water samples taken from three depths in and about the London Dock area; the report showed that "it did not contain the smallest appreciable quantity of copper."

Speaking as a medical man, Roget felt that the water, as provided, was subjecting the Londoner to "the continued use of a noxious ingredient," which lowered the general health of the users and made them overly susceptible to various diseases which they might otherwise fight off. Moreover, he was pessimistic about the future: "We apprehend that there are no grounds for assuming the probability of any improvement in the state of the Water drawn from the London District of the river."

The final conclusions of the commission might be summed up in this sentence:

> We are of opinion that the present state of the supply of Water to the Metropolis is susceptible of and requires improvement; that many of the complaints respecting the quality of the Water are well founded, and that it ought to be derived from other sources than those now resorted to, and guarded by such restrictions as shall at all times ensure its cleanliness and purity.[35]

Despite the strong hints from the Home Secretary's office that he refrain from suggesting improvements, Roget managed to insert here and there (besides the material submitted as appendixes) the following specific suggestions:

1. Institution of sand or sand and charcoal filtration.
2. Establishment of public baths in the neighborhoods of reservoirs to reduce the temptation to bathe in the water supply.
3. Redesign and relocation of intake valves.

4. Location of new sources of supply.

5. Appointment of another commission to go into the whole matter thoroughly.

6. Some governmental control of public water supply.

The following sentence, from the last page of the report, is illustrative of the way the commissioners booby-trapped their report:

> Some part of the evidence offered to us by one of the companies, relating to projected alterations and improvements, and which was not in a sufficiently mature state to be made public, has, at the request of the company, been withdrawn, on their finding that we had not the power of prosecuting the inquiry to the extent originally contemplated.[36]

Such a masterful stroke was not missed by the press, which took up Roget's report and, being a good deal freer than he to hammer away loudly, and often rudely, at reluctant officialdom, shouted and insinuated and satirized in campaign after campaign. Finally, Peel himself, in 1843, advised appointing a Royal commission, which found a serious condition of national ill health. This finding was the lever to move legislation establishing the general Board of Health (1845), and that, in turn, was the means of bringing a whole train of sanitation reforms into action, and eventually, the creation of the Metropolitan Water Board.[37]

Roget's water supply report—the first of its kind—was, apparently, a sound piece of work, well organized, resourcefully thought out, painstaking in detail and substantiation. The report showed Roget to be more than competent to carry through a job to his own satisfaction despite the opposition of the most powerful office in the land. Had the commission's recommendations been acted upon with dispatch, the Government might have spared thousands the agonizing diarrhetic and vomiting cramps, the withering and discoloration of the skin, and the final, fatal collapse characteristic of the water-borne Asiatic cholera. But by 1831, when the cholera actually struck Britain, the water companies, with few exceptions, had made no changes. Roget's excellent report remained filed away by a government that condemned its people to horrible pain and death before it would interfere with business as usual.

XIII [1834 ❧

Bridgewater Treatise

IN many ways the appearance in two volumes, early in 1834, of *Animal and Vegetable Physiology Considered with Reference to Natural Theology* by Peter Mark Roget, M.D. (London: William Pickering), marked the peak of his professional life. He and his contemporaries were convinced it would be the work for which he would be remembered. Ironically, it remains one of his least known, certainly least read, achievements.

Mary's fatal disease, which he was so dismally unable to cure, had pointed out to him with painful clarity the vulnerability of man in general, the rudimentary nature of medical science, and the inevitability of changes that would leave man alone and fossilized in a forgotten set of ideas and values. Close to the sources of professional power and authority, Roget was too conscious of the rising generation and the increasing demand for medical reform not to have sensed that he himself was at a critical turning point.

Nearly twenty years before, as an up-and-coming young physician, he saw what happened when the venerable and hopelessly stodgy Royal College of Physicians refused to assist the apothecaries in their attempt to bring about some order in those lower reaches of medical practice. In the early nineteenth century, the apothecaries were, in effect, the general practitioners of London. Of the three levels of medical men—the physicians, the surgeons, and the apothecaries—the last were the lowest on the scale of professional status, only a cut above the teeming quacks and charlatans that preyed on the sick, and yet they performed perhaps the most needful service of all. While the physicians and surgeons generally limited their practice to the wealthy and the middle classes, it was the apothecaries who treated the poor. Yet, when the apothecaries launched a determined attempt to improve and regularize their profession—culminating in the Apothecary Act of 1815—the Royal College of Physicians ignored their pleas for help and thus lost, for many years, control of the largest and most industrious group of practitioners in London. Roget remembered his and Marcet's discussions of the proposed Apothecary Act, perhaps recalling particularly a letter of Marcet's (March 24, 1813, RCP) in which he expressed their common resistance to the apothecaries' effort.

In the years immediately following publication of the Bridgewater Treatise, Roget himself became briefly part of the ruling caste of the Royal College of Physicians. On September 30, 1834, he was installed as a member of the powerful Board of Censors of the college, a small group of distinguished physicians who examined all applicants for licenses to practice medicine in London.[1] It was precisely in this year that the college came under the concerted fire of Thomas Wakley's committee of inquiry, and as a result, the college made some gestures toward an internal reform. Roget attended several meetings, most of them concerned with a reworking of the statutes of the body, but on September 30, 1835, he declined continuing to serve as a Censor because it was interfering with his work at the Royal Society.[2] Roget had been faced with a difficult choice: accept the opportunity to move up into a position of leadership in the Royal College by identifying himself with the agencies of change that were finally at work there, or sacrifice the advancement to avoid becoming involved in the disturbing currents of reform. His decision was moved more by a fundamental ambiguity than by a simple conservatism.

Since the founding of *Lancet,* Wakley had increased the pressure of his campaign to improve medical practice and education. Some of the most prominent men in the field—John Abernethy and Astley Cooper, for example—were among Wakley's targets, and in that very year, 1834, the House of Commons approved a bill calling for an inquiry into the state of the medical profession. Week after week, Wakley published evidence to back up the charges he made against the "dull, feeble exclusiveness of the Royal College of Physicians, the tyranny and ineptitude of the Royal College of Surgeons, the pettyfogging malice of the Society of Apothecaries."[3] Finally, it seemed, the nation itself was about to lend a hand. The hearings produced a stream of witnesses to the incompetency, the nepotism, the corruption, the lack of standards, the exclusiveness, the poor education, the resistance to change that characterized most of the profession at that time. In 1840, trying to apply the momentum gained with the 1834 investigation, Wakley's partner, Henry Warburton, proposed a Medical Act that would have set up a national College of Medicine to register and license practitioners in all branches of medicine.

In short, what was happening in the 1830's was what Charles Newman has lucidly described, in his *Evolution of Medical Education in the Nineteenth Century,* as the great transformation from medieval to modern medicine: a profound revolution comparable to the political revolution of the same period. Placing this enormous sequence of changes between 1825 and 1850, Newman dates the real beginning with the first practice of auscultation by the French physician Théophile Laënnec in 1819.[4] This choice of a particular diagnostic technique is appropriate, for the most distinct sign of significant change was the beginning of actual examination and observation of the patient by the physician. Implausible as it may seem, English doctors, who started the rebirth of science, had generally failed to apply the most rudimentary precept of the scientific method—actual observation —to their own profession. They relied far more on what their patients told them than on actual examination, a fact that goes a long way toward explaining why so many of the letters written to Roget were nothing but long catalogs of the patient's notions of how they felt. Catherine, Annette, Sophia Romilly, both Samuel and Anne Romilly, and any number of friends poured out their descriptions of complection, appetite, elimination, pains in the back, stoppages of breath, etc., in such interminable detail that in reading the letters through for the first time one is almost certain to conclude that the whole lot of them were unredeemable hypochondriacs.

The use of the stethoscope—at first simply a stick of wood— produced such startling results that great impetus was given to other sorts of physical examination. By the mid-1830's doctors had tumbled to the study of pathology itself. A whole new breed of doctors was thus appearing—people like Thomas Addison, Richard Bright, and James Paget—in the wards of London hospitals, and they began to make themselves felt in the rising demand for changes in the teaching of medicine. Where in earlier decades medical teaching was almost entirely confined to lectures —hence the importance of the many medical lecture halls about London in the first few decades of the century—the new men demanded more and more clinical experience and training. Ironically enough, they based much of their new techniques upon a study of such French physiologists of Roget's generation as Bichat, whose life and work Roget had researched without recognizing the revolutionary importance of Bichat's substitution of "tissues" for the notion of organs made of nebulous "living substance." The remarkable changes in medical education amounted to a whole new method of work for the physician—inspection, palpation, percussion, clinical and laboratory tests—a kind of work that Roget could see only as a threat to his established professional life.

Just as the shape of his familiar medical world was changing before his eyes, so was the larger geography of Roget's metaphysical world undergoing fundamental change. One might even say diastrophic change, considering the part that geology played in this alteration.

It is altogether fitting that the man who eventually would have so much to do with the unseating of Roget at the Royal Society was Charles Lyell, whose *Principles of Geography,* which appeared in three volumes from 1830 to 1833, effectively capped the loud and turbulent argument among the contending theorists on the origin of earth forms. For in the faith-shattering controversies arising out of the stormy birth of geology and the geological teachings of such men as Adam Sedgwick, James Hutton, John Playfair, Abraham Werner, and William Buckland lay the makings of a description of the universe that had little or nothing to do with the reigning theology. How this must have affected Roget might be seen in the brief and poignant objection of Sedgwick to Robert Chambers' *Vestiges of the Natural History of Creation,* a book that defended Lyell's *Principles:* "The world," cried Sedgwick, "cannot bear to be turned upside down." As Gillispie comments, "This was a cry from the heart of a scientist upon whom had suddenly flashed the full implications of his own endeavors, and who refused to understand them." [5] When one recalls that it was Lyell's book that Darwin described as opening the way to evolution—Darwin dedicated his *Voyage of the Beagle* to Lyell—Roget's confused state in 1834 might better be appreciated. Gillispie might well have been describing this confused state when, in the preface to his fine book, he writes:

Indeed, during the seven decades between the birth of modern geology and the publication of *On the Origin of Species,* the difficulty as reflected in scientific literature appears to be one of religion (in crude sense) *in* science rather than one of reli-

gion versus science. The most embarrassing obstacles faced by
the new sciences were cast up by the curious providential mate-
rialism of the scientists themselves. . . .[6]

Against this heightened consciousness of change and contradiction—in his own home, with the death of Mary; in his own profession, with the revolution in medicine; in the world at large,
with the overturning of a God-propped universe—with all the
pain, bewilderment, and challenge that these changes suggest—
Roget wrote his Bridgewater Treatise.

The treatise itself was one of a series of eight lengthy tomes
commissioned to fulfill the terms of the will of Francis Henry
Egerton, eighth Earl of Bridgewater, who died in February 1829
and directed that £8,000 of his estate be set aside for that purpose.
The money was to be paid to the person or persons nominated
by the President of the Royal Society who would write, print,
and publish one thousand copies of a work

on the power, wisdom, and goodness of God, as manifested in the
creation; illustrating such work by all reasonable arguments, as
for instance the variety and formation of God's creatures in
the animal, vegetable, and mineral kingdoms; the effect of
digestion and thereby of conversion; the construction of the
hand of man, and an infinite variety of other arguments; as
also by discoveries ancient and modern, in arts, sciences, and
the whole extent of literature.[7]

Davies Gilbert, then President of the society, solicited the aid
of the Archbishop of Canterbury and the Bishop of London, and
announced the following Bridgewater Treatises:

1. The Rev. Thomas Chalmers, D.D., On the Power, Wis-
dom, and Goodness of God as Manifested in the Adaptation of
External Nature to the Moral and Intellectual Constitution of
Man.

2. John Kidd, M.D., F.R.S., On the Adaptation of External
Nature to the Physical Condition of Man.

3. The Rev. William Whewell, M.A., F.R.S., Astronomy and
General Physics considered with Reference to Natural Theology.

4. Sir Charles Bell, K.G.H., F.R.S., L.&E., The Hand; its
Mechanism and Vital Endowments as Evincing Design.

5. Peter Mark Roget, M.D., Animal and Vegetable Physiology Considered with Reference to Natural Theology.

6. The Rev. William Buckland, D.D., F.R.S., On Geology
and Mineralogy.

7. The Rev. William Kirby, M.A., F.R.S., On the History, Habits, and Instincts of Animals.

8. William Prout, M.D., F.R.S., Chemistry, Meteorology, and the Function of Digestion, considered with Reference to Natural Theology.

To avoid any delay, the Duke of Sussex, who succeeded Gilbert as President of the RS in 1830, guaranteed to underwrite the immediate publication of the treatises if monetary assistance was needed. The works began to appear early in 1833, with Whewell's, Kidd's, and Bell's, and those were quickly followed by Roget's and the others.

Despite their forbidding appearance and their expensive bindings—full calf covers with gold stamping on the spine—all of the treatises were successful in the sense that they went through several editions. Roget's work reached a fifth edition in 1870. He completed work on the fourth edition in June 1867, at the age of eighty-eight.

The treatises were met with the anticipated applause of the establishment. The *Quarterly Review,* for example, in a joint review of the first four treatises, began, "It is impossible to peruse the titles of these books, without feeling an emotion of gratitude towards the memory of the noble and reverend person to whose munificence we are indebted for their publication." [8] Reviews in the *Christian Examiner,* the *North American Review,* and other periodicals spoke warmly of the clarity and orderliness of Roget's presentation, and even the *Edinburgh Review* complimented Roget for the "acuteness and sobriety of argument and the tone of piety and religious feeling" in which his treatise was composed.

There were, on the other hand, some criticisms of the way in which Gilbert had carried out the stipulations of Bridgewater's will. Typical of these comments was that of the *Quarterly Review* writer, who, after praising the individual works, charged that Bridgewater's will had been "strangely misinterpreted," that Gilbert had "essentially mistaken the purpose which Lord Bridgewater had in view." This criticism was based, first, on the argument that Bridgewater had in mind a *single* work—not eight of them. Possibly the reviewer was suggesting that Gilbert had used the nobleman's will to pay off a number of useful friends. Secondly, said the reviewer, the volumes were priced too high to make it likely that they would "attain any wide circulation in these days of cheap literature." This same criticism is echoed by

Sir John Barrow, whose book is full of gossip about Royal Society personalities: ". . . never, I believe, were the intentions of a pious and benevolent testator more completely frustrated." [9]

A final and rather ludicrous comment on the whole series was the appearance in 1837 of *The Ninth Bridgewater Treatise—A Fragment,* by Roget's former friend and foe, Charles Babbage. As Babbage pointed out, his volume was an entirely unauthorized and independent venture—he enjoyed not the backing of wealthy and influential men, nor had he any expectation of realizing a profit from his work. This was a dig, apparently, at the Bridgewater writers, for their benefactor had specifically written into the arrangements that all profits arising from the sale of the subsidized works should go to the authors.

A curious, rather disconnected volume, Babbage's book argues that the Bridgewater writers did not go far enough, that in effect, "the effect of the Treatises is to support a general prejudice . . . that the pursuits of science are unfavourable to religion." Of the individual writers, he singled out only Whewell whom he soundly criticized for attempting to invalidate the arguments of others by inquiring into their intellectual or their moral character.[10]

Babbage's argument, which runs to 179 pages, is an interesting commentary on the philosophical predicament Roget found himself in, and a criticism of the competence of the Bridgewater writers to cope with that predicament. He makes a stalwart attempt—which none of the Bridgewater writers did—to answer David Hume's posthumous attack (*Dialogues Concerning Natural Religion,* 1799) on the design idea so successfully espoused later by Paley, by showing that Hume knew little or nothing about the laws of probability. Babbage then proceeds to use his mathematical prowess to disprove Hume's statement that a miracle could *never* take place.

Roget's Bridgewater Treatise remains as a monument to Roget's capacity for work—prolonged, resourceful, highly organized labor—and can serve as a testament to the real need of a talented man to reaffirm order in human existence at a difficult time in his life. It deserves, then, a more than passing glance here.

Ransacking his own library, and the libraries and museum collections of most of the scientific institutions in town, and drawing on his own writings as well as the current work appearing in British and European journals, Roget put together a text, running well over a quarter of a million words, in less than three years. At the same time he nursed a dying wife, maintained his medical practice, prepared lectures and articles and carried on a variety of activities at the Royal Society, the Royal Institution, and the Royal Society of Arts. Moreover, his editorial work with the Society for the Diffusion of Useful Knowledge was continuing at an even heavier rate than before.[11] Not only was he reading and reporting on many manuscripts submitted to the society, but he was readying his own treatises—"Electricity," "Galvanism," etc.—for publication in a collected volume in 1832.

Roget acknowledges his indebtedness in his preface to the treatise, where he notes that his chief sources have been the works of Cuvier, Johann Blumenbach, Carl Gustav Carus, Everard Home, J. F. Meckel, Henri de Blainville, P. Latreille, and Geoffroy Saint-Hilaire, as well as the volumes of the *Philosophical Transactions, Mémoires and Annales du Muséum,* and *Annales des Sciences Naturelles.* He particularly mentions as helpful the lectures at the Royal College of Surgeons delivered by Everard Home, Astley Cooper, William Lawrence, Benjamin Brodie, Joseph Henry Green and Charles Bell, and those at the University of London by Robert Edmund Grant. Roget also drew heavily upon such contemporaries as his good friends Marcet and Bostock. Nor was Roget shy about quoting his own works. On pages 9, 189, 524, 532, and 582 of Volume II he refers the reader to fuller discussions in such earlier writings as his article "Age," his Gulstonian Lectures, his paper on optical illusion, and his conclusions about diet at the Milbank penitentiary. Of the 463 engravings, small but vigorously executed woodcuts, dozens were taken directly from the works of Cuvier, Carus, Home, de Candolle, Grant, and Müller. The only drawings labeled "original" were some ten or twelve executed by George Newport, a rising young entomologist.

Thus, the treatise pretended to no original discoveries or observations; it was what we might call today a library paper, a compendium of facts and illustrations drawn from the work of other investigators. Its chief claim to value was—and this might have been anticipated by anyone aware of Roget's philosophical concerns—whatever organization and sense of unity could be brought to physiology and comparative anatomy:

> These facts I have studied to arrange in that methodized order, and to unite in those comprehensive generalizations, which not only conduce to their more ready acquisitions and retention to memory, but tend also to enlarge our views of their mutual

connexions, and of their subordination to the general plan of creation. My endeavours have been directed to give to that subject that unity of design, and that scientific form, which are generally wanting in books professedly treating of Natural Theology, published prior to the present series; not excepting even the unrivalled and immortal work of Paley.[12]

In addition to fulfilling the requirements laid down by Bridgewater's will, Roget hoped that his treatise would serve as a "useful introduction to the study of Natural History; the pursuit of which will be found not only to supply inexhaustible sources of intellectual gratification, but also to furnish, to contemplative minds, a rich fountain of religious instruction"—a statement that reminds one strikingly of a similar remark by Ralph Waldo Emerson just three years later. A moment's comparison of the two statements may suggest one of Roget's limitations as a philosopher. In his famous address "The American Scholar," delivered to the Phi Beta Kappa society at Harvard on August 31, 1837, Emerson, concerned with the relationship between science and man, took the intellectual step that Roget could not:

He shall see that nature is the opposite of the soul, answering to it part for part. One is seal and one is print. Its beauty is the beauty of his own mind. Its laws are the laws of his own mind. Nature then becomes to him the measure of his attainments. So much of nature as he is ignorant of, so much of his own mind does he not yet possess. And, in fine, the ancient precept, "Know thyself," and the modern precept, "Study nature," become at last one maxim.[13]

Roget's hope that the treatise might induce the study of natural history no doubt accounts for the fact that the work (especially Volume I) is full of entertaining descriptions of animal behavior, and rather elementary explanations of such phenomena as the arrangement of leaves on a stem, the operation of long muscles, the ready absorption of dyes by certain bones. The presence of such natural history notes—of a kind beloved by newspaper editors in need of half inches of filler material—should by no means lead one to conclude that Roget's treatise was a mere scrapbook of odds and ends. It was carefully and consistently organized, and in all but a few instances, he made such notes do double duty: first, to heighten the interest of his amateur reader in natural history, and second, to demonstrate his single, pervasive thesis—that wherever one turns in nature, he finds evidence of order and design.

The treatise is conveniently divided. The first volume, opening with a full reprinting of the outline of Cuvier's classification of animals that Roget used earlier in his 1826 book, consists almost entirely of a class-by-class discussion of "the mechanical functions" of the several phyla of animals—in other words, a comparative anatomy. After a sixty-page introduction, Roget explains generally how both animals and plants are organized. He then takes up, with a chapter to each, the "mechanical" (zoological) features of the "zoophytes" (under which term he lumped all sorts of "lower forms," ranging from sponges to starfish), the molluscs, the "articulata" (annelid worms, spiders, and crabs), the insects, the vertebrates, fishes, the reptiles, mammals, and birds. Cuvier had begun with mammals, then birds, then reptiles, fish, molluscs, "articulata," and "zoophytes," just the reverse of Roget's arrangement of the animals. Just why Roget altered Cuvier's classification scheme, which he had so often lauded and used, is not explained. Another curious difference in Roget's scheme is his leaving the birds to last, an alteration probably due to a last-minute desire to say something about flight, perhaps because of his long interest in animal locomotion. To forestall any temptation to attribute a symbolic significance to this placement of the birds, I must report that Roget, like Cuvier and all of his contemporaries, unequivocally placed man at the top of the animal heap:

. . . disclaiming any close alliance with inferior creatures, he proudly stands alone, towering far above them all. . . .[14]

The second volume treats what Roget called the "Vital Functions," in a way that would probably today be called comparative physiology, offering, first, an exposition, "Nutrition in Vegetables," and then, in more detail, chapters on animal physiology under the following headings: "Animal Nutrition," "Digestion," "Chylification," "Lacteal Absorption," "Circulation," "Respiration," "Secretion," "Nervous Power," "Sensation," "Touch," "Taste," "Smell," "Hearing," "Vision," "Perception," "Reproduction," "Organic Development," and "Decline of the System." His final chapter, "Unity of Design," like his introductory chapter, summarizes the generalizations that he developed throughout the book and attempts to bring all in line with his announced thesis.

It is in his first chapter, "Final Causes," and his last, "Unity of Design," that a modern reader might find matters of interest, for

it is there that Roget's determined views about the relation of
God to Man are set forth, and it is there that he reveals the pain
and confusion of a man trying at once to celebrate science and to
contain it within the restrictions of a dogmatic faith. In "Final
Causes," for example, he opens with a four-page extolling of science, how it is revealing ever greater realms to man's understanding. This is promptly followed up with a reminder that

> . . . we are sure to arrive at boundaries within which our powers
> are circumscribed. Infinity meets us in every direction, whether
> in the ascending or descending scale of magnitude; and we feel
> the impotence of our utmost efforts to fathom the depths of
> creation, or to form any adequate conception of that Supreme
> and Dominant Intelligence, which comprehends the whole
> chain of being.[15]

Roget then takes up again, as he had some years before in writing his "Physiology" article for the *Supplement* of the *Encyclopaedia Britannica,* the importance of discovering relationships. That, he says, is the proper object of all human knowledge; therefore we must consider the two chief *kinds* of relationships that we are likely to discover.

> The phenomena of the universe may be viewed as connected
> with one another either by the relation of *cause and effect* or
> by that of *means and end;* and accordingly these two classes or
> relations give rise to different kinds of knowledge, each of
> which requires to be investigated in a peculiar mode and by a
> different process of reasoning. The foundation of both these
> kinds of knowledge is, indeed, the same; namely, the constant
> uniformity which takes place in the succession of events, and
> which, when traced in particular classes of phenomena, consti-
> tutes what we metaphorically term the *Laws of Nature.*[16]

Roget explains that, because the forces that govern the inorganic
phenomena of the universe are "undeviatingly regular and uniform," the cause-and-effect relationship is applicable in that area.
But when one turns to the world of living matter, then an entirely different approach must be adopted.

In his attempts to suggest the marvel and the multiplicity of
life on the planet, Roget's stilted prose *almost* comes alive itself:

> Can there be a more gratifying spectacle than to see an animal in
> the full vigour of health, and the free exercise of its powers,
> disporting in its native element, revelling in the bliss of exis-
> tence, and testifying by its incessant gambols the exuberance of
> its joy?

. . . if we review every region of the globe, from the scorching sands of the equator to the icy realms of the poles, or from the lofty mountain summits to the dark abysses of the deep; if we penetrate into the shades of the forest, or into the caverns and secret recesses of the earth; nay, if we take up the minutest portion of stagnant water, we still meet with life in some new and unexpected form, yet ever adapted to the circumstances of its situation. . . .

Roget carefully footnoted the word "Nature" as follows:

In order to avoid the too frequent, and consequently irreverent, introduction of the Great Name of the SUPREME BEING into familiar discourse on the operations of his power, I have, throughout this Treatise, followed the common usage of employing the term *Nature* as a synonym, expressive of the same power, but veiling from our feeble sight the too dazzling splendour of its glory.[17]

What must a modern reader make of this explanation—Roget's fondness for euphemism? a tendency toward pantheism? an ostentatious or a genuine piety?

It should be obvious, says Roget, that the simple cause-and-effect relationship is inadequate to explain the world of the physiologist. He thus arrives at the means-and-end relationship, from which are derived laws "which are usually denominated *final* causes."

Upon this framework Roget builds his entire argument for design, an argument that is little more than that of William Paley's *Natural Theology, or Evidences of the Existence and Attributes of the Deity Collected from the Appearances of Nature* (1802). So closely, indeed, does Roget follow Paley that he even appropriates Paley's famous opening device of the man finding a watch on the heath and reasoning from its operation and parts that it had to be designed by an external and superior intelligence.

Roget's entire treatise is simply an elaboration of his basic argument that the existence of God (and thus a purposeful universe) is proved by the appearance of design in every part of every living thing. All of Roget's hundreds of animals and vegetables treated—their parts, their functions, their adaptations to soil, weather, food, and their fellows—demonstrate the same conviction. Although Roget does not write quite as dogmatically as Paley—Paley laid down the law flatly: any view other than that design in nature proved the existence of God was atheism[18]—Roget arrived at very nearly the same conclusion, as we shall see in examining his final chapter.

Admitting the difficulties posed by a common argument—
what evidence of God was provided by the terror, injury, and disease produced by life forms preying upon each other?—Roget reminds us that "our more sober judgment should place in the
other scale the great preponderating amount of gratification,"
which is also the result of this animal warfare. He then goes on
quickly to point out that such systems of hostilities are merely
devices for "preserving the proper balance between different
races," and, thus, are simply additional evidence that "each separate species of animals, far from being isolated and independent,
performs the part assigned to it in the system of nature."

He rejected as too "hypothetical and figurative" the popular
idea that all living things could be arranged in a linear series,
commencing with the simplest and "regularly ascending to the
most refined and complicated organizations till it reached its
highest point in man." Roget declared that

> instead of one continuous series, we are presented with only de-
> tached fragments and interrupted portions of this imaginary
> system: so that, if, for the sake of illustration we must employ
> a metaphor, the natural distribution of animals would appear
> to be represented, not by a chain, but by a complicated net-
> work, where several parallel series are joined by transverse and
> oblique lines of connexion. A multitude of acts, however, tend
> to show that the real types or models of structure, are more
> correctly represented by circular, or recurring arrangements.[19]

In short, despite the many anomalies and adaptations reported,
Roget, like the great majority of his fellows, insisted that all living beings existed as part of a preconceived scheme or system of
nature. The presence of vestigial organs, for example, merely
confirmed the wisdom of the Divine maker, who foresaw the altered conditions which made that organ no longer necessary. The
discovery of unclassifiable types merely confirmed "the law of variety," and so on.

It is in his final chapter, "Unity of Design," after a six-
hundred-page review of animal anatomy and physiology, that
Roget's philosophical difficulties are most clearly revealed. To
begin, he finds it necessary to rely heavily upon analogy; in fact,
setting aside the unkind things he said about the phrenologist's
use of analogy, Roget raises this device to

> a principle, the recognition of which has given us enlarged views
> of a multitude of important facts, which would otherwise have

remained isolated and unintelligible. Hence naturalists, in arranging the objects of their study, according to their similarities and analogies, into classes, orders and genera, have but followed the footsteps of Nature herself. . . .[20]

Leaning upon his knowledge of comparative anatomy, Roget states again his belief in the constancy of species and in the law of gradation, and he elaborates a kind of "sequential creationism." Thus, each new form discovered is merely following an ascending scale of creation, retaining a strong likeness to that which preceded it and impressing its own features on those which immediately succeed it. He notes that the embryos of "higher" forms possess in their early phases a marked resemblance to that seen in the permanent condition of the lowest animals in the same series.

But for all his admiration of the "law of gradation," Roget balked when it came to suggestions of an evolutionary machine at work. He was particularly antagonistic to the ideas of Lamarck:

The pursuit of remote and often fanciful analogies has, by many of the continental physiologists, been carried to an unwarrantable and extravagant length; for the scope which is given to the imagination in these seductive speculations, by leading us far away from the path of philosophical induction, tends rather to obstruct than to advance the progress of real knowledge. By confining our inquiries to more legitimate objects, we shall avoid the delusion into which one of the disciples of this transcendental school appears to have fallen, when he announces, with exultation, that the simple laws he has discovered have now explained the universe. Nor shall we be disposed to lend a patient ear to the more presumptuous reveries of another system-builder, who, by assuming that there exists in organized matter an inherent tendency to perfectibility, fancies that he can supersede the operations of Divine agency.[21]

Roget appends a footnote here, identifying Lamarck as the source of such a heretical idea:

He believes that tribes, originally aquatic, acquired by their own efforts, prompted by their desire to walk, both feet and legs, fitting them for progression on the ground; and that these members, by the long continued operation of the wish to fly, were transformed into wings, adapted to gratify that desire. If this be philosophy, it is such as might have emanated from the college of Laputa.

The succeeding pages of Roget's final chapter make it clear that
what he is objecting to is not so much the idea that individuals
could *will* themselves and their species into change—although he
thought that silly enough—but the suggestion that there could
exist an evolutionary machine operating independently of an
all-seeing, all-planning God. He compared Lamarck invidiously
with "the humble spirit of the great Newton, who struck with
the immensity of nature, compared our knowledge of her
operations . . . to that of a child gathering pebbles on the sea
shore," and reverted again to his earlier dithyrambic insistence
on the ineffable mystery of existence.

The final two paragraphs of Roget's treatise offer the clearest
illustration of the confusion and contradiction into which Roget's ideas fall. Further, they suggest the pathos—not only of Roget's situation, but of his entire generation (and much of our
own)—of man trying desperately to hold together a world that
seemed to be flying apart at the seams. These passages, in all their
difficult turns and relapses, with all their unhappy reliance upon
clichés and generalities and wishful thinking, reveal the anguish
of an intelligent, sensitive, and aging man trying to reaffirm a
world view that was no longer tenable, and seeing himself as some
sort of lonely survivor upon whom had fallen the burden of explaining away the dilemmas of human existence.[22]

The Great Author of our being, who, while he has been pleased
   to confer on us the gift of reason, has prescribed certain limits
   to its powers, permits us to acquire, by its exercise, a knowledge of some of the wondrous works of his creation, to inter-
   pret the characters of wisdom, and of goodness with which they
   are impressed, and to join our voice to the general chorus
   which proclaims "His Might, Majesty, and Dominion." From
   the same gracious hand we also derive that unquenchable
   thirst for knowledge, which this fleeting life must ever leave
   unsatisfied; those endowments of the moral sense, with which
   the present constitution of the world so ill accords; and that
   innate desire of perfection which our present frail condition is
   so inadequate to fulfil. But it is not given to man to penetrate
   into the counsels, or fathom the designs of Omnipotence; for
   in directing his views into futurity, the feeble light of his reason is scattered and lost in the vast abyss. Although we plainly
   discern intention in every part of the creation, the grand object of the whole is placed far above the scope of our compre-
   hension. It is impossible, however, to conceive that this enormous expenditure of power, this vast accumulation of

contrivances and of machinery, and this profusion of existence resulting from them, can thus, from age to age, be prodigally lavished without some ulterior end. Is Man, the favoured creature of nature's bounty, "the paragon of animals," whose spirit holds communion with celestial powers, formed but to perish with the wreck of his bodily frame? Are generations after generations of his race doomed to follow in endless succession, rolling darkly down the stream of time, and leaving no track in its pathless ocean? Are the operations of Almighty power to end with the present scene? May we not discern, in the spiritual constitution of man the traces of higher powers, to which those he now possesses are but preparatory; some embryo faculties which raise us above this earthly habitation? Have we not in the imagination, a power but little in harmony with the fetters of our bodily organs; and bringing within our view purer conditions of being, exempt from the illusions of our senses and the infirmities of our nature, our elevation to which will eventually prove that all these unsated desires of knowledge, and all these ardent aspirations after moral good, were not implanted in us in vain?

Happily there has been vouchsafed to us, from a higher source, a pure and heavenly light to guide our faltering steps, and animate our fainting spirit, in this dark and dreary search; revealing those truths which it imports us most of all to know; giving to morality higher sanctions; elevating our hopes and our affections to nobler objects than belong to earth, and inspiring more exalted themes of thanksgiving and of praise.[23]

Read against the context of Roget's grief over the painful and untimely death of Mary, against a grinding history of devoted work and tragic losses, against an increasing awareness that the world to whose peaks he had labored to aspire was crumbling away beneath him—this closing passage of Roget's treatise becomes something more than cluttered and clumsy and highly artificial prose. The feeling of the man rides up from beneath all the contrivance, and it becomes a poignant human document.

XIV [1832–1848 ℰ

Panizzi, Royal Society Reform

At just about the same time that Roget began working on his Bridgewater Treatise, he inadvertently launched another project—one that turned out to be much more important insofar as science was concerned and much more difficult to see to completion—the writing of a new catalog for the library of the Royal Society. The catalog became the source of an exhausting controversy, which Roget weathered—not without a few bruises—only to be plunged into a series of heightening conflicts that finally ousted him from his entrenched position at Somerset House. It is particularly ironic that the whole row, which lasted some seven years and very nearly cost Roget the friendship of one of the most unusual luminaries of the nineteenth century—Antonio Panizzi [1]—evolved from Roget's having tried to do Panizzi a favor.

In 1832, its library swelled by books received in a transaction with the British Museum, the Royal Society needed a new catalog. Some of its members began working on the task, but they had not gone far before they conceded that they needed professional assistance. Meeting Panizzi at a dinner party, Roget, a member of the RS Library and Catalogue Committee, suggested that perhaps Panizzi would look over what had been done thus far and make recommendations. Panizzi complied, but after a brief examination of the proof sheets, he characteristically expressed himself in no uncertain terms and immediately alienated himself from the men with whom he would have to work on the project for the next several years, particularly Lubbock and Baily. In effect, he said, the work thus far was so ineptly done that it was impossible to repair. He would, he said, be willing to write a new catalog himself, but he could not be a party to "a work which I felt satisfied would be disgraceful to the Royal Society and to any person who should venture to meddle with it." [2]

This was the inauspicious beginning of Panizzi's association with the Royal Society. He was, however, again through Roget's good offices, retained by the RS to make the new catalog, for which he was to be paid at the rate of £30 for every thousand titles, such remuneration not to exceed £500.[3]

At the outset, Panizzi and the Library Committee worked at cross purposes. The terms of his contract forced Panizzi to work within a classification system devised by the committee. The classes were ill devised, ill defined, and wholly inadequate. Panizzi saw the system as the work of amateurs, and he said so, with the result that the Library Committee stubbornly determined to retain the classes. Thus, much of the abrasiveness of the contact Panizzi had with committee members, including Roget, arose from the difficulties Panizzi ran into in trying to work within the system, and the sometimes ludicrous attempts of the committee to make stopgap revisions in the system of classes.

A second point of contention was the society's refusal to allow the hired professional to make professional decisions, a fact illustrated by the Council's explicit order that Panizzi be ruled by the members of the committee—individually and collectively—on all matters concerning the catalog.[4]

With his impetuous, imperious nature, Panizzi was simply incapable of steering a course between the Charybdis and Scylla of these two fundamental disagreements. Everything he did, everything the committee did became a source of argument, of challenge, of recrimination. The committee went so far as to act on long-discussed plans to build a gallery around the society's library. The committee deliberately chose that moment in August 1835 when Panizzi had begun to send copy to the printer and when it was essential that the books, as Panizzi had arranged them for his work on the catalog, not be disturbed and that he have easy access to all parts of the collection. "The workmen took possession of the library, the books were covered over, the room turned into a workshop without one syllable being ever spoken to me on the subject." [5] To retaliate, Panizzi simply appropriated all the page proofs, hid them away to be used as evidence in his own defense, and locked up the drawers of title slips and pocketed the key.

Roget tried to remain a neutral figure and act as a buffer between the two warring parties. But in July 1836 Panizzi made this no longer possible. He laid down an ultimatum: either the committee must give him the freedom he deemed necessary to do the work properly, or he would proceed no further.[6] Roget made one more effort to keep the peace. From his Bernard Street study he wrote a personal letter, marked "private," urging Panizzi to retract his demands. The letter well expresses Roget's essential reasonableness, and suggests the genuineness of his attempt to serve Panizzi as well as the society.

My dear Panizzi,

I wish you to consider this letter as not official, but as conveying to you private information and as springing purely from my friendship towards you, and my anxious wish that you should not involve yourself in a dispute with the Council of the Royal Society, especially with such a thorough misconception of the real state of things as your letter of yesterday shows you are labouring under; and which letter, after I have pointed out its total inapplicability to the subject under consideration, I hope you will be induced to retract. . . .

Here, Roget referred to an earlier letter of Panizzi's, that of June 17, which first suggested that the whole matter be turned over to a referee.

Not a single person present could understand what it meant: not a soul could comprehend the nature of your objections to go on with the Catalogue, or could penetrate the motives which prompted the vague and unlooked for complaints interpreted through that letter. What the interpretation which you put on your contract with the Council is and in what points it differs from that of the Catalogue Committee or Council, nobody has yet had the sagacity to divine. . . .

Roget reminded Panizzi that in response to the earlier letter, the committee had invited him to a meeting, so that the members could better understand his grievances, and that he had flatly refused to attend. He had done so, partly at least, because the invitation had been sent him by an *assistant* secretary rather than by Roget.[7]

Now let me beg you to consider what, under the circumstances, would be the effect of your last letter to me should you persist

in obliging me to lay it before the next Council, which is summoned for next Thursday. Recollect that in it you speak of
"Disadvantages you have laboured under, and which you have
in vain endeavoured to remove"; and that "your exertions to
give satisfaction are useless"; that you "have been put to inconveniences," "made sacrifices," "suffered hardships," etc., etc. I
should like to ask you what impression is likely to be received
from such expression by persons who know nothing of the
grounds on which they proceed? Of what earthly use these general and indefinite complaints can be to you until they are distinctly specified and made intelligible to those to whom they
are addressed?

Secondly, you reiterate, in the letter I am criticizing, the profession of your willingness to fulfill your contract, while at the
same time it appears that you refuse to go on with the work,
without furnishing the least clue by which anyone can tell
wherein you consider that you have been called upon to de-
viate from the said contract. You require a categorical answer
from the Council, "Yes or No," to the proposal of a reference
[of the dispute to a third party] while they are all the while
not aware of any grounds for dispute. You surely ought not to
demand the redress of grievances before acquainting them with
what those alleged grievances are . . .

In the hope that you will consider in a most amicable spirit
what I have said to you in this letter, and that you will re-
model that which I shall have to present to the Council from
you, I send it back to you, and remain, etc., etc.[8]

Apparently, Panizzi's only answer to this effort by Roget was to
redeliver his original letter of July 8. The society's answer was to
fire him forthwith.

There followed a furious flurry of letters and finally the publication of Panizzi's *Letter*—some sixty pages of detailed and satirical "animadversions" on the bibliographical ignorance of the
committee and its lack of courtesy and cooperation. Roget drew
up, under the orders of the Duke of Sussex, then President of the
society, a "Statement of the Council relative to Mr. Panizzi's
Pamphlet," which was released to the press following the Duke's
presidential address to the society at its anniversary meeting of
November 30, 1837.[9]

Panizzi promptly brought out another pamphlet, tearing into
Roget's point-by-point defense of the society, and arguing that
the society still owed him some £300 for services rendered.

The battle was taken up by others. More pamphlets appeared,
including at least one more by the unquenchable Panizzi. Paniz-

zi's demands for compensation were turned over to a neutral third party, and the dispute was not settled until 1839, when the referee, John Elliot Drinkwater Bethune, found for Panizzi. The only mention of the termination of the affair is a discreet note under "extraordinary disbursements" in the RS Council minutes, authorizing payment of £328 to Panizzi.[10]

That same year—1839—also marked the final appearance of the Royal Society catalog, and Roget, the Council, and Panizzi could turn to other matters. Panizzi, meanwhile, had undertaken the enormous job of rewriting the catalog of the British Museum, and he was well launched on a career there that resulted not only in an incomparable library but in a legend for the Italian refugee, who became indeed the "Prince of Librarians."

As to subsequent relations between Roget and Panizzi, I can say very little, for I have found but one brief bit of evidence of any further association—a letter in the British Museum collection. Roget, writing Panizzi on March 18, 1859 (Roget was then eighty), thanked Panizzi for an earlier letter explaining why the committee closed the list of contributors to the Neapolitan Exile Fund (one of Panizzi's many campaigns) without including Roget's name on the published list of contributors. "The offer I made of my name was prompted by my desire to testify in the public manner my sympathy for the victims of tyrannical oppression. Of this feeling I gave a small token yesterday by a contribution paid in at the banker's."

During the seven long years of the Panizzi affair, Roget was busy, as usual, with a good many other activities. His Bridgewater Treatise appeared, Thomas Wakley's campaign for medical practice reform culminated in a special committee of inquiry, Catherine Roget died, Roget was appointed to the Senate of the University of London, Victoria was crowned, Roget's articles in the seventh edition of the *Encyclopaedia Britannica* appeared— with the subsequent renewal of warfare with the phrenologists— and, on June 17, 1839, Roget was appointed Examiner in Comparative Anatomy and Physiology at the University of London.[11]

A signal honor was Roget's appointment in 1834 as the first Fullerian Professor of Physiology at the Royal Institution, a chair created by the donation of £6,000 in investments by John Fuller. The only stipulation Fuller made was that one Peter Mark Roget, M.D., be appointed the first Professor.[12] In his letter of acceptance, Roget wanted the terms carefully understood before he began preparing his lectures: 1) that the dividends from Fuller's gift should be paid to Roget as long as he continued to be Professor, beginning with and inclusive of the dividends which would be due on July next; 2) that he should not be required to give the lectures until the spring of the next year (1835).[13] The dividends would have amounted to £100 per annum through the three years Roget held the professorship.[14]

Little is known of Fuller, a somewhat eccentric landowner and onetime sheriff of Sussex. He is only barely mentioned in one of Roget's letters to Marcet in August 1822. Roget said he had spent a few days at Fuller's place, Rose Hill, in Sussex, that summer. Judging from a letter from Fuller, read at the general meeting of March 24, 1834, Fuller's gift to the institution may have been a reaction against the clamor of such critics of British science as Babbage and Granville: ". . . it never shall be said that Britains, who are now at the head of all science, shall at any time shrink beneath the level of the rest of mankind." [15]

Roget's Fullerian Lectures consisted of three distinct courses, the "Physiology of Animals": eleven lectures between January 20 and April 7, 1835; twelve lectures between January 26 and April 26, 1836; and eleven lectures between January 17 and March 14, 1837.[16]

In May of 1837, Roget wrote to the institution that it was not his intention to offer himself as a candidate for the Fullerian professorship at the ensuing election. In November, a successor was chosen—Robert Edmund Grant, Professor of Comparative Anatomy and Zoology at London University from 1827 to 1874, and one of Roget's most telling antagonists in the warfare about to break out at the Royal Society. Of all the men who pretended to knowledge in physiology and comparative anatomy, Grant was undoubtedly Roget's strongest competitor. Of Grant, Thomas Henry Huxley later wrote:

> Within the ranks of the biologists at that time (1851–58) I met nobody, except Dr. Grant, of University College, who had a word to say for evolution;—and his advocacy was not calculated to advance the cause.[17]

Some fourteen years younger than Roget, Grant early established himself as an accurate and resourceful observer, and his generalizations, based on careful dissections, eventually carried much more weight than Roget's. Sir Norman Moore called Grant "the English Cuvier."

Among other problems at the Royal Institution in 1837 was a

"Gilbert-and-Sullivan" contest on the design of the new facade for the building on Albemarle Street. This prodigious row boiled down to whether the institution should have pilasters decorating the front or three-quarter pillars. Members were hit up for donations, and one man offered to increase his donation by £20 if they could have the pillars rather than the pilasters. The remodeling job with pilasters was originally estimated to cost £1,400, but the pillars faction pushed the donations up to £1,740 and carried the day. Roget contributed £2 to the impressive new front,[18] which remains the first view of the institution a visitor gets today. As a member of the Board of Visitors, Roget had also to worry about a leaking water closet at the RI, but across town, at Somerset House, far more serious trouble was brewing.

For many years, storms had threatened at the Royal Society over two particular practices—the awarding of medals for outstanding work, and the selection of papers for *Philosophical Transactions*. Part of the revolt in 1830 was an expression of dissatisfaction with the committees responsible for assigning these honors. Roget, who often served on five or six committees,[19] was therefore directly involved. Early in 1833, in response to charges of irregularities in awarding the two annual Royal Medals (valued at 50 guineas each), Roget served on a committee that drew up specific regulations governing the adjudications and the awards. But on May 13, the Council rescinded the resolutions of January 31 regarding the Royal Medals, and the maneuverings began all over again.

In 1834, Roget was appointed to a committee to decide the awarding of the Royal Medal in Physics, which was given in December to Charles Lyell for his *Principles of Geology*. The committee was careful to note that they "decline to express any opinion on the controverted portions contained in that work"—a rather understated recognition of the thundering battle over the "new geology" that had gone on for four decades, but which was virtually ended by the appearance of Lyell's work.

Continuing to pour his industry into the business of the Royal Society, Roget attended at least eighteen meetings of the Council in 1835 and an unspecified number of committee meetings. The number of meetings is also suggestive of the restiveness of the society, for it would appear that the number of Council meetings increased in direct proportion to the wrangles and conflicts within the society. On January 15 of that year, Roget proposed as honorary foreign members Frédéric Cuvier, Christian Ehrenberg, and Pierre Flourens. At the same meeting Faraday proposed Roget's old friend de La Rive as an honorary foreign member. On May 5, 1836, Roget had the pleasure of seeing to it that Marcet's son, François, was elected an FRS.

The submerged discontent that had been growing in the society surfaced in May 1836 as the result of an action taken by the Council in January. The Council interpreted the fifth section of Chapter XI of the society's statutes as intended to "prevent the discussion of any subject not immediately connected with the usual business of the ordinary meetings." Charging that this ruling had, through the spring of the year, been applied in a discriminatory fashion, and that the journal-book of the society thus contained a number of "informal and invalid" motions and remarks, a petition was filed requesting the President to convene a special general meeting to discuss the matter. The petitioners also criticized a resolution which withheld the thanks of the society to the author of a work presented by him to the society (this referred to Babbage's and South's critical tracts),

. . . thereby establishing the dangerous precedent of substituting for an act of mere courtesy on the part of this Society one of discriminating responsibility in the acknowledgement of books received as presents—an act utterly at variance with the usages of any scientific or literary society in this country, and which would involve the Royal Society in endless difficulties and controversies.[20]

The "requisition" was signed by S. B. Granville, J. A. Paris, W. R. Hamilton, W. M. Leake, Gore Ouseley, Joseph Sabine, S. D. Broughton, Benjamin Oliveira, H. Earle, John Knowles, A. Baird, Marshall Hall, T. J. Pettigrew, and James Copland. The Council unanimously declared that no special meeting had the power of expunging minutes of past proceedings, but did call a general special meeting for June 23.

The meeting was noisy, undignified, and marked by many extreme statements. But nothing happened. The old Council held tight to the reins, and effectively quashed attempts to bring about changes in the society's statutes to the following ends: 1) achieve the election of a scientist as President; 2) have a majority of scientists on the Council; 3) open the records of the Council in order to clear away administrative abuses; 4) confine membership to genuine scientists; 5) limit the number of Fellows elected each year. Through the 1830's there were increasing signs that without these changes the society could no longer maintain its reputation as the leading scientific organization in England. These signs were various. As an example of how badly the society's affairs were being run, the Leeuwenhoek collection of microscopic lenses—"like solitaire diamonds to the Royal Society"—had simply disappeared sometime between 1800 and 1830.[21] Another sign was the falling off of interest in the Royal Society Club, a dining club composed of forty members, who dined together immediately before scheduled meetings of the society and Council. In years past, much of the decision-making of the Council was accomplished over after-dinner port, but attendance dropped steadily in the 1830's. In 1834, for instance, from July to December, only twenty-nine members and eleven visitors attended. There were several meetings to which no one came, although the meals were prepared all the same. On July 23, 1829, two visitors showed up but neither of the members who had invited them made their appearance. Often there were only four or five at the meetings. In July 1830 the whole company consisted of the President and the Treasurer.[22]

One frequent subject of cries for reform was more careful editing of the prestigious *Philosophical Transactions*. Reformers charged that entirely too many papers were published and that much of the supervision, including selection of these papers, was handled by nonscientific men. Despite some related improvements accomplished during the presidency of the Duke of Sussex— some of them attributed to Roget's devotion to his job: publication of the minutes of the Council, distribution of the *Proceedings,* and the publication of abstracts of *Philosophical Transactions* papers—progress was far too slow to suit the younger men, and the 1830's and the 1840's were marked by frequent clashes.

One of these burst into the medical press when, in November 1836, Roget's Zoology and Physiology Committee recommended that the Royal Medal go to George Newport (1803–1854), entomologist, for his study, "Investigations on the Anatomy and Physiology of Insects," published as a series of papers in *Philosophical Transactions*. The following brief and vicious note appeared in *Lancet:*

> I wish one of your correspondents who is able would show in its true light, the affair of the Royal Medal, given by Dr. Roget, the plagiarist of Grant, to his friend Newport. Dr. M. Hall could supply the necessary information.[23]

The charge of plagiarism refers to Roget's Bridgewater Treatise, which leaned heavily upon Grant's work on sponges and other marine animals. It should be noted, however, that Roget repeatedly acknowledged Grant throughout the Bridgewater Treatise. Newport, too, was a very great help to Roget in that section of the Bridgewater Treatise dealing with insects. It was later alleged that Roget paid off his debt to Newport by awarding him the Royal Medal.

The next issue of *Lancet* carried this edged response from Hall:

"T. J." in your last number is wrong in appealing to me. His appeal ought to have been made to Dr. Grant and Mr. Kiernan. I know nothing of the question which he would agitate. I accompanied Mr. Kiernan and Dr. Grant, with a view of comparing Mr. Newport's papers with the works of the anatomists who have preceded him. The result of our comparison was, that we were all as much at a loss as "T. J." to discover on what ground the Royal medal, certainly the highest reward of science in this country, could be awarded to Mr. Newport.[24]

In view of exchanges that followed, it is clear that Hall's remark was but a thinly disguised declaration that Newport had indeed been guilty of plagiarizing the work of earlier entomologists.

A third writer, who identified himself simply as an "F.R.S. not a member of the Council," wrote a longer reply to both "T. J." and Hall, opening with the opinion that "The Royal Medals are public property, and should not only be awarded with judgment and justice, but, like woman's honour, so as to be above all suspicion." At first appearance a defense of Roget, "F.R.S." 's article was curiously qualified—"It does not appear to me, however, that the insertion of Dr. Roget's name into 'T. J.' s' communication is either just, or warranted by any thing which has yet been made public." At least, said "F.R.S.," it was unfair to attribute the award solely to Roget, unless "T. J." could show that the committee was composed of Roget only, or Roget's influence was paramount in the committee.

On the propriety of that award, I offer no opinion, as the subject is one upon which my knowledge is literally nothing. When I see the names of Dr. Marshall Hall and Dr. Grant standing in opposition to it, I own it leads me to hesitate in approving it; but, at all events, should Mr. Newport's researches be less valuable than they have been considered to be by that committee, I

am sure that no member of the Council of the Royal Society
has been actuated by other than proper motives in the
award.[25]

"F.R.S." suggested that, rather than air such matters in the
press, a more proper course would be to gather the necessary information and present it in the form of a memorial to the President and Council of the Royal Society. "Should this memorial be
passed over by the Council without due attention, *which I am
sure would not be the case,* then other methods would be requisite—and obvious, too."

This writer closed with the remark that it was generally understood that the Newport affair was being promoted by Francis
Kiernan (1800–1874), who was chagrined because he had been
awarded the society's Copley Medal rather than the Royal
Medal.

Kiernan's friends responded indignantly to this suggestion, of
course, and the status of the argument was admirably summed up
by one further letter to *Lancet,* signed "Scrutator (not an
F.R.S.)":

The question at issue is one of considerable interest and importance, and has become one of notoriety, and of much discussion
amongst the Fellows of the R.S., and I quite agree with your
sensible correspondent "F.R.S." in thinking that "the matter is
now in a state which calls imperatively for explanation, as well
for the credit of the Committee, as for individual justice."

Dr. Roget is charged with having imposed upon the Committee, and palmed upon them papers as containing *discoveries,* which, in reality, *contain none;* and with having rewarded
some sinister services rendered to himself by Mr. Newport, by
obtaining for Mr. Newport the Royal Medal.

The Committee is charged with having wished, but not
dared, to revoke their award of the Royal Medal to Mr. Newport, and with having endeavoured to correct one mistake by
the commission of another, in the further award of the Copley
Medal to Mr. Kiernan.

Mr. Kiernan is charged with having meanly acquiesced in an
arrangement of the Committee to give him the Copley Medal,
to quiet his disappointment at having been unjustly deprived
of the Royal Medal.

If these charges be true, a flagrant outrage has been committed upon the interests of science, the munificence of Royalty,
the reputation of the R.S., and the sacred trusts of office, by
an individual, which demands public exposure. But if they be

not true, the character of that individual should be cleared from such a serious imputation. I call upon Dr. Roget, Mr. Kiernan, and Mr. Newport, I call upon the Committee and Council of the R.S. to place this matter in the light of day.[26]

Aside from subsequent arguments in Council about the composition of the Zoology and Physiology Committee, I have found no evidence that the Newport case did, indeed, come into the light of day.

Marshall Hall attempted to reopen the case in 1839 with a long, complaining letter to Sir John Herschel, then Vice-President of the society, detailing his arguments with Roget, his objections to Newport's getting the medal, and the injustice Hall had suffered at the hands of the Physiology Committee. In essence, Hall's charges amounted to the following:

1. Favoritism. Hall said that both he and Dr. A. P. W. Philip read papers on the capillary vessels in 1831, but that because Philip was a member of the Council, his paper was published, and Hall's was not. Moreover, Philip's conclusions were wrong, Hall declared.

2. Plagiarism. Hall claimed that Grant and Roget had had a falling out as Grant was reading proofs on Roget's Bridgewater Treatise and discovered that Roget had appropriated much of Grant's work. Grant refused to read further. It was at this point, Hall charged, that Roget persuaded Newport, a pupil of Grant's, to help on the treatise.

3. Collusion. Roget persuaded Newport to assist him with the promise that he would see that Newport got the Royal Medal.

4. Incompetence. Hall said that along with Kiernan and Grant, he had compared Newport's work with previous works on the same subject—a step that Roget's committee should have taken. The result of that comparison was a resummoning of the committee. It was at this time, Hall said, that the committee, "to appease Mr. Kiernan, awarded to him the Copley Medal, leaving the previous award of the Royal Medal undisturbed, and thus, as one of the Vice Presidents of the Royal Society expressed it, 'attempted to correct one blunder by committing another.'"

5. Distortion. Hall declared that in writing an abstract of one of his papers, Roget "prejudged it with a sneer" and entered a false notation that the drawings and diagrams had not yet been supplied the committee. Hall said that not only were the drawings and diagrams in the hands of the committee, but Roget knew it at the time. Further, Hall said, Roget, in editing the *Pro-*

ceedings of the society, barely mentioned what Hall considered to be a definitive answer he had given to an insinuation made against him in Newport's paper.[27]

Hall was unhappy because of the failure of the committee and the Council to accept a number of his papers. Apparently suffering from lack of a sense of humor, Hall's dignity had been more than ruffled when some waggish Council member, reading in a Hall paper a reference to an experiment on the movements of a decapitated tortoise, scrawled in the margin, "Will they live after they are made soup of?" Hall was so incensed he printed up a note of protest which he distributed to the Council: "Such an observation needs no remark from me. It is rather an indignity put upon the Royal Society itself."

Humorless or no, Hall was highly respected by many, who maintained that he was unjustly maligned and persecuted by the Royal Society and most of the medical press, and his reputation surmounted this antagonism in the 1840's and 1850's. He was very active in the British Association for the Advancement of Science, and in medical reform efforts of the 1840's. In 1850, 1852, and 1856, he published pamphlets proposing sewage treatment works to reduce the pollution of the Thames. It would be interesting to determine whether, in these writings, he drew at all on Roget's 1827 study of the water supply.

It would seem that Hall's charges were not given any serious hearing at the Royal Society, although they may well have contributed ammunition to Herschel's successful reform campaign in the late 1840's. At any rate, Roget successfully rode out both the Newport and the Hall storms, surviving them only to be caught in another—his last—the Beck-Lee Affair.

The long and confused dispute between Roget's Physiology Committee and the anatomists Robert Lee and Thomas Snow Beck became a hopelessly tangled skein of meetings, hearings, position papers, newspaper accounts, correspondence, Council actions and rescinded actions, petitions, and protests that stretched from November 1839 to November 1849. For ten long years the cumulative arguments mounted without interruption and with increasing complexity until what had begun as an ostensibly simple disagreement over the awarding of a Royal Medal was finally seen for what it was: a large-scale revolt against Roget's old guard, a revolt that fed on the unresolved dissatisfactions of a decade before and which finally swept the Royal Society clean with a series of major reforms. Confusing the lines of this prolonged reform movement were many petty disputes, professional jealousies, and personality clashes that caused many a Fellow to despair of the society's ever coming to grips with the underlying basic problems. Not the least of the confusing elements was the delight of the popular press in publishing the most invidious accounts of the squabbles within the society.

If a distinct event can be isolated as the locus of all the prolonged wrangle, it would be the Physiology Committee's decision, in 1845, to award the Royal Medal to Beck for his work on the nerves of the uterus. An impressive number of Fellows were outraged at this decision: charge after charge was filed against the committee for alleged irregularities in the decision, against Beck for claiming precedence in an area where Lee was a recognized pioneer, against the Council for refusing to investigate.

After a number of ineffectual, individual protests, several important Fellows, including Richard Bright, Marshall Hall, Robert Grant, and T. Wharton Jones (probably the "T. J." whose letter to *Lancet* launched the controversy over Newport's award in 1836), petitioned in 1847 for a special meeting of inquiry into the 1845 Royal Medal award in physiology. At the special meeting, February 11, the Jones faction almost succeeded in forcing the rescinding of the award, but the Council preferred to bury the matter and scuttled the enabling resolution with an amendment which concluded, "it therefore does not seem expedient . . . that any further proceedings should be taken in the matter." [28]

But times were a-changing, in the Royal Society as well as in the larger world outside; members would no longer accept such arbitrary actions of the Council. The reformers tackled the Physiology Committee itself, forcing a resolution to expand its membership and thus reduce Roget's influence. The Council promptly rescinded the resolution. The President of the society was pressured into reporting on correspondence between Lee and himself on the 1845 award, but the Council again tried to quash the matter by resolving unanimously "that it is inexpedient to re-open the question."

Through 1847 and 1848 the pressure mounted to an irresistible climax. A growing faction threatened to invoke a governmental inquiry. The newspapers were in full cry of what was being revealed bit by bit, as the Establishment became desperate and at times ruthless in its attempts to preserve its power and position. When the full story was known of the shoddy treatment given Lee,[29] Roget and the society's President, the Marquis of North-

ampton, were forced to resign from the Council; the reformers
swept into office and immediately set about restructuring the institution.

The repudiation of Roget and the belated recognition of Lee
were overwhelming. In a biographical sketch, *Lancet* listed some
thirty-nine major papers—obstetrical studies—as indicative of
Lee's work and credited him with essential contributions to the
ovular theory of menstruation. The attempts by the Royal Society in 1845, said *Lancet,* to throw discredit on Lee's discovery of
the ganglionic nervous system of the uterus and the heart

> only ended in the exposure and disgrace of all the individuals
> concerned in the transactions. The erasure of confirmed min-
> utes from the journal-book of the Council to conceal the ille-
> gal deed was discovered; the resignation of the Marquis of
> Northampton and Dr. Roget and the entire destruction of the
> Committee of Physiology and all the other committees
> followed.[30]

The whole complicated controversy was the best evidence of
what the reformers had been maintaining for twenty years—that
the Royal Society was hopelessly mired in the machinations of
its cliques and in the hardened accretions of its antique procedures. That this conclusion was shared by a majority of the Fellows by the end of 1848 is confirmed by the rapid strides made
from that time toward real reform of the society. To the outside
world, and increasingly so to subsequent generations, the Beck-
Lee controversy was an obscure argument at an obscure moment
in history. However, as the dismal account of Roget's declining
years as Secretary of the Royal Society, the affair, in all its convo-
lutions, maneuverings, and reprisals, preserves the peculiar
drama of good men and bad floundering in the coils of their own
ambitions and consciences. That this drama was played out
within the laughably solemn walls of the Royal Society certainly
does not deny the pathos that was as real to Lee, to Beck, to Jones,
Hall, Grant, and above all to Roget, as any encounter played
today in the larger theater of national or world politics.

Meanwhile, as the Beck-Lee struggle held the public eye, an
even more serious battle was being waged underground as reformers tried to push past Roget certain procedural changes that
were, finally, the framework for eventual reform of the society at
large. Chief among these opponents of Roget were Herschel,
Leonard Horner, Charles Lyell, and perhaps the most effective

organizer of the lot, William Robert Grove, mathematician, physicist, and later President of the Royal Society.

Shortly after the first outcry over the awarding of a Royal
Medal to Beck, Horner, Grove, Lyell and others formed a
"charter committee" to revise the statutes of the society. Roget set
himself up as a stumbling block to the work of this committee,
sometimes going to the length of refusing to call or to sanction
the calling of a meeting by the committee.[31] The reformers simply met informally and carried forward their plans and arguments in each other's homes. Katherine Horner Lyell (Horner's
daughter had married the geologist) cites a letter of Lyell's in
which he spoke of Roget and friends as "a set of obstructives,
compared to whom Metternich was, I presume, a progressive
animal." [32] One of the principal points at issue was the reformers' insistence on imposing a limit on the number of new Fellows
to be taken into the Royal Society each year. Roget stubbornly
opposed the scheme, despite a series of courteous and well-rea-
soned letters Horner wrote him during 1846. Another series of
Horner letters—these to Grove—shows the disgust and frustration that lay just under the surface of the polite battle:

> You have undoubtedly seen that Dr. Roget has not inserted in
> the minutes the series of Resolutions moved by me, seconded
> by you, read *seriatim* from the chair, partly discussed, and
> partly decided upon.
>
> Immediately on getting the published pages, I wrote to him,
> calling his attention to the omission, and his answer to me is,
> "I think I can show that I was right in not inserting your pro-
> posed resolution." I gave him a second opportunity of correct-
> ing his error (now proved to be a deliberate act by his note to
> me) this morning, but he adheres to it. To what length will he
> not go! [33]

Or, in another letter, on February 5, ". . . Roget's conduct . . .
is most reprehensible and he ought to be told so in plain terms."

Another crucial issue, one that came even closer to Roget,
arose over the reformers' demand that one of the two secretaries
of the society be a man from the physical sciences and one from
the life sciences. Roget fought this move with equal subbornness,
particularly when Grove was nominated to fill a vacancy.[34]

Grove pushed forward on another front by organizing the Philosophical Club, a dining club of Fellows very much like the old
Royal Society Club, but determinedly scientific in its composition. Founded on April 12, 1847, the Philosophical Club served

as a watch-dog group, monitoring the changes in the making at
the Royal Society and in every way promoting the trend toward
excluding nonscientific figures from the society. Most of its
members—membership was limited to forty-seven—were adher-
ents of the Horner-Grove-Lyell faction. Roget was conspicuous in
his refusal to participate in the new club. Instead, he remained
with the old Royal Society Club and watched its activity and influence diminish even as he himself lost ground to the hard-press-
ing reformers.

Thus Roget was left very much alone, his solid reputation considerably shaken, his former supporters in the medical press fled,
and the remainder of his oldest friends gone. Babington died in
1833; Yelloly in 1842; Bostock in 1846. In 1846 Roget's son John
went off to Cambridge. In the ten years between 1838 and 1848,
Roget attended at least sixty meetings of the Physiology Committee, not to mention scores of other meetings of committees, Council, and society. In his own eyes he had worked hard and worked
well. Compared with those of some of his colleagues, his reports
on papers submitted to the committee are admirably serious,
objective attempts to review the work of his contemporaries. In
1840 he had given up his medical practice, partly because of his
increasing deafness, partly because he wanted to be free for more
research and writing and for the heightening battles at the Royal
Society. He had found the battles right enough, and now the battles had found him.

In that great meeting hall in Somerset House on the evening
of November 30, 1847, Roget read his final message as senior Secretary. To him the hall must have seemed filled with opponents,
the young, the eager, the indignant men of a new age, barely
concealing their impatience to be done with the seventy-year-old
man who now addressed them:

> I wish to take the opportunity afforded me by the present assem-
> blage of the Fellows to announce to them my intention of re-
> tiring, at the next anniversary, from the office I have so long
> had the honour of holding in the Royal Society. This determi-
> nation, as many of my friends well know, has not been formed
> hastily; and I would have carried it into effect some time ago,
> had it not been for the peculiar circumstances in which I
> found myself placed.

After a dignified sketch of the changes he had witnessed in the
society during his lengthy tenure, Roget made his only allusion

to the battles which had driven him to the necessity of making this swan song:

> . . . Having now grown grey in that service, I feel that it is time for me to retire, while my strength is yet unbroken, and before the changes which the Society is now undergoing shall cause fresh demands to be made upon it; that I may dedicate the remaining term of life that may yet be spared me to those pursuits of science to which I have always been warmly attached, and with which the labours and the cares of office have seriously interfered.
>
> I have alluded to the existence of some peculiar circumstances which had prevented my taking this step some time ago. These circumstances must be fresh in the memory of most of those I am now addressing: they sprung from a series of malignant attacks, carried on with extraordinary pertinacity during nearly two years, against the Society, its President, and above all, the Committee of Physiology; and these attacks were pointed more particularly against myself, under the erroneous notion that I was especially responsible for the proceedings of that Committee; whereas, in reality, of all its members, I was the one who was least implicated in them. While the battle was raging, I could not, in honour, withdraw from the field; my duty was to remain at my post and abide the pelting of the storm. But these squalls having now blown over, I feel at liberty to retreat, and to resign into your hands the trust you have so long and so liberally confided to me.

A striking irony—one that Roget himself was keenly aware of —is the fact that at that same anniversary meeting, November 30, 1847, when Roget read his retirement speech, Grove was awarded the Royal Medal for Physics, and Sir John Herschel the Copley Medal for Astronomy.

At the end of 1847, Roget was a wise old bird, and a durable one too. He had had far too much experience in the competitive jungle of London not to know when the odds were against him, and increasingly so with every additional year, every new encounter with the new forces then at work. Change was in the air. Change had been turning institutions upside down for nearly two decades; now it had finally come to the Royal Society. He had too many things yet to do to destroy himself in the mills that were now turning and reshaping the old society, and he may even have acknowledged to himself that the changes were long overdue. He had not studied and written on the phenomenon of human aging without understanding that which many another investigator has yet to learn—that the findings applied to himself as well as to mankind in general. He simply no longer could command the physical resources in himself that were necessary to do battle with the younger men. Moreover, there seemed little point in it. Practically all of his own generation—people who would best have understood what he fought for—were gone, and many of the succeeding generation were gone as well. Certainly few in that meeting hall, including Roget himself, could suspect that he would live for another twenty years, active and productive to the last.

The fact that he relinquished the secretaryship and thus his position as a leader of the old guard did not mean that Roget was through with the Royal Society. On the contrary, he continued to sit on committees, and ironically, as Vice-President, chaired many a meeting of the Council as the whole structure of the society changed beneath him. He remained on the Council until 1851, and was active on committees as late as 1853. On June 29, 1854, he had the pleasure of seeing Marcet's son awarded £50 for his researches into the excretions of man and the animals. At the same meeting, Huxley was awarded £300 for publication of his zoological studies. At the next meeting, November 2, 1854, Roget saw Charles Darwin elected to the Council.

XV [1848–1852

Thesaurus

FROM the beginning of his professional life, Roget had toyed with a project that an objective observer might well insist lay quite outside the scope and powers of the Secretary of the Royal Society, the Fullerian Professor, the physiologist, the water expert, the chess master, the physician, or any of the other competencies attained by Peter Mark Roget. Neither literarily nor philologically was Roget equipped to create the work that has made his name as much a household word as that of Noah Webster. None of his other works, as he moved from chemistry to mathematics to optics to comparative anatomy, gives any suggestion that Roget was even interested in such a project, let alone capable of carrying it off. Yet from 1805 onward, he had been compiling and testing lists of words arranged in certain orders; and in 1849, in his seventieth year, when he no longer had to fight the battles of the Royal Society, he settled down in his study in Upper Bedford Way, opened his files, and began writing the *Thesaurus of English Words and Phrases.*

In this paradoxical fact—that it was Roget, the aged London doctor, who wrote the *Thesaurus,* rather than any number of his better equipped contemporaries—we can read the distinctive signature not only of Roget but of his age. The *Thesaurus* was, for Roget at least, not a literary tour de force but the culminating effort of a lifetime devoted to discovering a way of presenting the unity of man's existence.

While he was mildly interested in and even vaguely proud of his literary style, Roget was certainly no stylist. He made no innovations, started no trends, attempted no experiments in literature, made no explicit study of rhetoric. From start to finish, his long record of published and private writings shows that he had quickly and easily adopted a kind of formal eighteenth-century style that seemed to be designed more to establish a kind of decorum or mien than to communicate ideas or feelings. It was characterized by a reliance on the balanced sentence, the antithesis, a ponderous parallelism, and an abstract and highly latinate vocabulary. His tendency to string clauses and phrases together reminds one of the cautionary legal device of writing an entire document as one sentence. The effect was that of a stiff sort of rationality, almost as though the writer were setting up an opaque and rigid screen between himself and his reader to prevent any personal or emotional contact during the painful but necessary interview to follow. Roget's style was certainly no worse than that of most of his age—but it was no better either. Significantly, there is no evidence that he had *any* literary pretensions beyond that competence expected by his largely scientific audience. His reading and abstracting of papers for the various society publications gave him a kind of workaday editorial training, but again, it was only such that enabled him to make the papers of his fellow scientists presentable. Some idea of his standards can be gained by the following excerpt from his manuscript report on a paper submitted to the Royal Society:

> His style is marked throughout by want of perspicuity and precision; his meaning is often obscured by a diffuseness and laxity of expression, rendering it difficult to follow the course of his argument [Roget then listed samples of the author's "grossly incorrect spelling"] . . . *fulcri* for *fulcra*, "aeria" for "area," "fiber" for "fibre," "born out" for "borne out," "principal" for "principle," etc., etc. . . . Taking into consideration the inconclusiveness of the author's mode of reasoning and the unsatisfactory manner in which he has treated the subject, I am of opinion that this paper, on either ground, is unworthy of a place in the *Philosophical Transactions*.[1]

In all of his writings up to this time, Roget had composed only one on a literary subject, an article on Dante—or, to be more exact, one half of an article. Written in collaboration with Ugo Foscolo, this study of the Italian poet appeared in the February 1818 issue of the *Edinburgh Review*.[2]

Nor did his reading habits suggest a literary interest. The periodicals he read, the volumes that he accumulated into a formidable library, as one might expect, were predominantly scientific.

In other words, Roget's interest in style was chiefly utilitarian.

He would have seen the efforts of literary folk to achieve some sort of elegance or grace or vivacity as the very kind of wasteful expenditure that he deplored in those who pursued elegance in dress or society. As his mother had so rightly prophesied, Roget had no distinguishable literary bent.

Moreover, by no stretch of the terms could Roget have been called a linguist or a philologist. He was a competent reader of Latin, German, and Italian, and a more than competent reader and writer of French, but the few translations he attempted—for example, those paragraphs in his *Edinburgh Review* essays on Huber—simply did not involve him in language per se. The words were only means to an end, in that case the facts of Huber's work with ants and bees. Aside from his first year's work in classical literature at Edinburgh, which no doubt helped form his heavy, foursquare style of expression, there is no indication that he had any linguistic training—no studies, for example, in the origins of his language, nor any letters suggesting that he was at all concerned with such linguistic problems as the relationship between spoken and written language, the conflict between denotative and connotative aspects of words, or the natural pressure of linguistic change versus the desire to preserve and to purify.[3]

In short, nowhere in the not inconsiderable surviving remnants of Roget's life is there a sign of that sort of inconsequential fiddling with language that denotes a fascination with language itself—the sort of playing with sounds, significations, structures, that if continued might lead the player into writing poetry, or studying the attributive influence of the demonstrative pronoun. Roget was so little interested in language for itself that it is only in a very occasional letter, rather late in life, that he even barely mentions his "word book." Yet he says himself, in his preface to the original edition of the *Thesaurus*, that he had worked on it since 1805.[4]

Why then would Roget have so devoted himself, in those four years between 1848 and 1852, to a work that he was so eminently unqualified to produce? One might reasonably argue that he simply followed the pattern long established in his life—that whenever he suffered a defeat, he remembered his uncle's fears about the family weakness of despondency, and deliberately lost himself in work. However, the larger patterns of his life, those shaped by his most consistent intellectual and emotional needs, suggest a more satisfying explanation.

In nearly every phase of his life, not excluding his marriage,

Roget's most characteristic concern was for the organization of activity. His chief contributions were not medical innovations, scientific discoveries, ingenious experiments, or profound insights—although, as we have seen, he contributed modestly in all these modes—but in organization. His real intellectual gift and joy was the ability to bring about order in that which lacked it. Whether one examines his efforts in public health, in physiology, in comparative anatomy, or his dedication to the Medical and Chirurgical Society and to the Royal Society; whether one surveys his Bridgewater Treatise, his papers for the Society for the Dissemination of Useful Knowledge, or his articles for various encyclopaedias, one is struck first by his determination to present that material in an orderly manner. His early contribution to medical education—the lectures at Manchester—as well as his later efforts in the same field as Examiner at the University of London, speak of his awareness of the imperative need for an *organized* body of knowledge and its *orderly* presentation. His dogged work for the many scientific societies, old and new, again expressed his conviction that what was needed was an organized approach. In a prefatory note attached to his essays on magnetism and electricity, written for the SDUK, Roget said he had been chiefly motivated by the gathering together into a "didactic order" of the many recent discoveries and theories in the field. Even in projects of personal improvement he looked to organization first, as is seen in his delight with Feinagle's elaborate but highly organized memory system.

This devotion to organization, to rationality, to order, is most clearly manifest in his lifelong fascination with problems of classification. And he was, of course, in the midst of an age of classifiers, for, it would seem, the successful emergence of modern science depended on the primacy of a workable classification of its elements. In geology, biology, chemistry, physics, the enormous strides made in the early nineteenth century were steps taken upon a groundwork of systems of classification. Linnaeus was a demigod, and improvers on his system were consistently elevated as well.[5] Bentham's elaborate attempts to classify the "springs of human action" in a tabular breakdown under his major headings, "Pleasure" and "Pain," are still preserved in Volume I of his *Works*. Much of the appeal of the phrenology scheme can be explained by the apparent order the doctrine brought to psychology through its analysis of human motives into distinct classes. Throughout the midcentury decades, men were struggling toward classification in the physical sciences as well, as is seen in Mendeleev's devising of the periodic table of chemical elements in 1869.

In Roget's own fields—medicine and physiology—real progress was made when men like him insisted upon establishing clear-cut orders of things and procedures. Roget's admiration for his contemporary, the Swiss botanist Augustine de Candolle, was based primarily upon the latter's lifelong efforts to develop a principle of classification according to the natural, as opposed to the Linnaean or artificial, method.[6] Significantly, the science of comparative anatomy came into being only after the organizational influence of newly established classification systems. To Roget, Georges Cuvier was a gigantic figure primarily because of the clarity of his scheme of classifying the animal kingdom. That Darwin himself realized that a firm classification of life forms was the essential fundament for his theories of origin and evolution is abundantly clear in his writings. Darwin's organized view and way of life are suggested by an appendix to his autobiography, in which, upon pondering whether or not to marry, he neatly drew up the pro and con arguments in facing columns on a single page.

A beautiful expression of the near-worship with which Roget's contemporaries approached the achievements of classifiers is the opening sentence of an essay in Bentham's *Westminster Review,* in the same year that the *Thesaurus* appeared. The writer, in treating four volumes on botany that had been published in recent years, centered his remarks on the great value of the "systematists: Solomon, Dioscorides, Linnaeus!—three full-sounding names, names with a presence. We utter them as an incantation, an 'open sesame!' . . ."[7]

Thus, organization—and particularly classification, with all its attendant problems of establishing relationships, recognizing correlations, distinguishing between large and small orders of things, and rendering visible the spatial, chronological, numerical, causal, and constituent relations among all the things and happenings of existence—became early and remained late Roget's primary intellectual challenge and joy and frustration.

Roget was no philosopher in the modern sense of the term, but he saw clearly (as in his Bridgewater Treatise) the fact that without order, without organization, there could be no design; and without design, there could be no God. Without God, there could be no purpose, and without purpose, there was no meaning.

That classification is just as viable today as it was in 1852 in

the hopes and struggles of men to unify and systematize their
knowledge of existence can be realized by the briefest consideration of modern problems of information retrieval, data process-
ing, and machine translation.[8] Roget's distinctive contribution—
the classification of ideas into a skeleton outline of commonly
understood terms—is, in effect, the heart of information retrieval
systems now in operation or in an advanced stage of development. Researchers and experimenters at such institutions as Cornell University, International Business Machines, Mitre Corporation, and Arthur D. Little, Inc., develop their own "thesauri" from
various sources, including Roget's *Thesaurus*. Roget's title word
"thesaurus" has now come into the language as a common noun.
The term, as it is now used in information retrieval work, is the
bridge between the searcher for information and the source of
that information.

This bridge, in information retrieval circles (frequently called
an authority list, dictionary, or thesaurus) is a set of descrip-
tors or subject headings which are being used to describe or
characterize something and upon which the user can rely when
he frames a question.

A thesaurus would be a structured list of words showing au-
thorized terms, broad terms or narrow terms, "see also" references, and scope notes to explain the use of the term.

Frequently nowadays such dictionaries or thesauri are stored
in the computer so that they can be updated readily and referred to by the indexer and the user from remote terminals. A
typical thesaurus would be the one developed by the Engineers
Joint Council in New York City. This is a project on which
many people worked for many months. This thesaurus is now
available in printed as well as in machine-readable form.[9]

A case in point is Roget's interest in the classification of books,
first at the Medical and Chirurgical Society, then at the Royal
Society. Panizzi's struggle to establish workable rules for classifying the collection at the British Museum has become a virtual
legend. John Latham, long in disrepute as a do-nothing president
at the Royal College of Physicians, was remembered with respect
because many years earlier he had brought order out of the chaos
of the library at the college. John Lubbock, one of Roget's cohorts in the old guard at the Royal Society, expressed a widespread concern of the age when he published a curious pamphlet,
*Remarks on the Classification of the Different Branches of Human
Knowledge* (London, 1838). Lubbock complained that such con-

temporary philosophers as Dugald Sewart had not paid sufficient attention to the problem of classifying knowledge. Lubbock's own system was an unwieldy tripartite arrangement under the major headings of "History," "Philosophy," and "Fine Arts," and may help explain why he and Panizzi were so much at cross purposes in cataloging the library of the Royal Society. Melvil Dewey was not to begin work on his decimal system of classifying books until 1876, and the Library of Congress system was not devised until 1899.

From the classification of books to the classification of ideas and language was an easy, even a natural, step. Even as Roget worked on his *Thesaurus,* John Stuart Mill was developing his *System of Logic,* which begins with a consideration of meaning in individual words—that is, an attempt to systematize the means with which we construct logical, or illogical, propositions. Within the long tradition of the Royal Society itself was a continuing philosophical concern for a more logical, more precise language. One of the society's earliest publications was an essay by John Wilkins, *Towards a Real Character and a Philosophical Language* (1668), in which the author anticipated Roget's central scheme and tried to arrange all human ideas into a series of classes. Beginning with the most general, and devising ever-smaller compartments to accommodate the increasingly specific subdivisions of those large ideas, Wilkins offered a tabular outline of all human knowledge—precisely what Roget did more successfully by constructing a mammoth word list.

Nor was Roget unaware of the philosophical effort he was making in the *Thesaurus.* In the introduction to the first edition, he noted that he had studied Wilkins' work, as well as two other works, which, with Wilkins', were the only attempts he could find "to construct a systematic arrangement of ideas with a view to their expression": an ancient Indian work, the *Amera Cosha,* or *Vocabulary of the Sanscrit Language,* translated by Roget's colleague Henry Thomas Colebrooke in 1803, and an anonymous work that appeared in Paris in 1797 under the title *Pasigraphie, ou premiers éléments du nouvel art-science d'écrire et d'imprimer une langue de manière à être lu et entendu dans toute autre langue sans traduction.* "It contains a great number of tabular schemes of categories, all of which appear to be excessively arbitrary and artificial, and extremely difficult of application, as well as of apprehension," said Roget. Moreover, Roget saw his own book as a tool for the philosopher:

Metaphysicians engaged in the more profound investigation of the Philosophy of Language will be materially assisted by having the ground thus prepared for them, in a previous analysis and classification of our ideas; for such classification of ideas is the true basis on which words, which are their symbols, should be classified. It is by such analysis alone that we can arrive at a clear perception of the relation which these symbols bear to their corresponding ideas, or can obtain a correct knowledge of the elements which enter into the formation of compound ideas, and of the exclusions by which we arrive at the abstractions so perpetually resorted to in the process of reasoning, and in the communication of our thoughts.[10]

Finally, Roget's analysis of the language, as seen in the *Thesaurus*, was absolutely necessary, he felt, to the determination of the principles on which a "strictly *Philosophical Language* might be constructed." Of course, such a language would be adopted by every civilized nation, "thus realizing that splendid aspiration of philanthropists—the establishment of a Universal Language."

While modern linguistic studies have all but abandoned the feasibility of an artificial universal language, the idea of order and system in language is as prominent in the writings of linguists now as it was in Roget's introduction. There are enormous differences, of course—Roget seeing order as that which had to be imposed from without, and modern students seeing it as that which is inherent in the growth of language itself—but the preoccupation of both the nineteenth-century and the twentieth-century minds with a *systematic* understanding of language is significant. Consider, for example, the contribution of Noam Chomsky in generative grammar, or that of Benjamin Whorf, who writes convincingly of the causal relationship between modes of language and modes of thought.[11]

It is in this context, then, that we must look at Roget's *Thesaurus*, despite the fact that the book has never, to my knowledge, been considered a philosophical work. In fact, the instant and virtually unanimous reception of the book as a device for adding a ready-made veneer of words and phrases and thus a semblance of style to the untrained writer's repertory is the ultimate irony of Roget's laborious endeavor. What he conceived, in all sobriety and dutiful conscience, as a philosophical sextant, became, in its dime-store editions, a gimmick beloved by the crossword puzzle fan. We must thus see the *Thesaurus* as a philosophical effort, not for the sake of a philosophical exercise, but in order to recognize in it the ultimate signature of a man whose very intellectual and emotional being demanded an ordered and a charted (or at least a chartable) universe.

To understand Roget's unique contribution, it is necessary to see it in the sequence of earlier attempts at gathering the synonymies of the language into book form, for it is only with the *Thesaurus* that the synonymy becomes other than 1) a word-finding list, or 2) a series of related words more or less carefully discriminated.[12] The earliest work known is an anonymous seventeenth-century manuscript, "An Essay Towards a New English Dictionary, Wherein the Terms of Art are Cast Together, as Likewise Words and Phrases of the Same Import, so That Every Reader May Without Trouble Find Words and Expressions Proper to His Subject."

Some forty printed works on English synonymy had appeared before Roget's book in 1852. Actually, these represent only twenty different titles, the remainder being revised editions. First is a 1766 work by John Trusler, *The Difference Between Words Esteemed Synonymous in the English Language; and the Proper Choice of Them Determined; Together with So Much of Abbé Girard's Treatise on This Subject as Would Agree with Our Mode of Expression.*[13] The next and perhaps most amusing work of this type was that of Hester Lynch Piozzi (1741–1821). Better known as Mrs. Thrale, the close friend of Dr. Johnson (who may have written some sections of the book), Mrs. Piozzi "was attempting to indicate and establish idiomatic English." Her book, therefore, was highly prescriptive, as is suggested by its full title: *British Synonymy; or, an Attempt at Regulating the Choice of Words in Familiar Conversation.*[14] Mrs. Piozzi's book, published in Dublin in 1794, contained some 427 pages, consisting of an alphabetically arranged series of longish paragraphs, each devoted to a group of synonymous words. Her chief concern was that her book be of use to those coming up in society and to eligible foreigners, whose inadequate grasp of the nuances of English synonymies might lead them into embarrassing situations. It is Mrs. Piozzi who remarked in her preface, "Synonymy has more to do with elegance than truth"—a statement that would have disgusted Roget. Two samples of her method and her characteristic attitude will explain her statement adequately:

AFFABILITY, CONDESCENSION, COURTESY, GRACIOUSNESS

Are nearly synonymous, though common discourse certainly admits that an equal may be affable, which I should still think wrong in a printed book, and unpleasing everywhere, because the word itself seems to imply superiority. We will allow however that the *lofty courtesy* of a princess loses little of its *graciousness,* although some *condescension* be left visible through the exterior *affability;* but that, among people where talents or fortune only make the difference, a strain of polished familiarity, or familiar politeness (call it as you will) is the behaviour most likely to attract affectionate esteem.

DESPONDENCY, HOPELESSNESS, DESPAIR

Form a sort of heart-rending climax rather than a parallel—a climax, too, which time never fails of bringing to perfection. The last of these words implies a settled melancholy, I think, and is commonly succeeded by suicide.

While Mrs. Piozzi evidently had a very delicate ear indeed, her book was not universally applauded. In a cantankerous article in *Fraser's Magazine,* an unsigned writer, reviewing what had been accomplished in books on synonyms up to 1851, put his opinion of Mrs. Piozzi's book very plainly:

Good, bustling, lively Mrs. Piozzi was much better qualified to defend her husband, and vindicate the rights of an imprudent love-match . . . than to compile a guide to British synonymy; and if her evil genius had prompted her to do something to justify the charge of flippancy and shallowness flung so coarsely upon her by Dr. Johnson, she could not have more effectually responded to the temptation than by giving these foolish volumes to the world. Mrs. Piozzi was absolutely ignorant of the nature of the task she had undertaken. . . . The work is utterly destitute of any governing principle. Mrs. Piozzi runs in amongst words like a child at romps, and tosses them about apparently more in sport than earnest. . . .[15]

There is little point in discussing each of the synonymy works antedating Roget's except to the extent necessary to show the chief directions taken by his predecessors. As suggested above, they generally fell into two types: those that were simple lists of words—word-finding lists, and those that tried to explain the distinctions within the several synonymies treated. One interesting variation was the attempt by the translator William Taylor (1765–1836), who brought out *English Synonymes Discriminated* in 1813. Taylor's innovation—one that has been dropped in modern works—was the use of etymologies to explain original meanings of words and thereby establish synonymic relationships. While the *Fraser's Magazine* writer found much to admire in Taylor, he pointed out—and modern linguists would agree—

that *original* meanings may or may not have anything to do with *current* meanings.

The most important and most durable precursor to Roget's *Thesaurus* appeared first in 1816: *English Synonymes Explained, in Alphabetical Order; with Copious Illustrations and Explanations Drawn from the Best Writers,* by George Crabb. Running to 772 pages in the first edition, Crabb's work, by its sheer massiveness, cast a shadow over all the others, and it attempted to combine the useful features of all that had gone before. Thus, Crabb is a word-finding list, alphabetically arranged; it is a discriminating synonymy; it makes considerable use of etymologies; and it provides appropriate citations from respectable literature.

The value of early editions of Crabb was greatly lessened by several serious weaknesses: it was weighted down by the many authorities quoted; it was puffed up out of all compass by Crabb's tendency to insert his opinions on a variety of topics; his knowledge of etymologies was often faulty. An unsigned essay in the *Quarterly Review* complained of Crabb's "unbearable prolixity," and condemned as maddeningly circular Crabb's ingenious, if cumbersome, attempt to provide cross references throughout the work. Crabb had devised a system of large and small capitalized key words to lead his readers from one related word to another —surely a foreshadowing of Roget's apparatus—but

> PREMEDITATION, for example . . . [refers one to] another set of capitals . . . in another part of the volume, FORETHOUGHT; there we are sent to seek FORECAST; and at FORECAST we are desired to consult FORESIGHT: and after being thus bandied about, we are at length favoured with the author's sentiments on PRE-MEDITATION.[16]

At midcentury Crabb's work still offered the greatest body of synonymic material, and it ran through at least sixteen revisions and reprintings in England and America before 1852. Apparently its success encouraged other lexicographers, for in the ten years immediately before Roget's *Thesaurus* appeared, no less than fourteen new synonymy volumes appeared on the market (some of them new editions of older works), including works by William Carpenter (1842), John Platts (1845), George F. Graham (1846), James Jermyn (1848), James Rawson (1850), and Elizabeth Whately (1851). Only Crabb's and Whately's have been reprinted in recent years.

Why Roget's work could enjoy the instant acceptance it did in

1852, with what would seem a plethora of wordbooks already in the field, can be answered only by the fact that the *Thesaurus* offered something entirely new. It is here that Roget's philosophical objectives come into view.

As has often been noted, Roget described his book as the exact converse of a dictionary: instead of presenting a vocabulary of words for the purpose of finding the ideas they represent, the *Thesaurus* presents the ideas arranged in a way to reveal the words that can be used to express them. The scheme seems simple enough at first glance, but what it finally entailed was the arrangement and classification of *all human knowledge* under a graduated system of headings and key words. Even to attempt this prodigious feat meant a careful sorting out of kinds of relationships among ideas, a penetrating study of semantic correlations, and the invention of a mechanism that would make possible a workable layout of these ideas and their corresponding words. The task was virtually impossible, but the thin old doctor, noting "it is of the utmost consequence that strict accuracy should regulate our use of language," accepted the challenge as a duty.

Working from his knowledge of classification systems in biology and in bibliography, Roget first set up six major classes of ideas:

   I   ABSTRACT RELATIONS
   II   SPACE
   III   MATTER
   IV   INTELLECT
   V   VOLITION
   VI   SENTIENT AND MORAL POWERS

His choice of these major classes, of course, reveals a good deal about the elements into which Roget divided his world. Each of these major "classes," which might be thought of as analogous to *phyla* in the zoological classification, was divided into from three to eight "sections" (*classes* in zoology), and each section into as many as twenty "heads" (*orders*). Finally, all of these divisions —some thousand in all—were laid out in outline and tabular form and carefully numbered. A sample of the types of subdivisions he called "sections" and "heads" is the following drawn from Class IV, Intellect:

   I   *Intellectual Operations in General*
       450   Intellect

Each number, then, designated a particular paragraph of the book, a particular idea, under which the reader would find all words expressive of that idea. Thus, when one opens the *Thesaurus,* he finds an initially confusing arrangement of paragraphs or groups of words—not set up alphabetically, but numerically. Obviously, an additional device—an alphabetical index—was necessary for one to locate that numbered paragraph dealing with the idea for which he needed appropriate words. It is in augmenting and improving the index that subsequent editors have made their most useful contributions to Roget's *Thesaurus.*

The *Thesaurus* offered no definitions, no etymologies, no discriminating explanations of the differences between any given pair of synonyms, no citations of "best authors." Again and again, Roget emphasized that the purpose of his work "is not to explain the signification of words, but simply to classify and arrange them according to the sense in which they are now used, and which I presume *to be already known to the reader* [italics added]."

It almost seems as though he found the idea of defining or explaining words to his readers distasteful—a far remove from Mrs. Piozzi's heavy-handed didacticism. Roget appears to have paid his readers an enormous compliment: that they knew the meaning of the words before they looked them up. His contribution was arranging those words according to distinct relationships so that the reader could bring order out of the chaos of thought and language. Rather than having an interest in "elegance," as Mrs. Piozzi would have it, his whole concern was with "truth," and he saw that it was in their relationships to each other that words could approximate truth.

As in any sorting-out process, Roget was plagued by the big problem inherent in classification: the validity of categories vs. the continuum of nature. It is this problem, of course, that Panizzi fought so hard to avoid in objecting to the Royal Society scheme of classes for its new library catalog; it is this problem that Dewey tried to meet in his decimal system by inventing a means of infinitely expanding his ten major classes. Roget tried to solve the problem by providing copious cross references and by cataloging rather than classifying, entering the same word again, under as many classes, sections, and heads as seemed necessary.

Other difficulties of the synonymist Roget confronted manfully: what to do about words that have two meanings, quite opposite to each other (e.g., "to cleave," "to let," "to ravel," "priceless"); how to distinguish between common *phrases* (which he wanted to include) and common *proverbs* (which he excluded); how to clarify the confusion caused by inconsistent prefix significations (while "dis" and "un" and "in" normally reverse the meanings of the words to which they are attached, in a good many, such as "dissever," "disannual," "unloose," and "inebriety," the prefixes do not affect the meanings at all). Roget refused to become entangled in etymologies and word changes—he saw that subject as quite outside the scope of his book. Nor would he attempt to discriminate among synonyms, as most of his predecessors had: "far less do I venture to thrid the mazes of the vast labyrinth into which I should be led by any attempt at a general discrimination of synonyms. The difficulties I have had to contend with have already been sufficiently great, without this addition to my labours."

Moreover, Roget did not see himself as a linguistic arbiter. He left to the Mrs. Piozzis and the Crabbs the doubtful duty of purifying the language and thus ranged himself with the modern descriptive linguist who finds it difficult enough to *describe* the language as it is without attempting to *prescribe* what it ought to be.

With regard to the admission of many words and expressions, which the classical reader might be disposed to condemn as vulgarisms, or which he perhaps might stigmatize as usage of the day, I would beg to observe, that, having due regard to the uses to which this Work was to be adapted, I did not feel myself justified in excluding them solely on that ground, if they possessed an acknowledged currency in general intercourse. It is obvious that, with respect to degrees of conventionality, I could not have attempted to draw any strict lines of demarcation; and far less could I have presumed to erect any absolute standard of purity. My object, be it remembered, is not to regulate the use of words, but simply to supply and to suggest such as may be wanted on occasion, leaving the proper selection entirely to the discretion and taste of the employer.

In short, Roget paid his readers still another compliment—not only of knowing the meanings of his words, but also of having the taste to use them appropriately.

On the subject of neologisms, Roget was liberal within rather unspecified limits. He accepted gladly new words that inevitably arose from innovations in the sciences and arts, describing these as "perfectly legitimate and highly advantageous; and they necessarily introduce those gradual and progressive changes which every language is destined to undergo." He was severely critical, however, of "some modern writers" who arbitrarily fabricated new words and newfangled phraseology "without any necessity, and with manifest injury to the purity of the language." He put this sort of thing down as a "vicious practice, the offspring of indolence or conceit, and an ignorance or neglect of the riches in which the English language already abounds." On this subject, Roget undoubtedly would have nodded agreement to Chaucer's line, "Men loven of propre kinde newefangelnesse." In fact, he suggested modestly that his book might well be used as a standard vocabulary, tending to limit the fluctuations to which the language is always subjected.

With admirable clearheadedness and singleness of purpose, Roget adhered to his plan—a kind of "synopticon" of the language. Criticisms that he was too arbitrary in devising his main classes and that many of his headings could appear as well under one section as another were met with a steady expanding and improving of the massive index.[17]

Roget's "happiest inspiration," according to Professor Dutch, was an arrangement within a given section to show antonymic as well as synonymic relationships among words. Roget did not call similar terms "synonyms" or opposing terms "antonyms." In fact, according to Miss Egan, the latter term was not coined until 1867, with the appearance of *A Complete Collection of Synonyms and Antonyms,* by the Rev. Charles J. Smith.[18] Roget, like most synonymists, insisted that there *were* no real synonyms in the sense of two words having identical meanings. Instead, he called them "analogous" words and "correlative" words. In his introduction to the 1852 *Thesaurus*—still the best explanation of his methods and objectives—Roget explained why he printed analogous words and correlative words in facing columns on the page. In devising this arrangement, he became aware of many problems that plague the semanticist today, and he enunciated a sociolinguistic principle that such modern linguists as Otto Jespersen have readily adopted:

The study of correlative terms existing in a particular language, may often throw valuable light on the manners and customs of the nations using it. [Roget here acknowledges with a foot-note his indebtedness to David Hume for this observation, and he quotes several examples from Hume's "Essay on the Populousness of Ancient Nations."] . . .

In many cases, two ideas which are completely opposed to each other, admit of an intermediate or neutral area, equidistant from both; all these being expressible by corresponding definite terms. . . .

Identity	Difference	Contrariety
Beginning	Middle	End
Past	Present	Future

In other cases, the intermediate word is simply the negative to each of two opposite positions—

Convexity	Flatness	Concavity
Desire	Indifference	Aversion

Sometimes the intermediate word is properly the standard with which each of the extremes is compared—

Insufficiency	Sufficiency	Redundance

Or, as later editors pointed out, the intermediate word signifies an imperfect degree of each of the qualities set in opposition:

Light	Dimness	Darkness
Transparency	Semitransparency	Opacity
Vision	Dimsightedness	Blindness

Roget's study of these correlative relationships caused him to conclude that his book should be made up in triple instead of double columns, but he recognized the practical difficulties of getting such an arrangement on the page, and he limited himself to the two columns. Later editors found that even the task of maintaining an orderly face-to-face double column layout was too much for the rigid page size and the variable lengths of articles involved. Both British and American publishers finally scrapped the facing columns but preserved the useful propinquity of correlative articles by keeping them in numerical order.

Accompanying Roget's philosophical interests in devising the *Thesaurus* was his *secondary* concern for the stylistic value of the book to the speaker or writer. He did comment on problems of style—and some of these were very astute comments indeed—and he did see the book as useful to those without a philosophical notion in their heads. But underlying these remarks, his pervading concern lay in the utilitarian management of language as an instrument of truth. The following passage, from his 1852 introduction, is characteristic in its strictures against those who express themselves carelessly:

> Few, indeed, can appreciate the real extent and importance of that influence which language has always exercised on human affairs, or can be aware how often these are determined by causes much slighter than are apparent to a superficial observer. False logic, disguised under specious phraseology, too often gains the assent of the unthinking multitude, disseminating far and wide the seeds of prejudice and error. Truisms pass current, and wear the semblance of profound wisdom, when dressed up in the tinsel garb of antithetical phrases, or set off by an imposing pomp of paradox. By a confused jargon of involved and mystical sentences, the imagination is easily inveigled into the belief that it is acquiring knowledge and approaching truth. A misapplied or misapprehended term is sufficient to give rise to fierce and interminable disputes; . . . a verbal sophism has decided a party question; an artful watchword, thrown among combustible materials, has kindled the flame of deadly warfare, and changed the destiny of an empire.

Since its inception, the *Thesaurus* has been the favorite, both in Britain and America, of hundreds of thousands of students, writers, lecturers, word-game enthusiasts. The continuous rewriting of the *Thesaurus* became a family industry. Roget himself

was collecting additions and changes right up to his last days in
1869 and had personally seen twenty-five new editions and printings through the press. Upon his death, his son, John L. Roget,
took over and saw to innumerable corrections and additions and
many new editions until his death in 1908. At this time, *his* son,
Samuel Romilly Roget, carried on the dynasty and energetically
advanced the fortunes of the *Thesaurus* until he died in 1952.
Shortly before his death, he sold the family rights to the original
and continuing publisher, Longmans, Green, who have strengthened what would seem to be a self-perpetuating and utterly
unique literary phenomenon. By the most modest estimate, approximately twenty million copies of Roget's *Thesaurus* have
been issued by various publishers since 1852.

Despite more than a century of consistent praise, Roget's *Thesaurus* enjoyed something less than universal critical acclaim
when it first appeared. Roget's book, after all, had some rather
potent competition: 1852 was also the publication year of many
other important works, including Dickens' *Bleak House,* Hawthorne's *The Blithedale Romance,* Melville's *Pierre,* Cardinal
Newman's *Scope and Nature of a University Education,* Harriet
Beecher Stowe's *Uncle Tom's Cabin,* Thackeray's *Henry Es-
mond,* and Herbert Spencer's *Philosophy of Style.*

Most journals and papers that reviewed the *Thesaurus* were re-
servedly complimentary and somewhat bewildered as to how one
would use the thing. All of them expressed admiration for the
labor and ingenuity that Roget had expended, a sure sign that
they really didn't know what to make of it. "Whatever may be
thought, however, of the general aim of Dr. Roget's work, there
can be no doubt as to the ability of its execution," said *The
Athenaeum.*[19] "This is at least a curious book, novel in its design, most laboriously wrought, but, we fear, not likely to be so
practically useful as the care, and toil, and thought bestowed
upon it might have deserved," began *The Critic,* which concluded its article: "The labour of getting up such a work as this
must have been enormous, but will its usefulness repay the toil
by profit as much as its ingenuity will entitle him to honour?" [20]
The Eclectic Review was a little warmer:

> It seems scarcely fair to give only a "brief notice" of so elaborate
> a work as this; and yet it would be difficult to do it justice even
> in a long review. We regard it very highly. . . . We should re-
> joice if our warm commendation promoted the circulation of
> so *thoroughly useful* a book.[21]

Bentham's *Westminster Review,* which Roget might have expected to have been mischievous, gave him the most unqualified approval of all the reviewers. It alone seemed to understand Roget's classification of ideas (perhaps out of habitual dealing with Bentham's fondness for classification); at least its writer did something more than others, who simply filled up the column or page of space between their opening and closing remarks with quotations from Roget's introduction.

It is a dictionary; but not a dictionary of definitions, nor even of synonyms, but of verbal and phraseological equivalents or correlates. A person accustomed to use a biblical concordance, knows the value of the book at once. . . . No literary man should be without such a help, as none can pretend to be above using it. Byron used "Walker's Rhyming Dictionary," and Macaulay himself will not despise Roget. . . . The labour must have been immense, but the author's reward is sure. Roget will rank with Samuel Johnson as a literary instrument-maker of the first class.[22]

Putnam's severely criticized the first American editor, Rev. Barnas Sears, D.D., for "meddling with Professor Roget's book," specifically for omitting a large part of the English edition consisting of what Sears called "vulgar words and phrases," a curiously convincing example of the sense of false gentility and prudery that has plagued American letters ever since. *Putnam's* protested "on the ground that the words and phrases, so excluded, were not vulgar, in any offensive sense, but simply idiomatic; that they were used by the best writers, and of indispensable service to an easy and popular style of composition." [23] Thus the *Putnam's* writer revealed an infinitely keener understanding of Roget's eclectic approach and of the real nature of style than did the fastidious Reverend Sears, who was Secretary of the Massachusetts Board of Education.

The criticism of this tampering with Roget's book was so widespread in the United States that, in a subsequent edition, Sears made himself look even more foolish by reinstating the "vulgar words and phrases," but setting them up in a separate category as an appendix. The reviews, including *Putnam's,* had great sport with this, pointing out that Sears could not have a better guarantee of attracting the attention of tender youth to these forbidden expressions. They included, by the way, such dangerous phrases as "fiddle-faddle," "neither rhyme nor reason," "a wild-goose chase," "a mare's nest," "a cock and bull story." Why, asked the mischievous *Putnam's* writer, was "fiddle-faddle" not as good as "wishwash," "moonshine," "monkey-trick," "rigamarole," "Twaddle," "fudge," "balderdash," or "bull," all of which appeared in the respectable body of the book?

Within a few years of its appearance, the *Thesaurus*, despite the lukewarm reception of many papers, was now being defended. And so it has been since. With each new edition of the book, dozens of reviewers dutifully crib from Roget's original introduction, quote the publisher's claims for so many thousand new entries, and state again that no serious student or writer should be without one. The absence of serious examination of the *Thesaurus* or of the whole idea of a book of synonyms—with the rare exception of Miss Egan's essay and perhaps the hypercritical remarks of the anonymous *Fraser's Magazine* writer—is an amazing phenomenon in itself, considering the widespread use of the *Thesaurus* and similar works. One other exception must be noted, a review-essay in the *North American Review*, appearing two years after the first appearance of the *Thesaurus*. The writer, identified as E. P. Whipple by Allibone,[24] stood alone in his attitude, resoundingly critical and skillful in his ridicule:

We congratulate that large, respectable, inexpressive and unexpressed class of thinkers, who are continually complaining of the barrenness of their vocabulary as compared with the affluence of their ideas, on the appearance of Dr. Roget's volume. If it does nothing else, it will bring a popular theory of verbal expression to the test; and if that theory be correct, we count upon witnessing a mob of mute Miltons and Bacons, and speechless Chathams and Burkes, crowding and tramping into print. Dr. Roget, for a moderate fee, prescribes the verbal medicine which will relieve the congestion of their thoughts. All the tools and implements employed by all the poets and philosophers of England can be obtained at his shop. The idea being given, he guarantees in every case to supply the word. . . . Indeed, if the apt use of words be a mechanical exercise, we cannot doubt that this immense mass of the raw material of expression will be rapidly manufactured into history, philosophy, poetry, and eloquence.

Seriously, we consider this book as one of the best of a numerous class, whose aim is to secure the results without imposing the tasks of labor, to arrive at ends by a dexterous dodging of means, to accelerate the tongue without accelerating the faculties. It is an outside remedy for an inward defect. In our opinion, the work mistakes the whole process by which living thought makes its way into living words, and it might be thoroughly mastered without conveying any real power or facility of expression.[25]

Commenting freely on the teaching of composition—"rhetoric is not a knack, and fluency is not expression"—Whipple deplored the tendency to divorce words from feeling, "to shrivel up language into a mummy of thought," which he charged was the result of expecting too much from too many. He pointed to the literature of the day, "so-called," as suggestive of the "marasmus under which the life of language is in danger of being slowly consumed." Whoever his particular targets were, Whipple went on for many pages, threshing out the mediocre and, incidentally, castigating poor old Roget for his part in producing more mediocrity. The following passage—surely an awesome sentence— is typical:

This fluent debility, which never stumbles into ideas nor stutters into passion, which calls its commonplace comprehensiveness, and styles its sedate languor repose, would, if put upon a short allowance of words, and compelled to purchase language at the expense of conquering obstacles, be likely to evince some spasms of genuine expression; but it is hardly reasonable to expect this verbal abstemiousness at a period when the whole wealth of the English tongue is placed at the disposal of the puniest whipsters of rhetoric,—when the art of writing is avowedly taught on the principle of imitating the "best models,"—when words are worked into the ears of the young in the hope that something will be found answering to them in their brains,—and when Dr. Peter Mark Roget, who never happened on a verbal felicity or uttered a "thought-executing" word in the course of his long and useful life, rushes about, book in hand, to tempt unthinking and unimpassioned mediocrity into the delusion, that its disconnected glimpses of truths never fairly grasped, and its faint movements of embryo aspirations which never broke their shell, can be worded by his specifics into creative thought and passion.

Whipple's essay offers, in addition to the general criticism already shown, many pages of examples of what he regarded as live literature, drawn from his wide reading of British literary, legal, and political writers. Throughout he urges that what is needed is not more information, but inspiration; not more words to facilitate the expression of ideas, but something which would facilitate the conception of ideas. A remarkably insightful—if somewhat cavalier—critic, Whipple and his essay deserve to be better known.

Notwithstanding the keenness of Whipple's remarks, he remained a very exclusive minority as is amply attested by an impressive 112-page scrapbook owned by Mr. John Romilly Roget, the only son of Samuel Romilly Roget and the sole surviving male of the British Rogets. The large folio sheets are covered by hundreds of clippings from newspapers all over the English-speaking world, celebrating the appearance of one or another edition of the *Thesaurus*. Without exception, the reviews and notices are more than favorable; they are laudatory, congratulatory, with a distinct tendency toward eulogy as they approach the present. Moreover, this collection covers only the *Thesaurus* editions appearing between 1916 and 1940, about a sixth of the long life of Roget's book. Presumably a full collection would run well into the thousands of items. There is little point in dwelling on these reviews for they all sing the praises of each new edition and remind their readers again and again that no one pretending to a serious interest in the language should be without the current edition of Roget's *Thesaurus*. In addition to repeated reviews in the standard literary weeklies—e.g., *Saturday Review, The New York Times Book Review,* and *John O'London's Weekly*—the *Thesaurus* has frequently been praised in metropolitan papers of leading cities around the world and in hundreds of lesser-known provincial papers and specialized journals, indicating the widespread devotion of Englishmen, Americans, Indians, Canadians, and Australians to Roget's work.

Browsing through this collection of keepsakes, one becomes aware of the birth and development of a British tradition, for by this time the *Thesaurus* certainly had become a tradition. Dozens of affectionate jokes and bits of light verse reveal the growth of affection and pride in the book. *Punch* in its *New Yorker*ish way, picking up a slip in some Scottish paper which mentioned "The Saurus," noted, "The title, 'The Saurus' is widely recognized. It was assumed by the head of the Ichthyo branch of the Saurus family." [26] Again and again, letters to *The Times* and other papers call upon other writers and readers to consult their "Roget" before making such execrable use of the language. Repeatedly, newspaper writers turn to the *Thesaurus* to settle some stylistic issue. Perhaps the most clever of the many playful uses of the *Thesaurus* was that of the following letter writer in satirizing Futurism, a short-lived literary school, of the first decade of the century, that sought to throw out English syntax and punctuation entirely and rely solely upon lists of vivid nouns:

To the Editor,

Sir, Mr. Philip Gibbs, in his amusing article on Signor Marinetti's scheme of Futurist literature, has overlooked, I think, an earlier writer who should receive credit as being the first exponent of the style. The first edition of his book was issued in 1852, and this fact establishes a clear claim to precedence. My own edition of the work is dated 1908, but a comparison with the original publication shows that in all essentials the author's style suffered no marked change. The work is divided into 1,000 chapters and deals with an immense range of subjects. As an instance of the method of dealing with war, I quote from chap. 722:
    "Battle array, campaign, crusade, expedition; mobilization; state of siege; battlefield (arena), 728."
It will be noted that punctuation is used here, and the deletion of that may be claimed by Signor Marinetti as original, although I have known many instances of the method in private letters. Another great difference is that my author has no prejudice against the use of adjectives, but he usually separates them from any noun, thus giving them a peculiar value which is practically substantival. Thus, in the following moving passage on this same subject of war, he writes:
    "Contending, 720, armed,—to the teeth—cap-a-pie; sword in hand; in—, under—, up in-arms; at war with; bristling with arms; in—battle array,—open arms—the field; embattled."
The author's name is Peter Mark Roget, M.D., F.R.S.

—J. D. Beresford
St. Ives, Cornwall.[27]

Schoolmasters, in journals like *The Class Teacher*, the *Educational Review*, *The Librarian*, urged their charges to keep the *Thesaurus* at their elbows and recommended copies as ideal gifts for young persons. It became a journalistic cliché for writers to begin their pieces with an apt quotation from the *Thesaurus*. *The Daily Express*, for example, in May 1916, in its lead story on a shake-up in Parliament, opened the account, after a series of headlines, "SYNONYMS FOR MUDDLE (from Roget's Thesaurus): Confusion, disarray, jumble, huddle, litter, lumber, farrago, mess, muddle . . ."

As the long march of new editions continued, the reviews be-

came more and more mellow, with more and more frequent references to "an old friend," and less and less inclination toward
any critical examination of the book. The appearance of a new
edition was predictably the occasion for full-length feature stories
on one phase or another of the life of its "amiable old doctor
and savant," Peter Mark Roget, often with a rather smeary reprint of the Eddis engraving. Medical journals, from *Lancet* to
the *Journal of Laboratory and Clinical Medicine* (St. Louis),
would suddenly, and periodically, rediscover their claim to Roget
and print eulogistic articles on his accomplishments in many
fields. Throughout the 1920's and the 1930's, there were occasional interviews with Samuel Romilly Roget, who, in addition
to editing the *Thesaurus* all his life, had been trained as an
electrical engineer and produced a *Dictionary of Electrical
Terms* (1924). Perhaps the most useful of these interviews produced a front-page article by Claude F. Luke in *John O'London's
Weekly*, on June 4, 1937, in which Luke drew an engaging picture of Samuel Romilly Roget in his book-lined study at 13 Phil-
limore Gardens, Kensington.

Self-appointed guardians kept watch on successive editions of
the *Thesaurus,* and any interesting changes became news. On October 5, 1930, the *Sunday Express,* under inch-high headlines, recorded one of these changes:

WHAT THE WORD 'JEW' MEANS

OFFENSIVE TERMS
CUT FROM A
BOOK

reporting that uncomplimentary synonyms given under the word
"Jew" had been omitted in a new edition of the *Thesaurus* published in the United States.

The crossword puzzle craze of the 1920's gave the *Thesaurus* a
whole new reason for being and gave its sales an enormous shot
in the arm. It began with the regular publication of puzzles in
the *New York World* in 1913, gradually spread across the United
States, and in the early 20's hit England like a tidal wave. Reaching its peak in about 1925, the enormous popularity of the puzzles proved a windfall to publishers of dictionaries and wordbooks of all sorts. But the undisputed king was Roget's
Thesaurus. At the height of the craze, booksellers could not keep
the volume in stock, and new printings were exhausted as fast as
they came off the press. With this new demand for the *Thesau-*

rus, feature writers had a new peg on which to hang their perennial Roget commemoratives. A good example is the feature story in *The New York Times Magazine,* of February 8, 1925. Under a large headline, "ROGET BECOMES SAINT OF CROSSWORDIA," William S. Odlin described the effects of the crossword puzzle and the belated popularity of Roget:

> Until the word in six letters meaning this or that, or what have you, threw its tantalizing shadow across a hitherto tranquil land, the meaning to the layman of either Roget or Thesaurus might be described, chemically, as "a trace." . . . This, then, was Roget's 'Thesaurus' until the crossword puzzle became the preoccupation of our citizens. The victim of cross-wordophobia first called in the dictionary and that alleviated his suffering a little. But something more potent was demanded by many of the complications that developed, and the 'Thesaurus' proved the efficacious poultice for his aching brow. In homes where a few weeks ago volume and compiler were not even names, the book found a place where in the Age of Innocence the family Bible might have rested.

One of the most amusing—and puzzling—evidences of the nation's preoccupation with the *Thesaurus* is found in a newspaper column by G. Ward Price, appearing in the *Daily Mail* on March 26, 1940:

> This morning when I presented myself at the aerodrome some 20 or 30 pieces of baggage were taken on board the Paris aeroplane without examination. Having admitted, however, that I was going on to Turkey and offered an attaché case full of books for inspection, I was made the subject of investigation and scrutiny for a full half-hour. At the end of that time the three officials concerned confiscated as dangerous literature:
>   Three Baedeker guide books in English—dealing with Turkey, Syria, and Palestine;
>   A Roget's Thesaurus of words and phrases, and
>   A French dictionary.
>   It cannot have been coded messages that they feared, for they allowed me to take a full set of this morning's papers without examination.

The publication history of the *Thesaurus,* like that of most famous and often-printed books, is so complicated by the many publishers and editors who have become involved, by the loss of key documents, by national and international copyright agreements and arguments, by the necessity for preserving trade secrets, and so forth, that it is extremely doubtful whether a clear and complete picture will ever emerge. Some idea of the expanding inflorescence of Roget's *Thesaurus* in these later years can be gained from the fact that the main catalog of the Library of Congress now contains thirty printed cards under the main entry "Peter Mark Roget," and another twenty cards under the main and added entry "Mawson" (the best-known American editor).[28]

It is first necessary to understand that all of the several varieties of Roget's *Thesaurus* still in print are offshoots of two main stems which I shall call the British *Thesaurus* and the American *Thesaurus*. The American was, of course, based upon the British, but through the many revisions, deletions, and changes necessary to adapt the original to American English, the American *Thesaurus* has become in effect a root-stock itself, and thus the parent work of many subsequent varieties.[29]

In the original agreement, dated January 17, 1852, between Peter Mark Roget, of 18 Upper Bedford Place, and Messrs. Longman, Brown, Green, and Longmans, Longmans agreed to publish an edition of one thousand copies of the *Thesaurus*, and, after deducting all costs, to divide the profits remaining between Roget and the firm. Corrections above 10s. per sheet were to be charged to the author, and Roget was to be allowed twelve copies gratis, with any additional copies at the trade sale price (twenty-five for the price of twenty-four). The retail price of the original *Thesaurus* was set at 14s. The book appeared in May 1852.

A second agreement, of November 8, 1852, made possible a second edition, from which Roget was to receive two thirds of the profits instead of half. The edition amounted to fifteen hundred copies, and was ready in March 1853.

The third edition, that of February 1855, was issued as a result of an agreement dated November 25, 1854, in which Longmans, Green paid Roget a flat £140, with all remaining profits to go to the company. The retail price was ½ guinea, and the edition amounted to fifteen hundred copies.

Demand for the book continued, and again, on October 6, 1855, Roget and Longmans agreed to bring out a fourth edition (in December), for which Roget was to get £133 on the day of publication.

Thus began the steady march of *Thesaurus* editions through the years. Roget personally supervised the publication of twenty-five editions and printings, although a few remnant letters suggest that as early as 1866 his son, John Lewis Roget, was assisting him. All in all, up to the end of 1960, Longmans, Green issued 108 different editions and printings, ranging from two hundred fifty copies (September 1858) to twenty-five thousand copies (March 1949). The most important revised editions of the British *Thesaurus* were those of 1879, 1925, 1933, 1936, 1952, and 1962. The total issued by Longmans, Green up to 1960 amounted to just under a half million copies. One complication arose in 1933, when the London firm began issuing an American edition as well. I do not have production figures for that edition.

The effect of the crossword puzzle craze is dramatically shown by a comparison of the figures from 1910 to 1929 and those for the two decades preceding. From October 1890 to 1908, Longmans, Green issued a printing about every other year, averaging two thousand copies each. Beginning in February 1911, at least one new printing was required each year (five of them in 1925), and these printings ran from three thousand to ten thousand each.

That the *Thesaurus* has become an increasingly profitable property is indicated by the increase in royalties to the family. Where Roget considered himself as doing well to collect £150 for an edition, a few remaining receipts at Longmans, Green show that John Lewis Roget received anywhere from £300 to £500 for editions issued from 1874 to 1890, and that Samuel Romilly Roget's share through the 1920's, 30's, and 40's amounted to over £1,000 per year. Samuel Romilly's record royalty check (November 1947) came to £3,753.

In 1950, with a major revision needed and S. R. Roget growing old and tired, Longmans, Green bought out the rights of the family for £4,500. Since that time, Longmans, Green alone has held the copyright for the British *Thesaurus*.

The first American *Thesaurus* was that edited by Barnas Sears and issued by Gould and Lincoln, Boston, in 1854. This ran through several printings, to at least as late as 1867. However, in 1886 Thomas Y. Crowell & Company entered the field and brought out its first American edition, which was a copy of John Lewis Roget's 1879 edition. From that time forward, Crowell was to be the major American publisher. In the years just before 1911, Crowell issued several printings, variously revised and amended to suit American needs. These changes were incorporated by the American lexicographer C. O. Sylvester Mawson into the completely reset 1911 edition, which for many years was the standard *Thesaurus* in the United States. Mawson completed another major overhaul in 1922, with the first "International Edition," so called because of the number of non-English words included. This remained the standard in the United States until 1946, when *Roget's International Thesaurus,* New Edition, was published by Crowell, and that, in turn, stood at the head of American thesauri until *Roget's International Thesaurus,* Third Edition, appeared in 1962, a volume containing 1,258 pages compared with an original Crowell edition of approximately 600 pages. The fact that Dutch's edition of the British *Thesaurus* and Crowell's third *International Thesaurus* both appeared in 1962 is purely coincidental. While both of the books adhere to Roget's original classification scheme, their vocabularies have developed along such different lines that both houses are now agreed that they are quite different works.

This agreement makes any attempt to determine priorities rather futile—not that over the years the two companies have not had words over their respective rights. Both companies attempted to establish their individual rights to publication and distribution of the *Thesaurus.* In 1932, Mawson, in answer to accusations of copyright infringement, countered with a lengthy document and a twelve-page textual analysis to show that, on the contrary, his 1922 first *International Thesaurus* had been drawn on by Samuel Romilly Roget in preparing the 1925 British *Thesaurus,* and that "no less than ninety-four percent [of the new matter in the 1925 edition] has been purloined from my International Edition of 1922." The British firm studied Mawson's statements seriously and drew up an even longer memo (including some thirty pages of comparative analytical data), purporting to show that Mawson's 1931–32 edition had borrowed freely from the British *Thesaurus.* Longmans, Green's legal aides, attempting to pin the whole matter down to an actionable issue, found that while the 1909 Crowell *Thesaurus* was, indeed, "simply a reprint of the 1879 edition," Crowell was in the clear because their edition was published only in the United States, "and in that country neither John L. Roget nor his executors have ever had any copyright. . . . Therefore, the executors were not in a position to complain of the conduct of the Thomas Y. Crowell Company."

While these exchanges make interesting reading, particularly for one interested in detailed comparisons of American and British thesauri, the question would seem to have been mooted by the larger laws of language itself. Even as American English has strayed far from the Queen's English, so the American and British thesauri have gone their separate ways. And we are left with another irony: now, nearly one hundred and twenty years after the *Thesaurus* first appeared, both American and British publishers claim to have preserved the essential Roget.

Other complications in the publication history arose from branches off these two main stems. In England, several publishers other than Longmans, Green have published some form of Roget's *Thesaurus*—some of them by arrangement with Longmans, Green; some not. Examples are the *Penguin Thesaurus*, the *Everyman Thesaurus*, the *University Thesaurus* (Jones), and Collins' *International Thesaurus*. The last turns out to be the British title of Mawson's American *International!*

In the United States, Garden City, by arrangement with G. P. Putnam's Sons, brought out in 1931 the *Dictionary of Synonyms and Antonyms; Being a Presentation of Roget's Thesaurus . . . the Whole Compiled in Alphabetical Form . . .* , again edited by C. O. S. Mawson.[30] In dropping Roget's classification system, Mawson, of course, should have dropped the name "Roget," for it was that system, as we have seen, that was the one distinctive feature of Roget's book. In effect, the dictionary form put the work back into the same simple word-finding system characterized by Crabb and other pre-Roget attempts.

A sensationally successful branch of the American stem was the Pocket Books edition—*Roget's Pocket Thesaurus* (1946), which in turn was based upon still another Crowell edition, *Roget's Treasury of Words*, edited by Mawson and Katharine Aldrich Whiting in 1924. The Pocket Books *Thesaurus* sold 1,725,000 copies in the first ten years of its existence, and between 1956 and 1965 increased that total to 5,416,857.[31] A second paperback Roget, Signet's *New American Roget's College Thesaurus in Dictionary Form* (1958), is a thriving newcomer, and to date has sold just under four and a half million copies in fifty-four printings.[32]

At least a dozen other American synonymic works not claiming kinship with the original Roget's *Thesaurus* are still in print. There are many offshoots even further removed from the parent Roget but falling within the same genus, such incredible collections of trite and hackneyed expressions that the ghost of E. P. Whipple could only say, "I told you so." [33]

As Roget himself suggested in his 1852 introduction, his idea has proved to be adaptable to other languages. Since 1852 at least two French thesauri have appeared,[34] and more than a dozen German synonymies.

However, it does not seem likely that our age will see the fulfillment of one of Roget's dreams: "In a still higher degree would all those advantages be combined and multiplied in a *Polyglot Lexicon* constructed on this system"—unless, of course, electronic translating systems can be seen as a ramification of Roget's scheme. It does so happen that Roget's *Thesaurus* has been of use in the development of such systems. The Cambridge University Language Research Unit has used the work to explore the extent to which the ambiguity of words encountered in sentences undergoing machine translation could be resolved. Taking the ambiguous term, the Cambridge researchers examined the various *Thesaurus* headings in which that term occurred. All the words used in each such category were matched against the other meaning-bearing words of the sentence. For example, if the term to be translated were the ambiguous German word *Mutter,* meaning either "mother" or "nut," all of the terms found under both meanings would be matched against the other words of the sentence being translated—the degree of overlap would determine which of the two meanings would be appropriate to the translation.[35]

Thus has Roget's modest book, which first took form as a hundred-page penny notebook containing some fifteen thousand words written in the neat script of Peter Mark Roget, grown into one of the most substantial, most ubiquitous works of the English-speaking world. Nor would Roget be surprised. As the preceding discussion has shown, he saw his *Thesaurus* not simply as the crowning achievement of his own industrious life, but as an outline for an infinitely greater accomplishment yet to be realized —the construction of a utilitarian device to harness into the service of his Age of Progress those inestimable and hitherto unmanageable forces: thought and word.

Had Roget fallen out with the Royal Society a few months earlier, and begun compiling his *Thesaurus* in 1847, say, instead of 1848, the *Thesaurus* would have appeared in time to be exhibited at that climactic glory of the early Victorian age, the Great Exhibition of 1851, along with all manner of inventions and artifacts drawn from all corners of the world: the McCormick reaper, an envelope-folding machine, the Koh-i-noor diamond, a silver-gilt toilet table, model houses for workingclass families, and a papier-mâché piano case. Surely, for all Roget's gentlemanly sense of restraint, the *Thesaurus* would have been welcomed as a proud exhibit in that hall of wonders, the Crystal Palace, which opened to a crowd of over twenty-five thousand on May 1, 1851.

Home of Sir Samuel Romilly at 21 Russell Square, London, now in the shadow of the towering Senate House of the University of London. An upstairs bedroom of this house was the scene of Romilly's suicide in 1818.

Alexander Marcet (1770–1822), Roget's closest friend, fellow physician, scientific researcher, and, with Roget, one of the earliest promoters of the Medical and Chirurgical Society of London, precursor of the Royal Medical Society.

John Bostock (1773–1846), physician, physiologist, and close friend of Roget. Bostock took his medical degree with Roget on the same day at Edinburgh, worked with Roget and Marcet in promoting the Medical and Chirurgical Society of London, and carried out analyses of water samples for Roget's pioneer study of the London water supply in 1827.

Painting of Roget in 1824, the year of his marriage. The portrait was done by North of Liverpool as a companion piece for the painting of Mary Roget (J. Romilly Roget)

Painting of Mary Hobson Roget in 1824, the year of her marriage. The daughter of a wealthy Liverpool manufacturer, she was twenty-nine, Roget forty-five. Mary died of cancer only eight years after their marriage. (J. Romilly Roget)

The London Institution, designed by William Brook, erected in 1815 in Finsbury Circus, was typical of the many scientific and literary societies in which Roget worked and which played such an important part in the emergence of modern sciences during the first three decades of the nineteenth century. Roget was a featured lecturer at the London Institution in 1826. The building was demolished in 1936.

St. Pancras Church, still standing at Euston Road and Woburn Place, was designed in 1819 by W. and H. W. Inwood. This building was Roget's place of worship for nearly fifty years. He and Mary customarily walked there from Bernard Street.

A page from Mary Roget's "Archives of the Nursery," a journal she kept from 1826 to 1828. In it she wrote detailed accounts of her children's behavior and development. (J. Romilly Roget)

First page of a report on optical studies that Roget read before the Royal Society in 1824. A landmark paper, it enunciated the principle on which modern motion picture photography is based.

[131]

V. *Explanation of an optical deception in the appearance of the spokes of a wheel seen through vertical apertures.* By P. M. ROGET, *M. D. F. R. S.*

Read December 9, 1824.

A CURIOUS optical deception takes place when a carriage wheel, rolling along the ground, is viewed through the intervals of a series of vertical bars, such as those of a palisade, or of a Venetian window-blind. Under these circumstances the spokes of the wheel, instead of appearing straight, as they would naturally do if no bars intervened, seem to have a considerable degree of curvature. The distinctness of this appearance is influenced by several circumstances presently to be noticed; but when every thing concurs to favour it, the illusion is irresistible, and, from the difficulty of detecting its real cause, is exceedingly striking.

The degree of curvature in each spoke varies according to the situation it occupies for the moment with respect to the perpendicular. The two spokes which arrive at the vertical position, above and below the axle, are seen of their natural shape, that is, without any curvature. Those on each side of the upper one appear slightly curved; those more remote, still more so; and the curvature of the spokes increases as we follow them downwards on each side till we arrive at the lowest spoke, which, like the first, again appears straight.

Somerset House on the Strand, headquarters of the Royal Society during most of Roget's active work with the society. Roget was elected Secretary of the prestigious RS in 1827 and reigned in this post through many a stormy political and scientific battle, until he was forced to resign in 1848.

Peter Mark Roget in 1839. This engraving, made from a painting by E. Y. Eddis for an impressive *Medical Portrait Gallery* (Pettigrew, 1840–41), has become the best-known likeness of Roget. It has appeared in many American and British editions of the *Thesaurus* and in dozens of reviews and magazine articles.

THESAURUS

OF

ENGLISH WORDS AND PHRASES,

CLASSIFIED AND ARRANGED

SO AS

TO FACILITATE THE EXPRESSION OF IDEAS

AND ASSIST IN

LITERARY COMPOSITION.

BY PETER MARK ROGET, M.D., F.R.S., F.R.A.S., F.G.S.

FELLOW OF THE ROYAL COLLEGE OF PHYSICIANS;
MEMBER OF THE SENATE OF THE UNIVERSITY OF LONDON;
OF THE LITERARY AND PHILOSOPHICAL SOCIETIES ETC. OF MANCHESTER, LIVERPOOL,
BRISTOL, QUEBEC, NEW YORK, HAARLEM, TURIN, AND STOCKHOLM.
AUTHOR OF
THE "BRIDGEWATER TREATISE ON ANIMAL AND VEGETABLE PHYSIOLOGY,"
ETC.

"It is impossible we should thoroughly understand the nature of the SIGNS, unless
we first properly consider and arrange the THINGS SIGNIFIED."—*Esea Hrepierra.*

LONDON:
LONGMAN, BROWN, GREEN, AND LONGMANS.
1852.

Title page of the first edition of Roget's *Thesaurus*. First published by Longmans, Green in London, 1852, the *Thesaurus* went through twenty-five editions before Roget's death and has since appeared in dozens of modified forms throughout the English-speaking world. (British Museum)

ROGET'S
INTERNATIONAL THESAURUS

OF

ENGLISH WORDS AND PHRASES

A COMPLETE BOOK OF

SYNONYMS AND ANTONYMS

FOUNDED UPON
AND EMBODYING ROGET'S ORIGINAL WORK
WITH NUMEROUS ADDITIONS AND
MODERNIZATIONS

BY

C. O. SYLVESTER MAWSON, LITT. D., PH.D.

*Associate Editor of Webster's New International Dictionary, Webster's Collegiate
Dictionary, etc.; Revising Editor of Sanskrit and Anglo-Indian Terms
in the Century Dictionary; Consulting Specialist to the late
Sir James Murray of the Oxford English Dictionary;
Member of the Royal Asiatic Society,
Société Asiatique, etc.*

NEW YORK
THOMAS Y. CROWELL COMPANY
1922

Title page of Thomas Y. Crowell's original 1922 *International Thesaurus,* which established itself as the authoritative American *Thesaurus.* Subsequent editions, revised and amplified, have secured the *International* as the standard work in the United States.

Peter Mark Roget at eighty-one. Through his last years, attended only by his daughter Kate, he followed a strict regimen of work and study, and was engaged in emending and correcting his *Thesaurus* a few days before his death in 1869. (J. Romilly Roget)

John Lewis Roget (1828–1908), Peter Mark Roget's only son, who took over the editing of the *Thesaurus* with his father's death and carried it on until his own passing. John Lewis Roget was also a talented watercolorist and a well-known art critic. (J. Romilly Roget)

Samuel Romilly Roget (1875–1952), Peter Mark Roget's grandson, shown here in the uniform of the Royal Naval Anti-Aircraft Corps in 1917. An electrical engineer, S. R. Roget picked up the family *Thesaurus* project on the death of his father and edited it until 1950, when he sold the family rights to Longmans, Green, the original and continuing publisher of the British *Thesaurus*. (J. Romilly Roget)

Mr. John Romilly Roget and Miss Ursula Roget, great-grandchildren of Peter Mark Roget, and the last surviving members of the British line. They are shown in Mr. Roget's home in Kent, where he has been long established as a professional horticulturist. (Gordon Dixon)

Bookplate used by Peter Mark Roget for the approximately four thousand volumes of his private library. (Royal College of Physicians)

Peter M. Roget M.D.

Acknowledged by most social historians as the ultimate expression of early Victorian values, the Great Exhibition was a thoroughly human compound of the admirable and the silly, the truly serious and the merely pretentious, and thus would have made an entirely appropriate mounting for Roget's elaborate and ambitious work:

There was yesterday witnessed a sight the like of which has never happened before and which in the nature of things can never be repeated. They who were so fortunate as to see it hardly knew what most to admire, or in what form to clothe the sense of wonder and even of mystery which struggled within them. The edifice, the treasures of art collected therein, the assemblage and the solemnity even more than sense could scan, or imagination attain. . . . It was felt to be more than what was seen, or what had been intended. Some saw in it the second and more glorious inauguration of their Sovereign; some a solemn dedication of art and its stores; some were most reminded of that day when all ages and climes shall be gathered round the Throne of their Maker; there was so much that seemed accidental, and yet had a meaning, that no one could be content with simply what he saw.[36]

XVI [1853–1869 ❦

Last Years

FROM the publication of the *Thesaurus* until his death in 1869, Roget was increasingly aware that he had outlived not only most of his contemporaries but most of their children too. In effect, he had enjoyed (and suffered) three normal lifetimes and half a dozen different careers—enough activity to provide memories for a hundred old men. For a man who had waited until his fiftieth year to have a son, he was among the fortunate few who could watch his boy grow into young manhood, acquit himself well at Cambridge, return to London, establish his own career, marry, and present the old man with a lively grandchild.

By the time he was well into his sixties, Roget had become used to the idea that his subsequent years would be a necrology of his friends and associates. Nearly every year recorded the deaths of two or three old friends or foes, so that the years became a succession of familiar names winking out like so many candles: Cooper, de Candolle, Edgeworth, Yelloly, Bell, Sussex, Bostock, Napier, Combe, Peel, Northampton, Children, Newport, Whewell, Bright, Wakley, Lansdowne, Horner, Southey, Lubbock, Brande, Faraday, Brougham . . .

Roget busied himself, of course, with the rapid succession of new editions of his *Thesaurus*. In 1852, the first year of its publication, he had the pleasure of noting the passage of a special act of Parliament, partly based on his water report, forbidding London water companies to draw from the Thames from below Teddington Lock. While he no longer engaged in their organizational battles, he retained a more or less active membership in the Senate of the University of London, the British Association for the Advancement of Science, and the Royal, the Medical and

Chirurgical, and many other societies. He spent more time with his chess, contributing problems and solutions to various newspapers. His 1840 paper "Description of a Method of Moving the Knight over Every Square of the Chess-board Without Going Twice over Any One; Commencing at Any Given Square, and Ending at Any Other Given Square of a Different Colour" [1] had brought him into correspondence with chess masters all over England and Europe, and prompted him to attempt to market a traveler's chessboard, the "Economic Chess-board," in 1845. This was made of cardboard, with small pasteboard pieces lying flat on the board and kept in place by the insertion of their bases into folds or pockets.[2]

Roget indulged his latent interest in machines as an avid spectator at the many mechanical and industrial exhibitions that were held in London in those years. He was particularly interested in calculating machines and such contraptions as the Maelzel chess automaton, and he is said to have spent much time and labor in attempts to construct a calculating machine. The Royal Society obituary states that "he also made some progress towards the invention of a delicate balance, in which, to lessen the effect of friction, the fulcrum was to be within a small barrel floating on water." Combining his considerable mathematical skill with his mechanical aptitude, Roget worked out a series of conversions of plane rectilinear figures of equal areas—"cutting out pieces of card so that they could be differently put together to prove the equality, and thereby forming a series of geometrical recreations." [3] By such means he made "considerable progress" toward developing mechanical or visual proofs of particular Euclidian propositions. The same source comments perceptively that while

. . . the doctrine of utility, which had been impressed upon him in early life by his friends, Dumont and Bentham, was ever present to his mind, he was also incited to the pursuit of his researches by an innate and ardent love of his subject for its own sake. He would exhibit the same keen relish for analysis undertaken in the construction of a toy as when employed in the establishment of a physical principle.[4]

Well into his last few years, Roget thus occupied himself with diversions that would have taxed much younger and more vigorous men. He investigated difficult problems in optics, played with permutations and combinations, and composed four-move stratagems of chess of acknowledged beauty and merit. He developed a new interest in these last years—the collecting and (of course!) the classifying of light, epigrammatic literature, a curious turn of mind for a man who had never been known for his sense of humor. And always, there was more work to be done on the *Thesaurus*. According to the Royal Society obituary, Roget continued to make additions and corrections in that redoubtable work until the last day of his life.

He refused to be drawn into any further disputes although there were plenty of them still raging at the Royal Society and elsewhere. He was the target once again of an indignant reader who objected to one of his early papers for the *Encyclopaedia Britannica*. In 1858, one David Buxton, Principal of the Liverpool School for the Deaf and Dumb, published a pamphlet [5] damning the reprinting of Roget's article "Deaf and Dumb," charging that the article was little else than a simple reprint of the preceding edition; that with a few minor exceptions, it contained no new information and repeated "the most ludicrous errors of fact"; that it was outdated by the advance of knowledge in the field; that it did not mention English institutions for the deaf and dumb; that it spoke of men as alive who had died thirty years before; that it misquoted from published tables of statistics; and that its bibliography contained not one work more recent than 1833.

Buxton's accusation, which subsequently appeared in the *Athenaeum*, prompted Adam and Charles Black, who were bringing out the eighth edition of the *EB* in separate volumes from 1853 to 1860, to respond in the same journal. The Blacks claimed that Buxton was all wrong, but they rather carefully avoided discussing that particular article. Instead, they referred to the whole encyclopaedia. Volume XV, in which "Deaf and Dumb" appeared, was more than nine tenths new, they said, and of the remaining tenth, all the articles had been revised and corrected. Their only defense of the article itself was an allusion to Roget as an authority: "it was contributed by Dr. Roget, the well known author of one of the Bridgewater Treatises, and not one likely to make 'the most ludicrous errors of fact.' "

Buxton retorted that the Blacks' answer was vague and that it avoided his specific criticisms. He acknowledged that Roget's essay was undoubtedly "an admirable production *at the time it was written* [about 1820; italics added]. It probably did good service for it described an art which was in its infancy. . . . The art has advanced . . . and Dr. Roget's original article has become one of the antiquities of the subject." Roget refused to enter the fray, and Mr. Buxton had the last word.

Roget thus lived at peace with midcentury London, secure in his Upper Bedford Place home, surrounded by his beloved library and attended by his daughter Kate, who stayed with the old man through the rest of his life.

Roget enjoyed walking, even in his last few years, and a familiar figure about Russell Square and the Bloomsbury area was the tall, thin, clean-shaven, white-haired doctor, dressed in his customary black, right down to the many-buttoned gaiters that kept his old ankles warm, and carrying with a certain dignified flair his favorite slender, round-handled stick. He knew, after all, nearly every paving block and iron paling in the district, had seen its trees grow, its buildings rise from mud and meadows. He had walked every street and alley of it as a hurrying young doctor on his rounds, as a proud husband strolling with his beautiful wife, as an imperturbable elder statesman of those professional purlieus. As at Bernard Street, Roget remained close to his favorite haunts—the British Museum, the University of London, Queen's Square, St. Pancras Church. Like most Londoners, he prided himself not only on his ability to walk long distances but also in his enjoyment of walking. And, like most Londoners still, he would describe distances as a five-minute or a ten-minute walk, rather than in blocks or miles. He would much rather walk the mile south to Lincoln's Inn Fields or north to Regent's Park than take one of the thousands of hackneys, but he no longer made the extensive treks that he and Mary once enjoyed.

Roget's son was a consolation as well, although he was by no means a permanent resident of No. 18 Upper Bedford Place.[6] Two years after Mary's death, seven-year-old John Lewis Roget was sent to a private school in Hampstead, where he remained for two years. After additional tutoring, he was placed in the Blackheath Proprietary School, and then (in September 1840) the University College School in Gower Street. From July 26 to September 7, 1844, Roget and his children enjoyed an extensive tour of Europe: Antwerp, Liège, Aix-la-Chapelle, Cologne, Coblenz, the Rhine, Mannheim, Heidelberg, Strasbourg, Basle, Pavannes, Berne, Fribourg, Geneva, Chamonix, Milan, and over the Saint Gothard. John entered Trinity College, Cambridge, in 1846, and took his B.A. in 1850. During holidays he frequently visited his Aunt Annette, still living alone at Ilfracombe.

Roget saw a good deal of his son from 1851 onward, as the

young man had commenced a serious study of the profession of barrister-at-law, and thus divided his time between Upper Bedford Place and Lincoln's Inn Fields. Roget delighted in John's progress as an artist as well, and a good many of the young Roget's pencil sketches are preserved in *his* son's charming book *Travel in the Two Last Centuries of Three Generations.*

In 1853, John took his M.A. degree at Cambridge, was called to the bar, and commenced legal practice with two friends at 39 Chancery Lane. He continued his artistic interests through his life, becoming a recognized critic and watercolorist, and publishing in 1891 *A History of the Old Water-Colour Society,* and in 1911 a collection of his own work, *Sketches of Deal, Walmer, and Sandwich.*

John assisted his father in the final editions of the *Thesaurus* before 1869, and assumed the editorship of the work upon his father's death,[7] bringing out many important revisions. His most important contributions to the *Thesaurus* was a new and greatly expanded index for the 1879 edition.

In 1865, John Roget married Frances Ditchfield, and they made their home at No. 14 Warwick Road, Paddington. In 1868, a year before Peter Mark's death, John announced the birth of their first child, Elinor. A second daughter, Isabel, was born in 1870, and a son, Samuel Romilly Roget, arrived in 1875, shortly after the family had moved to a larger house at No. 5 Randolph Crescent, Maida Hill.

Judging from his many contributions to art and to literary publications, as well as to such organizations as the Burlington Fine Arts Club and the Royal Society of Painters in Water-Colours, which met in Pall Mall East—directly opposite the Royal College of Physicians, where his father attended occasional lectures until 1869—John Lewis inherited not only the artistic bent of his grandmother but the lively sense of humor of his mother. He was much sought after for literary and art reviews as well as for performances in amateur theatricals.

Neither of the daughters of John Lewis Roget married; thus the line was carried on by Samuel Romilly Roget, who, upon his father's death on November 11, 1908, assumed the family *Thesaurus* enterprise with a vigor that greatly renewed public interest in the venerable reference work. Trained as an electrical engineer, Samuel Romilly Roget was a hard-driving worker, more like Peter Mark than John Lewis had been. He had none of the artistic or literary interests of his father, it would seem.

Again, the methodical and the utilitarian emerged in the family. S. R. Roget produced a textbook on electricity,[8] a dictionary of electrical terms, the travel book covering three generations of Rogets, and articles on engineering subjects in many journals and papers. His works received many laudatory reviews. Expressive of his organizing impulse, S. R. Roget subscribed to a clipping service, and neatly pasted the clippings in his scrapbook in chronological order, carefully adding identification of the source of each item. Alert to the promotion of the *Thesaurus,* he wrote letters to *The Pall Mall Gazette, The Times,* and others, in which he stepped forward as authority to resolve arguments over the signification of particular words. One of these little arguments— whether the word "suffragette" should or should not be used in the *Morning Post*—was ended by S. R. Roget's forthright application of the sound linguistic principle that custom is law. He took occasion to point out in a letter to *The Pall Mall Gazette,* April 22, 1914, that both terms—"suffragette" and "suffragist," which had been offered as an alternative—were indeed "in common use by English writers and speakers, and are therefore 'part of the English Language.' "

This question came before me recently in connection with their inclusion in future editions of "Roget's Thesaurus," and I decided upon placing them, when that work is reprinted, in different categories . . . placing "Suffragette" under the heading of "disobedience," among such words as "rebel," "revolter," and "rioter"; while including "Suffragist" among the words denoting a desire for improvement, in company with "reformer," etc.

Like his grandfather, S. R. Roget was an energetic organization man. He was particularly active in promoting the work of the Huguenot Society of London, serving on its Council for many years, and as its President at the time of his death in 1952.

Two years before his death, seeing little interest in the *Thesaurus* on the part of his son, S. R. Roget sold his family's interests in the work to the original publisher, Longmans, Green. That was the end of the *Thesaurus* as a dynastic enterprise of the Rogets, but the hearty reception of the completely revised new edition by Professor Dutch (1962) and the third "International" edition (Crowell, 1962) indicates that the sturdy old book is still very much alive.

S. R. Roget's son, John Romilly Roget, also a Cambridge man, veered away from traditional family interests, early became inter-

ested in horticulture, and for many years now has been living in
Kent, where he has established a thriving nursery, specializing in
orchids and other exotic tropical plants.[9] Both Mr. Roget and his
sister, Miss Ursula Roget, are active members of the Huguenot
Society.

Little is known of the feminine side of the Rogets after the
death of Peter Mark Roget's wife. Roget's daughter Kate, who
never married, remained with her father until his death. Of John
Lewis Roget's daughters Elinor and Isabel, only the latter had
any recorded public life. She was a knowledgeable student of various sociological problems and wrote and lectured on the care
and treatment of epileptics. Like her brother, Isabel was a long-
time member of the Huguenot Society. Elinor died on October 3,
1920; Isabel on July 28, 1943. Neither of them had married.

Neither John R. Roget (born 1905) nor his sister Ursula
(born 1908) has married, and they are, therefore, the last members of the British Rogets, a long and productive line. While the
Roget name is being carried forward by a good many living representatives, they are all descendants of cousins of Roget's father,
Jean Marc Roget, whose only brother, Jean Samuel Roget, had
no sons. Thus the direct-line genealogy beginning with the
short-lived Geneva pastor ends with John R. and Ursula Roget
in England.

The world, of course, had changed enormously just in the sixty
years that Peter Mark Roget lived in London, and to give the old
man credit, once he had accustomed himself to the fact that he
was no longer in the forefront of a fast-running century, he
thought the changes, in general, were all to the good. By the year
of his death, at least the beginnings of programs were under way
to alleviate the sufferings of the poor in the squalid slums of
London, and other farseeing programs had been constructed, partially on ground that Roget himself had prepared, to forestall
even greater foreseeable problems in public health. Sadler's committee had opened British eyes at last to the horror of child
labor in the mines: Shaftesbury's campaigns had made great in-
roads on the national reluctance to help the poor, the ignorant,
and the mentally ill. Roget, in fact, lived to see some of the measures of the Second Reform Act of 1867 put into practice.[10] In
the same issue of the *Lancet* that reported Roget's death (September 25, 1869) were accounts of plans to control pollution of
rivers in the suburbs, of prosecutions against butchers for sell-
ing contaminated meat, of the condemnation of several houses at

West Hackney as "unfit for human habitation and a hotbed of fever for many years past," of an Order in Council directing that a ship lately arrived from the West Indies be held in quarantine until further orders, some passengers having come down with yellow fever. There was also a severe letter on the dangers of tight lacing.

Despite his determinedly optimistic view of his world, Roget, even in his eighties, was too much a scientific observer to blind himself to how much remained to be done. But it is also true that he looked back at metropolitan conditions in the 1820's, 30's, and 40's with real horror at what had passed for sanitation. Thus, as he walked slowly along Bernard Street—so brightly new when he moved there in 1808, and now so dingily smoke-stained —the old man could, with some satisfaction, nod with the knowledge that Londoners starting out in the 60's had infinitely better chances for longer and healthier lives. During his last thirty years, the state of legislative enlightenment had improved considerably beyond what it was in 1833, when Parliament reluctantly provided £20,000 for educational purposes and in the same session voted £50,000 to improve the Royal Stables.[11]

Whether, in thinking about his whole self-congratulatory "age of progress," Roget would have wagged his head with Brougham over the madness of it all—"The folly of 700 people going fifteen miles an hour in six carriages on a narrow road, exceeds belief [12] —or celebrated with Tennyson—"Forward, forward let us range,/ Let the great world spin for ever down the ringing grooves of change" [13]—we do not know. We do know, however, that he did not wither into a bitter old man. On the contrary, his disposition seemed to mellow with old age, and his sense of humor quickened—witness the following couplet he scribbled on a note in his eightieth year:

> Time wastes us all, our bodies and our wits;
> But we waste time—so Time and we are quits.[14]

The few fragmentary accounts of his last few years—namely, the obituaries published by his several societies—are uniformly complimentary. Aside from a deafness that barred him from profiting further from lectures and meetings, Roget's angular frame and sturdy internal machine functioned perfectly until a few weeks before his death. Charles Knight recorded a pleasant conversation with Roget in 1863 and remembered him as "full of animation, with undimmed intelligence—his age was 'as a lusty

winter, frosty but kindly.' " Others spoke of his constant cheerfulness, his beaming face, and his "unremitting kindness and benevolence, which endeared him to all around." [15]

Roget was not a man to collect things—with one exception.
All his life he had sought after books. They were, as we have
seen, his stock in trade, his working tools, and a well-fitted library
was to him the center of his home and his life. Thus, perhaps no
better final view of the man, the work, and the words that were
Peter Mark Roget can be provided than by a glance into the library at No. 18 Upper Bedford Place, a glance that is made possible by the survival of a bookseller's catalog announcing that
"the important library of P. M. Roget, M.D., F.R.S., Etc., will be
sold by auction at No. 13 Wellington Street, Strand, at one
o'clock precisely." [16] The individual books and journals reminiscent of particular features and phases of Roget's long life loom
up like beacons in the dim past, and a brief quantitative analysis
of the library reveals the sweep as well as the limitations of his
interests.[17]

Roget's library, at least as it was described in the catalog, consisted of approximately four thousand volumes, which might
be broken down into the following classes:

SCIENCE (including mathematics, engineering, and medicine)	1,732 vols.
LITERATURE (including drama and philology)	607 vols.
HISTORY (including biography and travel)	420 vols.
GENERAL PERIODICALS	329 vols.
GENERAL ENCYCLOPAEDIAS	256 vols.
PHILOSOPHY (including theology)	177 vols.
SOCIOLOGY (politics, taxation, legislation)	117 vols.
GAMES, JOKES, EPIGRAMS (including chess)	70 vols.
ART, MUSIC	17 vols.
BUSINESS (mainly banking)	8 vols.
OTHERS (undescribed)	356 vols.

4,089 [18]

It is not surprising, of course, that Roget's library should have
been dominated by scientific works, nor that within this large
category, books on medicine, physiology, and anatomy should be
most numerous. A sample list of some of these volumes is, in effect, a recapitulation of Roget's industrious and at times tempes-
tuous scientific life. Standing on his shelves as mute witnesses to

his own accomplishments and to those of his friends and opponents were most of the landmark volumes of that wholesale emergence of individual sciences from the last decade of the eighteenth century to the middle of the nineteenth. Names like those of Bichat, Mill, Huxley, Humboldt, Babbage, Grove, Tyndall, Watt, Herschel, Davy, Combe, Cuvier, Lyell, Müller, Bentham, Darwin, Mayo, Owen, Huber, Biot, Brewster, Hall, Grant, Bell, Lee, Quételet, Faraday not only were markers of Roget's own life but remain as unfaded guideposts of the rapid development of modern science.

More than nine hundred French titles in Roget's library suggest his lifelong connections with France and Geneva as well as the importance of Continental culture in the eyes of nineteenth-century Englishmen.

Second to science in Roget's library was that section devoted to literature and language, including almost one hundred volumes of dramatic works, such as Sharpe's eighteen-volume *British Theatre* (1804–5) and the thirteen-volume *Théâtre Français* (1767–8). Roget was very weak on the classics—perhaps a half dozen Greek and Latin titles in all—and his library simply did not recognize the United States, with one strange exception—one copy of Joe Miller's joke book. Of Cooper, Irving, Poe, Hawthorne, Emerson, Thoreau, Melville, Whitman, Longfellow, Whittier, Bryant—nothing.

While Byron, Shelley, Wordsworth, Scott, Campbell, Beattie, Goldsmith, Swift, Hazlitt, Spenser, Chaucer, Richardson, and Mrs. Hemans were represented, there was not one volume of Shakespeare in the catalog. There were, however, two works of Shakespearian criticism! Nor were there any volumes of Southey or Coleridge, although Roget knew both men. Even more surprising is the almost total absence of Victorian writers—unless they were included in such lots as No. 738: "Modern cheap literature —15 v." Roget had one volume of Tennyson and a three-volume set of Harriet Martineau's *Forest and Game-Law Tales* (1845), but he had no Dickens, Thackeray, Newman, Macaulay, Brontë, Eliot, Peacock, Browning, Austen, Ruskin, Carlyle, Kingsley, Meredith, Gaskell, Arnold, Disraeli, Bulwer-Lytton, nor Trollope. It seems unbelievable that he would not have read with particular interest *Mary Barton* (1848), which is still one of the best accounts of life in Manchester, where he had begun his medical practice; or *Coningsby* (1844); or *Felix Holt, the Radical* (1866); or *Oliver Twist* (1838); or *Pelham* (1828); or *Barchester Towers* (1857);

or any number of other sociologically revealing novels that were
to be so important in opening Englishmen's eyes to the true nature of the conditions of their poor, their middle, and their idle
classes.

Approximately one hundred works on language, many of
which he no doubt used in working on the *Thesaurus,* included
many dictionaries in English, French, Italian, and Latin; several
synonymies, including an original Crabb and a French thesaurus;
several treatises on language per se (e.g., Farrar, *Essay on the Origin of Language*); and several volumes on literary style.

Roget's reading in history was spotty, with the bulk of the volumes in that section being biographies and such biographical
sourcebooks as Munk's *Roll of the Royal College of Physicians
from 1518 to 1800,* Debrett's *Baronetage and Knightage,* and
Lucy Atkins' *Memoirs, Miscellanies, and Letters.* Presumably he
would have drawn on this section in writing his many biographical articles, such as the pieces for the *Encyclopaedia Britannica.*

Travel books, perhaps half a hundred of them, were also very
miscellaneous in Roget's library, and, for the large part, more
fashionable than technical or professional. They included folio
views of the Thames, pictures of Holland, traveler's handbooks
for Scotland, France, and Germany, and the beginnings of a
collection on the new continent: F. Bailey's *Journal of a Tour in
Unsettled Parts of North America in 1796–1797;* E. Burke's *Account of European Settlements in America* (1777); *Report of the
United States Coast Survey* (1856–58).

In the last decade or two of his life, one of Roget's little hob-
bies was the collection of books dealing with jokes, parlor magic,
and witticisms. He had about twenty such items as *Charades, En-
igmas, and Riddles Collected by a Can'tab;* Sydney Smith's *Wit
and Wisdom; London Budget of Wit;* R. Kempt's *American Joe
Miller; Wit's Red Book or Calendar of Gaiety for 1822; Pun-
niana;* and *Punch's Twenty Almanacks in One Volume.*

Considering the fact that Roget lived through the tempests of
the great British reform acts, and that he was intimately acquainted with many of the prime movers of that bloodless revolution, his library was very meager in political and sociological
materials. He had Adam Smith's *Wealth of Nations,* Romilly's
speeches, Francis Horner's memoirs, one belated history of the
French Revolution, Harriet Martineau on political economy and
the poor laws, Brougham on leaders of the times, Mackinnon's
On the Rise and Present State of Public Opinion, several tracts

by Thomas Paine, a few volumes each of Sir James Mackintosh, Sydney Smith, and Richard Whately, but that was about all. Some of the unclassified lots at the auction, of course, probably included a sampling of the many sociopolitical pamphlets of the day—for example, lot No. 1008: "Biographical tracts, scientific and political, some scarce—a parcel." Surprisingly, there was almost nothing on education, a subject in which both Roget and his wife were keenly interested.

Philosophically, Roget's library ran heavily toward the empiricists, the utilitarians, and the common-sense men: Locke, Hume, James Mill, Bentham, Dugald Stewart, Sir James Mackintosh— with a slanting off into Dr. Hartley, J. D. Morell, H. T. Buckle, and M. F. Tupper. It did include Kant's *Critique of Pure Reason* and a twenty-six-volume set of Rousseau, which had been so important to his father. His theological reading was not distinguished—surprisingly, he did not even have a copy of Paley's *Natural Theology,* although his Bridgewater Treatise was a demonstration of Paley's thesis, and although Mary Roget studied Paley as a girl.

In addition to the journals of his scientific societies, Roget subscribed to several general periodicals: *Edinburgh Review, Argosy, Athenaeum, Literary Gazette, Spectator, Saturday Review, National Review,* and *Penny Magazine.* He had a wealth of general encyclopaedias, reminiscent of the common practice among doctors of increasing their incomes and reputations by contributing to the many encyclopaedias appearing in the first three decades of the century. The *Encyclopaedia Britannica; Rees's Cyclopaedia of Arts, Science, and Literature; Encyclopaedia Metropolitania; Library of Useful Knowledge; Library of Entertaining Knowledge; Lardner's Cyclopaedia* appeared in multivolume sets on his shelves.

The fact that the whole library brought less than £200 suggests why Sotheby called Roget's an "important" library rather than a "valuable" one. The learned doctor did not spend his time nor his money on rare books; like his mind, his library was not an ornament nor a plaything, but a practical tool to aid one in getting on with the day's work. Several well-known booksellers, including Quaritch, Walford, and Wheldon, attended the sale, but they were not generous bidders. Apparently they didn't have to be. Judging from the number of titles—often multivolume works— that were knocked down for a shilling, one might guess that there was little, if any, contest over most of the items. The great

majority of the 454 lots, ranging from three or four volumes to as
many as sixty or seventy, were sold for very small amounts—
scores of them going for one, two, or three shillings. All of Roget's
beloved chess books (more than fifty of them), for example,
brought less than £5. The highest bids—Walford's £20 for the
long run of RS *Philosophical Transactions,* and Quaritch's £16
for eighty-three volumes of the two journals *Philosophical Magazine* and *London and Edinburgh Philosophical Magazine*—were
the only purchases that might have generated some excitement
among those present. Only 31 lots reached as high as a one-pound
bid. The *Edinburgh Review,* a complete run from its commencement to July 1869, brought only 15s.

Over and over again, as he paced his gas-lighted library at
night, turning some mathematical puzzle this way and that,
Roget saw on the gilt spines of his books the same constellation
of names: Stewart, Edgeworth, Beddoes, Davy, Romilly, Bentham, Faraday, Marcet, Dumont, Wollaston, Babbage, Lee, Panizzi, Peel, Latham, Lyell, Whewell, Roget . . . and for each
name, a face—sober, affectionate, mischievous, indignant, visionary, earnest, excited, pompous, hostile . . . and for each face, a
time and a place and a happening, across ninety years of life.
The library lamp glinted on those names, illuminated those
faces, threw shadows among those volumes tall and short, slim
and stout, as the street lamps ("There is gas in the Park!") cast
the variegated shadows of men on the streets and walls of Roget's
Edinburgh, Geneva, Manchester, and London. A working library,
the library and portrait of a man working all his life, Roget's
study was truly a hall of echoes, perfectly audible, in all their insistent clamor, to a deaf old man.

As had been his custom for several years, Roget left the city in
August 1869, for a retreat in the hilly resort of West Malvern,
near Worcester, appropriately enough about halfway between
London and Liverpool. He and Kate took their usual rooms in a
hillside residence, Ashfield House (now No. 225 West Malvern
Road), with a broad westerly view toward the Cambrian Moun-
tains of Wales.[19] Enjoying his usual walks in the neighborhood
and meditative evenings on the broad veranda of the place, Roget
retained his strength until the resort was struck by a prolonged
and intense heat wave. The unyielding high temperatures were
too much for the efficient machine that Catherine Roget had
nursed into action ninety years before. He weakened visibly, and
on September 12 he expired, "peacefully and without suffering,

from the natural decay of that vital power, the mysterious working of which he had so laboured to illustrate." [20]

After a quiet family service in St. James Church, West Malvern, Roget's long body was laid to rest in the grassy slope of the churchyard, and his grave covered by a large, plain granite slab bearing the simple inscription:

PETER MARK ROGET
M.D. F.R.S.
DIED AT WEST MALVERN
SEPT. 12TH 1869
AGED 90

Kate's name—Catherine Mary Roget—and her dates were added in 1905 when her body was buried under the same slab.

Notes

Notes

THE FOLLOWING abbreviations have been used throughout the notes:

AGR	= Anne Garbett Romilly	RCP	= Royal College of Physicians
AM	= Alexander Marcet		
AR	= Annette Roget	RI	= Royal Institution
BM	= British Museum	RS	= Royal Society
CR	= Catherine Roget	SDUK	= Society for the Diffusion of Useful Knowledge
EB	= *Encyclopaedia Britannica*		
ED	= Etienne Dumont	SR	= Samuel Romilly
JLR	= John Lewis Roget	SRR	= Samuel Romilly Roget
JRR	= John Romilly Roget		
MC	= Medical and Chirurgical Society	UE	= University of Edinburgh
MR	= Mary Roget	UL	= University of London
PMR	= Peter Mark Roget		

CHAPTER I

[1] The *Dictionary of National Biography* article perpetuates this misinformation, as do introductory sketches in the most recent editions of Roget's *Thesaurus*. The few brief accounts of Roget in print are chiefly dependent upon the *DNB*, which in turn drew upon the obituary memoir published by the Royal Society of London in 1870. That obituary has been the source of several erroneous statements about Roget. The location of Jean Roget's church was determined authoritatively fifty years ago by George B. Beeman and reported in his "Notes on the Sites and

History of the French Churches in London," *Proceedings of the Huguenot Society of London,* Vol. VIII (1905–8), pp. 36–39. Basing his conclusions upon a search of the registers of the churches, and the minute books of the consistorial meetings, Beeman found that Roget's church was that known as Le Quarré ("The Square"), from its original location in the seventeenth century in the chapel of Monmouth House, on the south side of Soho Square. A few years before the turn of the eighteenth century, the congregation moved to a dingy building in Berwick Street, now the site of St. Luke's Church. There they met for worship until 1769, when the congregation built a small church on the south side of Little Dean Street (formerly Milk Alley). Jean Roget preached there from 1775 to 1781, when his ill health forced him to resign. The church was closed about 1853, when the congregation and the church property were absorbed by La Savoie, the Savoy Church.

[2] "Notes on the Life and Work of John Lewis Roget," *Proceedings of the Huguenot Society of London,* Vol. IX (1910), pp. 545–48.

[3] Samuel Romilly, *Memoirs of the Life of Sir Samuel Romilly,* with a selection from his correspondence, edited by his sons, 2nd edition (London: Murray, 1841), Vol. I, p. 31.

[4] *Ibid.,* p. 39.

[5] *Ibid.,* p. 145.

[6] S. R. Roget (ed.), *Travel in the Two Last Centuries of Three Generations* (New York: Appleton, 1922), p. 21.

[7] Several pages of excerpts from Catherine's journal of this trip make up Chapter II of her great-grandson's book *Travel in the Last Two Centuries . . .* (pp. 32–47). I have been unable to find the journal itself, and it is the opinion of the surviving members of the family that it was among the bulk of the family papers lost in subsequent fires and removals.

[8] Letter, ED to CR, June 24, 1787, tr. Geoffrey Selth. (JRR)

[9] I do not know whether this was Catherine's own composition or a mere translation of some fashionable French writer.

[10] Letter, ED to CR, August 10, 1787, tr. Geoffrey Selth. (JRR)

[11] Apparently Catherine also had trouble understanding Jean Samuel's letters, judging by a remark in a letter to SR on February 25, 1793: "I never can comprehend my Brother in Law's letters, they are the most puzzling I ever read. I can only make out that the Genevan affairs go on very bad—that a dreadful scarcity of corn prevails, that he and our friend Dumont are not of the same mind, and what above all I fear, that they (that is, our family) talk of leaving the town and seeking refuge *en pays étranger.*"

[12] *Letters Containing an Account of the Late Revolution in*

France and Observations on the Constitution, Laws, Manners, and Institutions of the English . . . During the Years 1789 and 1790 (London, 1792). There is a copy in the British Museum.

[13] An annuity scheme in which the subscribers share a common fund with the benefit of survivorship, the survivors' shares being increased as the subscribers die, until the whole goes to the last survivor.

[14] Letter, CR to SR, July 2, 1791. (JRR)

[15] Letter, CR to SR, October 11, 1791. (JRR)

[16] Letter, CR to SR, December 26, 1791. (JRR)

[17] Letter, CR to SR, February 10, 1793. (JRR)

[18] Letter, CR to SR, February 25, 1793. (JRR)

[19] Letter, SR to CR, October 25, 1792. It is not completely clear whether this is St. James Street (W.1.) or St. James's Street (S.W.1.), but from the handwriting it appears to be the former.

[20] Professional economists point out that there are so many variable factors involved that it is simply impossible to establish precise twentieth-century equivalents for eighteenth-century sums. However, after studying the information provided us by my colleague, John Soares, who queried economists at the Federal Reserve Banks of San Francisco and New York City, we have decided to use a rough equivalency of $25 (1967) to every £1 (1840) and to use this ratio throughout the book. Thus, Catherine's annual income of £200 was roughly the equivalent of $5,000 today.

[21] "Consols": abbreviation for Consolidated Bank Annuities, a form of British Government stock originated in 1751. Through the period under discussion, the Government did not borrow money at various rates of interest, but kept the interest rate constant—3 percent—and varied the amount of principal offered to the investor. At the close of the war with France in 1815, for example, one could get as much as £174 in consols for £100 cash.

[22] Letter, SR to CR, April 29, 1793. (JRR)

CHAPTER II

[1] S. R. Roget (ed.), *Travel in the Two Last Centuries of Three Generations* (New York: Appleton, 1922), offers an amusing account of this journey.

[2] Letter, CR to SR, December 2, 1793. (JRR)

[3] Mr. D. Bisset, Secretary to the Faculty of Medicine, UE, has kindly identified the following members of the faculty as those attended by Roget during his years at the university:

John Hill, appointed to the Chair of Humanity in 1775.

Andrew Dalzel, appointed to the Chair of Greek in 1772.

Joseph Black, appointed to the Chair of Chemistry in 1766.

Daniel Rutherford, appointed to the Chair of Botany in 1786.

Alexander Monro II, appointed to the Chair of Anatomy in 1754.

Thomas Charles Hope, appointed to the Chair of Chemistry in 1795.

James Gregory, appointed to the Chair of Medicine in 1790.

Alexander Hamilton, appointed to the Chair of Midwifery in 1780.

Francis Home, appointed to the Chair of Pharmacology in 1768.

Andrew Duncan, appointed to the Chair of Physiology in 1789.

James Russell, lecturer in clinical surgery.

[4] Letter, PMR to SR, December 31, 1793. (JRR)

[5] D. B. Horn, *A Short History of the University of Edinburgh, 1556–1889* (Edinburgh: University Press, 1967), p. 89.

[6] Letter, CR to SR, April 11, 1794. (JRR)

[7] Letter, ED to CR, February 28, 1794, tr. Geoffrey Selth. (JRR)

[8] Letter, CR to SR, December 22, 1795. (JRR)

[9] Letter, CR to SR, October 15, 1795. (JRR)

[10] Letter, CR to SR, November 27, 1795. (JRR)

[11] Letter, CR to SR, November 6, 1795. (JRR)

[12] Letter, CR to SR, March 19, 1797. (JRR)

[13] Letter, CR to SR, July 22, 1797. (JRR)

[14] Letter, PMR to SR, September 21, 1797. (JRR)

[15] William Wilberforce (1759–1833), philanthropist and religious writer, best remembered now for his leadership in outlawing slavery in England, but widely thought of at the end of the eighteenth century as a prying, self-righteous, self-appointed keeper of the public morals and supporter of the repressive measures of Viscount Sidmouth. In 1802 Wilberforce formed the Society for the Suppression of Vice. He was a favorite target of William Cobbett (in *Rural Rides*), who repeatedly described Wilberforce as an archhypocrite and suppressor of the poor. It is significant that Catherine, who, for all her sympathetic statements about the conditions of the poor, was fearful of genuine reform, should write so strongly about Wilberforce.

[16] Letter, ED to CR, December 19, 1797, tr. Geoffrey Selth. (JRR)

[17] Letter, CR to SR, December 22, 1795. (JRR)

[18] Personal letter, Charles P. Finlayson, Keeper of Manuscripts, UE Library, January 15, 1967.

CHAPTER III

[1] Maria Edgeworth has recorded that so keen was Beddoes on the curative properties of gases that he more than once "conveyed Cows into invalids' bedrooms that they might inhale the

breath of the animals." Cited in J. G. Crowther, *Men of Science* (New York: Norton, 1936), p. 22.

[2] It is probably through his friendship with Anna's brother Lovell Edgeworth, whom he knew at Edinburgh, that Roget decided to visit Beddoes.

[3] There is some argument about whether it was Josiah or his cousin, Thomas, who donated this sizable grant.

[4] Barbara M. Duncum, *The Development of Inhalation Anaesthesia with Special Reference to the Years 1846–1900* (Oxford: University Press, 1947), p. 69.

[5] F. F. Cartwright, *The English Pioneers of Anaesthesia* (Bristol, 1952), p. 103.

[6] *Ibid.,* p. 107.

[7] Duncum, p. 74.

[8] John Davy, *Memoirs of the Life of Sir Humphry Davy* (London, 1839–40), Vol. I, p. 64.

[9] Duncum, p. 75.

[10] Thomas Beddoes and J. Watt, *Considerations on the Medicinal Use and on the Production of Factitious Airs,* 2nd ed. (Bristol, 1795).

[11] Humphry Davy, *Researches . . .* (London, 1800), pp. 458–60.

[12] Crowther, p. 32.

[13] William Wordsworth, "Preface to the Second Edition of *Lyrical Ballads,*" in Charles S. Holmes, Edwin Fussell, and Roy Frazer (eds.), *The Major Critics* (New York: Knopf, 1957), p. 188.

[14] Lawrence Hanson, *The Life of S. T. Coleridge: The Early Years* (New York: Russell & Russell, 1962), p. 361.

[15] Cartwright, p. 120.

[16] PMR, in Humphry Davy, *Researches . . .* , pp. 509–12.

[17] Letter, ED to CR, September 10, 1799, tr. Geoffrey Selth. (JRR)

[18] Letter, SR to CR, October 26, 1799. (JRR)

[19] John Bowring (ed.), *Life and Letters of Bentham* (London, 1843), Vol. X, p. 342.

[20] Letter, PMR to AM, December 13, 1799. (RCP)

[21] Letter, ED to CR, undated, tr. Geoffrey Selth. (JRR)

CHAPTER IV

[1] The nature of Peter Roget's work with Bentham provides a good illustration of the inadequacy of most of the accounts of Roget's life. Beginning with Pettigrew, and running on through the RS *Proceedings* and the *DNB* to such current attempts as that of Ober, these sources hazily describe Bentham's project as a scheme for the utilization of the sewage of the metropolis. Neither in the John Romilly Roget papers nor in the Bentham

collection at University College do I find any evidence that Roget had anything to do with any of Bentham's projects other than that of the Frigidarium. One exception to these misleading accounts is that of the memoir published in the *Minutes of Proceedings of the Institution of Civil Engineers,* which correctly notes the Frigidarium as a cold-storage scheme.

[2] Richard Rush, *A Residence at the Court of London* (London: Bentley, 1833), pp. 286–88.

[3] These papers, along with the bulk of Bentham's manuscripts and jottings, are housed at University College, where archivists have sorted and catalogued them and stored them in several hundred boxes.

[4] John Bowring, *Life and Letters of Bentham* (London, 1843), Vol. X, p. 346 ff.

[5] *Ibid.*

[6] *Ibid.,* p. 347.

[7] *Ibid.,* pp. 348–49.

[8] Letter, PMR to CR, November 7, 1800, tr. Jay Louis Hall. (JRR)

[9] *Ibid.*

[10] Letter, PMR to CR, December 7, 1800, tr. Jay Louis Hall. (JRR)

[11] Charles Milner Atkinson, *Jeremy Bentham: His Life and Work* (London: Methuen, 1905), p. 211. The fact that Roget rubbed shoulders with both Coleridge and Bentham, the two figures selected by John Stuart Mill thirty years later as most responsible for the intellectual revolution of the age, is a fruitful subject for speculation. How that association may have influenced Roget's idea of "culture," for example, might well prove worthy of investigation. A good starting point, in addition to Mill's essays on the two men, would be Raymond Williams' discussion in Chapter III of his *Culture and Society* (New York: Columbia University Press, 1958).

[12] *Ibid.,* p. 168.

[13] Letter, PMR to AR, December 29, 1800, tr. Jay Louis Hall. (JRR)

[14] Letter, PMR to AR, December 29, 1800. (JRR)

[15] *Ibid.*

[16] George Frederick Cooke (1756–1811), who, with Mr. Siddons, joined Kemble at Covent Garden.

[17] John Philip Kemble (1757–1823), then manager of Drury Lane.

[18] Letter, PMR to CR, January 16, 1801. (JRR)

[19] *Ibid.*

[20] Letter, PMR to CR, February 22, 1801, tr. Jay Louis Hall. (JRR)

[21] Letter, PMR to CR, February 27, 1801, tr. Jay Louis Hall.

(JRR) The reference to secret writing may suggest that Peter was feeling the expense of his heavy correspondence with his mother. In 1800, the postage for a "single-sheet" letter, from London to Sidmouth, would have amounted to about half a shilling, or, using our $25-to-£1 ratio, about 65¢.

22 Letter, PMR to CR, March 2, 1801, tr. Jay Louis Hall. (JRR)

23 Letter, AR to PMR, March 1801. (JRR)

24 Letter, PMR to CR, March 17, 1801, tr. Jay Louis Hall. (JRR)

25 Letter, PMR to CR, April 11, 1801, tr. Jay Louis Hall. (JRR)

26 Letter, SR to PMR, September 16, 1801. (JRR)

27 Letter, PMR to AGR, January 1, 1802. (JRR)

28 Letter, PMR to CR, January 24, 1802, tr. Jay Louis Hall. (JRR)

29 *Ibid.*

CHAPTER V

1 Henry Crabb Robinson, *Diary, Reminiscences, and Correspondence,* edited by Thomas Sadler (Boston: Fields, Osgood, 1870), Vol. I, p. 68.

2 Philips had not satisfied himself with his own observations. He had written to friends who had met young Roget, and received, he said, highly laudatory reports on the young man's character and abilities. One of Philips' informants was Richard "Conversation" Sharp (1759–1835), who was a familiar in the best drawing rooms—and counting rooms—of London. Sharp's intimate friendship with such influential figures as Samuel Rogers, Sir James Mackintosh, Sydney Smith, David Ricardo, William Wordsworth, Lord Holland, was more than once employed to Peter's advantage. Another recommending letter came from Roget's friend Arthur Aikin, chemist and scientific writer best known as Secretary of the Royal Society of Arts, a position he held for twenty-three years.

3 Herbert Philips (ed.), *Continental Travel in 1802–03: The Story of an Escape* (Manchester, 1904), p. 9. The bulk of the following account is drawn from this small collection of letters, edited by a nephew of the two Philips boys. It is an exceedingly rare volume—see my "Peter Mark Roget: Travels and Letters," *Bulletin of the New York Public Library,* Vol. 71 (October 1967), pp. 542–45. The only other published account of Roget's Geneva adventure is that in his grandson's book (see note 5 below), which is based primarily upon the Philips volume. In the family papers surviving are perhaps eight unpublished letters that deal with various aspects of the adventure.

4 Philips, p. 22.

[5] S. R. Roget (ed.), *Travel in the Two Last Centuries of Three Generations* (New York: Appleton, 1922), pp. 66–67.

[6] *Ibid.*, p. 69.

[7] Etienne de Lessert (1735–1816), financier, arrested during the Reign of Terror, but reinstated under Napoleon.

[8] Son of Shelburne, first Marquis of Lansdowne. Henry Petty, who later became third Marquis of Lansdowne, occupied important posts in the reform Government, and assisted Roget at several points during his life.

[9] Madame Gautier was a revered friend of both Samuel Romilly and the Roget family.

[10] Philips, p. 37.

[11] *Ibid.*, p. 33.

[12] *Ibid.*, pp. 36–37.

[13] *Ibid.*, p. 47.

[14] S. R. Roget, pp. 73–84.

[15] *Ibid.*, p. 81.

[16] Auguste Fournier, *Napoleon I: A Biography*, tr. Margaret Bacon Corwin and Arthur Dart Bissell (New York, 1903), p. 39.

[17] Philips, p. 52.

[18] S. R. Roget, p. 84.

[19] Philips, p. 72.

[20] *Ibid.*, p. 73.

[21] S. R. Roget, p. 90.

[22] Philips, p. 82.

[23] *Ibid.*, p. 83.

[24] Fournier, p. 267.

[25] Philips, p. 94.

[26] S. R. Roget, p. 100.

[27] *Ibid.*, p. 91.

[28] *Ibid.*, p. 93.

[29] *Ibid.*, p. 104.

[30] Philips, p. 106.

[31] S. R. Roget, p. 94.

[32] *Ibid.*, p. 107.

[33] *Ibid.*, pp. 105–6.

[34] William Edward Hartpole Lecky, *Historical and Political Essays* (London, 1908), p. 141.

[35] S. R. Roget, p. 108. From this point on, through the critical phase of the escape, the only surviving sources conflict on some dates and some of the sequences. However, since there are no significant differences in the three separate stories, we have deemed it justifiable to combine the three accounts into one coherent narrative. Thus, the next few pages should be considered a composite of 1) letters in the Philips collection, 2) surviving family letters, and 3) Roget's grandson's version, as presented in S. R. Roget's volume.

[36] S. R. Roget, pp. 109–10.

[37] Letter, CR to AGR, June 25, 1803. (JRR)

[38] S. R. Roget, pp. 114–15.

[39] *Ibid.*, pp. 115–16.

[40] Following is the text of the *acte de vérité*, certifying Roget's Genevan citizenship:

Le Maire de la Ville de Genève certifie que le Citoyen Jean Roget, né le 30 mars 1751, étoit citoyen de la ci-devant République de Genève, et que son fils Pierre Marc Roget, né le 18 Janvier 1779 à Londres, a conservé sa qualité de ci-devant Genevois, en vertu de laquelle, et d'après l'article 1er due traité de réunion, en ces termes, 'Les Genevois absens ne seront point considerés comme émigrés. Ils pourront en tous tems revenir en France et s'y établir,' etc. Le dit Pierre Marc Roget a déclaré voulour de fixer dans sa patrie et jouir des droits attachés à la qualité de Citoyen français. Et s'est fait incrire sur le tableau de la Commune.

   Genève le 29 messidor an 11.
   (signed) Picot, adjt.
   Gervais, S. en chef.

S. R. Roget, p. 112. The document was endorsed by the following residents of Geneva, including Roget's paternal uncle, the first named: Samuel Roget, René Guillaume Prévost Dacier (lawyer), Pierre Prévost Marcet (professor), J. Peschier (pastor), Antoine Roustan (pastor), Jean Lequaint (pastor), Jean Pescier (doctor), and Louis Odier (doctor).

[41] Philips, pp. 137–39.

[42] S. R. Roget, p. 118.

[43] *Ibid.*, pp. 119–21.

[44] Philips, pp. 114–15.

[45] S. R. Roget, p. 125.

[46] Philips, p. 128.

[47] Letter, PMR to SR, September 18, 1803. (JRR)

[48] Letter, CR to AGR, October 17, 1803. (JRR)

[49] Philips, p. 130.

[50] *Ibid.*, pp. 133–34.

CHAPTER VI

[1] Thomas Percival (1740–1804), long a stalwart of the Manchester medical community, published in 1803 a code of medical ethics which was later used as the basis for the code drawn up by the American Medical Association in 1847. John Ferriar (1761–1816) was largely responsible for Manchester's first public health services.

[2] Letter, AR to PMR, May 20, 1804. (JRR)

[3] The Misses Pick were close friends of the Rogets at Ilfracombe. They kept in touch with Catherine and Annette through most of their subsequent wanderings.

[4] There are three letters addressed to Peter at that address—Annette's of May 20, Romilly's of May 21, and Catherine's of June 26.

[5] Asa Briggs, *Victorian Cities* (London: Odhams, 1964), especially Chapter III; W. H. Chaloner, "The Birth of Modern Manchester," in *Manchester and Its Region,* British Association for the Advancement of Science (Manchester: University Press, 1962), pp. 131–46; J. L. and Barbara Hammond, *The Town Labourer: 1760–1832, the New Civilization* (London: Longmans, Green, 1966); G. M. Young (ed.), *Early Victorian England, 1830–1865* (Oxford: University Press, 1934); Elizabeth Cleghorn Gaskell, *Mary Barton: A Tale of Manchester Life* (London: Everyman's Library, 1965).

[6] *Annual Register* (London, 1808), pp. 132–34.

[7] John Ferriar, *Medical Histories and Reflections,* 3 vols. (London, 1810). This extremely interesting work suggests another tie between Roget and Ferriar, for it was dedicated to the same Richard "Conversation" Sharp who had given Roget such a high recommendation to John Philips in December 1801.

[8] See Appendix I.

[9] Personal letter, Jean M. Ayton, August 10, 1967.

[10] Edward Mansfield Brockbank, *Sketches of the Lives and Work of the Honorary Medical Staff at the Manchester Infirmary, 1752–1830* (Manchester, 1904), p. 218.

[11] P. Roget, B. Gibson, and J. Hutchinson, *Syllabus of a Course of Lectures on Anatomy and Physiology* (Manchester, 1805), p. 21. A photostat copy of this item, classified by the National Library of Medicine (Bethesda, Md.) as an "extremely rare" publication, was provided me by that library.

[12] Brockbank, p. 218.

[13] Personal letter, A. L. Smyth, February 8, 1967. Unfortunately, the society's quarters suffered a direct hit during enemy air raids in 1940, and most of its records were destroyed in the ensuing fire. An examination of volumes of the *Memoirs* of the society up to 1860 turned up some interesting facts, e.g., that the society was the first to publish Benjamin Franklin's paper "Meteorological Imaginations and Conjectures,"—but very little on Roget except that he was, in 1805, a member of the Committee on Papers, and that he was listed as a "Corresponding member" as late as 1819.

[14] Frank Renaud, *A Short History of the Manchester Royal Infirmary* (Manchester, 1898), p. 76.

[15] Letter, SR to PMR, November 10, 1804. (JRR)

[16] Letter, CR to PMR, March 16, 1805. (JRR)

[17] Letter, PMR to AR, September 6, 1808, tr. Howard Shipman. (JRR)

¹⁸ See Frank Peel, *The Risings of the Luddites* (London, 1888), for a fascinating account of the distressed and riotous artisans who, in 1811, attempted to prevent the use of power looms.

¹⁹ For example, see the "Chronicle" section of the *Annual Register* of 1808 for accounts of negotiations between owners and workers and of uprisings in towns throughout Lancashire.

CHAPTER VII

¹ John Romilly Roget pointed out to me this passage in *Peter Pan* (London: Hodder and Stoughton, 1928), pp. 3–4.

² *Survey of London: King's Cross Neighborhood (The Parish of St. Pancras, Part IV)*, ed. J. R. Howard Roberts and Walter H. Godfrey, Vol. XXIV (London: London County Council, 1952), p. 46. In addition, the tax rolls for the parish of St. George's, Bloomsbury, show Roget as paying, in 1809, a tax of £8 3s. 14d. against a valuation of £65. He paid twice this amount in 1819, but in 1829 his contribution had dropped to £7 4s., in 1839 to £3 16s., and in 1842, his last year at Bernard Street, to £4 2s. 4d. Cited in *Poor Rate, 1809, for Parish of St. George's, Bloomsbury.* (The rate books can be examined at the Holborn Central Library, 32 Theobalds Road, W.C.1.) My thanks are due Mr. F. R. Pryce, Reference Librarian, who graciously assisted me in searching these manuscript record books.

³ John Summerson, *Georgian London* (Harmondsworth, Middlesex: Penguin, 1962), p. 170.

⁴ *Survey of London*, p. 46.

⁵ Summerson, p. 65.

⁶ Letter, SR to PMR, August 8, 1809. (JRR)

⁷ *London and Provincial Medical Directory for 1861* (London, 1861).

⁸ Arnold Chaplin, *Medicine in England During the Reign of George III* (London, 1819), p. 134.

⁹ Zachary Cope, "The Private Medical Schools of London (1746–1914)," in F. N. L. Poynter (ed.), *The Evolution of Medical Education in Britain* (London: Pittman Medical, 1966), p. 93.

¹⁰ William Thomas Brande (1788–1866), chemist and influential member of the Royal Institution, Royal Society, etc.; served with Roget on many committees and projects.

¹¹ Sir Joseph Banks (1743–1820), wealthy English naturalist, President of the Royal Society for forty-one years.

¹² Cope, p. 93.

¹³ Marc Auguste Pictet (1752–1825), Professor of Philosophy at Geneva, family friend of Roget, one of the deputation of Gen-

evese who negotiated for the union of the State of Geneva with the French Republic in 1798.

[14] Paulina B. Granville (ed.), *Autobiography of A. B. Granville* (London, 1874), Vol. I, pp. 445–46.

[15] *Ibid.*, Vol. II, p. 47.

[16] *Transactions of the Medical and Chirurgical Society,* Vol. I (1809). The introductory pages of the first volume list the following members, from its formation to March 1809: John Abernethy, John Aiken, William Babington, Matthew Baillie, Sir Joseph Banks, George Birkbeck, Gilbert Blane, Alexander Marcet, Sir William Blizard, John Cooke, John Bostock, Henry Cline, Astley Cooper, Humphry Davy, Everard Home, John Hunter, Edward Jenner, John [sic] Roget, Benjamin Travers, James Wilson, William Hyde Wollaston, and John Yelloly. William Saunders, M.D., was the first President, Yelloly the first Secretary, and Marcet the first Foreign Secretary. Both Marcet and Yelloly remained on the Council of the society for many years and were simultaneously Trustees.

[17] *Transactions,* Vol. II (1811), pp. 136–60. In addition to listing the following new members: William Henry, William Laurence, Robert Sutherland, and John Want, this volume notes Yelloly and Roget as Secretaries, Marcet as Corresponding Secretary, Sir Henry Halford as President, Astley Cooper as Treasurer, and James Curry, Thompson Forster, John Sims, and Everard Home as Vice-Presidents.

[18] Thomas Joseph Pettigrew, *Medical Portrait Gallery: Biographical Memoirs of the Most Celebrated Physicians, Surgeons, etc., etc., Who Have Contributed to the Advancement of Medical Science* (London: Whittaker, 1840) Vol. IV, p. 6.

[19] *Transactions,* Vol. VII, pp. 284–95.

[20] *Minute Book of the Council of the Medical and Chirurgical Society,* Vol. I (1809), p. 84. (Two folio manuscript volumes, bound in green leather, were graciously made available to my inspection by Mr. P. Wade, Librarian, Royal Society of Medicine.

[21] P. Wade, "The History and Development of the Library of the Royal Society of Medicine," *Proceedings of the Royal Society of Medicine,* Vol. 55 (August 1962), p. 627.

[22] *Minute Book,* Vol. X (1819).

[23] *Ibid.,* Vol. V (1814).

[24] Letter, PMR to AM, August 27, 1819. (JRR)

[25] In addition to those already named, the following sample, taken from the membership list printed in July 1822, is representative: Henry Alexander, John Armstrong, Robert Bree, John Bright, Richard Cartwright, William Frederick Chambers, Samuel Cleverly, Thomas Copeland, Sir Alexander Crichton, David

D. Davies, Sir David Dundas, Henry Earle, John Elliotson, John Richard Farre, William Henry Fitton, Charles Ferguson Forbes, Algernon Frampton, Robert Gooch, John Alexander Gordon, Joseph Henry Green, George Gregory, James Harding, John Haviland, Henry Holland, Robert Hume, William Hunter, Alexander Copland Hutchison, Edward Jenner, James Johnson, Edwin Godden Jones, James Laird, William Lambe, Patrick Macgregor, Sir James McGrigor, William Macmichael, Herbert Mayo, Samuel Merriman, Benjamin Fonseca Outram, Sir Christopher Pegge, William Prout, Henry S. Roots, John Shaw, John Sims, Southwood Smith, William Somerville, Henry Herbert Southey, Duncan Stewart, Alexander Robert Sutherland, Honoratus Leigh Thomas, Sir Matthew John Tierney, Benjamin Travers, Martin Tupper, John Vetch, James Wardrop, Robert Williams, Thomas Young. Honorary members included John Aikin, Humphry Davy, William Hyde Wollaston, Jakob Berzelius, George Cuvier, John Frederick Meckel.

26 *Index to Minute Books,* RI, p. 319. (This and other manuscript record books of the Royal Institution were made available to me by Mr. Oliver Stallybrass, Librarian.)

27 *Ibid.,* p. 320. Roget was joined during these courses of lectures by other speakers: W. T. Brande, on vegetable chemistry; Campbell, on poetry; John Flaxman, on sculpture; T. S. Evans, on astronomy; Smith, on botany; Rev. E. Forster, on oratory; and J. Landseer, on philosophy of the arts.

28 For an account of the formation of the Royal Institution, see C. Harrison Dwight, "Count Rumford," *Notes and Records of the Royal Society of London,* Vol. II (March 1955), pp. 189–201.

29 Henry Holland, *Recollections of Past Life* (New York: Appleton, 1872), p. 111.

30 Walter E. Houghton (ed.), *The Wellesley Index to Victorian Periodicals 1824–1900* (Toronto: University Press, 1966), p. 1068.

31 Henry Crabb Robinson, *Diary, Reminiscences, and Correspondence,* edited by Thomas Sadler (Boston: Fields, Osgood, 1870), Vol. I, p. 241.

32 *Gentleman's Magazine,* Vol. 86, Part I (January 1816), pp. 45–49.

33 *Proceedings of the Royal Society* (1870), p. xxxix.

34 Gregor von Feinagle, *The New Art of Memory, Founded on the Principles Taught by M. G. von Feinagle* (London, 1812), p. 42.

35 *Philosophical Transactions,* Vol. 105 (1815), pp. 9–28, with 3 plates.

36 Florian Cajori, *A History of the Logarithmic Slide Rule and Allied Instruments* (New York, 1909), pp. 48–49.

CHAPTER VIII

[1] Archibald Constable (1774–1827), Scottish publisher of Sir Walter Scott and, after 1812, the *EB*.

[2] Thomas Robert Malthus (1766–1834), English political economist.

[3] I have been unable to identify this man positively, but it is not unreasonable to assume that Stewart referred to his fellow philosopher and contributor to the *Edinburgh Review*, Sir William Hamilton (1788–1856). Another possibility is Robert Hamilton (1743–1829), who wrote on the national debt. The *EB Suplement* was very strong on economics and included articles by Malthus, J. R. McCulloch, James Mill, and David Ricardo.

[4] Possibly William Emerson Tennent, Scottish merchant.

[5] Macvey Napier, Jr. (ed.), *Selection from the Correspondence of the Late Macvey Napier, Esq.* (London: Macmillan, 1879), p. 6.

[6] Personal letter, D. G. C. Allan, Curator-Librarian, Royal Society of Arts, May 22, 1967. According to the *Transactions* and the *Proceedings* of the society, Roget was most active with this group under the presidency of the Duke of Sussex, who at the same time headed the Royal Society—another example of the associations that formed a tight weave of relationships among the leaders of London scientific, political, and literary society. Still another is provided by Roget's friendship with J. F. Daniell, who not only brought Roget into the Royal Society of Arts but served with him on the Board of Visitors for the Royal Institution, as noted below.

[7] Untitled manuscript record of minutes of the Visitors, 1800–1828, p. 184. (In the archives of the Royal Institution)

[8] Letter, PMR to AM, September 7, 1815. (JRR)

[9] Thomas Joseph Pettigrew, *Medical Portrait Gallery* (London: Whittaker, 1840), Vol. IV, p. 6.

[10] P. M. Roget, "On the Kaleidoscope," *Annals of Philosophy*, Vol. XI (May 1818), p. 375.

[11] *Proceedings of the Royal Society* (1870), p. xxxiv.

[12] Henry Holland, *Recollections of Past Life* (New York: Appleton, 1872), p. 165. Another successful doctor, John Cheyne, after a rather slow start, began practicing in Dublin in 1809. By 1820 his practice was £5,000 a year, which remained its annual average during the next ten years. Cited in Pettigrew, Vol. III, p. 7.

[13] Letter, SR to PMR, February 8, 1817. (JRR)

[14] Romilly's entire speech, in which he castigated the Alien Bill, is printed as a lengthy footnote in his *Memoirs* (London, 1840), Vol. II, pp. 502–4.

15 *Ibid.,* p. 506.

16 *Ibid.,* p. 513.

17 Cecil G. Oakes, *Sir Samuel Romilly* (London: Allen & Unwin, 1935), p. 368.

18 Letter, AM to PMR, October 8, 1818. (RCP)

19 Letter, AM to PMR, October 21, 1818. (RCP)

20 The will reposes in the subterranean vaults of Somerset House, where I examined it in the summer of 1967. It is written in a uniform but rather crabbed hand on very large folio sheets of thick parchment, and included with other wills of the period in a heavy volume bound in thick canvas-covered boards, brass-studded, with brass hinges and lock, the whole volume about 14 by 20 inches. The elderly clerk who fetched it for me could barely hoist it to the table.

21 According to *The Morning Chronicle* of November 4, 1818, the death occurred about 11 P.M.; *The Times* for the same date puts the time at about 10 P.M.

22 This testimony by Dumont, as well as that following by Marcet, Bowen, and the rest, is taken from the very full report of the coroner's inquest as reported in *The Times* of November 4, 1818. Other reports of the inquest, such as that in *The Morning Chronicle,* are, except for minor points, the same. The inquest was called at 11 A.M. November 3, at the Colonnade public house, Bernard Street, before Thomas Stirling, Esq., coroner for the County of Middlesex, and lasted well into the afternoon.

23 Shortly after the inquest had begun, Dumont interrupted the testimony with an announcement that he had just been handed a note from Henry Brougham, requesting Dumont to confer with him immediately on matters of importance to the hearing. The coroner granted Dumont's request to leave, talk to Brougham (who was himself ill), and return to make his deposition. When Dumont returned, the hearing had adjourned to the Romilly home, and he hurried there to advise the coroner that it was of utmost importance to hear the testimony of the doctors who had attended Romilly *previous* to his death.

24 Romilly's house still stands at No. 21 Russell Square. It is now filled with bookcases as part of the library of the Institute of Eastern European Studies, University of London. The house is marked with a commemorative plaque. The next house to the west, No. 23, was Marcet's, and the last house on the block, No. 24, is the house of the publisher, Faber and Faber, in the top floor of which T. S. Eliot pursued his editorial work and wrote many of his finest productions.

25 Letter, PMR to AM, November 2, 1818. (JRR)

26 Oakes, p. 376.

27 E.g., Thomas Belsham, *Reflections upon the Death of Sir*

Sam'l Romilly, in a Discourse Delivered at Essex Street Chapel, November 8, *1818* (London, 1818); M. R. Stockdale, *A Shroud for Sir Samuel Romilly: An Elegy* (London, 1818).

[28] *The Times,* December 2, 1818.

[29] Letter, AM to PMR, November 18, 1818. (RCP)

CHAPTER IX

[1] "Encyclopaedia," *Encyclopaedia Britannica,* Vol. 8 (1947), pp. 428–430B.

[2] *Supplement to the Fourth, Fifth, and Sixth Editions of the Encyclopaedia Britannica,* Vol. I (1816), pp. xx and xxii. Contributors were identified by coded initials—Roget as "W." In the seventh edition, his letter was "Y."

[3] Letter, PMR to Macvey Napier, August 8, 1829. (BM)

[4] Letter, PMR to Macvey Napier, May 29, 1823. (BM)

[5] *Philosophical Magazine,* Vol. LIX, pp. 389–392.

[6] [Peter Mark Roget,] "Barthez," *Supplement,* Vol. II, p. 301.

[7] [Peter Mark Roget,] "Physiology," *Supplement,* Vol. VI, p. 180.

[8] *Ibid.,* p. 181.

[9] [Peter Mark Roget,] "Physiology," *Encyclopaedia Britannica,* 7th ed., Vol. XVIII (c. 1838), p. 577.

[10] I have verified these dates of Roget's participation, either by examination of documents of the institutions or by personal correspondence with their representatives.

[11] "Physiology," *EB,* 7th ed., Vol. XVIII, p. 578.

[12] *Ibid.,* p. 592.

[13] *Ibid.,* p. 629.

[14] Letter, PMR to Macvey Napier, July 11, 1817. (BM)

[15] Johann Kaspar Spurzheim (1776–1832), who, with Franz Joseph Gall (1758–1828), promulgated phrenology as a scientific discipline. The writings of the two men were considered the fundamental documents of the doctrine.

[16] [Peter Mark Roget,] "Cranioscopy," *Supplement,* Vol. III, p. 419.

[17] *Ibid.,* p. 433.

[18] *Ibid.*

[19] I have in hand a copy of *Education and Self-Improvement Founded on Physiology and Phrenology: Or, What Constitutes Good Heads and Bodies, and How to Make Them Good by Enlarging Deficiencies and Diminishing Excesses,* by O. S. Fowler, a "Practical Phrenologist." This, the second edition of Fowler's work (New York, 1844), is an American sample of the many volumes issued on the subject during the first half of the nineteenth century. Fowler begins with a graphic presentation of the "meta-

physical labyrinth" that Roget refers to—a chart and list of the particular "organs" into which Gall and Spurzheim had subdivided the brain. Fowler's list runs only to twenty-four rather than to the thirty-three referred to by Roget, but that should be sufficient. The organs are named for the mental attribute for which they are responsible: amativeness, philoprogenitiveness, adhesiveness, inhabitiveness, concentrativeness, combativeness, destructiveness, alimentiveness, aquativeness, acquisitiveness, secretiveness, cautiousness, approbativeness, self-esteem, firmness, conscientiousness, hope, marvelousness, benevolence, constructiveness, ideality, sublimity, imitation, mirthfulness.

[20] *Lancet,* first issued on October 5, 1823, by Thomas Wakley (1795–1862), was making itself felt as a crusading medical weekly. Heartily disliked as a muckraking, sensation-seeking penny paper by the more prominent and well-entrenched of the profession, *Lancet* exposed malpractice and fought to improve hospital conditions and medical education. It did not hesitate to do battle with such influential men as Sir Astley Cooper and others of Roget's friends.

[21] *Lancet,* Vol. VI (August 14, 1824), pp. 203–4.

[22] Dr. Andrew Combe (1797–1847); George Combe (1788–1858).

[23] Letter, George Combe to PMR, May 5, 1819, in *Gall, Vimont, and Broussais: On the Functions of the Cerebellum,* translated by George Combe (Edinburgh, 1838), pp. 217–21.

[24] Letter, PMR to George Combe, May 18, 1819, in *Gall, Vimont, and Broussais,* p. 221.

[25] *Ibid.,* p. 223.

[26] Letter, PMR to George Combe, June 3, 1819, in *Gall, Vimont, and Broussais,* p. 226.

[27] George Combe, *Essays on Phrenology* (Edinburgh, 1819), p. 63.

[28] *Ibid.,* p. 65.

[29] *Ibid.,* p. 91.

[30] John Abernethy, *Reflections on Gall and Spurzheim's System of Physiology and Phrenology* (London, 1821), pp. 7–9.

[31] "Cranioscopy, by Dr. Roget," *The Phrenological Journal and Miscellany,* Vol. I, No. 2 (1824), p. 166.

[32] *Ibid.,* p. 176.

[33] William Thackeray credited Elliotson with saving his life and dedicated his novel *Pendennis* to Elliotson.

[34] *Lancet,* Vol. VII (April 16, 1825), p. 41.

[35] John Bostock, *Elementary System of Physiology,* Vol. III (London, 1824–27), p. 276.

[36] *The Phrenological Journal,* Vol. X (September 1837), p. 153.

[37] G. M. Young, *Victorian England: Portrait of an Age* (London: Oxford University Press, 1966), p. 36, n. 2.

[38] Philip Magnus, *King Edward the Seventh* (New York: Dutton, 1964), p. 12.

[39] *The Phrenological Journal*, Vol. XI (Vol. I of new series) (1838), p. 456.

[40] Letter, PMR to Macvey Napier, February 19, 1838. (BM)

[41] P. M. Roget, *Treatises on Physiology and Phrenology*, Vol. I (Edinburgh, 1838), p. vi.

[42] *Ibid.*, p. 93.

[43] Andrew Combe, *Strictures on Anti-Phrenology in Two Letters to Macvey Napier and P. M. Roget, M. D., Being an Exposure of the Article Called "Phrenology" Recently Published in the Encyclopaedia Britannica* (London, 1838), pp. 30–31.

[44] "Book of the Week," *The Aldine Magazine of Biography, Bibliography, Criticism, and the Arts*, Vol. I (January 19, 1839), pp. 121–22.

[45] *The Phrenological Journal and Magazine of Moral Science*, Vol. XII, p. 283.

[46] *British and Foreign Medical Review*, Vol. IX (1839), pp. 190–215; Vol. X (1840), pp. 534–35.

CHAPTER X

[1] Benjamin Travers, *Synopsis of Diseases of the Eye* (London, 1820), pp. 71–75. Only five years younger than Roget, Travers spent 1806 and 1807 in Edinburgh, where he met Professors Dugald Stewart, Playfair, Leslie, etc., and where he repeated on a large scale the experiments of Bichat on the effects of unarterialized blood on the heart and nervous system. It was Travers' experiments that confirmed Bichat as an accurate experimentalist. Travers was a fellow member with Roget on the Council of the M-C Society.

[2] Letter, AM to PMR, September 20, 1819. (RCP)

[3] Roget identified him only as "Forbes." There were, at this time, several physicians named Forbes practicing in London; thus, a positive identification is not practicable. Two of these— Charles Fergusson Forbes and James David Forbes—had close connections with the military (as inspectors of military hospitals) and thus possibly with Wellington. A third possibility is the John Forbes who ten years later was one of the editors of the *Cyclopedia of Practical Medicine*, to which Roget contributed two substantial essays.

[4] Letter, AM to PMR, February 3, 1820. (RCP)

[5] Letter, AM to PMR, November 16, 1820. (RCP)

[6] Gaspard Charles de La Rive (1770–1834) took his M.D. at

Edinburgh in June 1797, and practiced with success and distinction in Geneva. He is listed in the Royal Society catalogues as the author of fourteen papers in French and German, mostly on physics and electricity. His son, Auguste Arthur de La Rive, and Marcet's son, François, worked together for many years in Geneva on temperature and electrical experiments.

[7] Letter, AM to PMR, April 2, 1820. (RCP)

[8] An excellent account of the institutional politics set afoot by Banks's death is provided by L. F. Gilbert, "The Election to the Presidency of the Royal Society in 1820," *Notes and Records of the Royal Society of London*, Vol. II, No. 2 (March 1955), pp. 256–79. Quoting J. F. W. Herschel's diary, Mr. Gilbert notes that Wollaston had the same opinion of Davies Gilbert's fitness for the presidency as Roget. Herschel and Babbage were instrumental in persuading Wollaston to stand for election. Ironically, Gilbert was the man to propose Wollaston for President during the interim between Banks's death and the regular election, November 30. Mr. L. F. Gilbert quotes from letters by Marcet, Bostock, and Babington on the appropriateness of Humphry Davy's being elected when Wollaston retired from the contest.

[9] Letter, PMR to AM, May 12, 1820. (RCP)

[10] Letter, AM to PMR, August 2, 1820. (RCP)

[11] This was perhaps the most heartbreaking year for the liberals in Italy in the long struggle for Italian unity and constitutionalism. In both Naples and Piedmont, Carbonarist mutinies broke out, resulting in the institution of constitutional governments, only to have those swept away again by autocratic forces.

[12] Letter, PMR to AM, March 19, 1821. (RCP)

[13] *Literary Gazette,* No. 269 (March 16, 1822), p. 168.

[14] *Literary Gazette,* No. 266 (February 23, 1822), p. 121.

[15] Letter, AM to PMR, July 28, 1822. (RCP)

[16] Letter, PMR to AM, August 9, 1822. (RCP)

[17] Letter, ED to PMR, October 22, 1822, tr. Geoffrey Selth. (JRR)

[18] Personal letter, Dr. E. W. Maddison (Librarian, Royal Astronomical Society), August 14, 1967.

[19] Letter, AM to PMR, September 11, 1822. (RCP)

[20] The foregoing account of Marcet's death is taken from a letter from J. L. Mallet to Leonard Horner, October 20, 1822, published in Leonard Horner (ed.), *Memoirs and Correspondence of Francis Horner, M.P.* (London, 1849), Vol. II, pp. 205–7. Leonard Horner later figured in the successful revolt against Roget and the old guard of the Royal Society.

[21] P. M. Roget, "Alexander Marcet," *Annual Biography and Obituary,* Vol. VII (1823), pp. 290–98.

[22] The spelling of this word varies considerably. Generally, it

was spelled with one "l" in Roget's day and is spelled with two "l"'s today. Since most of the original sources use the shorter version, I have followed that throughout.

[23] James Elmes, *Metropolitan Improvements,* Vol. I (London, 1827), p. 150.

[24] My chief sources of information are the official Roget-Latham report published by the House of Commons and the testimony taken by a select committee of the House. Several pamphlets published by Latham and others involved, included in the fine collections of medical tracts at the Royal College of Physicians and the British Museum, have also been very helpful. The best single source (because it reprints the significant parts of most of the others) is Latham's lengthy pamphlet *An Account of the Disease Lately Prevalent at the General Penitentiary* (London, 1825). Unless otherwise noted, my version of the epidemic depends primarily upon Latham. It should be recognized that Latham was careful in his pamphlet (p. xiv) to say that he was speaking for both Roget and himself:

> As the labour and responsibility of our charge were equally divided between Dr. Roget and myself, so the practical measures adopted were the result of our consultations. I am not aware that there ever arose between us the smallest disagreement either in opinion or practice; and I reckon it among the best fruits of my labours on this occasion that they have procured for me in my colleague a faithful friend. To Dr. Roget, I am also indebted for suggestions most useful to me in drawing up this account of the disease, and I am allowed to appeal to him in confirmation of its truth.

[25] Latham, p. 6.

[26] *Ibid.,* p. 10.

[27] *Ibid.,* p. 23.

[28] *Minutes of Evidence Before Select Committee on the General Penitentiary at Milbank* (May 16, 1823), p. 26.

[29] Latham, p. 76.

[30] These were called *A Short Vindication . . . , A Second Vindication . . . ,* and *Third Vindication of the General Penitentiary, Showing That There Is No Ground Whatever for Supposing That the Situation of That Prison Had Any Share in Producing the Late Disease Among the Prisoners Confined There, Being an Answer to Some Observations Contained in a Work Published by P. Mere Latham.* All were published in London in 1824 and 1825 and are part of the British Museum's medical-tract collection.

[31] *Lancet,* Vol. I (1823), pp. 95–6.

[32] "Extract from the *Report of the Select Committee,*" reprinted in *Lancet,* Vol. I (1823), pp. 95–102.

[33] This account is derived from Hutchinson's pamphlets *Correspondence Between the Committee of the General Penitentiary*

at Milbank and Mr. A. Copland Hutchison . . . (London, 1823), and *A Statement on Occasion of the Extraordinary Sickness Which Has Lately Occurred at the General Penitentiary at Milbank.* (London, 1823).

34 Latham, p. 175.

35 *Ibid.,* p. 196.

36 *Ibid.,* p. 158.

37 *Ibid.,* p. 237–38.

CHAPTER XI

1 Letter, CR to PMR, August 7, 1820, tr. Geoffrey Selth. (JRR)

2 Letter, AR to PMR, August 7, 1820, tr. Howard Shipman. (JRR)

3 Rough draft of letter, PMR to AR, August 10, 1820, tr. Howard Shipman. (JRR)

4 Letter, AR to PMR, August 27, 1821, tr. Jay Louis Hall. (JRR)

5 Letter, AR to PMR, August 15, 1822, tr. Christiane Saint Jean Paulin. (JRR)

6 Letter, ED to PMR, January 7, 1825, tr. Geoffrey Selth. (JRR)

7 Letter, AR to PMR, December 26, 1827, tr. Jay Louis Hall. (JRR)

8 According to a "Certified Copy of an Entry of Marriage," kindly provided me by the Rev. F. L. Jones, the present vicar of St. Philip's, where the Register Book of Marriages preserves the original record. Witnesses were the bride's parents; a friend, Ellen Potter; and John Bostock.

9 Letter, ED to PMR, n.d., tr. Geoffrey Selth. (JRR)

10 Letter, MR to Samuel Hobson, June 19, 1811, tr. Christiane Saint Jean Paulin. (JRR)

11 William Paley (1743–1805), famous for his book on design as evidence of the existence of God.

12 Letter, MR to Samuel Hobson, December 4, 1812. (JRR)

13 Excellent samples of Sam Hobson's journal make up the bulk of Chapter VI of S. R. Roget's *Travel in the Two Last Centuries of Three Generations,* pp. 136–57.

14 E.g., *The European Magazine and London Review,* Vol. 86 (November 1824), p. 472; *Liverpool Mercury* (November 19, 1824), p. 167.

15 Letter, Tom Hobson to MR, March 13, 1825. (JRR)

16 Letter, AR to MR, December 2, 1824. (JRR)

17 Confirmed by personal letter from A. C. C. Peebles (Secretary, Athenaeum Club), April 24, 1967.

[18] Edgar Johnson, *Charles Dickens: His Tragedy and Triumph*, Vol. I (New York: Simon & Schuster, 1952), p. 232.

[19] Published the next year in *Philosophical Transactions*, Vol. 115, Part I, pp. 131–40.

[20] *The Liveliest Art: A Panoramic History of the Movies* (New York: New American Library, 1959), p. 14. I am indebted to John Bigby for pointing out this passage and for advising me generally in evaluating the importance of Roget's paper. Among other accounts, an especially helpful one is that in Terry Ramsaye, *A Million and One Nights: A History of the Motion Picture* (New York: Simon & Schuster, 1926).

[21] Faraday, in an article in 1831, cited Roget's study in his opening paragraph and mentioned Roget's pioneer study five more times in describing a device he (Faraday) had constructed to experiment with the optical effects of the wheel phenomenon and persistence of vision. See "On a Peculiar Class of Optical Deceptions," *Journal of the Royal Institution*, Vol. I (1831), pp. 205–23, 334–36; and Michael Faraday, "Radial Images," *Literary Gazette* (January 7, 1843), p. 7. Sir John Herschel also produced an instrument to show apparent motion from an inanimate drawing. He called it the Thaumatrope, and first published a notice of it in 1826, two years after Roget's paper. Roget himself toyed with some practical applications of the wheel phenomenon and constructed several wheel and disc devices which he showed to his friends in the spring of 1831, but he was too busy, he said, to pursue the project.

[22] Joseph Plateau (1801–1883), Belgian physicist and long-time professor at Ghent, received his doctorate from the University of Liège on June 3, 1829, with his thesis "Certain Properties of the Impression Produced by Light upon the Organ of Sight." It is in a letter to Quételet (Dec. 5, 1829) that he acknowledges his indebtedness to Roget's paper. In 1831, Plateau and Faraday carried on a written argument over priority of observations of the wheel phenomenon.

[23] Simon Stampfer (1792–1864), a professor at Vienna, treated Roget's wheel phenomenon mathematically. A practical man, he took out an Austrian patent on his invention, which he called Stroboscopic Discs, on May 7, 1833.

[24] Lambert Adolphe Jacques Quételet (1796–1874), Belgian astronomer, meteorologist, and statistician. A prominent lecturer at the Royal College and at the Museum of Science and Letters, Quételet became Roget's Belgian counterpart when he was appointed perpetual secretary of the Brussels Academy in 1834.

[25] Probably the best and most curious panoramic description of London during those years when Roget and Mary were enjoying their walks about the city is the lengthy account of an enor-

mous painting, "A Panoramic View of London, as Seen from the Summit of the Cross of St. Paul's Cathedral," in Elmes's invaluable *Metropolitan Improvements* (London, 1828), pp. 68–79. Possibly the largest canvas ever exhibited anywhere, the "Panoramic View" occupied the interior walls of a building, the Colosseum, erected for that purpose on Cambridge Terrace, just north of the elegant Park Crescent entrance to Regent's Park. It was the work of Thomas Hornor, who made his original sketches from a temporary observatory erected above the cross of St. Paul's, and then through nearly four years, with the aid of a host of artists and students, painted the detailed, representational view of the city. It was finished in time for Elmes to use a description of it in 1828. Hornor's vast painting would have been the 1830 equivalent of the dizzying composite photographs now available of the whole of London as seen from the six-hundred-foot Post Office Tower off Tottenham Court Road.

[26] In all, Roget wrote four separate treatises for the society: "Electricity" (1827), "Galvanism" (1829), "Magnetism" (1831), and "Electro-Magnetism" (1832). Each of these papers ran to well over one hundred pages, and they were later issued as a book by the society as Volume II of its Library of Useful Knowledge.

[27] Charles Knight, *Passages of a Working Life* (London: Bradbury and Evans, 1864), Vol. 2, p. 123.

[28] "On an Apparent Violation of the Law of Continuity," November 5 and 12, 1825.

[29] Letter, MR to Sam Hobson, October 20, 1827. (JRR)

[30] Letter, Charlotte Parks to Sam Hobson, March 27, 1827. (JRR)

[31] Letter, MR to Sam Hobson, September 3, 1832. (JRR)

[32] An incredibly bad novel by Rousseau (1762). The Rogets' interest in the book is significant, however, because it presents in story form Rousseau's educational theories—how to bring up a child according to the so-called principles of nature.

[33] It is necessary here to correct a piece of misinformation that has been perpetuated by recent magazine writers—that Roget took an active part in founding the University of London. It is true that he knew the poet Thomas Campbell (described by Bellot as the first to express the idea of the university), and had been active in the Society for the Diffusion of Useful Knowledge with Brougham. He was also an associate of other prime movers such as Bentham, Leonard Horner, James Mill, John Leslie, James Mackintosh—a predominantly Utilitarian group. But my own search of the minutes of the Senate of the university and the independent research of Mr. A. H. Wesencraft, of the university Library, have failed to show any Roget connection with the uni-

versity until 1836. This is ten years after the *original* institution —now called University College—was organized. In fact, an entry in the university Council minutes of 1828 shows that Roget was among a list of *un*successful applicants for professional chairs. Roget's connection with the university began in 1836 when he was one of the "eminent persons" invited to join the Senate. He served on a number of important committees for the Senate during the next ten years, including those that established requirements for examinations in various fields and prepared the draft of an important medical reform bill in 1848, and he remained a member of the Senate until his death. Between 1839 and 1842 he served as Examiner in Physiology and Comparative Anatomy, but resigned when the university, caught in an economy wave, reduced the £250 paid the Examiners, asked a lot of impertinent questions about the number of hours devoted to the task, and refused to respond to Roget's insistence that there should be separate Examiners for physiology and for comparative anatomy.

[34] The "Annals of the Nursery," surely a useful document for a social historian, has lain out of sight with the other family records until Mr. John Romilly Roget graciously released it to us for use in this account of his great-grandfather. As in the excerpts of the earlier part of Mary's journal, I have modernized the spelling, punctuation, and paragraphing.

[35] Letter, PMR to Samuel Hobson, August 21, 1832. (JRR)

[36] Letter, MR to Sam Hobson, September 3, 1832. (JRR)

[37] Letter, MR to Sam Hobson, December 18, 1832. (JRR)

[38] Letter, Mrs. A. Bostock to Mrs. W. Swainson, March 19, 1833. (JRR)

[39] *The Times,* April 16, 1833, and *Liverpool Mercury,* April 19, 1833.

CHAPTER XII

[1] The discoverer of platinum, Wollaston is listed as the author of thirty-nine papers published in *Philosophical Transactions.*

[2] Henry Crabb Robinson, *Diary, Reminiscences, and Correspondence,* edited by Thomas Sadler, Vol. II (Boston: Fields, Osgood, 1870), p. 424.

[3] Letter, PMR to Charles Babbage, July 27, 1820. (BM)

[4] Letter, PMR to Charles Babbage, July 21, 1821. (BM)

[5] Letter, PMR to Charles Babbage, August 11, 1819. (BM)

[6] Charles Babbage, *Reflections on the Decline of Science in England and on Some of Its Causes* (London: Fellowes, 1830).

[7] *Ibid.,* App. 3, p. 2.

[8] *Ibid.,* App. 4, p. 1.

[9] *Ibid.,* p. 2.

[10] L. Pearce Williams, "The Royal Society and the Founding of the British Association for the Advancement of Science," *Notes and Records of the Royal Society of London,* Vol. 16, No. 2 (November 1961), p. 226.

[11] Letter, PMR to Charles Babbage, February 5, 1830. (BM)

[12] Letter, PMR to Charles Babbage, February 13, 1830. (BM)

[13] Letter, PMR to Edward Sabine, May 31, 1830. (RS)

[14] "Minutes of the Council of the Royal Society" (November 4, 1830). Roget's salary as senior Secretary was £105 per year.

[15] James South, *Charges Against the President and Councils of the Royal Society,* 2nd ed. (London, 1830), p. vi.

[16] The "public expostulation," for example, of Dr. A. B. Granville, *Science Without a Head; or, The Royal Society Dissected* (London, 1830), ran to 120 closely printed pages, plus appendixes.

[17] *The Athenaeum* (November 27, 1830), p. 747.

[18] Quoted in Arundell Esdaile, *The British Museum: A Short History and Survey* (London: Allen & Unwin, 1946), p. 212.

[19] Letter, J. F. W. Herschel to Charles Babbage, August 15, 1830. (RS)

[20] Letter, J. F. W. Herschel to Charles Babbage, November 26, 1830. (RS)

[21] I have used a copy of the announcement preserved at the University of London Library in the notes and tracts of Augustus de Morgan.

[22] Williams, p. 229.

[23] "Minutes of the Council of the Royal Society" (November 18, 1830), p. 130.

[24] Peter Mark Roget, a single manuscript sheet, untitled, dated July 4, 1833, in the RS manuscript collection.

[25] Roget's lectures, "On the Laws of Sensation and Perception," were published in the *London Medical Gazette,* beginning in May 1832, and were translated into German and published as "Ueber die Gesetze der Empfindung und Perception," *Froriep Notizen,* Vol. XXXIV, pp. 241–50, 257–66.

[26] *Ibid.,* Vol. VIII (July 9, 1831), p. 508.

[27] For samples, see almost any issue of *The Times* from February or March of 1827. Items range from the relatively mild protest of a Mr. "J. W.," of No. 8 Ewer Street (in the Southwark district south of the Thames), that his neighborhood "had not had a drop of water for nearly a fortnight, and this frequently occurs," to discussions of a highly damaging pamphlet, *The Dolphin; or Grand Junction Nuisance: Proving That 7,000 Families in Westminster and Its Suburbs Are Supplied with Water in a*

State Offensive to the Sight, Disgusting to the Imagination, and Destructive to the Health. The most convincing material in the pamphlet was a series of testimonials by medical men, including Henry Halford, John Abernethy, William Lambe, Wilson Philip, Benjamin Robert Hume, John A. Paris, H. L. Thomas, Robert Keate, Henry Holland, Robert Bree, James Johnson, and William Macmichael, attesting to the filthy state of the water supplied. *The Dolphin* was answered by W. M. Coe, Secretary of the Grand Junction Water Company. Coe was particularly incensed by the frontispiece of the pamphlet, which showed the main intake of the Grand Junction company directly opposite the mouth of the great Ranelagh sewer. The intake "is much more distant from the sewer than the plate represents, but what is still more material to observe," protested Coe, "it is completely above so as to make it utterly impossible that one drop of sewer water can reach it."

[28] Charles Knight, *Passages of a Working Life During Half a Century*, Vol. I (London: Bradbury and Evans, 1864), p. 30.

[29] G. M. Young (ed.), *Early Victorian England, 1830–1865*, Vol. I (Oxford, 1934), p. 85.

[30] Telford (1757–1834), an accomplished civil engineer, was responsible for many major improvements in England, particularly its system of roads and highways.

[31] "Copy of the Commission Issued for Inquiring into the State of the Supply of Water to the Metropolis, and of the Correspondence Between the Commissioners and the Secretary of State for the Home Department Respecting the Objects of the Commission," Sessional Paper 897, Public Record Office, p. 1. Roget was chairman, according to a letter from Mary Roget to Samuel Hobson, January 12, 1828. (JRR)

[32] *Ibid.*, p. 4.

[33] Bostock used these data as the basis for his first paper in *Philosophical Transactions* (1829).

[34] *Report of the Commissioners Appointed by His Majesty to Inquire into the State of the Supply of Water in the Metropolis* (London, 1824), p. 1.

[35] *Ibid.*, p. 11.

[36] *Ibid.*, p. 12.

[37] The state of the London water supply was, indeed, a favorite target of attack in Dickens' early crusading numbers of his *Household Words*. Dickens' brother-in-law, Henry Austin, Secretary of the Sanitary Commission in 1850, supplied the facts for a series of hard-hitting reform articles directed against the excessive charges, the dirty water, and the lack of supply to the poor. See Edgar Johnson, *Charles Dickens: His Tragedy and Triumph* (New York: Simon & Schuster, 1952).

CHAPTER XIII

[1] *Annals of the Royal College of Physicians* (1834), p. 66. (Examined on microfilm at RCP)

[2] *Ibid.* (1835).

[3] Charles Newman, *Evolution of Medical Education in the Nineteenth Century* (London: Oxford University Press, 1957), p. 150.

[4] Newman's statement is illustrated by an entry in a widely used medical dictionary in my possession, which first appeared in 1857: "Laënnec introduced auscultation to appreciate the different sounds which can be heard in the chest, and in the diagnosis of diseases of the heart, lungs, etc. This may be done by the aid of an instrument called a stethoscope. . . ." Robley Dunglison, *Medical Lexicon, A Dictionary of Medical Science* (Philadelphia: Blanchard and Lea, 1860), p. 108.

[5] Charles Coulton Gillispie, *Genesis and Geology: A Study in the Relations of Scientific Thought, Natural Theology, and Social Opinion in Great Britain, 1790–1850* (Cambridge: Harvard University Press, 1951), p. 149.

[6] *Ibid.*, p. ix.

[7] Peter Mark Roget, *Animal and Vegetable Physiology Considered with Reference to Natural Theology* (London: William Pickering, 1834), Vol. I, p. xv. All subsequent references to this work will be noted as "Roget, Bridgewater Treatise."

[8] *Quarterly Review*, Vol. 50 (October 1833), pp. 1–34. The nobility and reverence of the Earl of Bridgewater (Francis Henry Egerton, 1756–1829) are not revealed in the *DNB* sketch of his life. A classicist and genealogist, Egerton retained the preferments of several church appointments, but for many years their duties were performed by proxy. Described as "a man of great eccentricity," Egerton spent many of his later years at Paris in a mansion he called the Hôtel Egerton, and which he filled with cats and dogs, some of which were dressed up as men and women, and were driven out in his carriage and fed at his table.

[9] Sir John Barrow, *Sketches of the Royal Society and the Royal Society Club* (London, 1849), pp. 106–7.

[10] Whewell's methods were often so attacked. See my brief treatment of this in "A Memorandum Composed Mainly of Quotations from an Anonymous Critic of Schoolmen of One Hundred Fourteen Years Ago," *Phi Delta Kappan*, Vol. XLVII (April 1966), pp. 444–46.

[11] A series of surviving letters between Roget and Thomas Coates, another editor for the SDUK, shows Roget to have been a fair-minded but a rather difficult editor to please. Reporting to

Coates on a manuscript from one P. Cooper, who had claimed to
have discovered a simple theory, Roget comments sarcastically:
"If his own representation of this theory were correct, it would
infallibly be the greatest discovery ever made by human genius;
for when compared with it, that of universal gravitation must be
esteemed a mere trifle. My opinion is that the SDUK is not worthy of the honor of being the organ by which so important a secret, which is to effect a complete revolution in science, shall be
revealed and promulgated to the world." Letter, PMR to
Thomas Coates, March 19, 1833. (University College)

On the other hand, Roget returned another manuscript—one
on physiology—unread to Coates because he himself was planning such an article for the society: "I think it would be better if
some other person were referred to for an opinion. . . ." Letter,
PMR to Thomas Coates, January 10, 1827. (University College)

[12] Roget, Bridgewater Treatise, Vol. I, p. ix.

[13] Ralph Waldo Emerson, *Works* (New York: Walter J. Black,
n.d.), p. 557.

[14] Roget, Bridgewater Treatise, Vol. I, p. 536.

[15] *Ibid.*, p. 5.

[16] *Ibid.*, pp. 5–6.

[17] *Ibid.*, pp. 11–14.

[18] William Paley, *Works* (Philadelphia: Crissy and Markley,
1853), p. 390.

[19] Roget, Bridgewater Treatise, Vol. I, pp. 53–54.

[20] *Ibid.*, Vol. II, p. 626.

[21] *Ibid.*, pp. 637–38.

[22] I have examined the following passage in some detail elsewhere. See "Peter Mark Roget: Style as Symptom," *College Composition and Communication*, Vol. XVII (October 1966), pp. 135–
39.

[23] Roget, Bridgewater Treatise, Vol. II, pp. 639–41.

CHAPTER XIV

[1] Antonio Panizzi (1797–1879) came to England as a political
refugee in 1823 after being involved in the Italian revolutionary
movement of 1821. His work in translating Italian literature; in
reorganizing the entire British Museum, carrying through sweeping reforms; in fending off attacks upon the museum; and in
erecting the present library and reading room is well known, particularly since the recent publication of Edward Miller's *The
Prince of Librarians* (London: Deutsch, 1967). For a more detailed account of the Roget-Panizzi row, see my "Roget vs. Panizzi
—a Collision," *Journal of Library History*, Vol. IV (January
1969), pp. 9–39.

[2] Antonio Panizzi, *A Letter to His Royal Highness the Presi-*

dent of the Royal Society on the New Catalogue of the Library of That Institution Now in Press (London, 1837), p. 6. This pamphlet, which displays in all its sharpness Panizzi's talent for satire and invective, is one of the several surviving documents of the long-winded battle. It is particularly useful, if one makes allowances for Panizzi's point of view, as a running account of the affair up to 1837.

3 "Minutes of the Council of the Royal Society," October 25, 1832.

4 "Minutes of the Library and Catalogue Committee," April 25, 1836.

5 Panizzi, *A Letter . . .* , p. 24.

6 Letter, Antonio Panizzi to PMR, July 8, 1836. (RS)

7 "Minutes of the Council of the Royal Society," July 7, 1836.

8 Letter, PMR to Antonio Panizzi, July 9, 1836. (RS)

9 [Roget,] "Statement of the Council," following "Address of the President," *Proceedings of the Royal Society*, Vol. 4.

10 "Minutes of the Council of the Royal Society," December 12, 1839.

11 Personal letter, A. H. Wesencraft, Middlesex South Library, UL, February 17, 1966.

12 "Minutes of the General Meetings of the Royal Institution," Vol. IV, p. 299.

13 "Minutes of the Managers of the Royal Institution," April 7, 1834, p. 156.

14 Personal letter, W. R. Westhead, Assistant Secretary and Clerk of Accounts, RI, July 11, 1967.

15 "Minutes of the General Meetings of the Royal Institution," Vol. IV, pp. 270–71.

16 Manuscript list of lecturers in an album designated "Guard Book No. 1," at the library of the RI.

17 Nora Barlow (ed.), *The Autobiography of Charles Darwin* (New York: Harcourt, Brace, 1958), p. 49 n.

18 "Minutes of the Managers of the Royal Institution," entries throughout 1837.

19 In 1833, for example, Roget was a member of the Library and Catalogue, the Donation Fund, the Finance, the Meteorological, the Tide, and the Medal committees, in addition to two or three *ad hoc* committees. "Minutes of the Council of the Royal Society," December 1, 1832.

20 Petition dated May 21, 1836, and read to the Council by Roget on June 8.

21 Dorothy Stimson, *Scientists and Amateurs: A History of the Royal Society* (New York: Schuman, 1948), p. 221.

22 A. Geikie, *Annals of the Royal Society Club* (London: Macmillan, 1917), pp. 297–320.

23 *Lancet*, January 21, 1837, p. 624.

[24] *Ibid.*, January 28, 1837, p. 656.

[25] *Ibid.*, February 4, 1837, p. 715.

[26] *Ibid.*, February 18, 1837, pp. 899–900.

[27] All of these charges above are paraphrased from the letter from Hall to Herschel, October 1, 1839. (RS)

[28] The following summary of the Beck-Lee controversy is drawn from the minutes of the Council of the Royal Society, the manuscript minute book of the Committee of Zoology and Physiology, and correspondence preserved at the Royal Society. I am grateful to the RS library staff for making these sources available to me.

[29] The fullest account is that by Dr. Lee himself. Buried in the back pages of a highly technical description of his life's work (*Memoir on the Ganglia and Nerves of the Uterus* [London, 1849]) are some fifty pages of careful exposition of the whole affair: the visits of leading surgeons and physicians to inspect his dissections, the voluminous correspondence with members of the Physiology Committee and with Northampton, testimonials from dozens of influential medical men of the day, detailed accounts of the relevant meetings of the Council and the Physiology Committee, reports of his many conversations with Roget and of his many attempts to convince the committee of the genuineness of his discoveries by repeated dissections and demonstrations. Roget's only public reply to Lee's charges was to have published, over his signature, the committee's report of its examination of Lee's paper. See *Medical Times*, Vol. 17 (January 15, 1848), p. 261; *London Medical Gazette*, January 14, 1848, p. 82.

[30] *Lancet*, March 22, 1851. Thirty years later, the medical profession itself went on record confirming Lee's account, as seen in the concluding remarks of the brief biography of Lee by the official scribe of the Royal College of Physicians:

> . . . his dissections of the nerves of the heart and the uterus entitle him to a place in the foremost rank of anatomists and physiologists of his time and country. It is on these remarkable dissections that Dr. Lee's fame with posterity will chiefly rest. They gave occasion to much painful controversy at the time, and the treatment which Dr. Lee received in reference to them from the Royal Society did not conduce to the honor of that learned body. . . . Dr. Lee's account of the whole transaction . . . must be assumed to be substantially accurate, for it passed, so far as I know, without challenge or contradiction, and his threat of legal proceedings was followed by the resignation of the noble president and somewhat later by that of the senior secretary of the society, and by the dissolution of the Committee of Physiology.

See William Munk, *The Roll of the Royal College of Physicians of London*, 2nd ed., rev. (London: Royal College of Physicians, 1878), Vol. III, pp. 268–69.

31 Letter, Leonard Horner to W. R. Grove, November 12, 1846. (RI)
32 Katherine Lyell, *Life, Letters, and Journals of Sir Charles Lyell* (London, 1881), Vol. II, p. 145.
33 Letter, Leonard Horner to W. R. Grove, January 18, 1847. (RI)
34 Letter, Charles Lyell to W. R. Grove, July 7, 1848. (RI)

CHAPTER XV

1 Manuscript report, single page, dated July 31, 1848. (RS collection)
2 *The Wellesley Index to Victorian Periodicals 1824–1900* (Toronto: University of Toronto Press, 1966), p. 1068.
3 Compare, for example, the qualifications of Roget with those of such linguists as Francis Andrew March, or Charlton Laird, or S. I. Hayakawa, whose later contributions to synonymy might have been expected to throw Roget's work quite in the shade. While *March's Dictionary-Thesaurus* (1902) developed a small but loyal following and has recently been reprinted (Hanover House, 1958), it remains relatively unknown, and *Laird's Promptory* (1948) is no longer in print. Hayakawa's work *Funk & Wagnalls Modern Guide to Synonyms and Related Words* (1968) has too recently appeared to predict its success.
4 According to a personal letter from John Romilly Roget, April 25, 1966, all the letters to and from Peter Mark Roget about the actual making of the *Thesaurus* were destroyed by fire during the great air raid on London in the last week of December 1940.
5 See letter of Sir Joseph Banks praising the classificatory contributions of de Jussieu, in J. Barrow, *Sketches of the Royal Society and the Royal Society Club* (London, 1849), pp. 50–51.
6 Roget's admiration for de Candolle may also have been strengthened by the fact that the Swiss botanist published a highly complimentary biography of Etienne Dumont—*Notice sur la vie et les écrits de M. Dumont* (Geneva, 1829). Roget's RS medals committee named de Candolle for the Royal Medal in Physiology in 1833.
7 *Westminster Review,* Vol. LVIII (October 1852), p. 207.
8 As an excellent introduction to this fascinating field, see Lawrence Sandek, "Man's World of Facts," *Data Processor,* Vol. X (November 1967), pp. 4–34.
9 Personal letter, Mr. Stephen E. Furth, International Business Machines Corporation, August 9, 1968. For a thorough discussion of the application of the thesaurus principle to information retrieval, see Gerard Salton, "Automatic Content Analysis in Infor-

mation Retrieval," Technical Report No. 68–5 (January 1968), Department of Computer Science, Cornell University.

Professors Walter and Sally Sedelow, of the Department of Information Science, University of North Carolina, have written me (August 19, 1968) that they have made direct use of Roget's *Thesaurus* "as one source of help in the compiling of search thesauri, which are in turn used by the computer to generate thesauri for specific works." The Sedelows are also making comparisons of various computer thesaurus outputs for identical texts, and hope soon to have all of *Roget's International Thesaurus*, 3rd ed. (Crowell, 1962) on tape.

Perhaps the closest thing to an official definition in this new field is the following, issued by the Committee on Scientific and Technical Information, Federal Council for Science and Technology:

> . . . a thesaurus is a compilation of selected terms with appropriate term interrelationships displayed in such a way as to promote maximum consistency in the description of concepts for indexing and searching. A thesaurus provides a means of translating the language of the literature and of the information user into a formalized vocabulary for optimum storage and retrieval.

Guidelines for the Development of Information Retrieval Thesauri (Washington, D.C., 1967), p. ii.

[10] From the introduction to the first edition of the *Thesaurus*.

[11] Benjamin Whorf, *Language, Thought, and Reality* (Cambridge, Mass.: Massachusetts Institute of Technology, 1956), p. 252.

[12] My most useful guides (and practically the only ones in print) in tracing the history of English synonymies were *A Bibliography of Writings on the English Language from the Beginning of Printing to the End of 1922*, by Arthur G. Kennedy (Cambridge, Mass., and New Haven: Harvard University Press and Yale University Press, 1927), and a thorough and perceptive essay by Miss Rose F. Egan, "Survey of the History of English Synonymy," which appeared as part of the introductory matter of *Webster's Dictionary of Synonyms* (Springfield, Mass.: Merriam, 1942), pp. vii–xxv.

[13] 2 vols. (London, 1766). The allusion in the title is to Abbé Gabriel Girard (1677–1748), who in 1718 published in France *La Justesse de la langue françoise, ou les différentes significations des mots qui passent pour être synonymes.*

[14] The copy I examined in the British Museum, and from which the passages below are quoted, was that of a later edition, published in Paris in 1804.

[15] "English Synonyms," *Fraser's Magazine*, September 1851, p. 261.

16 "Article IV," *Quarterly Review,* Vol. XXXV (1827), p. 415.

17 In the current British *Thesaurus,* the 1962 edition done by Professor Robert A. Dutch, the index runs to 646 pages, just 14 pages shorter than the main vocabulary section of the *Thesaurus* proper. The current American *Thesaurus* offers 1,258 pages, of which 601 are index. The original 1852 edition of 418 pages was about one third the size of the present volume.

18 Egan, "Survey of the History of English Synonymy," p. xvii.

19 September 4, 1852, p. 939.

20 Vol. XI (June 15, 1852), p. 320.

21 N.s., Vol. IV (July–December 1852), p. 623.

22 *Westminster Review,* Vol. LIX (April 1853), pp. 309–10.

23 *Putnam's Monthly Magazine of American Literature, Science, and Art,* Vol. VI (September 1855), pp. 318–19.

24 S. Austin Allibone, *A Critical Dictionary of English Literature and British and American Authors* (Philadelphia: Lippincott, 1872), Vol. II, p. 1857.

25 [Edwin P. Whipple,] "The Use and Misuse of Words," *North American Review,* Vol. LXXIX (July 1854), pp. 137–57.

26 April 28, 1926.

27 *Daily Chronicle* (London), August 31, 1912.

28 Personal letter, Robert H. Land, Chief, Reference Department, Library of Congress, February 17, 1966. While many publishers have simply refused to reveal anything about their involvement with Roget publication, through the ready cooperation of Longmans, Green and Company and Thomas Y. Crowell Company, the chief publishers, British and American respectively, the major outlines of this history can be set down.

29 Thanks to the kindness of Miss Beryl Hurst of Longmans, Green, I was permitted to examine what is left of that firm's correspondence with the Rogets. Many documents and letters were destroyed when that London publisher's building in Paternoster Row was hit during the fire-bombing of London on December 29, 1940. Miss Hurst told me that the company had just laid in seven tons of coal in the basement, and that the fire burned for a month, consuming millions of printed books, and leaving Longmans, Green with just six titles of their long and respected list. In the strong room at the present Longmans, Green location, 48 Grosvenor Street, are several iron boxes filled largely with cinders—the remains of documents lost in that fire. Surviving, however, are a good many letters, receipts, copies of contracts, and interoffice memos that give a fairly detailed account of the first years of the British *Thesaurus.*

30 This was my first acquaintance with Roget's *Thesaurus.* My copy was given me by my mother on my eighteenth birthday, October 5, 1936.

[31] Alice Payne Hackett, *70 Years of Best Sellers: 1895–1965* (New York: Bowker, 1967), p. 13. Miss Hackett's fascinating study of best-sellers reveals that among reference books the *Pocket Thesaurus* is topped only by two other titles: *Pocket Atlas* (1917), and the *English–Spanish, Spanish–English Dictionary* (1948). In a list of all paperbacks, the *Pocket Thesaurus* is the tenth best-seller, trailing Benjamin Spock's *Pocket Book of Baby and Child Care,* and such fiction mileposts as *Peyton Place, God's Little Acre, Lady Chatterley's Lover,* Charles Monroe Sheldon's religious novel *In His Steps,* and Mickey Spillane's *I, the Jury.*

[32] Personal letter, Miss Susan Hoff, The New American Library, Inc., August 12, 1968.

[33] E.g., *Putnam's Phrase Book* (New York, 1922), or, more recently, *The Word Finder* and *The Phrase Finder* (Emmaus, Pa., 1956).

[34] *Dictionnaire analogique de la langue française* (Paris), and *Dictionnaire logique de la langue française* (Paris, 1882).

[35] Personal letter, Mr. P. B. Baxendale, International Business Machines Corporation, August 23, 1968.

[36] *The Times,* May 2, 1851.

CHAPTER XVI

[1] *Philosophical Magazine and Journal,* Vol. 116 n.s., pp. 305–9.

[2] I have been unable to find one of these, but Mr. John Romilly Roget told me that he remembered playing with one as a child.

[3] *Proceedings of the Royal Society* (1870), p. xl.

[4] *Minutes of the Institute of Civil Engineers,* Vol. XXX (1870), p. 424.

[5] *Observations on the Article "Deaf and Dumb" in the Eighth Edition of the Encyclopaedia Britannica* (Liverpool, 1858).

[6] Far and away the best source of information on John Lewis Roget is the article by his son, S. R. Roget, "Notes on the Life and Work of John Lewis Roget," *Proceedings of the Huguenot Society of London,* Vol. IX, pp. 545–63, from which the bulk of the following material on Roget's son is taken.

[7] Public Records Act No. 990, Somerset House, London, is a grant authorizing John Lewis Roget to act as executor of Peter Mark Roget's estate. Edward Romilly was named as coexecutor. The same depository holds the wills of all the Rogets. On Peter Mark Roget's death, his estate was valued at about £60,000;

John Lewis Roget's at £75,000; Samuel Romilly Roget's at £100,000.

⁸ *A First Book of Applied Electricity* (London: Macmillan, 1922).

⁹ Mr. John Romilly Roget has been a source of constant aid and encouragement in this piecing together of the jigsaw puzzle that is his great-grandfather's life and work. Certainly one of our happiest memories of England is that of a high tea one sunny afternoon on the broad, sloping lawn that runs down from Mr. Roget's eighteenth-century house to the Dover highway.

¹⁰ That these reforms did not come about easily is brought out lucidly in Michael Wolff's study, "The Uses of Context: Aspects of the 1860's," *Victorian Studies*, Supplement to Vol. IX (September 1964), pp. 47–63. Concentrating on three literary works that appeared during the turmoil of the 1867 Reform Act— George Eliot's *Felix Holt, the Radical*, Thomas Carlyle's *Shooting Niagara: And After?*, and Matthew Arnold's *Culture and Anarchy*—and their relationship to the Hyde Park riots and other manifestations of reform agitation, Professor Wolff questions the capacity of the cultural leaders of the time to recognize and to identify with social change. He suggests that a similar phenomenon is all too familiar today.

¹¹ Cyril Bibby, *T. H. Huxley: Scientist, Humanist, and Educator* (London: Watts, 1959), p. 22.

¹² Letter, Henry Brougham to Macvey Napier, printed in Macvey Napier, Jr. (ed.), *Selection from the Correspondence of the Late Macvey Napier, Esq.* (London: Macmillan, 1879), p. 88. Brougham, writing in 1830, referred to the death of William Huskisson, former President of the Board of Trade and leader of the Liverpool backers of the first British railroad, opened with great ceremony by the Duke of Wellington on September 15, 1830. A crowd of fifty thousand saw the first engine start off and the ironic accident that fatally injured Huskisson.

¹³ *Locksley Hall* (1842), ll. 181–2.

¹⁴ Fragment of a note, signed by PMR and dated May 23, 1859, name of addressee torn away. (Holborn Central Library, Camden Libraries, London)

¹⁵ *Proceedings of the Royal Society* (1870), p. xl. In the same year, 1863, Roget was fit enough to arrange and carry through a tour of the north Devon coast with two friends; his manuscript letter of August 26, 1863 (JRR) makes reservations for three places (two inside and one outside) in the coach from Bideford to Bude. In September of the year following—he was then eighty-five—he enjoyed a weekend visit in Bath, where he attended the annual meeting of the BAAS. His letter to Charles Lyell, September 27, 1864 (JRR), is to this effect. The family papers include

correspondence to and from Roget well into 1869, most of these items being brief acknowledgements of invitations, birthday greetings, etc.

[16] My thanks are due Mr. L. M. Payne, Librarian of the Royal College of Physicians, for helping me find at the British Museum the 1870 catalog of the venerable firm of Sotheby, Wilkinson and Hodge, a company that still does business in London today under the single name Sotheby. The Sotheby catalog is a sixty-three-page printed book, of which twenty-three pages are devoted to Roget's library—the auctioneers were, in the same sale, disposing of two other libraries and an Amati violincello. The copy preserved in the British Museum includes bids that the individual lots finally fetched and the names of successful bidders. The British Museum staff generously allowed me to photocopy the whole catalog and thus provided the means of our studying the single source of information extant on what was, in effect, a unique expression of the interests and actions of Roget and his times. Certainly the hours we have spent studying the catalog have given us understandings and insights into the life of Roget that no other source could have provided. The sale was held on March 12, just six months to the day since Roget's death.

[17] Readers interested in examining Roget's library more closely are referred to my earlier study of his collection, "The Library of Peter Mark Roget: A Centenary Inspection Tour," *The Book Collector* (England), Vol. 18, No. 4 (Winter 1969), pp. 449–70.

[18] An accurate total of the volumes in Roget's library is impossible to determine because the Sotheby catalog was prone to describe many lots as "a parcel," or "a bundle," or "and others." For purposes of this tabulation, I have arbitrarily (and, I think, conservatively) counted a "bundle" or a "parcel" as five volumes.

[19] A search of the church records by Rev. N. S. Peter Baron, present vicar of St. James, West Malvern, and of the files of newspapers in towns of the area has turned up nothing of interest about Roget as a regular summer resident. However, we enjoyed the hospitality in 1967 of an elderly couple, Dr. and Mrs. W. G. Shakespeare, in their new home directly across from "Ashfield House," which the Shakespeares had formerly owned and lived in for many years. They reported to us (I'm not sure how seriously) that the place had also been inhabited by a ghost in a black cloak. Dr. Shakespeare said that among other guests staying in the place during the summers of Roget's last years were Benjamin Jowett, the great classicist, and his protégé Algernon Charles Swinburne, and some years later, the great Hungarian violinist Joseph Joachim.

[20] *Proceedings of the Royal Society* (1870), p. xl.

Appendices

[Appendix 1 ☙

Advice to the Poor

"Advice to the Poor," published as an appendix to John Ferriar's *Medical Histories and Reflections* (London, 1810) was originally a paper written for and distributed to the poor of Manchester during Ferriar's work there as a physician in the Manchester infirmary (1790–1815). Roget worked with Ferriar and contributed to some of the earliest attempts to organize public health services for the poor in that teeming capital of the textile industry.

You are requested to read the following paper with attention, by persons who are endeavouring to relieve you from the misery and fatality of fevers, and other infectious diseases. A great deal has been done by the establishment of the fever-wards, the good effects of which you daily experience; but much dpends upon your own conduct, for preventing the first occasions of sickness. We can only stop the progress of diseases after they have once begun, but it is greatly in your power to prevent them from beginning at all, by attending to the simple directions which follow.

Avoid living in damp cellars: they destroy your constitutions, and shorten your lives. No temptation of low rents can counterbalance their ill effects. You are apt to croud into the cellars of new buildings, supposing them to be clean. This is a fatal mistake. A new house is always damp for two years, and the cellars, which you inhabit under them, are generally as moist as the bottom of a well. In such places, you are liable to bad fevers, which often throw the patient into a decline, and you are apt to get rheumatic complaints, that continue for a long time, and disable you from working.

If you cannot help taking a cellar, be attentive to have all the windows put in good repair, before you venture into it, and, if possible, get it whitewashed. If you attempt to live in a cellar with broken windows, colds and fevers will be the certain consequences.

In many parts of the town, you sleep in back-rooms, behind the front-cellar, which are dark, and have no proper circulation of air. It would be much more healthy to sleep to the front: at least, when you have large families, which is often the case, you ought to divide them, and not to crowd the whole together in the back-cellar.

Keep your persons and houses as clean as your employments will permit, and do not regret the loss of an hour's wages, when your time is occupied in attending to cleanliness. It is better to give up a little time occasionally, to keep your houses neat, than to see your whole family lying sick, in consequence of working constantly, without cleaning. It would be of great service, if you could contrive to air your beds and bed-clothes out of doors, once or twice a-week.

Always wash your children from head to foot with cold water, before you send them to work in the morning. Take care to keep them dry in their feet, and never allow them to go to work without giving them their breakfast, though you should have nothing to offer them but a crust of bread, and a little water. Children who get wet feet, when they go out early fasting, seldom escape fevers, or severe colds.

If you know that any of your neighbours are in a starving condition, apply to some opulent persons in the neighbourhood; get them recommended to the overseer; or, if they are sick, to the Infirmary. Want of necessary food produces bad fevers; and many of you may suffer from neglecting poor distressed persons, whom timely relief would have preserved from the disease.

When you know, or have reason to believe that any of your neighbours are afflicted with fevers, and that they have not taken care to procure the assistance afforded by the Infirmary, you ought, both from a regard to them and to yourselves, to give immediate information to the physicians, or some trustee of the Infirmary, or to Mr. Bellott, Secretary to the Board of Health. The Board allows the sum of two shillings, for every well-founded information of this kind.

You ought to be very cautious in purchasing old clothes, or second-hand furniture; as they may be brought from houses infected with fever, and you may introduce the infection with them, into your own dwellings. Every article of this kind ought to be stoved or ventilated, before it is admitted into your houses.

Your sick neighbours, when the fever gets into their houses, may often require assistance from you. It would be cruel to refuse them, yet it is hard that you should be obliged to expose your health, and that of your family. You ought never to visit them from idle curiosity. But when they require your help in making their beds, washing, or turning the sick, you may preserve yourselves from being infected, by tying a handkerchief across your face, just below the eyes, to prevent the exhalations from the bodies of the sick from entering your mouth and nostrils. As soon as you return to your own house, wash your hands and face in cold water, and avoid touching any of your family, for half, or three quarters of an hour.

Your health will always be materially injured by the following circumstances: living in small back buildings, adjoining to the open vaults of privies; living in cellars, where the streets are not properly soughed, or drained: living in narrow bye streets, where sheep are slaughtered, and where the blood and garbage are allowed to stagnate and corrupt; and, perhaps, more than all, by living crowded together, in dirty lodging-houses, where you cannot have the common comforts of light and air.

It should be unnecessary to remind you, that much sickness is occasioned among you, by passing your evenings at alehouses, or in strolling about the streets, or in the fields adjoining to the town. Perhaps those who are most apt to expose themselves in this manner, would pay little attention to dissuasive arguments of any kind. However, those who feel an interest in your welfare, cannot omit making the remark.

There is another subject of great importance to you, on which you seem to want information. A great number of children die of the natural small-pox, almost every year. This mortality must be imputed, in a great degree, to your own negligence; for the faculty at the Infirmary offer to inoculate your children, and give public notice of the proper time for making your application, twice a-year. The next period for inoculation will be in March; the succeeding period in September. The chance of recovery from the small-pox received by inoculation, is so much greater than the chance of recovery from the natural kind, that you ought to consider yourselves as performing a duty to your children, and to the public, in bringing those who have not yet had the small-pox, to be inoculated at the Infirmary.

You ought to be informed, that there is scarcely any thing more injurious to the health of children, than allowing them to work at night in the cotton-mills. It may not always be in your power to prevent their being employed in this manner, but you should be made acquainted with the danger to which you expose them. There is no hazard incurred by their working during the day, in clean, well-managed cotton-mills.

It is also proper to inform you, that you may be infected with fevers, by working in the same place with persons who have just recovered from fevers, or by people who come from infected houses, where they are at no pains to keep themselves clean. It is a fact well-known to this Board, that infectious fevers have been conveyed from Manchester to neighbouring towns, and cotton-mills, by persons going from infected houses. You had better collect something among yourselves, to support such persons for a fortnight after their recovery, than expose yourselves to the risk of catching a fever, by their returning too early to work.

People who are discharged from the fever-ward, bring no infection out with them; their clothes being aired and cleaned, during their stay in the House of Recovery.

[Appendix 11 ℰ

*The Published Writings of Peter Mark Roget**

Fᴏʟʟᴏᴡɪɴɢ each item is listed in parentheses the location of at least one copy of the work. Items I have been unable to verify have been set aside in a separate list. The following abbreviations are used throughout:

BM	= British Museum	SFPL	= San Francisco Public Library
NLM	= National Library of Medicine	UC	= University of California
NYPL	= New York Public Library	UL	= University of London
PRO	= Public Record Office		
RCP	= Royal College of Physicians	UM	= University of Missouri
RS	= Royal Society of London	US	= University of Sussex
RSM	= Royal Society of Medicine	WHML	= Wellcome Historical Medical Library

1798
1. "Tentamen physicum inaugurale de chemicae affinitatis legibus." University of Edinburgh, 69 pp. (ʙᴍ, ʀᴄᴘ) [Roget's M.D. dissertation]

1799
2. "Observations on the Non-prevalence of Consumption Among Butchers, Fishermen, etc.," in *Essay on the Causes of Pul-*

* Reprinted, with additions, from "Peter Mark Roget: A Centenary Bibliography," *The Papers of the Bibliographical Society of America*, Vol. 62 (Third Quarter, 1968), pp. 436–47.

monary Consumption, by Thomas Beddoes. London, pp. 48–51. (BM, RCP)

1800

3. ["Reports from Medical Men,"] *Researches, Chemical and Philosophical; Chiefly Concerning Nitrous Oxide, or Dephlogisticated Nitrous Air, and Its Respiration,* by Humphry Davy. London, pp. 509–12. (BM) [A letter from Roget, detailing his reactions to inhaling nitrous oxide]

1805

4. *Syllabus of a Course of Lectures on Anatomy and Physiology,* by P. M. Roget, B. Gibson, and J. Hutchinson. Manchester, 33 pp. (NLM) [An outline of lectures similar to those delivered by Roget at various schools and institutions through the next forty years]

1811

5. "A Case of Recovery from the Effects of Arsenic, with Remarks on a New Mode of Detecting the Presence of This Metal," *Transactions of the Medical and Chirurgical Society,* Vol. II, pp. 136–60. (RSM)

1812

6. "A Note," *Transactions of the Medical and Chirurgical Society,* Vol. III, p. 342. (RSM) [A brief afterthought on the article of 1811]

7. "Recherches sur les moeurs des fourmis indigènes," *Edinburgh Review,* Vol. 20 (July), pp. 143–69. (UL) [A review-essay on a work by Huber surveying the status of entomology]

1815

8. "Nouvelles observations sur les abeilles," *Edinburgh Review,* Vol. 25 (October), pp. 363–89. (UL) [A review-essay on Huber's pioneer work]

9. "Description of a New Instrument for Performing Mechanically the Involution and Evolution of Numbers," *Philosophical Transactions,* Vol. CV, pp. 9–28, with 3 plates. (RS) [Paper read before the Royal Society on November 17, 1814, on the basis of which Roget was elected a Fellow of the society]

1816

10. "On a Change in the Colour of the Skin Produced by the Internal Use of Nitrate of Silver," by P. M. Roget and J. A. Albers, *Transactions of the Medical and Chirurgical Society,* Vol. VII, pp. 284–96. (RSM)

1818

11. "On the Kaleidoscope," *Annals of Philosophy,* Vol. XI, pp. 375–78. (RS) [In the form of a letter to the editor]

12. "Dante," by P. M. Roget and Ugo Foscolo, *Edinburgh Review*, Vol. 29 (February), pp. 453–64. (UL)

1819

13. "Sweating Sickness," *The Cyclopaedia or Universal Dictionary of Arts, Sciences and Literature*, ed. Abraham Rees. London, Vol. 34, no pp. (RCP)

14. "Symptom," in Rees's *Cyclopaedia*, Vol. 34.

15. "Synocha," in Rees's *Cyclopaedia*, Vol. 34.

16. "Synochus," in Rees's *Cyclopaedia*, Vol. 34.

17. "Tabes," in Rees's *Cyclopaedia*, Vol. 35.

18. "Tetanus," in Rees's *Cyclopaedia*, Vol. 35. [Items 13 through 18 range from one short paragraph to several pages.]

1820

19. "On a Voluntary Action of the Iris," *A Synopsis of the Diseases of the Eye and Their Treatment*, by Benjamin Travers. London, pp. 71–75. (RSM) [A report by Roget on his own experiments in controlling the muscles of the eye]

1821

20. "Observations on Mr. Perkins's Account of the Compressibility of Water," *Annals of Philosophy*, Vol. I n.s., p. 135. (RI) [Letter to the editor, correcting a computational error in a paper published in the journal]

1822

21. "On the Functions of Progressive Motion in Vertebrated Animals," *Philosophical Magazine*, Vol. LIX, pp. 389–92. (RI)

22. "On Respiration," *Philosophical Magazine*, Vol. LIX, pp. 305–8. (RI)

23. "Introduction to Physiology and the Functions of the Skeleton," *Literary Gazette and Journal of Belles Lettres, Arts, Sciences, etc.*, n.v., No. 266 (February 23), p. 121. (UL)

24. "Progressive Motion in Vertebrates," *Lit. Gaz.*, No. 269 (March 16), p. 168.

25. "Chemical Functions," *Lit. Gaz.*, No. 270 (March 23), p. 184.

26. "Digestion," *Lit Gaz.*, No. 271 (March 30), pp. 200–1.

27. "Respiration," *Lit. Gaz.*, No. 274 (April 20), pp. 249–50.

28. "The Capillaries," *Lit. Gaz.*, No. 276 (May 4), p. 280.

29. "Introduction to Perception and Feeling in Animals," *Lit. Gaz.*, No. 277 (May 11), pp. 295–96.

30. "Vision," *Lit. Gaz.*, No. 278 (May 18), pp. 311–12.

31. "Sensitive Functions," *Lit. Gaz.*, No. 279 (May 25), pp. 327–28.

1823

32. ["Opening Lecture,"] *Lit. Gaz.*, No. 317 (February 15), p. 105.

33. "Introduction to Comparative Physiology," *Lit. Gaz.*, No. 319 (March 1), pp. 137–38.

34. "Zoophites," *Lit. Gaz.*, No. 320 (March 8), p. 154.

35. "Insects," *Lit. Gaz.*, No. 321 (March 15), pp. 168–69.

36. "Insects," *Lit. Gaz.*, No. 322 (March 22), pp. 185–86.

37. "Insects," *Lit. Gaz.*, No. 323 (March 29), pp. 201–2.

38. "Molluscs," *Lit. Gaz.*, No. 325 (April 12), pp. 233–34.

39. "Vertebrates," *Lit. Gaz.*, No. 326 (April 19), pp. 249–50.

40. "Reptiles," *Lit. Gaz.*, No. 327 (April 26), pp. 267–68.

41. "Birds," *Lit. Gaz.*, No. 328 (May 3), pp. 282–83. [Items 21 through 41 are abstracts of lectures delivered at the Royal Institution.]

42. ["Use of Nitrate of Silver on Epilepsy,"] *A Treatise on Nervous Diseases,* by John Cooke. London, Vol. I, pp. 147–52, 215–16. (WHML) [Cooke quotes from various reports and case histories by Roget.]

43. "Biographical Memoir of Dr. Alexander Marcet," *Annals of Biography and Obituary,* Vol. 7, pp. 290–98. (US) [Marcet and Roget were active in the formation and promotion of the Medical and Chirurgical Society.]

44. "Report of Drs. Latham and Roget, upon the Penitentiary, 4th July, 1823," *Report from the Select Committee on the State of the Penitentiary at Milbank,* App. E, item 12 (July 8). Ordered printed by the House of Commons. (UL) [The report, minutes of evidence, and appendixes occupy 399 pages. Roget's and Latham's conclusions take up 2 pages, and their direct testimony 13 pages (17–29). The two doctors had been appointed to investigate charges of inadequate care of prisoners leading to a severe epidemic in the prison.]

1824

45. "Ant," *Supplement to the Fourth, Fifth, and Sixth Editions of the Encyclopaedia Britannica.* Edinburgh, Vol. I, pp. 455–62. (UL)

46. "Apiary," *EB Supp.,* Vol. I, pp. 467–69.

47. "Baldinger," *EB Supp.,* Vol. II, pp. 121–24.

48. "Barthez," *EB Supp.,* Vol. II, pp. 143–47.

49. "Beddoes," *EB Supp.,* Vol. II, pp. 206–10.

50. "Bee," *EB Supp.,* Vol. II, pp. 212–41.

51. "Bichat," *EB Supp.,* Vol. II, pp. 299–302.

52. "Brocklesby," *EB Supp.,* Vol. II, pp. 523–24.

53. "Broussonet," *EB Supp.,* Vol. II, p. 529.

54. "Camper," *EB Supp.,* Vol. II, pp. 589–93.

55. "Cranioscopy," *EB Supp.,* Vol. III, pp. 419–37.

56. "Crawford," *EB Supp.,* Vol. III, pp. 437–38.

57. "Currie," *EB Supp.,* Vol. III, pp. 432–56.

58. "Deaf and Dumb," *EB Supp.*, Vol. III, pp. 467–83.
59. "Kaleidoscope," *EB Supp.*, Vol. V, pp. 163–71.
60. "Physiology," *EB Supp.*, Vol. VI, pp. 180–97. [Items 45 through 60 appeared from 1818 to 1824, as the six volumes of the *Supplement* were issued separately.]

1825

61. *An Account of the Disease Lately Prevalent at the General Penitentiary*, by P. M. Latham [and P. M. Roget]. London. (BM) [This was a pamphlet amplifying some of the controversial aspects of the report to the House of Commons.]

62. "Explanation of an Optical Deception in the Appearance of the Spokes of a Wheel Seen Through Vertical Apertures," *Philos. Trans.*, Vol. CXV, pp. 131–40. (RS) [Several histories of the motion picture cite Roget's paper as contributing importantly to the discovery of the fundamental optical principle on which the cinematic process depends.]

63. "Explanation of an Optical Deception in the Appearance of the Spokes of a Wheel," *Quarterly Journal of Science and Arts*, Vol. XIX, pp. 298–99. (RI) [Abstract of the original paper]

64. "Explanation of an Optical Deception," *Annals of Philosophy*, Vol. X, pp. 107–12. (RS) [A reprinting of the *Philos. Trans.* paper]

1826

65. *An Introductory Lecture on Human and Comparative Physiology, Delivered at the New Medical School in Aldersgate Street*. London. (BM, RCP)

1827

66. "Electro-Magnetism," *Quarterly Review*, Vol. XXXV, pp. 237–69. (UL) [A review-essay on Ampère's *Recueil d'observations electro-dynamiques* and Peter Barlow's *Essay on Magnetic Attractions and on the Laws of Terrestrial Magnetism*]

67. *Electricity*, Library of Useful Knowledge. London: Society for Diffusion of Useful Knowledge. (UC) [First of a series of treatises that appeared as separate booklets and were later issued together (see item 75). *Electricity* was issued again separately in a second edition, according to Pettigrew, but I have been unable to locate a copy.]

68. "To the Editor," *The Times* (November 10), p. 2. (SFPL) [Roget's letter, signed "Aequitas," was written in response to another, signed "Humanitas," which asked some rather pointed questions about the fate of funds collected by the Ladies Patronesses of the Spanish and Italian Bazaar. I found a rough draft of the "Aequitas" letter in Roget's family papers.]

1828

69. "On an Apparent Violation of the Law of Continuity,"
Philosophical Magazine, Vol. III, pp. 118–21, 203–6. (RI) [The
editor notes that this was reprinted from the *Scientific Gazette* of
November 5 and 12, 1825, but I was unable to find the original
publication.]

70. *Supply of Water in the Metropolis: Report of the Commissioners Appointed by His Majesty to Inquire into the State of
the Supply of Water in the Metropolis* (April 21), pp. 3–12.
Ordered printed by the House of Commons. (PRO) [This official
report, prepared by Roget, Thomas Telford, and William
Thomas Brande, was accompanied by 110 pages of testimony
from hearings conducted by the Commissioners, analyses of
water, plans of remedies, copies of petitions, and correspondence.]

1829

71. *Galvanism*, Library of Useful Knowledge. London: Society
for Diffusion of Useful Knowledge. (UC)

1830

72. "Observations by Dr. Roget in Reply to Mr. Babbage," in
Charles Babbage, *Reflections on the Decline of Science in England and on Some of Its Causes*, App. 4, pp. 1–5. London. (UC)
[The same material by Roget was also published in the June
1830 issues of the *Philosophical Magazine* and *Annals of Philosophy*.]

1831

73. *Magnetism and Electro-Magnetism*, Library of Useful
Knowledge. London: Society for Diffusion of Useful Knowledge.
(UC)

74. "On the Geometric Properties of the Magnetic Curve, with
an Account of an Instrument for Its Mechanical Description,"
Journal of the Royal Institution of Great Britain, Vol. I, pp.
311–19. (RI)

1832

75. *Treatises on Electricity, Galvanism, Magnetism and Elec-
tro-Magnetism*, Library of Useful Knowledge, Vol. II, *Natural
Philosophy*. London: Society for Diffusion of Useful Knowledge.
(UC) [A reprinting of the earlier separate papers]

76. "The Laws of Sensation and Perception," *London Medical
Gazette* (June 2). (RCP) [Abstracts of papers delivered by Roget
as Gulstonian Lecturer before the Royal College of Physicians,
May 2, 4, and 9, 1832]

77. "Ueber die Gesetze der Empfindung und Perception," *Froriep Notizen*, Vol. XXXIV, pp. 241–50, 257–66. (RCP)

1833

78. "Age," *Cyclopaedia of Practical Medicine,* ed. John Forbes, Alexander Tweedie, and John Conolly. London, Vol. I, pp. 34–46. (RCP)

79. "Asphyxia," *Cyclopaedia of Practical Medicine,* Vol. I, pp. 167–83.

80. *Asphyxia.* London, 16 pp. (NLM) [A reprint from *Cyclopaedia of Practical Medicine*]

1834

81. *Animal and Vegetable Physiology Considered with Reference to Natural Theology, Being No. 5 of the Bridgewater Treatises.* London, 2 vols. (SFPL) [This work, an attempt to reconcile science and religion, was regarded by Roget's contemporaries as the work for which Roget would be remembered. A second edition came out in the same year, a third in 1840, and a fourth and final edition in 1867.]

1837

82. *Die Erscheinungen und Gesetze des Lebens, oder populäre Vergleichende Physiologie der Pflanzen- und Thierwelt,* tr. F. M. Duttenhofer. Stuttgart: P. Neff. (UC)

83. "Statement of the Council Relative to Mr. Panizzi's Pamphlet," appended to *Duke of Sussex's Address to the Royal Society on Its Anniversary Meeting, Thursday, Nov. 30, 1837.* London, pp. 20–22. (RS) [Part of an answering pamphlet by the Royal Society during a long dispute with Antonio Panizzi over his preparing a catalogue of the Royal Society Library]

84. "Joseph Banks," *Encyclopaedia Britannica,* 7th ed. Edinburgh, Vol. IV, pp. 348–51. (UL) [This edition was not completed until 1842, but because some of the volumes were issued earlier, including that containing item 85, which prompted immediate responses (see items 87 through 89), I have used 1837 here as the significant publication date.]

85. "Phrenology," *EB* 7th, Vol. XVII, pp. 454–73. [A revision of item 55]

86. "Physiology," *EB* 7th, Vol. XVIII, pp. 577–729.

1838

87. ["Correspondence,"] *On the Functions of the Cerebellum,* by Gall, Vimont, and Broussais [no first names given], tr. George Combe. Edinburgh, pp. 221–23, 226. (WHML) [Combe published here letters of Roget to Combe, dated 1819, which were originally written as responses to Combe's objections to Roget's "Cranioscopy," which Combe considered an unfavorable and unsatisfactory review of the progress of phrenology. Combe maintained that Roget's "Phrenology" was an inexcusable rehashing

of the earlier article; this attitude accounts for the subtitle to 87: *Answers to the Objections Urged Against Phrenology by Drs. Roget, Rudolphi, Prichard, and Tiedemann.*]

88. *Treatises on Physiology and Phrenology*, 2 vols. Edinburgh. (RCP) [Reprints of items 85 and 86]

1839

89. *Outlines of Physiology, with an Appendix on Phrenology*, 1st Amer. ed., rev., with numerous notes. Philadelphia, 516 pp. (NYPL) [Substantially a reprint and rearrangement of material in items 85 and 86]

1840

90. "Description of a Method of Moving the Knight over Every Square of the Chess-Board Without Going Twice over Any One; Commencing at a Given Square and Ending at Any Other Given Square," *London and Edinburgh Philosophical Magazine*, Vol. XVI 3rd s., pp. 305–9. (RI)

1845

91. "Galvanism," *Encyclopaedia Metropolitana*. London, Vol. IV, pp. 173–224. (UL)

1848

92. "Report of Physiology Committee on Dr. Lee's Paper on the Ganglia and Nerves of the Heart," *London Medical Gazette* (January 14), p. 82. (RSM)

93. "Report of Physiology Committee on Dr. Lee's Paper on the Ganglia and Nerves of the Heart," *Medical Times*, Vol. 17 (January 15). (RSM) [The "Report," printed in at least two medical papers, was part of Roget's defense in a long and tangled series of disputes within the Royal Society, culminating in 1848 with his retirement as Secretary.]

94. [Letter to editor,] *Medical Times*, Vol. 17 (February 5), p. 317. (RSM)

1851

95. "Address by Dr. Roget," *Proceedings of the Royal Society*, Vol. V, pp. 703–4. (RS) [Roget's announcement of his intention to retire. His short, somewhat bitter address was delivered in 1847.]

1852

96. *Thesaurus of English Words and Phrases, Classified and Arranged so as to Facilitate the Expression of Ideas and Assist in Literary Composition*. London: Longman, Brown, Green, and Longmans. (BM)

1904

97. *Continental Travel in 1802–03: The Story of an Escape,*

by Herbert Philips. Manchester. (UM, BM) [An account made up of letters from Roget and the two boys to whom he was a tutor and guide during a grand tour of Europe]

1916
98. *Un anglais prisonnier à Verdun, 1803–1814,* ed. François Frédéric Roget. Geneva. (BM) [This small volume is comprised of letters from Lovell Edgeworth, P. M. Roget's traveling companion in France and Geneva, and of some of Roget's replies. F. F. Roget was one of several nephews of P. M. Roget.]

1922
99. *Travel in the Two Last Centuries of Three Generations,* ed. S. R. Roget. New York. (SFPL, NYPL, BM) [Chapters 4 and 5 detail the 1802–3 adventure and include several important Roget letters. The editor, S. R. Roget, was P. M. Roget's grandson.]

The following items are listed by one or more of the secondary sources consulted (indicated in parentheses), but they eluded my best efforts to locate them in the libraries of Britain and the United States:

1a. *Syllabus of a Course of Lectures on Classification of Animals.* Manchester, 1807, 13 pp. (Brockbank)

2a. *A Memoir of Sir Samuel Romilly.* London, 1819, 22 pp. (Brockbank)

3a. Appendix to *Larkin's Introduction to Solid Geometry and to the Study of Crystallography.* London, 1820. (*Proc. RS, Min. ICE,* Pettigrew.)

4a. "On the Quarantine Laws," *Parliamentary Review,* 1826, pp. 785–804. (*Proc. RS,* Brockbank, Pettigrew, DNB)

5a. "Pauper Lunatics," *Parliamentary Review,* 1828, pp. 265–98. (*Proc. RS,* Brockbank, Pettigrew, DNB)

6a. *Description of the New Sliding Rule of Involution Invented by Dr. Roget, Sec., R.S., with Instructions for Using It.* London, 1828. (Brockbank)

7a. [A series of chess problems contributed to the *Illustrated London News.*] (DNB)

8a. *The Economic Chess-board.* London and New York, 1846. (Allibone, *Min. ICE*)

Finally, there are a number of Roget's works that were *probably* published, in some form, but which I was unable to locate:

1b. Lectures, or abstracts of them, delivered at the Manchester Infirmary, January 29 to March 31, 1806.

2b. Lectures (or abstracts) on physiology of the animal kingdom, delivered before the Literary and Philosophical Society of Manchester, beginning in January 1807.

3b. Lectures (or abstracts) delivered at the Russell Literary and Scientific Institution, London, 1809–10.

4b. Lectures (or abstracts) on the theory and practice of medicine, delivered at the Theatre of Anatomy, Great Windmill Street, London, 1810–15.

5b. Lectures (or abstracts) delivered at the Royal Institution, London, 1812–14.

6b. Lectures (or abstracts) on animal physiology, delivered at the London Institution, 1824–26.

7b. Lectures (or abstracts) delivered at the Royal Institution, 1835–37 (when Roget was first Fullerian Professor of the RI).

Bibliography

Bibliography

Abernethy, John. *Reflections on Gall and Spurzheim's System of Physiology and Phrenology*. London, 1821.

Aldine Magazine of Biography, Bibliography, Criticism, and the Arts. London.

Allibone, S. Austin. *A Critical Dictionary of English Literature and British and American Authors*. Philadelphia: Lippincott, 1872.

Annals of Philosophy. London.

Annual Register, The. London.

Athenaeum, The: A Magazine of Literary and Miscellaneous Information. London.

Atkinson, Charles Milner. *Jeremy Bentham: His Life and Work*. London: Methuen, 1905.

Babbage, Charles. *Reflections on the Decline of Science in England and on Some of Its Causes*. London, 1830.

———. *The Ninth Bridgewater Treatise, a Fragment*. London, 1838.

Barlow, Nora (ed.). *The Autobiography of Charles Darwin*. New York: Harcourt, Brace, 1958.

Barrow, J. *Sketches of the Royal Society and the Royal Society Club*. London, 1849.

Beddoes, Thomas. *Essay on the Causes of Pulmonary Consumption*. London, 1799.

———, and Watt, J. *Considerations on the Medicinal Use and on the Production of Factitious Airs*. Bristol, 1795.

Bellot, Hugh Hale. *University College, 1826–1926*. London, 1929.

Belsham, Thomas. *Reflections upon the Death of Sir Sam'l Romilly, in a Discourse Delivered at Essex Street Chapel, November 8, 1818*. London, 1818.

Berry, Mary. *Extracts of the Journals and Correspondence of Miss Berry, from the Year 1783 to 1852*, ed. Theresa Lewis. London: Longmans, Green, 1865.

Bettany, G. T. *Eminent Doctors: Their Lives and Their Work*. London: Hogg, 1885.

Bibby, Cyril. *T. H. Huxley: Scientist, Humanist, and Educator*. London: Watts, 1959.

Bostock, John. *Elementary System of Physiology*. London, 1824–27.

Bowring, John. *Life and Letters of Bentham*. London, 1843.

Briggs, Asa. *Victorian Cities*. London: Odhams, 1964.

British Association for the Advancement of Science. *Manchester and Its Region*. Manchester, 1962.

British and Foreign Medical Review. London.

British Medical Journal. London.

Brockbank, Edward Mansfield. *Sketches of the Lives and Work of the Honorary Medical Staff at the Manchester Infirmary, 1752–1830*. Manchester, 1904.

Buxton, David. *Observations on the Article "Deaf and Dumb" in the Eighth Edition of the Encyclopaedia Britannica*. Liverpool, 1858.

Cajori, Florian. *A History of the Logarithmic Slide Rule and Allied Instruments*. New York, 1909.

Cartwright, F. F. *The English Pioneers of Anaesthesia*. Bristol, 1952.

Chaplin, Arnold. *Medicine in England During the Reign of George III*. London, 1919.

Cobbett, William. *Rural Rides in the Southern, Western, and Eastern Counties of England, Together with Tours in Scotland and in the Northern and Midland Counties of England, and Letters from Ireland*, ed. G. D. H. and Margaret Cole. London: Davies, 1930.

Combe, Andrew. *Strictures on Anti-Phrenology in Two Letters to Macvey Napier and P. M. Roget, M.D., Being an Exposure of the Article Called "Phrenology" Recently Published in the Encyclopaedia Britannica*. London, 1838.

Combe, George. *Essays on Phrenology*. Edinburgh, 1819.

——— (tr. and ed.). *Gall, Vimont, and Broussais on the Functions of the Cerebellum*. Edinburgh, 1838.

Committee on Scientific and Technical Information of the Federal Council for Science and Technology. *Guidelines for the Development of Information Retrieval Thesauri*. Washington, D.C., 1967.

Cope, Zachary. "The Private Medical Schools of London, 1746–1914," in *The Evolution of Medical Education in Britain*, ed. F. N. L. Poynter. London: Pitman Medical, 1966.

Cottle, Joseph. *Early Recollections Chiefly Relating to the Late Samuel Taylor Coleridge During His Long Residence in Bristol.* London, 1837.

Crabb, George. *English Synonymes Explained.* New York: Harper, 1917.

Critic, The. London.

Crowther, J. G. *Men of Science.* New York: Norton, 1936.

Cyclopaedia of Practical Medicine, ed. John Forbes, Alexander Tweedie, and John Conolly. London, 1833.

Daily Chronicle. London.

Davy, Humphry. *Researches, Chemical and Philosophical; Chiefly Concerning Nitrous Oxide, or Dephlogisticated Nitrous Air, and Its Respiration.* London, 1800.

Davy, John. *Memoirs of the Life of Sir Humphry Davy, Bart.* London, 1839–40.

Dictionary of National Biography. London: Oxford, 1949–50.

Duncum, Barbara M. *The Development of Inhalation Anaesthesia with Special Reference to the Years 1846–1900.* Oxford, 1947.

Dunglison, Robley. *Medical Lexicon: A Dictionary of Medical Science.* Philadelphia, 1860.

Dwight, C. Harrison. "Count Rumford," *Notes and Records of the Royal Society of London,* Vol. II (March 1955), pp. 189–201.

Eclectic Review, The. London.

Edinburgh Review. Edinburgh.

Egan, Rose F. "Survey of the History of English Synonymy," *Webster's Dictionary of Synonyms.* Springfield, Mass.: Merriam, 1942.

Elmes, James. *Metropolitan Improvements.* London, 1827–29.

Emblen, D. L. "The Library of Peter Mark Roget: A Centenary Inspection Tour," *The Book Collector,* Vol. 18, No. 4 (Winter 1969), pp. 449–70.

———. "A Memorandum Composed Mainly of Quotations from an Anonymous Critic of Schoolmen of One Hundred Fourteen Years Ago," *Phi Delta Kappan,* Vol. XLVII (April 1966), pp. 444–46.

———. "Peter Mark Roget: A Centenary Bibliography," *The Papers of the Bibliographical Society of America,* Vol. 62 (Third Quarter, 1968), pp. 436–47.

———. "Peter Mark Roget: Style as Symptom," *College Composition and Communication,* Vol. XVII (October 1966), pp. 135–39.

———. "Peter Mark Roget: Travels and Letters," *Bulletin of the New York Public Library,* Vol. 71 (October 1967), pp. 542–45.

————. "Roget vs. Panizzi—a Collision," *Journal of Library History*, Vol. IV, No. 1 (January 1969), pp. 9–38.

Emerson, Ralph Waldo. *Works*. New York: Black, n.d.

Encyclopaedia Britannica.
> Third Edition. Edinburgh, 1797.
> Seventh Edition. Edinburgh, 1837.
> Eighth Edition. Edinburgh, 1853–60.
> Ninth Edition. Edinburgh, 1875–89.
> Tenth Edition. London, 1902–3.
> Eleventh Edition. Cambridge, 1910–11.
> Twelfth Edition. London, 1922.
> Chicago, 1947.
> Chicago, 1967.

Esdaile, Arundell. *The British Museum: A Short History and Survey*. London: Allen & Unwin, 1946.

European Magazine and London Review, The. London.

Farington, Joseph. *The Farington Diaries*, ed. James Greig, Vols. VII and VIII. London: Hutchinson, 1927–28.

Feinagle, Gregor von. *The New Art of Memory, Founded on the Principles Taught by M. G. von Feinagle*. London, 1812.

Ferriar, John. *Medical Histories and Reflections*. London, 1810.

Fournier, Auguste. *Napoleon I: A Biography*, tr. Margaret Bacon Corwin and Arthur Dart Bissell. New York, 1903.

Fowler, O. S. *Education and Self-Improvement, Founded on Physiology and Phrenology*. New York, 1844.

Fraser's Magazine. London.

Gaskell, Elizabeth Cleghorn. *Mary Barton*. London: Everyman's Library, 1965.

Geikie, A. *Annals of the Royal Society Club*. London, 1917.

Gentleman's Magazine. London.

Gilbert, L. F. "The Election to the Presidency of the Royal Society in 1820," *Notes and Records of the Royal Society of London*, Vol. 11 (March 1955), pp. 256–77.

Gillispie, Charles Coulston. *Genesis and Geology*. Cambridge, Mass.: Harvard, 1951.

Granville, A. B. *Science Without a Head*. London, 1839.

Granville, Paulina B. (ed.). *Autobiography of A. B. Granville*. London, 1874.

Hackett, Alice Payne. *70 Years of Best Sellers: 1895–1965*. New York: Bowker, 1967.

Hammond, J. L., and Hammond, Barbara. *The Town Labourer, 1760–1832*. London: Longmans, Green, 1966.

Hanson, Lawrence. *The Life of S. T. Coleridge: The Early Years*. New York: Russell and Russell, 1962.

Holford, G. *A Short Vindication of the General Penitentiary at*

Millbank with a Few Remarks on Juvenile Offenders, Second Edition. London, 1824.

————. *Second Vindication of the General Penitentiary at Millbank.* London, 1824.

————. *Third Vindication of the General Penitentiary, Shewing That There Is No Ground Whatever for Supposing That the Situation of That Prison Had Any Share in Producing the Late Disease Among the Prisoners Confined There, Being an Answer to Some Observations Contained in a Work Published by P. Mere Latham, M.D.* London, 1825.

Holland, Sir Henry. *Recollections of Past Life.* New York: Appleton, 1872.

Horn, D. B. *A Short History of the University of Edinburgh, 1556–1889.* Edinburgh, 1967.

Horner, L. (ed.). *Memoirs and Correspondence of Francis Horner, M.P.* London, 1843.

Hutchison, A. Copland. *Correspondence Between the Committee of the General Penitentiary at Millbank and Mr. A. Copland Hutchison in June, 1822, and Alluded to in Mr. Hutchison's Letter to the Committee.* London, 1823.

Johnson, Edgar. *Charles Dickens: His Tragedy and Triumph.* New York: Simon & Schuster, 1952.

Journal of the Royal Institution. London.

Kennedy, Arthur G. *A Bibliography of Writings on the English Language from the Beginning of Printing to the End of 1922.* Cambridge, Mass.: Harvard; New Haven, Conn.: Yale, 1927.

Knight, Arthur. *The Liveliest Art: A Panoramic History of the Movies.* New York: New American Library, 1959.

Knight, Charles. *Passages of a Working Life During Half a Century.* London: Bradbury & Evans, 1864.

Lancet. London.

Latham, P. Mere. *An Account of the Disease Lately Prevalent at the General Penitentiary.* London, 1825.

Lecky, William Edward Hartpole. *Historical and Political Essays.* London: Longmans, Green, 1908.

Literary Gazette and Journal of Belles Lettres, Arts, Sciences, etc. London.

Liverpool Mercury, The.

London and Provincial Medical Directory. London: Churchill, 1848–62.

London Medical Gazette, The.

Lyell, Katherine M. *Life, Letters and Journals of Sir Charles Lyell, Bart.* London, 1881.

Magnus, Philip. *King Edward the Seventh.* New York: Dutton, 1964.

Medical Times, The. London.

Meteyard, Eliza. *A Group of Englishmen, 1795–1815, etc.* London: Longmans, Green, 1871.

———. *The Life of Josiah Wedgwood.* London, 1865–66.

Miller, Edward. *The Prince of Librarians.* London: Deutsch, 1967.

Minutes of the Council of the Royal Society of London.

Minutes of the Evidence Before the Select Committee on the General Penitentiary at Milbank, May 16, 1823. London: House of Commons.

Minutes of the Proceedings of the Institution of Civil Engineers. London.

Morning Chronicle, The. London.

Mudford, Peter G. "William Lawrence and *The Natural History of Man,*" *Journal of the History of Ideas,* Vol. XXIX (July–September 1968), pp. 430–36.

Munk, William. *The Roll of the Royal College of Physicians of London.* London, 1878.

Napier, Macvey, Jr. (ed.). *Selection from the Correspondence of the Late Macvey Napier, Esq.* London: Macmillan, 1879.

Newman, Charles. *The Evolution of Medical Education in the 19th Century.* London: Oxford, 1957.

Oakes, Cecil G. *Sir Samuel Romilly.* London: Allen & Unwin, 1935.

Ober, William B. "Peter Mark Roget: Utilitarian and Lexicographer," *New York State Journal of Medicine* (July 1965), pp. 1804–7.

Paley, William. *Works.* Philadelphia, 1853.

Panizzi, Antonio. *A Letter to His Royal Highness the President of the Royal Society on the New Catalogue of the Library of That Institution Now in Press.* London, 1837.

———. *Observations on the Address by the President, and on the Statement by the Council to the Fellows of the Royal Society, Respecting Mr. Panizzi, Read at Their General Meeting, Nov. 30, 1837.* London, 1837.

Peel, Frank. *The Risings of the Luddites.* London, 1888.

Pettigrew, Thomas Joseph. *Medical Portrait Gallery: Biographical Memoirs of the Most Celebrated Physicians, Surgeons, etc., etc., Who Have Contributed to the Advancement of Medical Science.* London: Whittaker, 1840.

[Philips, Herbert.] *Continental Travel in 1802–03: The Story of an Escape.* Manchester, 1904.

Philosophical Magazine and Journal. London.

Philosophical Transactions. London.

Phrenological Journal and Miscellany. Edinburgh.

Piozzi, Hester Lynch. *British Synonymy; or, an Attempt at Regu-*

lating the Choice of Words in Familiar Conversation. Paris, 1804.

Proceedings of the Huguenot Society of London.

Proceedings of the Royal Society of London.

Putnam's Monthly Magazine of American Literature, Science, and Art. New York.

Quarterly Journal of Science and Arts. London.

Quarterly Review, The. London.

Ramsaye, Terry. *A Million and One Nights: A History of the Motion Picture.* New York: Simon & Schuster, 1964.

Renaud, Frank. *A Short History of the House of Recovery, or Fever Hospital, in Manchester, from Its Establishment in 1796 to the Present Time.* Manchester, 1885.

Report of the Commissioners Appointed by His Majesty to Inquire into the State of the Supply of Water in the Metropolis. London: House of Commons, 1824.

Robinson, Henry Crabb. *Diary, Reminiscences, and Correspondence,* ed. Thomas Sadler. Boston, 1870.

Roget, Samuel Romilly. *A Dictionary of Electrical Terms.* London, 1924.

——— (ed.). *Travel in the Two Last Centuries of Three Generations.* London, 1921.

Roget's International Thesaurus, Third Edition. New York: Crowell, 1962.

Roget's Thesaurus of English Words and Phrases, New Edition, Rev., ed. Robert A. Dutch. London: Longmans, Green, 1962.

Roget's Thesaurus of the English Language in Dictionary Form, ed. C. O. Sylvester Mawson. New York: Garden City, 1936.

Romilly, Samuel. *Memoirs of the Life of Sir Samuel Romilly, Written by Himself, Ed. by His Sons.* London, 1840.

[Romilly, Samuel; Scarlett, James; Dumont, Etienne]. *Letters Containing an Account of the Late Revolution in France and Observations on the Constitution, Laws, Manners, and Institutions of the English During the Years 1789 and 1790,* tr. from the German of Henry Frederic Groenvelt. London, 1792.

Rush, Richard. *A Residence at the Court of London.* London, 1833.

Salton, Gerard. *Automatic Content Analysis in Information Retrieval.* Ithaca, N.Y.: Cornell, 1968.

Sandek, Lawrence. "Man's World of Facts," *Data Processor,* Vol. X (November 1967), pp. 1–36.

Singer, Charles. *A History of Biology.* New York: Schuman, 1950.

South, James. *Charges Against the President and Councils of the Royal Society.* London, 1830.

Stimson, Dorothy. *Scientists and Amateurs: A History of the Royal Society.* New York: Schuman, 1948.

Stockdale, M. R. *A Shroud for Sir Samuel Romilly: An Elegy.* London, 1818.

Storer, Tracy I. *General Zoology.* New York: McGraw-Hill, 1943.

Summerson, John. *Georgian London.* London, 1965.

Supplement to the Fourth, Fifth, and Sixth Editions of the Encyclopaedia Britannica. Edinburgh, 1824.

Survey of London: King's Cross Neighbourhood (The Parish of St. Pancras, Part IV), ed. J. R. Howard Roberts and Walter H. Godfrey, Vol. XXIV. London: London County Council, 1952.

Survey of London: Tottenham Court Road and Neighbourhood (The Parish of St. Pancras, Part III), ed. J. R. Howard Roberts and Walter H. Godfrey, Vol. XXI. London: London County Council, 1949.

Times, The. London.

Transactions of the Medical and Chirurgical Society. London.

Travers, Benjamin. *Synopsis of Diseases of the Eye.* London, 1820.

Troyat, Henri. *Tolstoy,* tr. Nancy Amphoux. Garden City, N.Y.: Doubleday, 1967.

Webster's Dictionary of Synonyms. Springfield, Mass.: Merriam, 1951.

Wellesley Index to Victorian Periodicals 1824–1900, ed. Walter E. Houghton. Toronto: Toronto, 1966.

Westminster Review, The. London.

[Whipple, Edwin P.] "The Use and Misuse of Words," *North American Review,* Vol. LXXIX (July 1854), pp. 137–57.

Whorf, Benjamin Lee. *Language, Thought, and Reality.* Cambridge, Mass.: Massachusetts Institute of Technology, 1956.

Williams, L. Pearce. "The Royal Society and the Founding of the British Association for the Advancement of Science," *Notes and Records of the Royal Society,* Vol. 16 (November 1961), pp. 221–33.

Williams, Raymond. *Culture and Society.* New York: Columbia, 1958.

Wolff, Michael. "The Uses of Context: Aspects of the 1860's," *Victorian Studies,* Supp. to Vol. IX (September 1964), pp. 47–63.

Wordsworth, William. "Preface to the Second Edition of *Lyrical Ballads,*" in Charles S. Holmes, Edwin Fussell, Ray Frazer (eds.), *The Major Critics.* New York: Knopf, 1957.

Young, G. M. (ed.). *Early Victorian England, 1830–1865.* Oxford, 1934.

———. *Portrait of an Age.* Oxford, 1966.

Index

Index